"THE YELLOW KID" — the famous Pennsylvania Limited of 1898 — stands behind D16 4-4-0 No. 174 at the end of Rockville Bridge in a Pennsylvania publicity classic from the author's collection.

EASTWARD, WESTWARD
The "Centuries" at Buffalo Central Terminal
THE NEW YORK CENTRAL LINES

KALMBACH **K** BOOKS®

BY ARTHUR D. DUBIN

SOME CLASSIC TRAINS

Library of Congress Catalog Card Number: 64-14749

ISBN: 0-89024-011-6

Cover stamping insigne by courtesy of the Pullman Company.

First printing, 1964. Second printing, 1966. Third printing, 1970.
Fourth printing, 1972. Fifth printing, 1973. Sixth printing, 1975.

This book is dedicated to Lois, Peter,
and Polly — for their special contribution.

To the memory of my mother and father, Anne
and Henry Dubin — for their encouragement.

To my brother and partner in architecture,
Martin David Dubin — for his interest.

Foreword

1   IN the precisely compartmented and meticulously pigeonholed realm of historical scholarship, the specialized subdivision of land transport has been until comparatively recent times almost entirely dominated by students of economic science and the corporate record. Railroading as a factor in the national economy, railroading as an organized technology, or even railroading as an element in wartime logistics has received its appropriate study and commentary from a variety of skilled analysts — some of them, like Charles Francis Adams, railroaders in their own right. The economic and political bibliography of transport by land and through the agency of the flanged wheel on the steel rail is an ample one in any university library.

Only in approximately the last three decades — as the sun was setting on its more splendid destinies — has the appeal of railroading as the stuff of folklore, legend, and romance had an impact on any considerable body of general awareness. Just as the automobile as an artifact of wonder and individual character with a style of its own had long been submerged in the assembly-line product of universal acceptance before it began attracting the attention of *aficionados*, amateurs, collectors, and its own special body of admirers, so the transport of passengers by railroad had almost achieved the end of the line before it attracted a vocal group of partisans. Railroading as a cult and as the potential matter of popular literature is, in proper fact, no older than the 1930's. Indeed, only when the rise of internal combustion in one of its aspects threatened the supremacy of steam motive power and in another aspect the existence of railroading as a whole did the cars and engines begin to attract to themselves hard-core enthusiasts of the type already existing in the fields of, let us say, the Civil War or the Old West.

Suddenly, however, as though realizing the lateness of the hour, there came into being a relatively small but also relatively compact confraternity of amateurs who cherished the tradition of the steamcars, who dreamed of preserving some aspects of their wonderment, and most of all, who set about photographing the visual façade of rail transport while still it trailed clouds of glory from the ineffable past.

True, there had been dedicated railroad iconographers reaching back into the pioneering years of the 19th century — men such as William Henry Jackson, Fred Jukes, and a few years later, Herb Arey, J. Foster Adams, and Charles Chaney — who with the primeval equipment at their disposal set about preserving the picture record of an industry that was then so much a commonplace that they were viewed as mild eccentrics. Without them the gap in our knowledge of other times would be at once melancholy and insurmountable.

By the late 1930's taking railroad photographs and other evidences of interest in the steamcars abruptly lost their implications of eccentricity when it was discovered that a sufficient body of enthusiasts for the special mystery of the high iron existed to make the publication of books in the field a profitable commercial venture. Nothing absolves a preoccupation of oddness like a capacity for making money.

Of the proliferation of the cult of railroading no account can be encompassed here of its sects and subdivisions and heresies; of its allegiances and feuds and splinter groups; of the rise and fall of publishing houses and periodicals as frequent and as inevitably doomed as small French restaurants; and of its diversification into channels of railroad art, literature, artifacts, sound tracks, fan excursions, regional associations and national chapters, pen pals, post cards, museums, and affiliations beyond the seas. Its periodicals run the gamut from TRAINS Magazine, the official scriptural reading of the faithful, and the *Bulletins* of the Railway & Locomotive Historical Society to fugitive *feuilletons* imprinted presumably in conspiratorial cellars which fold their tents when the print bill falls due.

Publishing houses with impressive titles rose in evanescent splendor to leave their imprimatur on single volumes of ungrammatic letterpress and halftones that apparently had been photographed not through the conventional Ben Day screen but through a Navajo rug.

Internecine warfare broke out between dissident sects so that in Colorado a dynamite outrage obtruded itself in the record. The acquisition of railroad memorabilia and rare photographs achieved such passionate dimension that an accomplished art collector, to whom the theft of the Mona Lisa from the Louvre would have been a mere finger exercise, looted the New Haven Railroad of its picture file in its entirety and ended his days in jail. His collection now reposes — stolen goods and all — in the archives of a richly endowed and nationally respected foundation.

In the midst of these heady tumults and rich disorders there remained at their editorial desks, drawing boards, and file cabinets a dedicated group of authentic students and amateurs of the railroad legend for whom the term scholars would be no overstatement. They fulfilled and continue to fill the role of better recognized academic authorities in more conventional fields of specialized information as custodians of the heroic past and archivists of the great days that are gone in terminal and coach yard, in the high passes of the land, and on the tangents across the prairies.

One of the most truly notable of these is the author of the volume to which these brief sentiments serve as foreword. Arthur Dubin is recognized by his peers and contemporaries in the railroad field as the ranking authority without exception in the domain of passenger equipment — the beautiful and useful art of carbuilders known to the initiated as varnish by reason of the rich finish applied to passenger cars in the days of their wooden construction.

The cars and their specifications, their purpose, compartmentation, and assignment to the great name trains of lordly carriers have been his concern and preoccupation since his earliest remembrance. The consists of specials and limiteds and flyers of the *belle époque* of railroad travel are a matter as familiar to his awareness as, say, the details of the Rocky Mountain fur trade were to Bernard De Voto or the engagements of the Civil War to Bruce Catton.

The concern of Some Classic Trains is an aspect of surface transport in the age of the steamcars so narrowly defined as to be designed by its very nature to appeal to the specialist, the *aficionado*, the true connoisseur of railroading. The main concern of the author is not for the impact of the agrarian philosophy of James Jerome Hill on the economy of the Dakotas or the significance of the fact that the J. Edgar Thomson steel mills, one of the greatest concentrations of steel processing in the world, are handily adjacent to the tracks of the Pennsylvania Railroad and are named for the man who first surveyed the Horseshoe Curve, a location which has never been resurveyed.

Whether the luxury equipment of the New York Central & Hudson River Railroad's first *Lake Shore Limited* was built by Wagner or Pullman cannot be imagined as a matter of universal concern, but to the knowing and informed student the difference is as vital as the distinction between sauces Mornay and Béchamel to the accomplished gastronome. It is the essence of the advice of Lord Joseph Duveen to Jules Bache, one of Duveen's clients who was building the formidable collection of art that is identified with the memory of this New York archmillionaire. Bache had been running hog wild in the entire field, purchasing Gainsboroughs, Titians, and Van Eycks like a sailor loose among the potables of a water-front bar when Duveen wanted to sell him Raphaels. "Don't dissipate, Julie," he advised Bache. "Don't dissipate — concentrate."

Arthur Dubin has not dissipated. He has not wasted his *expertise* in frivolous excursions into the realms of trivia. He has concentrated his efforts and directed his energies down the rich vistas of potentiality suggested by the purview of his own intelligent interests.

Definitive is a risky word to use in the context of scholarship. It has a way of returning to embarrass those to whom its recourse has been casual or ill considered, but it is safe to say — without using the word and incurring its attendant risks — that for a long time no other historian need explore the avenues of fact which have been charted in this book. Classic, too, is a word not lightly to be invoked. Its implications suggest its prudent and considered use, but it is the belief of the author of this footnote that Some Classic Trains will vindicate its title and achieve the distinction in general appreciation that it is sure to engender in the serious student of the romance and glory that rode the steamcars only yesterday.

Lucius Beebe.

Hillsborough, Calif.
1964

Contents

Introduction

1 THE half century which concluded with the splitting of the atom and the ending of World War II was the age of the classic train. It was the era when most overland travelers chose the railway and those seeking the epitome of luxury and speed selected the distinguished trains described in this volume.

The stories of these great limiteds reflect the history of the land, the life, and the architecture of the times. Insofar as the preservation of documents and photographs permits, Some Classic Trains attempts to record the essence of what has been termed the Golden Age of Railroading in North America.

Primeval expresses and sleeping cars

EMPIRE, a Silver Palace sleeping car built by Jackson & Sharp at its Delaware Car Works, was part of the assets of the Central Transportation Company purchased by George Pullman from Andrew Carnegie on February 17, 1870. Central had been incorporated in Pennsylvania on December 30, 1862, by Theodore Woodruff, E. C. Knight, H. B. Myer (who contributed their sleeping car patents), and Andrew Carnegie, at that time superintendent of Pennsylvania Railroad's Pittsburg Division. Carnegie was instrumental in securing contracts to furnish sleeping-car service to the Pennsy, and Knight secured a similar contract for Baltimore & Ohio. It was during negotiations by Union Pacific with both Central and Pullman for sleeping cars that Pullman bought out the other firm. Inside a Silver Palace car (left) one found carpeted floors, spittoons, and low-back seats covered with red velvet plush. But there was no silver; all hardware was white britannia metal.

Both photos, author's collection.

IN 1837 Philip Berlin, manager of the Cumberland Valley (now the Pennsy), developed a crude sleeping car for operations between Harrisburg and Chambersburg, Pa. Chambersburg was an important terminus for stage coach travel from the West. The new sleeper, built in Philadelphia, began running in the winter of 1837-1838 and its crude accommodations were available to the public until abandoned in 1848. Photographs depict exterior and interior of a Cumberland Valley combined car built in 1855 and now preserved by the Pennsy. But in the interior note the model of Berlin's CV sleeper of 1837 — an unusual replica of his crude overnight equipment.

Pullman-Standard.

VASTLY more refined sleeping-car travel was available in the 1890's, as attest the interior of Wisconsin Central's Fond du Lac built in 1892.

Collection of Everett L. DeGolyer Jr.

AN early through train, the New York & Philadelphia Express of the New Jersey Railroad & Transportation Company (now the Pennsy), poses about 1870 near Jersey City. Forty years earlier on January 7, 1830, Baltimore & Ohio carried the first revenue rail passengers in the U.S.

Pullman-Standard.

THE body of a martyred President is guarded by soldiers as the Lincoln funeral train pauses in the Pennsylvania Railroad's Harrisburg station en route to Springfield, Ill. The Great Seal and a unique double-truck running gear identify the Presidential car. When the funeral party reached Chicago officials of the State of Illinois arranged for its transfer to George Pullman's newly completed luxury sleeper, the Pioneer. This car

had cost $20,174 in an age when no predecessor had cost over $4500; was furnished with fine woods, plate glass, burnished metals, and comfortable berths. The car had not been well received by the railroads, however, because it was longer, wider, and higher than ordinary equipment. However, for the Lincoln funeral train, bridges and platforms of the Chicago & Alton were hurriedly altered and the Pioneer's maiden run was thus made.

PRR.

Pullman Company.

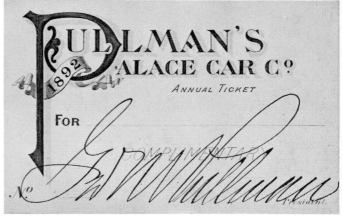

Author's collection.

GEORGE MORTIMER PULLMAN, founder of the carbuilding and operating companies which bear his name, was born at Brocton, N. Y., March 3, 1831, and died in Chicago October 19, 1897. His name appears in the dictionaries of 20 languages as a noun connoting luxury, comfort, and safety in overland transportation. Though he did not invent the sleeping car itself, Pullman did found the first long-distance sleeping-car company. His greatest contribution lay in persuading railroads to unify their operations for through-train service, and out of this movement mergers gained impetus. Today's mergers are a realization of his dreams.

No. 9 and its famous inventor

Pullman-Standard.

GREAT Pullman works constructed in 1880 at Lake Calumet, 14 miles south of Chicago, was planned in consultation with architects, engineers, and landscape specialists. George Pullman acquired 3600 acres, built a model plant and town which grew to a population of 12,000. Early Pullman-operated sleeping and parlor cars had been built by Barney & Smith, Harlan & Hollingsworth, and other railway car works. Prior to the Calumet site the first Pullman shops were located in Detroit, Elmira, N. Y., St. Louis.

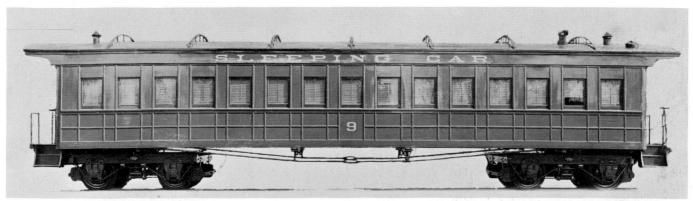

Pullman-Standard.

NO. 9 was George Pullman's first attempt to build a sleeping car. He remodeled two former Chicago & Alton coaches, Nos. 9 and 19, into sleepers at C&A's Bloomington (Ill). shops in 1859 for $2000. Photo shows replica of No. 9 rebuilt from Santa Fe coach 402.

17

THE SLEEPING COACHES

RUN UPON THE NIGHT TRAINS OF THIS LINE

BETWEEN CHICAGO AND BUFFALO

AND

CHICAGO AND CLEVELAND

Have Luxurious Hair Mattresses, Clean Linen Sheets, Feather Pillows with Clean Linen Slips, and are in charge of Competent and Courteous Conductors.

FOR TICKETS AND BERTHS APPLY AT 56 CLARK ST.

ONLY ONE CHANGE OF CARS

BETWEEN CHICAGO AND NEW YORK.

Author's collection.

ADVERTISEMENT for the Gates South Shore (Lake Erie) Sleeping Car Line operated by G. B. Gates over the Lake Shore & Michigan Southern between Buffalo and Chicago blurbed such travel inducements of 1869 as hair mattresses, clean linen sheets.

Author's collection.

WEBSTER WAGNER, inventor and politician, was born at Palatine Bridge, N. Y., October 2, 1817. In his youth he worked as an apprentice to his brother, a wagon builder. During September 1868 the Wagners completed four sleeping cars at a cost of $3200 each for Commodore Vanderbilt's Hudson River Railroad, which operated them overnight between New York and Albany. The cars were so successful that Vanderbilt organized the New York Central Sleeping Car Company with Wagner as president, and by 1880 there were 150 Wagner drawing-room and sleeping cars operating over the NYC. While serving as head of the firm Webster Wagner found time to be elected five times to the New York State Senate. But on Friday the 13th of January 1882 tragedy struck at Spuyten Duyvil, N. Y., on the northern tip of Manhattan Island in a train wreck in which Wagner was burned to death in one of his own palace cars, the Idlewild. The firm was reorganized as Wagner Palace Car Company.

All passes, collection of the author.

18

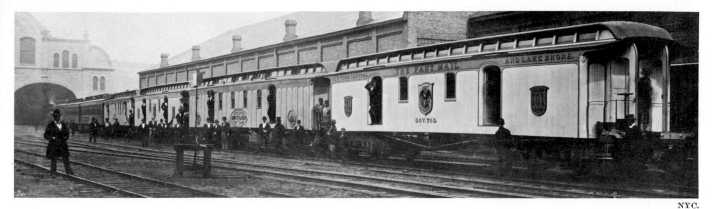

THE Lake Shore was famous as the route of the Fast Mail, whose equipment is displayed in fresh white paint for first run to Chicago.

In the beginning Pullman had company in the sleeping-car business

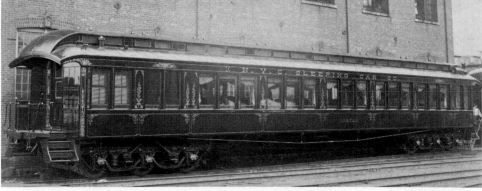

GARDEN CITY, alias drawing-room coach No. 21, was built in 1878 at Adrian, Mich., at a cost of $23,000 for Lake Shore & Michigan Southern service between Chicago-Cleveland.

URSULA, a drawing-room car of the New York Central Sleeping Car Company, stands outside Wagner's Buffalo Works in 1883. As part of the Vanderbilt railway empire, the Wagner firm built and operated nearly 700 palace cars before it was absorbed by Pullman Company in 1899.

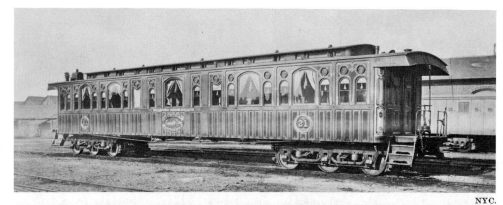

OAKLAND, a Wagner North Shore sleeping car, operated via the north shore of Lake Erie through Ontario on Vanderbilt's Michigan Central.

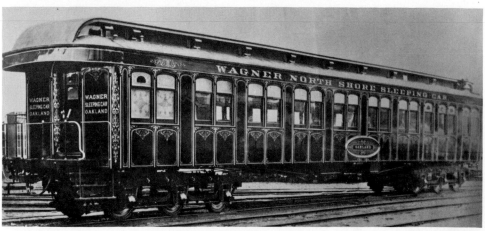

C&NW.

THREE sections of the Overland behind as many H-class 4-8-4's prepare to depart from Chicago & North Western's Chicago terminal.

Great terminals spawned great trains

NYC.

GREAT STEEL FLEET at La Salle Street Station, Chicago, in 1948; most famous of them all — the Century — is parked at the far right.

GRAND CENTRAL TERMINAL, one of the most renowned of the railway stations that double as famous and familiar urban landmarks, has long been home to New York Central's Great Steel Fleet and New Haven's Yankee flyers. It was designed by the architectural firms of Reed & Stem and Warren & Wetmore.

When completed on February 2, 1913, it was one of the costliest non-Governmental structures ever built. High above monumental concourse with "Golden Clock" atop information booth is night blue ceiling ablaze with stars depicting ecliptic and celestial equator intersecting at Vernal Equinox — mistakenly in reverse order.

21

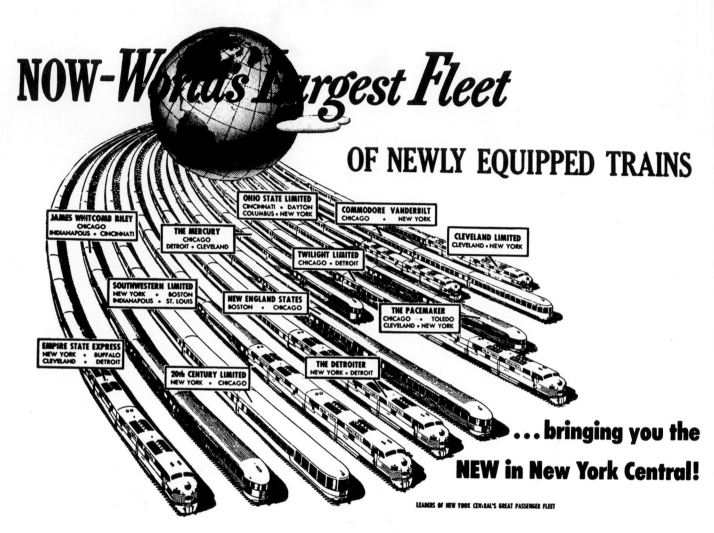

NOW—*World's Largest Fleet*
OF NEWLY EQUIPPED TRAINS

...bringing you the
NEW in New York Central!

LEADERS OF NEW YORK CENTRAL'S GREAT PASSENGER FLEET

20th CENTURY LIMITED—New York, Chicago. *World's Most Famous Train.* All-room sleeping cars; raised level observation car, club car with train secretary, radio telephone, valet and barber shop.

EMPIRE STATE EXPRESS—New York, Buffalo, Cleveland, Detroit. Reserved reclining seat coaches, tavern observation car, coach attendants, parlor car.

JAMES WHITCOMB RILEY—Chicago, Indianapolis, Cincinnati. Reserved reclining-seat coaches, observation-lounge car, coach attendants.

SOUTHWESTERN LIMITED—New York and Boston, Indianapolis, St. Louis. Sleeping cars, observation-lounge and lounge sleeping cars; through reclining-seat coaches.

THE DETROITER—New York, Detroit. All-room sleeping car train, two lounge-sleeping cars.

THE NEW ENGLAND STATES—Boston, Toledo, Chicago. Sleeping cars, observation-lounge and lounge-sleeping cars; reserved reclining-seat coaches, coach lounge, coach attendants.

THE MERCURY—Chicago, Detroit, Toledo, Cleveland. Reserved reclining-seat coaches, buffet lounge, coach attendants; parlor car, parlor-observation car.

TWILIGHT LIMITED—Chicago, Detroit. Reserved reclining-seat coaches, tavern-lounge coach, coach attendants; parlor car, observation parlor car.

THE PACEMAKER—Chicago, Toledo, Cleveland, New York. Reserved reclining-seat coaches, diner lounge, observation-lounge, coach attendants.

OHIO STATE LIMITED—Cincinnati, Dayton, Columbus, New York and Boston. Sleeping cars, observation sleeping car; reclining-seat coaches.

COMMODORE VANDERBILT—Chicago, New York. All-room sleeping car train, lounge car, observation lounge.

CLEVELAND LIMITED—New York, Cleveland. Sleeping cars, two buffet-lounge cars.

SLEEPING CAR PRIVATE ROOMS! *See cutaway views of various types and sizes.* **PAGES 42-43**

FULL-PAGE 1949 announcement of New York Central's vast re-equipment program after World War II displayed "world's largest fleet."

PULLMAN, COACH AND DINING CAR SERVICE

Regularly assigned cars are air-conditioned

Air-conditioned equipment is assigned as far as possible but the right is reserved to employ non air-conditioned cars as necessitated by volume of traffic or emergencies

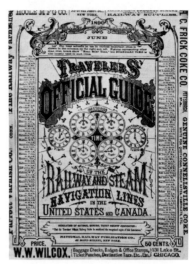

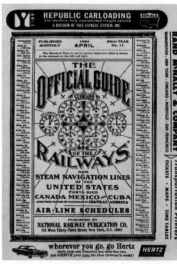

FOR YEARS more Pullman passengers were transported by New York Central than any other railroad, and this sample equipment page from its timetable dated December 11, 1949, indicates as much. The flagship of the fleet, the 20th Century Limited, bears the notice "Pullman Cars only; no coach passengers" — and the consist of No. 26 includes two transcontinental sleepers interchanged with Santa Fe's Chief streamliner.

Milwaukee Road.

THE downtown ticket office was a major point of sale for railway passenger transportation. Milwaukee Road customers in Milwaukee found marble-trimmed wood counter.

All photos, O. Winston Link.

THE Official Guide of the Railways, depicted in 1870, 1890, and 1964 editions, has been published in New York by the National Railway Publication Company since June 1868 and is the bible of the ticketseller, the railroad enthusiast's indispensable companion, and the "world's biggest pulp magazine." But its bulk has declined in recent years — from 1760 pages in December 1929 to 1440 in June 1944 to 1138 in July 1964 — as branch lines have gone "freight service only" and number of limiteds has waned.

23

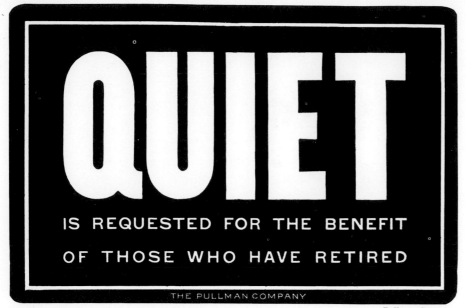

LOWER 8, Car 10 — the famous green receipt guaranteeing Pullman passage.

QUIET — the sign that has hushed conversation in green-curtained, carpeted aisles on journeys too numerous to contemplate.

Pullman travel was a world unto its own

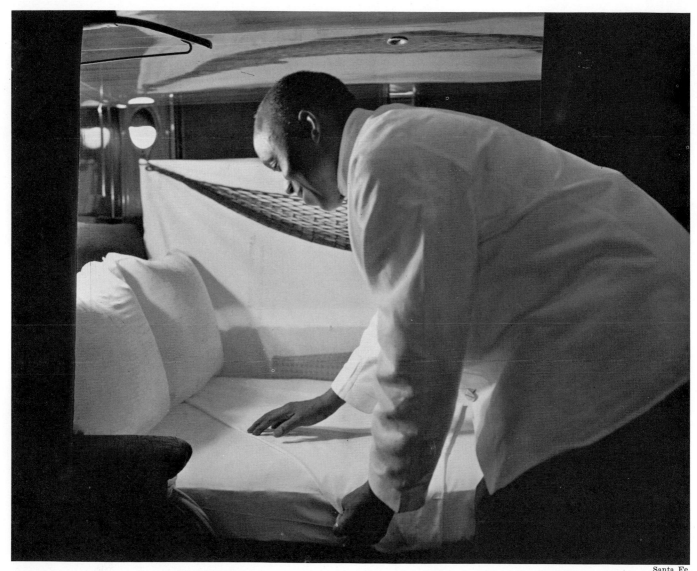

DURING the 1920's Pullman provided lodging for nearly 100,000 people every night (more than 35 million revenue passengers in 1927 alone), and for each passenger there were green curtains, crisp linen, a clothes hammock, a smiling white-jacketed porter.

Milwaukee Road.

FORUM for generations of male travelers was the end-of-car men's room. Smoke-heavy discussions of politics, women, and

GN.

the American scene continued past midnight. But next morning the quiet business of brushing teeth and shaving prevailed here.

Milwaukee Road.

NEVER quite resolved was how to undress in an upper or lower — as here aboard the Southwest Limited.

SP.

PRIVACY took a leap forward after World War II when toilets of two-person bedrooms were enclosed. Example displayed is aboard the Cascade of 1950.

NYC.

ABOARD the Century the diner is dark, the lounge empty; and up front the Hudson's screaming whistle is heard only by the R.P.O. clerks. In a quiet aisle the Pullman porter replaces a pair of freshly polished shoes.

25

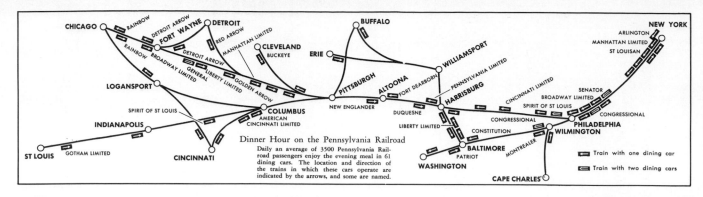

Dinner Hour on the Pennsylvania Railroad

Daily an average of 3500 Pennsylvania Railroad passengers enjoy the evening meal in 61 dining cars. The location and direction of the trains in which these cars operate are indicated by the arrows, and some are named.

Train with one dining car

Train with two dining cars

DURING THE 1930'S 3500 passengers dined in 61 dining cars each night on the Pennsylvania Railroad, and such trains as the Congressional, General, and Senator were so heavily patronized that their consists incorporated not one but two dining cars.

A world of snowy tablecloths and gleaming silverware

Milwaukee Road.

PRESIDENT Franklin D. Roosevelt, an enthusiastic railroad traveler, is reported to have said that the ultimate in gracious living was riding a Pullman train and watching the scenery pass by the diner while being served on a snowy tablecloth. Surely he would have enjoyed the onion soup that was a Milwaukee Road specialty in this Pioneer Limited dining car, not to mention such other railroad favorites as rib ends of beef on the New Haven; Lake Erie whitefish on the New York Central; chicken pot pie on the Great Northern; Alaska crab on the Union Pacific; trout on the D&RGW; fresh strawberries on the Illinois Central.

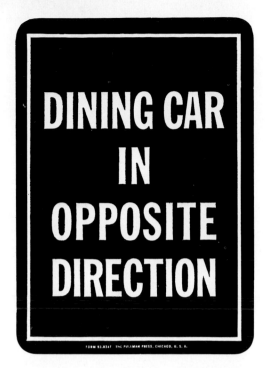

DINING CAR IN OPPOSITE DIRECTION

FORM 93-8747 THE PULLMAN PRESS, CHICAGO, U.S.A.

If you were hungry and encountered this sign, you were headed in the wrong direction.

THE TWENTIETH CENTURY LIMITED
DINNER SPECIALS

PEPPER POT *Biltmore*..Cup 30; Tureen 45	
CONSOMME, *Hot*..Cup 35; *Jellied,* Cup 45	
CLAM BOUILLON ....Cup 30	
OYSTERS *Stewed in Milk*..65; *Cream*..................75	

—+—

SHRIMP COCKTAIL, *20th Century*.. 65
BROILED SPANISH MACKEREL, *Anchovy Butter, Julienne Potatoes, Tomato Surprise* .. 95
FRIED OYSTERS, *Tartare Sauce, Saratoga Potatoes, Julienne of Beets* 85
BAKED SALMON STEAK *Creole, Potatoes Chateau, Wax Beans in Butter* 95

—+—

MINCED CHICKEN *on Toast, Green Peppers and Pimientos, Potatoes Persillade Parisienne* 95
PAPRICA OF VEAL *with Noodles, Carrots and Peas* 95
RACK OF PORK *Breaded Bordelaise, New Brussels Sprouts, Sweet Potatoes Glace* 95
ROAST RIBS OF PRIZE BEEF *with Vegetables* 1 10
OMELETTE *with Fresh Mushrooms in Cream* 95
HOME MADE NOODLES *Polonaise* 65
VIRGINIA HAM *with Fried Pineapple, Veloute of New Spinach, Baked Potato* 95

—+—

NEW CARROTS *in Butter with Chives* 40
NEW BRUSSELS SPROUTS *Polonaise* 45
GRILLED SPANISH ONIONS 40
VELOUTE OF NEW SPINACH 45
NEW CAULIFLOWER *Au Gratin* 45
BAKED SWEET POTATO 35

—+—

CARAMEL CUSTARD, *Red Currant Jelly* 35
BANANA SHORTCAKE *with Whipped Cream* 45
FRENCH VANILLA ICE CREAM *with Maple Syrup* 45
GREEN APPLE PIE.. 25; *with Cheese* 35 *A la Mode* 45
MINCE PIE, *Hot or Cold* 25
STEAMED FIG OR PLUM PUDDING, *Hard Sauce* 40
CREAM CHEESE *with Toasted Rye Bread, Guava Jelly* 40
GRAPE FRUIT, *Iced, Half* 35
N. Y. C. SPECIAL BAKED APPLE *with Cream* 35

— [SPECIAL PLATE COMBINATION] —
ROAST YOUNG TURKEY
FRESH MUSHROOM AND OYSTER DRESSING   CRANBERRY SAUCE
NEW BRUSSELS SPROUTS POLONAISE
SWEET POTATOES AND APPLES GLACE
ROLLS AND BUTTER   TEA, COFFEE, MILK
—+— [$1.35] —+—
ABOVE PORTIONS PER PERSON ONLY
AN EXTRA CHARGE OF 25 CENTS PER PERSON WILL BE MADE FOR MEALS
SERVED OUT OF DINING CAR

ROAST beef in 1929 was $1.10 on the Century.

WITH BEST WISHES FOR
A HAPPY HOLIDAY SEASON
PENNSYLVANIA RAILROAD
BROADWAY LIMITED
Christmas 1928

DINNER

OYSTER COCKTAIL

CELERY   QUEEN OLIVES

MOCK TURTLE   CONSOMME, JULIENNE

POACHED SALMON, SAUCE MOUSSELINE
POTATOES, NATURAL

1928 PRIZE LAMB CHOP WITH FRESH MUSHROOMS

ROAST STUFFED YOUNG TURKEY, CRANBERRY COMPOTE

POTATOES, FONDANTE   NEW PEAS

CREAMED ONIONS

GRAPE FRUIT AND LETTUCE SALAD, FRENCH DRESSING

PLUM PUDDING, HARD AND FRUIT SAUCE

HOT MINCE PIE

FRENCH ICE CREAM
WAFERS

ROQUEFORT CHEESE   TOASTED CRACKERS

TEA   COFFEE   MILK

CREAM MINTS

EGGS WILL BE SUBSTITUTED FOR MEAT COURSE UPON REQUEST

$1.50

A LA CARTE SERVICE ALSO AVAILABLE, IF DESIRED
SERVICE CHARGE OF TWENTY-FIVE CENTS WILL BE MADE FOR EACH
PERSON SERVED OUTSIDE OF DINING CAR
PAY ONLY UPON PRESENTATION OF CHECK
PASSENGERS ARE REQUESTED TO REPORT ANY UNUSUAL SERVICE OR
ATTENTION ON THE PART OF EMPLOYEES. THIS ENABLES US TO
RECOGNIZE THE EXCEPTIONAL EFFICIENCY WHICH WE WISH TO
ENCOURAGE IN OUR SERVICE.
D. N. BELL, PASSENGER TRAFFIC MANAGER, PHILADELPHIA
C. E. MILLIRON, SUPT. DINING CAR SERVICE, NEW YORK

_____, Steward in Charge

THE NAME OF YOUR WAITER IS _____

XXX·12·25·28

CHRISTMAS dinner, 1928, on the Broadway.

Precios en Pesos y Centavos Mexicanos
Money in Dollars and Cents, Mexican Money

ALMUERZO
BREAKFAST

FRUTAS
FRUITS

Naranja Rebanada 70   Cocktail, Jugo de Tomate 75   Jugo de Naranja 90
Sliced Orange   Tomato Juice Cocktail   Orange Juice

Jugo de Sauerkraut 75   Higos en Conserva, con Crema 1.00
Sauerkraut Juice   Preserved Figs with Cream

Jugo de Toronja Helado 75   Ciruelas Cocidas, con Crema 80
Chilled Grape Juice   Stewed Prunes with Cream

Duraznos, con Crema 90
Peaches with Cream

Frambuesas o Fresas en Conserva 80
Preserved Raspberries or Strawberries

Mermelada de Naranja 80   Miel, Porcion Individual 80
Orange Marmalade   Individual Honey

CEREALES
CEREALS

Cereal de Trigo Entero, con Crema 90
Whole Wheat Cereal with Cream

Todo de Salvado, con Crema 90   New Oata con Crema 90
All Bran with Cream   New Oata with Cream

Copos de Maiz o Salvado, con Crema 90
Corn or Bran Flakes with Cream

Grape Nuts con Crema 90
Grape Nuts with Cream

Biscochos (2) de Trigo Picado, con Crema 90
Shredded Wheat Biscuits (2) with Cream

Trigo o Arroz Esponjado, con Crema 90
Puffed Wheat or Puffed Rice with Cream

Copos de Arroz, con Crema 90
Rice Flakes with Cream

PESCADO
FISH

Arenque Hervido en Sal 1.90
Boiled Salt Mackerel

Arenque Ahumado con Huevos Escalfados en Crema 1.70
Kippered Herring with Shirred Eggs

HUEVOS Y TORTILLAS DE HUEVO
EGGS AND OMELETS

(2) Pasados por Agua, Fritos, Revueltos o Escalfados en Crema 90
Boiled, Fried, Scrambled or Shirred (2)

Escalfados (2) en Pan Tostado 1.20   Tortilla, Sencilla 1.20
Poached (2) on Toast   Omelet, Plain

Tortilla con Jamon o Jalea 1.80
Omelet with Ham or Jelly

BILINGUAL breakfast menu on Mopac in 1931.

AFTERNOON tea and cakes were a ritual aboard the Great Northern Empire Builder in 1929. Steward supervised proceedings carefully.

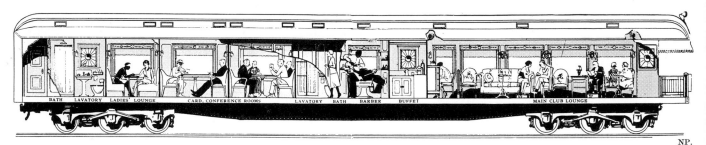

EVERY conceivable convenience could be found between vestibule and observation platform of lounge car in North Coast Limited of 1926: bath, maid, card room, barber, buffet, lounge, even a roomy observation platform fitted with campchairs, searchlight.

"Porter, which way is the club car?"

DEEP in the downstairs of Grand Central Terminal in 1930 the Advance 20th Century Limited waits to board its passengers.

DOUBLE signs on Fort Dearborn trailing North Western Limited of 1935 advertised both the train name and proprietor railroad.

28

TIME for a martini aboard the 1937 Santa Fe Super Chief.

THE PULLMAN COMPANY

SHOWER BATH

[FIFTY CENTS]

RING BELL FOR ATTENDANT OR PORTER

WANT to freshen up? Porter would bring towels and soap.

For your comfort

OBSERVATION CAR

OUTDOOR platform, parlor for men and women, periodicals, newspapers, women's lounge and bath, maid in attendance

CLUB CAR FORWARD

BARBER, valet service, bath, lounge for smoking, periodicals, newspapers, market reports

Refreshing drinks, cigars and cigarettes always available. Toilet articles may be purchased from barber.

A-876-27 O. L. *No Cigarettes will be Sold from this Car while in Iowa, Utah or Nevada*

DO not ask for cigarettes in Iowa, Utah, or Nevada, please.

OBSERVATION-CLUB CAR

Barber, valet service, bath, writing desk, periodicals, newspapers, market reports. Lounge for smoking.

Barber Shop
(Observation-Club Car)

Men

Hair Cut	.50
Shave	.25
Beard Trimmed	.35
Hair Singe	.25
Facial Massage	.50
Facial Massage (Boncilla)	1.00
Plain Shampoo	.50
Shampoo, Egg, Oil or Tonic	.75
Hair Tonics	.25
Bath	.50

Women

Hair Bob	.75
Hair Bob—Trim	.50
Neck Clip	.25
Plain Shampoo	1.00
Shampoo, Egg, Oil or Tonic	1.25
Hair Tonics	.25
Bath (Maid will arrange)	.50

VALET SERVICE
(Observation-Club Car)

Trousers (Pressing)	.35
Vest	.25
Coat	.65
Suit	1.00
Overcoat	1.00
Woman's Coat	1.00
Woman's Suit	1.25
Woman's Skirt	.75

Valet service from 6:30 in the morning to midnight. The porter of the sleeping car will arrange for this service. Please inform him at what hour you desire to have clothes returned.

Ladies' Maid

Skilled in manicuring, hair dressing and other personal services.

Manicuring	.75
Hairdressing	.75

Dining Car

Between Chicago, San Francisco and Los Angeles. A la carte service.

VALET was available from 6:30 a.m. until the midnight hour.

MOTHER of Charles Lindbergh helped to christen Spirit of St. Louis, shown here in 1928.

EACH winter morning in 1936 the Dixieland left Chicago snow in sections from ancient Dearborn Station, was in Miami warmth by the following evening.

29

FOR the young lady, a glass of Canada Dry ginger ale aboard Denver-bound Columbine's lounge in year 1930.

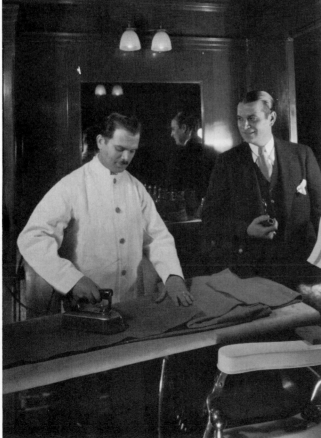

VALET had company as he wielded his iron aboard Great Northern's Oriental Limited in the 1920's. A quarter century later the barber of the newly re-equipped 20th Century Limited of 1948 (right) deftly co-ordinated his scissors and comb.

CENTURY passenger takes his office with him as he dictates to train secretary and has hostess place a radio-telephone call.

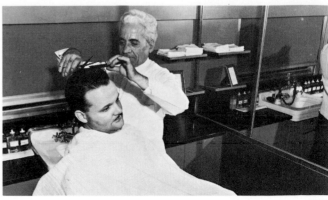

30

Both photos, Milwaukee Road.

MORE ginger ale — this time for two matrons in the ladies' lounge of the 1927 Olympian. On the Pioneer Limited of the same era the ladies gathered rather apprehensively before the tiny dial of the huge console, perhaps to hear of Lucky Lindy's fate.

The amenities of Pullman travel

Barney & Smith, courtesy Milwaukee Road.   GN.   NYC.

THREE decades of bathing aboard the steamcars — left to right, the 1912 Olympian . . . 1929 Empire Builder . . . 1948 Century.

COMING and going, the electrified Olympian of 1927 as photographed near Seattle by Asahel Curtis behind bi-polar gearless locomotive 10254, built in 1919 by Alco-GE. Equipped with 12 motors, the monster was 76 feet long and weighed 521,200 pounds, afforded Milwaukee Road passengers "the smoothest and most comfortable riding in the history of railroad travel." Thomas A. Edison was suitably impressed when he inspected one of the bipolars. "This is the last word in railway transportation," he observed, unaware that even Milwaukee's 660 route-miles of catenary across Western mountains would be shadowed by diesels.

Bi-polars, air conditioning, and American Flyer

Milwaukee Road.

ALTHOUGH experiments with "air cooling" dated back many years, the history of mechanical air-conditioning began with testing of equipment in Pullman sleepers in 1927-1929 and in coaches by Baltimore & Ohio in 1929. First completely air-conditioned train was B&O's New York-Washington Columbian. Date: May 24, 1931.

TINPLATE train manufacturers duplicated the classics in miniature. The author, a director of the Railway & Locomotive Historical Society of Boston, Mass., inspects the observation car of American Flyer's famous Mayflower train — the ne plus ultra of tinplate toys in the 1930's. Only 100 were built.

33

TWO brass bands are playing May 15, 1927, in Denver as UP's Columbine departs with Governor Adams (Colo.) on rear platform.

THOUSANDS entered Chicago's North Western Station May 5, 1930, to view newly equipped Columbine's blue-and-silver solarium.

THE roller-bearing 1938 Broadway is pulled by Charles ("I was a 97-pound weakling") Atlas.

FUR COAT and bathing suit combined on observation platform in Miami in January 1937 to celebrate Golden Jubilee of the winter season Florida Special.

34

"STREAMLINER" was the magic word at the railroad display of the 1934 edition of Chicago's Century of Progress Exposition. A white-coveralled engineer leaned out of the turret cab of Union Pacific's brown-and-yellow M-10000 (far left) as crowds gazed in wonderment at Winton distillate engine within. At Burlington exhibit (left) Zephyr shared space with 4-4-0 35 and Hudson on composite limited. In 1933 (above) England's Royal Scot parked alongside Q's 3000.

First runs, birthdays, exhibitions

TENTH birthday of Michigan Central's Detroiter on April 16, 1921, was reason for floral horseshoe hung on MC Pacific 8469.

ORIGINAL crew of 1902 Broadway posed on tank of D16sb 4-4-0 in Chicago June 15, 1927, when Limited observed 25th birthday.

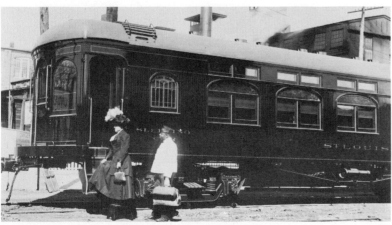

GOING NOWHERE: Publicity shot of 1910 of Illinois Traction's new sleeper St. Louis was actually staged at St. Charles plant of American Car & Foundry.

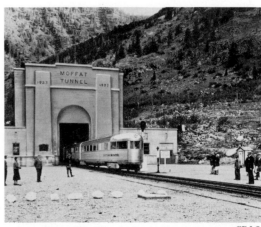

PIONEER ZEPHYR penetrated Moffat Tunnel June 16, 1934, to mark opening of D&RGW Dotsero Cutoff.

35

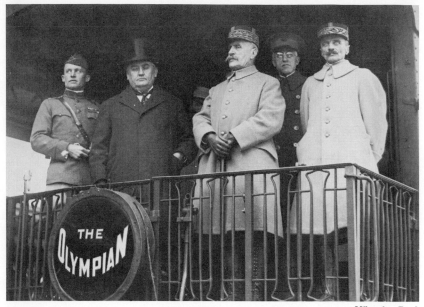

Milwaukee Road.

FIELD Marshal Foch of World War I fame aboard the Olympian in Seattle, Wash.

Milwaukee Road.

ON a journey from which he would not return alive, President Warren G. Harding posed in cab of Milwaukee Road electric locomotive 10305 in July 1923. On a goodwill tour, Harding traveled to Alaska (driving the Alaska Railroad's gold spike while there), then was stricken and died in San Francisco August 2.

CB&Q.

JACK DEMPSEY in cab of CB&Q's Denver Zephyr.

GENE TUNNEY, rival fighter of Dempsey, on the Oriental Limited in St. Paul.

GN.

PRESIDENTS: Harry S. Truman with Winston Churchill (left) leaves Washington on B&O in 1946 for latter's famous "Iron Curtain" speech at Westminster College in Fulton, Mo.; a jovial Herbert Hoover (above) waves from B&O train in Washington Union Station after radio talk.

Celebrated train travelers

PRINCE Olav and Princess Martha of Norway.

BABE RUTH, the New York Yankees' beloved Sultan of Swat, shook hands with Engineer W. L. Keene, his host on Milwaukee Road electric engine 10251.

DUKE and Duchess of Windsor ("Edward and Wally") smile aboard the Pennsy.

37

FIRST LIMITED TRAIN

Boston & Mt. Desert Limited Express

9 HOURS - Boston to Bar Harbor.

→ EXCLUSIVELY PULLMAN CARS. ←

VIA

Boston & Maine and Maine Central

RAILROADS.

This Train is composed of Pullman Vestibule Cars and Dining Car, and runs through to Bar Harbor (Mt. Desert Ferry)

WITHOUT CHANGE

BEING THE

FIRST LIMITED TRAIN IN NEW ENGLAND.

"9 HOURS to Bar Harbor" — 1887 brochure.

Boston and Mt. Desert Limited.

CONDENSED TIME-TABLE.

Leave BOSTON, Haymarket Sq. Station . . .	9.15 a.m.	
" EXETER	10.30 "	
" NORTH BERWICK	11.20 "	
Arrive PORTLAND, Congress St. Station . .	12.15 p.m.	
" BANGOR	3.40 "	
" MT. DESERT FERRY	5.20 "	
" BAR HARBOR	6.00 "	

Trains will commence running about July 1, 1887.

Leave BAR HARBOR	8.00 a.m.	
" MT. DESERT FERRY	8.50 "	
" BANGOR	10.30 "	
Arrive PORTLAND	2.00 p.m.	
" NORTH BERWICK	2.55 "	
" EXETER	3.40 "	
" BOSTON	5.00 "	

JAMES T. FURBER,   DANA J. FLANDERS,
GEN'L MANAGER.   GEN'L PASS'R AGENT.

VESTIBULES emphasized.   Author's collection.

IN NEW ENGLAND

Vestibules of the Mt. Desert Limited allowed ladies long walks

1 ONE of the vintage years for the classic train was 1887. During April of that year the new *Pennsylvania Limited*, crack flyer of the Pennsylvania Lines, was completed by the Pullman Company. It was the first train to be built with the vestibule, newly patented invention of H. H. Sessions, general manager of the Pullman Car Works in Chicago.

Arriving shortly thereafter was the color bearer for Down East, the *Boston & Mt. Desert Limited Express* — "The First Limited Train in New England." Popularly known as the *Mt. Desert Limited*, this sumptuous train was inaugurated on June 27, 1887, by the Boston & Maine and Maine Central railroads. It was composed of Pullman vestibule (parlor) cars and Pullman dining car which operated from Boston to Mt. Desert Ferry "without change." Advertised time, Boston to Bar Harbor, via Portland and Bangor, was 9 hours. The fashionable summer resort of Bar Harbor on Maine's Mt. Desert Island was the destination of the new train's well-to-do clientele en route from Boston, Philadelphia, New York, and Washington.

THE B&M 4-4-0 Columbia powered Mt. Desert Limited Express, which had a consist of unique four-door B&M baggage car No. 2; a Pullman dining car (with crew posed outside); and three Pullman parlors.

Railway & Locomotive Historical Society.

REAR-END view of the *Mt. Desert Limited Express* showing Pullman *Katrina*.

FIRST LIMITED TRAIN IN NEW ENGLAND

New England's first limited train

THE *Mt. Desert Limited* commenced operation in June 1887. It comprised five 70-foot Pullmans whose umber-colored exteriors were resplendent with gilding and filagree work. "All in one piece," as the Boston press commented, "a long-drawn serpentine creation, having, to be sure, joints to insure flexibility." The joints (vestibules) consisted of thick frames of steel, shaped like inverted ox bows. These were supported by strong elastic pressure derived from springs which bore against both top and bottom of the steel frame as well as against the timbers of the car superstructure. With the coupling of two vestibule cars, the steel frames were forced together by the springs, and the broad faces of the frames pressed upon each other with considerable force forming a passageway between cars which was completely protected from the elements. By means of this unique contrivance, the dining car, smoking car, and all other components of the train were made readily accessible in all weather and under all conditions. A brochure stated: "Ladies may make social calls or wander at will, may even take long walks for exercise or to relieve monotony, so perfect are the arrangements and appliances."

To permit special nonstop operation between Portland and Bangor — a distance of 135 miles — the Maine Central installed track pans to supply the *Limited*'s locomotives with water. Three pans, each nearly 1200 feet long, were installed between the rails at Mine Meadow, Dresden Tank, and Burnham Junction. Each pan was deep enough to receive a scoop which was lowered from the locomotive tender. Train speed was reduced to 15 mph while passing through the pans. Even at the reduced speed the entire area received a good wetting down.

Passengers detrained at Mt. Desert Ferry, known locally as "The Ferry," where they embarked on Maine Central steamer *Sappho* or *Sebenoa* for the half-hour voyage to Bar Harbor.

The *Limited* was a great success during its first season. Its new vestibuled equipment served to enhance Maine Central's reputation as the "Dude Line," a nickname applied because of the company's flower-decorated stations and courteous employees. When the last run of the season was completed on October 27, 1887, passenger traffic had increased 23 per cent over that of 1886.

Because of its fast schedule, the *Limited* became known locally as the "Cyclone." For the summer of 1888, it was reinstated on a speeded-up schedule. The *Pathfinder Guide* for September 1888 commented: "The fastest train in New England is the *Mt. Desert Limited* . . . making the run from Mt. Desert Ferry

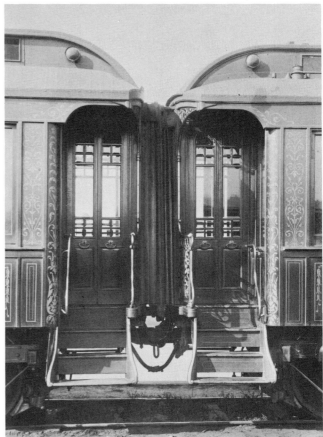

NARROW vestibules possessed recessed doors and brass grillwork; panels of carbody had scroll and filagree work in gold leaf.

to Boston, 306½ miles including five stops, in 7 hours 45 minutes, an average speed of about 40 mph."

The summer of 1889 was the last one for the *Mt. Desert Limited Express.* Short-lived though the operation was, it paved the way for the de luxe train in New England.

COMPLETE tea service was available from buffet for patrons of fringed chairs with foot cushions in this gorgeous parlor car.

ONE of Maine Central's two 4-6-4's with the southbound *Bar Harbor* at Waterville, Me., in 1946. Everett L. DeGolyer Jr.

FIRST LIMITED TRAIN IN NEW ENGLAND

The Bar Harbor Express

THE *Bar Harbor Express* — first through train from New York to the Ferry — commenced operation on June 16, 1902, via the New Haven to Springfield, Mass.; Boston & Albany to Worcester; Boston & Maine to Portland; and Maine Central to Mt. Desert. This arrangement continued until 1906 when Boston & Albany participation ceased and the New Haven carried the train through to Worcester. With minor changes in routing, the *Express* continued the New York-Bar Harbor operation until the end of the 1916 season.

On March 9, 1917, the first passenger train was operated from Pennsylvania Station, New York City, over the new 27-million-dollar Hell Gate Bridge to a connection with the New Haven. The new route permitted the *Bar Harbor* to become a Washington and Philadelphia train. On June 11, 1917, the first Pullmans rolled northward toward the Ferry from the nation's capital.

During the prosperous 1920's the *Bar Harbor* developed into one of the most celebrated railway trains in the land. Sepa-

rate sections operated from Washington, Philadelphia, and New York with passenger lists that read like pages from *Who's Who in America*. In addition, the *Bar Harbor* carried hundreds of children to summer camps. On the night of Labor Day 1923 the MEC turned over to the B&M at Portland 102 cars from the *Bar Harbor*, mostly filled with children.

As dependably as the seasons, the *Bar Harbor Expresses* made their bow early in June. Until Labor Day, long trains of Pullmans (and private cars, too) traveled the route to and from the Maine vacation spot. Then, after the last post-season trip, the silent, empty trains were backed into the coach yard to be disbanded until next season.

Year after year the great train carried on. During the 1920's the *Bar Harbor* operated daily. Through the '30's it ran six times a week. Operation was temporarily suspended during the emergency of World War II. With the return of peace the train was reinstated as a triweekly service, but as the operation of passenger trains in the East became less profitable, the train was cut back to week-end-only service. Finally on September 5, 1960, it began its final western movement from Maine. The end of the summer season also marked the end of a great era. ⌶

Charles E. Fisher.

PACIFIC powers the Bar Harbor across the Kennebec River in August 1926 with this consist: Maine Central baggage car; Philadelphia & Reading office car; Pennsy office car; 5 Pullmans; a Maine Central dining car; and a Maine Central coach. Highball!

Charles E. Fisher.

LESS than a month old, footboarded Pacific 470 of the Maine Central departs Bangor September 3, 1924, with the Bar Harbor. The train has a full complement of 14 cars in this photograph by the acknowledged dean of all New England railway historians.

Everett L. DeGolyer Jr.

IN its twilight years the Bar Harbor runs south at Ellsworth, Me., in August 1956 trailing a Pennsy baggage car behind three stainless-steel-sheathed New Haven sleepers. After ferryboats quit in 1931, the Bar Harbor terminated at Ellsworth and passengers transferred to buses for a ride over the causeway into Bar Harbor.

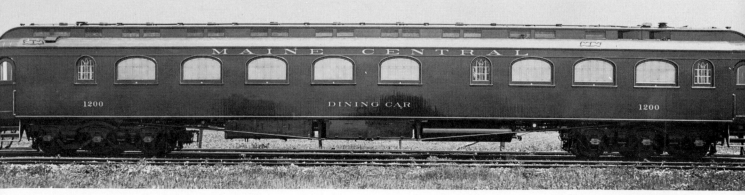

Pullman-Standard.

FIRST diner of Maine Central ownership was a graceful high-windowed 12-wheeler, No. 1200, built in 1906 for the Bar Harbor.

The Merchants

The moneymaker that became America's last daily all-parlor-car train

1 "THREE of the most magnificent trains in the United States, if not, indeed, in the entire world, are operated over the scenic Shore Line route by the New York, New Haven & Hartford Railroad.

"The *Bay State Limited*, the *Knickerbocker Limited*, and the *Merchants' Limited*, as they are known, are trains with marvelous equipment, and for trips occupying but little over 5 hours they are really palatial — truly Trains de Luxe!" — *The Shore Line Route, New York and Boston — 1913.*

New Haven.

TEN parlors and a diner are on the board at Track 26.

Limited

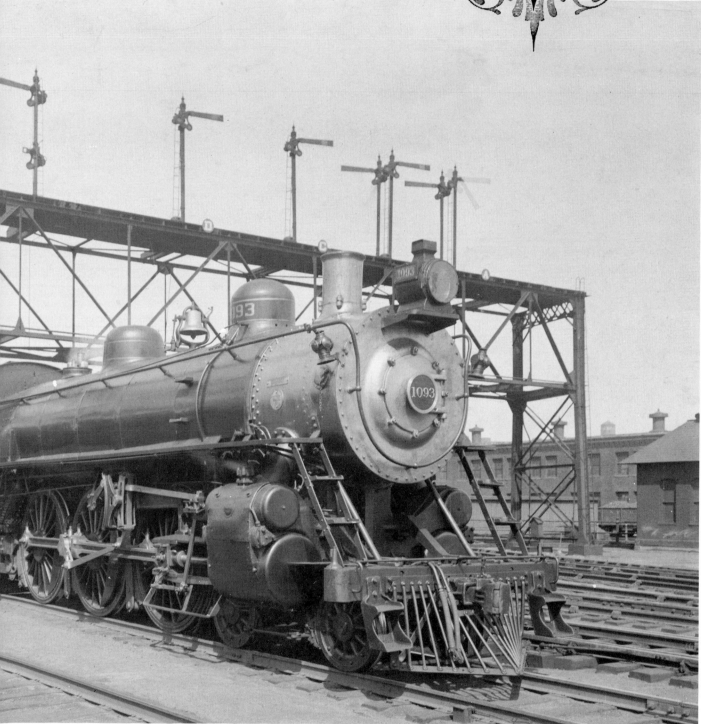

A NEW EDITION of the *Merchants'* stands poised behind Pacific 1093 at South Station, Boston, in 1913. Lucius Beebe collection.

The Merchants Limited

AT SPEED, with A-3a-class American 1203 (ex-No. 544, Rhode Island 1902) on the point. Everett L. DeGolyer Jr. collection.

Charles E. Fisher.

SCHENECTADY turned out high-drivered 4-4-0 No. 1213 (originally No. 539) in 1900. She headed the Merchants' first southbound trip from Boston at 5 p.m. on Monday, December 14, 1903.

The first Merchants'

AFTER the decline of the once-popular Sound steamboats and before the advent of the superhighway and the shuttle plane from Logan Airport, the only proper way to journey between Boston and New York was aboard the forest green cars of the New York, New Haven & Hartford Railroad.

In those happier days, three extra-fare all-parlor-car limiteds operated each day between South Station in Boston and Grand Central in New York City.* The first departure in the day was the morning train — the *Bay State*. At midday there was the *Knickerbocker*. Finally, in the late afternoon, came the greatest of all — the legendary *Merchants' Limited*. A symbol printed in the contemporary New Haven timetable indicated that the extra fare was charged for "limited and superior accommodations" in the parlor and stateroom cars. Favorite of the bankers and brokers from State and Milk streets, the *Merchants'* was the pride of the Shore Line Route.

The *Merchants'* began operation on Monday, December 14, 1903 — the New Haven road's answer to the businessmen of Boston who had expressed their desire for a train departing at the close of the business day. The Boston *Globe* for December 15, 1903, commented:

> Another Flyer Starts. New 5-hour train to New York leaves on first trip. Inauguration very successful.
>
> With wreaths of steam curling triumphantly around her cylinders, locomotive 539 of the New York, New Haven & Hartford Railroad last evening slowly drew from the train-shed of the South Station the *Merchants' Limited*, and the new 5-hour 5 p.m. train put on for the special benefit of Boston businessmen was on its first journey.
>
> Success of a pronounced kind attended the inauguration of the train, for not only were all the seats in the four parlor cars originally assigned to the train purchased in advance, but every seat in an additional car was taken.

In addition to locomotive No. 539, the first-run consist from Boston included No. 2269, a combination compartment and baggage car; dining car *Bronx*; 34-chair parlor cars 2173, 2183, 2172, and 2179; and a smoking and observation car with brass-railed open platform.

What the *Twentieth Century Limited* meant to overnight travel in America, the *Merchants'* was to daytime service. During what have been described as the golden years of railroading, both trains were the epitome of railroad passenger transportation.

*A fourth train, the *Mayflower*, operated as an extra-fare service from 1906 until 1907, when it reverted to a slower schedule. In 1930 the all-parlor-car *Yankee Clipper* was inaugurated for the midafternoon run.

Both photos, Pullman-Standard.

EARLY Shore Line diner Thames, built by Pullman in 1889, had dark green leather seats, bronze fittings; entered service on Gilt Edge.

The Merchants Limited

DINING CAR Bronx, No. 2303, was built by the New Haven in 1903, was used on first run of the Merchants', had vestibules.

THE 34-chair parlor car 2200, Pullman built in 1903, became Pullman Company's Campville in 1913, endured until 1933.

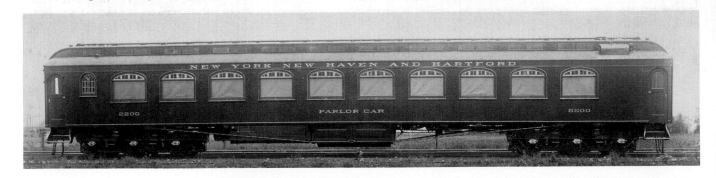

TWELVE-WHEEL elegance was the "state room car" 2195, fitted with two drawing rooms and a buffet. It became the North Shore in 1913 when Pullman assumed operation of New Haven parlor cars and sleepers. The 35-chair car was dismantled in 1926.

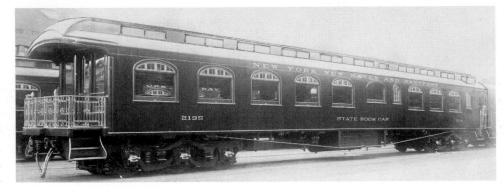

All photos Pullman-Standard except as noted.

PARLOR-BAGGAGE 2270—a unique car type—seated its patrons in deep plush and surrounded them with Victorian decoration.

ORNATE interior (above) of dining car 2313, the Lenox (below), complemented the majestic external look of Pullman product.

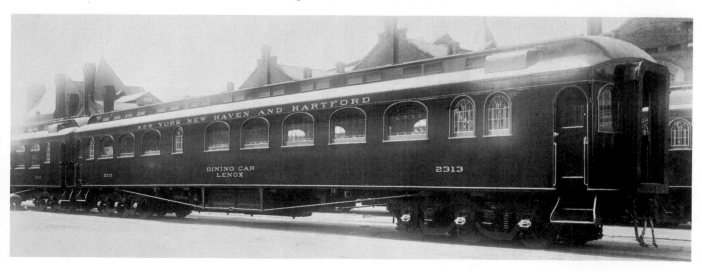

PACIFIC 1093 in a rods-down pose with the new 1913 *Merchants'* at South Boston. Charles E. Fisher collection.

ELECTRICS 01 and 05 (Baldwin-Westinghouse 1906) propel the 1913 *Merchants'* under catenary. Everett L. DeGolyer Jr. collection.

The Merchants Limited

A new Merchants' — 1913

THE PATRONAGE of the *Merchants'* was largely masculine. Ladies were rarely seen except in the private staterooms. Few ventured into the public cars except on their way to the diner. Many ladies, in fact, were reluctant to leave the sanctity of their rooms and had their dinner sent to them.

Dinnertime was awaited with great anticipation. The *Merchants'* Dollar Dinner was legend. Charles E. Fisher of Boston, president of the Railway & Locomotive Historical Society and dean of railway historians, has written nostalgically of meals enjoyed aboard the classic New Haven dining cars, particularly the high-windowed models with a sill upon which ferns and cut flowers were placed. The menu listed tempting delicacies supplied by S. S. Pierce, the traditional Boston grocer: cream of oyster soup, crab gumbo, curried eggs with rice, braised rib ends of beef with browned potatoes, Queen of Puddings. All drinking water served was purified by the Boston filter.

The *Merchants'* was considered the New Haven's best money-maker from ticket sales and also from the cascades of liquors and wines sold in the days before prohibition and after repeal. The wine card listed bottled goods of rare vintage together with the most elegant cigars. The latter, it was said, included J. P. Morgan's favorite smoke, carried at all times in order to be prepared for his once or twice a year patronage. Precious little remained to be desired — except, perhaps, the sale of wines and liquors in New York State (where the card notes their prohibition). Little wonder that the *Merchants'* was one of the few trains in the United States to carry two dining cars in its regular consist.

Until 1913 the New Haven was unique among Eastern roads in the ownership and operation of its own sleeping and parlor equipment. Certain of its heavy wooden private room cars built by Pullman and Barney & Smith were among the most unusual ever built. Reportedly they were replaced with Pullman-owned equipment in 1913 only when the passage of the law prohibiting wooden cars within New York City forced negotiation with the Pullman Company. By leasing from Pullman the New Haven was able to secure quickly, and with a minimum of capital, the enormous numbers of steel sleepers and parlor cars it required.

I-2 PACIFIC 1346 was built by Alco in 1913, possessed 73-inch drivers, exerted 37,600 pounds tractive force, and cost New Haven some $23,000.

Alco.

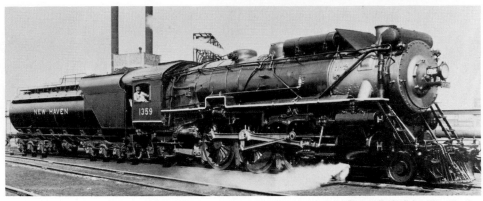

Everett L. DeGolyer Jr. collection.

ELESCO feedwater heater ahead of stack, air reservoirs mounted atop her boiler, and a 12-wheel Vanderbilt tender gave I-4-E Pacific 1359 an appearance that belied the fact that she was Alco constructed in 1916.

COMBINATION parlor-baggage car North Haven provided chairs for 24, was externally ribbed to simulate wood though built entirely of steel.

Pullman-Standard.

The Merchants Limited
DINNER

Grapefruit Cocktail

Puree of Tomato   Consomme

Olives   Radishes   Mangoes

Baked Savannah Shad, Allemande

Fricassee of Chicken

Spaghetti Italienne   Compote of Banana

Roast Prime Ribs of Beef au Jus
Roast South Shore Duckling with Currant Jelly
Roast Short Ribs, Brown Potatoes

Cold Roast Beef   Cold Ham   Sardines

Cardinal Punch

Boiled Potatoes   Spinach   Fried Egg Plant   Bermuda Onions

Dressed Lettuce, French Dressing

Strawberry Shortcake   Madeira Jelly

French Vanilla Ice Cream   Assorted Cake

Chocolates   Confections

Roquefort   Shefford Snappy Cheese   Camembert

Hard and Soft Crackers

Apples, Bananas, Oranges, Grapes

Demi-tasse

MEALS, ONE DOLLAR

The Table Water is purified by the Boston Filter

Unsatisfactory service should be reported promptly to the dining-car steward, and if not remedied at once by him, details to undersigned will receive prompt attention.

A. G. WEBB, Superintendent
Room 1629, Grand Central Terminal, New York

Wines
CHAMPAGNE.

	Large	Small
Great Western (Extra Dry)	$2.00	$1.00
Veuve Clicquot (Yellow Label)	4.00	2.25
Pommery & Greno (Sec)	4.00	2.25
G. H. Mumm's (Extra Dry)	4.00	2.25
Louis Roederer (Brut)	4.00	2.25
Krug (Private Cuvee)	4.00	2.25
Moet & Chandon (Imperial Crown Brut)	4.50	2.50
Ruinart (Vin Brut)	4.00	2.25

WHITE WINES.

Vine Cliff (Finest Riesling, Calwa Brand)	1.00	.60
Sauternes (Barton & Guestier)	1.25	.75
Chateau La Tour Blanche (Cruse & Fils Freres')	2.50	1.50

CLARET WINES.

Hillcrest (Finest Cabernet, Calwa Brand)	1.00	.60
St. Julien (Cruse & Fils Freres')	1.00	.50
St. Julien (Barton & Guestier)	1.00	.50
Pontet Canet (Barton & Guestier)	2.00	1.00
Chateau Larose (Cruse & Fils Freres')	2.50	1.25

BURGUNDY.

Pommard Red Sparkling (B. P. & F.)	3.00	1.50
Pommard (J. Regnier & Co.)	2.00	1.00
Chambertin (J. Regnier & Co.)	3.00	1.50

HOCK.

Laubenheimer (Carl Acker)		.50
Niersteiner (E. Saarbach & Co.)		.75
Rudesheimer (Carl Acker)		1.00

ALE, BEER, Etc.

	Bottle		Bottle
		P. B. Ale (A. Van Nostrand)	.25
Budweiser Beer (Anheuser-Busch)	.20	Delatour Club Soda	.15
Lemp's Falstaff Beer	.20	Siphon Soda, Bottle	.20
Schlitz Milwaukee Beer	.20	White Rock (Splits .15) .40	.25
Pabst Blue Ribbon Beer	.20	Apollinaris Water (Splits .15) .40	.25
Dog's Head Bass Ale	.30	Poland Spring Water, Still .30	.20
Bass' Ale (White Label)	.30	Red Raven, Splits	.15
Guinness' Dublin Porter (Burke's)	.30	Bromo Seltzer, Bottle	.10
Belfast Ginger Ale (C. & C.)	.25	French Vichy (Celestins) .50	.25
Clicquot Club Ginger Ale	.20	Russet Cider	.25

LIQUORS AND CORDIALS.

	Glass		Glass
Old Tom Gin	.20	Haig & Haig	.25
El Bart Dry Gin	.20	Amontillado Sherry	.15
Club Cocktails, "Manhattan"	.20	Benedictine (Pony)	.20
Club Cocktails, "Martini"	.20	Chartreuse Yellow (Pony)	.20
Tom Gin Cocktail	.20	Vermouth	.20
Maryland Rye Whiskey	.20	Creme de Menthe	.20
Private Stock Whiskey	.20	Apricot Brandy (Pony)	.20
Old Bourbon Whiskey	.20	Old Reserve Brandy (Pony, 20c.)	.35
Scotch Whiskey, "Dailuaine"	.20	French Vermouth	.20
Scotch Whiskey, "King Wm."	.25		

CIGARS.

	Each		Each
La Carolina (Perfectos)	.25	La Flor de Aliones (Bachelors)	.15
Romeo and Juliet (Perfectos)	.25	Don Rodrigo (Puritanos), 2 for .25	.15
Hoyo de Monterrey (Perfectos)	.25	Nottingham (Perfectos)	.10
Rey Eduardo (Escepionales), 3 for .50	.20		

Pall Mall Cigarettes			.25
Philip Morris (Cambridge)			.25
Egyptian Idols			.25
Rameses			.20

Playing Cards, 35 cents.
No wines or liquors sold in New York State.

BILL OF FARE on the Merchants' Limited listed prime ribs for 1 dollar, and a martini set one back only 20 cents.

52

A PORTER and a maid were in attendance on the 36-chair parlor car Millbury, an arch-windowed and ribbed but all-steel Pullman.

The Merchants Limited

WHITTENTON (above), Pullman-built in 1913, was equipped with 22 chairs (below) as well as a drawing room and a buffet.

STOCK QUOTATIONS were posted en route aboard the New Rochelle (above and below), a parlor-buffet-observation smoker.

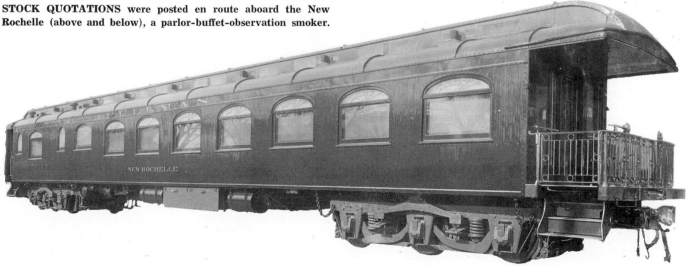

IN A CLASSIC STANCE, I-4-E Pacific 1384 departs New Haven for Boston with the brand-new all-parlor-car Yankee Clipper of 1930.

OBSERVATION *Charter Oak*. NH photo.

The last daily all-parlor-car train in America

FOR YEARS the *Merchants'* was a weekday-only operation, but with the arrival of new Pullman cars on November 19, 1924, a new Sunday service also became effective. Special features of the new equipment included stock market bulletins, special maid and porter service. No effort or expense was

spared to keep the *Merchants* (the apostrophe no longer appeared in any mention of the *Merchants Limited* after 1920) in immaculate condition. Replacement sets of Pullmans were built for the train in 1926, 1927, and 1929 — a record not equaled on any other road.

The clientele of the *Merchants* consisted largely of proper Bostonians: bankers and brokers, members of the finest Boston clubs — the Somerset, Algonquin, and Union. Lucius Beebe recounts a single trip during which he saw aboard the cars Robert Lincoln O'Brien, publisher of the Boston *Herald*; Abbott Lawrence Lowell, president of Harvard; Channing Cox of the Federal Reserve Bank and onetime Governor of Massachusetts; Hooper Hooper, dean of Boston wine merchants; Channing Wells, president of the American Optical Company; and financier Clarence Barron, owner of *Barron's* financial journal.

The *Merchants* reigned supreme on the Shore Line until March 18, 1930. On that date, with considerable ceremony at both South Station and Grand Central, the new *Yankee Clipper* was christened and went into service. During the 1930's the newer train appeared to be the fair-haired member of the New Haven family. Nonetheless, the core of *Merchants* patrons never waivered in their support of the time-honored train, and the *Limited* continued as the choice of the sophisticated traveler.

Final acclaim came late to the *Merchants*. In the 1949 refurbishing of New Haven passenger trains during the postwar reign of President Dumaine, the *Merchants* once again achieved

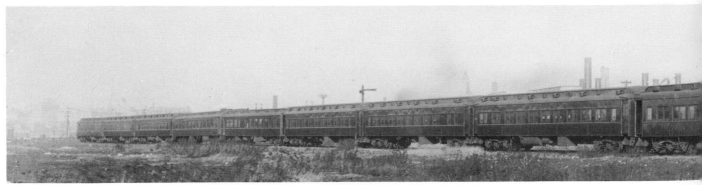

ALL-STEEL *Merchants* at South Boston in a mid-1920's publicity broadside. Charles E. Fisher collection.

COMPLETED January 2, 1930, for the Merchants, 32-chair, 1-drawing-room parlor Massachusetts Bay was 74 feet 6 inches long, weighed 158,200 pounds, had a fishbelly underframe.

All car photos this page, Pullman-Standard.

SOLARIUM-PARLOR Flying Fish (twin of Flying Cloud) was one of the last heavyweights; held 12 chairs, drawing room, buffet, and sunroom; and possessed just the suggestion of an observation's traditional railing.

The Merchants Limited

its unique status on the road. All of the famed Boston-New York limiteds received new streamlined stainless-steel parlor and dining cars. Both the *Yankee Clipper* and the *Merchants* were equipped with radio-telephones. But one train alone, of all the crack limiteds of the Shore Line, remained as an extra-fare operation. The *Merchants* survived as unchallenged king of the road and America's last daily all-parlor-car train.* ⚓

*On June 26, 1949, coaches were added to the *Merchants'* posh consist and an era came to an end.

THIRTY CHAIRS and a drawing room in colonial décor were inside the Northern Light, built in 1930 for the Yankee Clipper. Train's cars were named after clipper ships.

UNUSUAL stainless-steel-sheathed dining car Lewis Morris, built in 1949, rode on six-wheel trucks — odd fixture for a late-model streamlined car.

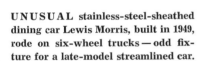

OBSERVATION-TAVERN Bunker Hill mixed stainless-steel sheathing with red-orange window trim, contained tavern section with bar as well as observation-lounge, was built in 1949 as a twin of the Watch Hill.

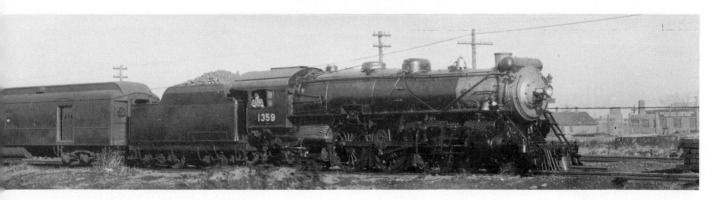

FIRST 26 picks up speed out of Englewood, Ill., behind new Alco Hudson 5268 on August 4, 1929. All photos these pages, A. W. Johnson.

"The 20th Century I

SECOND SECTION of 26 moves out of Englewood behind another 4-6-4. The date: August 4, 1929.

A chronicle of the land's most famous train

1   LITTLE ARGUMENT exists that the most famous passenger train in the United States is the *Twentieth Century Limited* of the New York Central System. Of the many hundreds of Limiteds, Specials, and Flyers that have traversed the land, few have ever stirred the imagination as has the *Twentieth Century*. The New York *Evening World* once said editorially that the name was "so magnificent that it should never be printed save in capital letters, thus: THE TWENTIETH CENTURY LIMITED."

There are those who lament the passing of such luxuries as the Century Club and the all-Pullman consist. Regrettably, these are gone. Indeed, life everywhere has changed! Nonetheless, today's newly refurbished *Century* offers the traveler between the nation's two largest cities a fast, reliable, and safe journey in a variety of accommodations ranging from economical comfort to maximum luxury.

FINAL SECTION of *Century*, minus flags, passes PRR's *Broadway Limited* at Englewood on August 4.

57

"The 20th Century Limited"

TASSELED draperies, high-backed chairs gave diner elegance.

Father of the Century

ON JUNE 15 in 1902 the *Twentieth Century Limited* was inaugurated between New York and Chicago as "the train a century ahead of its time."

The Father of the *Century*, the man who conceived, fought for, and christened this remarkable train, was a patent-medicine-salesman-turned-railroader by the name of George H. Daniels. Daniels, general passenger agent of the New York Central from 1889 to 1907, was a born showman with an uncanny sense of the dramatic. It was he who instituted railroad red caps and started the parcel checking service. George Daniels published for enduring fame, as part of the Central's Four Track advertising series, Elbert Hubbard's *A Message to Garcia*. In 1901 he arranged for a picture of the *Empire State Express* with famed **999** to be portrayed on a U. S. two-cent postage stamp — no small accomplishment, indeed.

It was also Daniels who conceived the Wagner-equipped *Exposition Flyer* and *Lake Shore Limited* — the trains that were the forerunners of the *Century*. The *Exposition Flyer* was operated during the summer and fall of 1893 on a daring 20-hour schedule via the Lake Shore Route to take travelers from New York to Chicago's Columbian Exposition (where the special train exhibited by the New York Central and Wagner Palace Car Company was one of the featured attractions). The new train met with great success but was withdrawn at the close of the fair.

The idea of a permanent fast de luxe New York-Chicago train obsessed Daniels, and finally with great flourish the *Lake Shore Limited* was placed in service in November 1897. A predecessor of today's *Twentieth Century Limited*, it was the New York Central's first regular de luxe all-Wagner operation from New York to the shores of Lake Michigan. Its 80-foot-long cars, among the longest of their day, were similar in pattern and décor to the celebrated World's Fair equipment in 1893.

These trains were designed and constructed by the Wagner Palace Car Company of Buffalo, and each consists of seven cars — a buffet smoking and library car, a dining car, a parlor car, three sleeping cars, and a private compartment stateroom observation car — all connected by standard wide plate glass vestibules and lighted by electricity as well as by Pintsch gas.

ANDES provided for gentlemen a club room with 14 club chairs and a writing desk fitted with stationery; buffet for serving cigars and wines; market reports by wire; barbershop; white-tiled bathroom with tub advertised as a "novel experience in railroad travel."

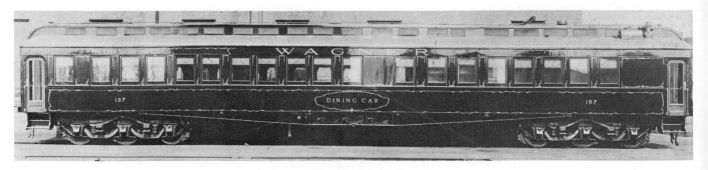

DINING CAR 197 seated 18 persons in the main dining room, which was finished in heavily carved English oak. Two other smaller dining areas could be partitioned off with heavy drapes for private dining. Of no slight importance was the wine and beer cooler.

PINZON contained large parlor with 20 revolving chairs. In opera box at one end of main room were four large chairs behind curved wainscot railing with heavy draperies which could be drawn for privacy. Reading room was equipped with library, and there was a buffet.

MALACCA, sleeping car with 10 sections, 2 staterooms, and buffet, was the Boston car and was routed over Boston & Albany. It was finished in St. Jago mahogany with olive green plush. Folding partitions turned two gold-and-ivory staterooms into bridal chamber.

ALHAMBRA was "furnished with particular reference to the comfort of the ladies." Observation-compartment car offered luxurious lounge, library, services of stenographer with typewriter. Eight compartment-staterooms were finished in different species of wood.

De luxe and all Wagner

THE Wagner Palace Car Company *Rules for Uniformed Employees, 1898* contains some priceless data:

Personal appearance: Avoid putting hand in pockets in tails of uniform overcoats in cold weather giving employee a decidedly loafering appearance, as well as spreading the tail of the coats and getting them out of shape.

Collars and cuffs: White linen only — celluloid are prohibited.

Passes: Individuals who from their large proprietary interests in roads are entitled to ride free in our cars should not be asked to show their passes.

Gambling and card playing: Not allowed on Sunday. Watch for "card-sharps." Card playing not allowed on cars in state of Texas.

Maids: Will wear the prescribed uniform while on duty, and must at all times carry sufficient clean linen for the round trip. They will also have the following personal equipment: Book of Rules, set of keys, bottle of smelling salts, liquid camphor, black and white thread, package of needles, and box of assorted pins for ladies' use.

Maids must be extremely careful to maintain a proper deportment while on duty. Under no circumstances will they allow any familiarity on the part of the crew or passengers, and they should at all times avoid even the appearance of it. No excuse will be accepted for a violation of this rule.

"The 20th Century Limited"

New 20-hour train: surely an experiment

A meteor palace, o'er a path of steel,
Glides, like a comet, on through fairy-land.
— Bingham Thoburn Wilson.

GEORGE DANIELS scored his greatest triumph with the inauguration of the *Twentieth Century Limited* on June 15, 1902. His selection of the *Century* name was pure genius. With this one move he imparted to the new train the historical thrill of passing from one century to another. With the new 20-hour schedule he symbolized the growth of American mechanical superiority.

On the appointed day a large number of railroad men and other spectators gathered in Grand Central Terminal, New York, to see the *Century*'s first westward departure at 2:45 p.m. A similar scene was enacted at Grand Central (La Salle Street) Terminal in Chicago (see ad at right).

Said an English newspaper:

Surely it is only an experiment. There are over 900 miles between the two American cities. Can so high a rate of speed as will be necessary to accomplish the feat be maintained daily without injury to the engine, the rails, and the coaches? The operators will soon find that they are wasting fortunes in keeping their property in condition and then, loving money better than notoriety, the 20-hour project will be abandoned.

Engine 2960, buffet-library car, two sleepers, dining car, and compartment-observation car made up the first train. Although there were accommodations for 42 passengers, only 27 persons, including "Bet-a-Million" Gates, braved the first trip.

In an age when the finest in railway travel was front-page copy, the new equipment was described by the press in glowing terms:

These trains express the latest art in carbuilding. No effort nor expense has been spared to provide the traveling public with all the comforts and conveniences that are afforded by the highest grade hotels, the furnishings and fittings being complete in every detail. The exterior of the cars is painted Pullman standard green color, the ornamentation in gold being simple, but very artistic; gothic lights and oval windows of stained glass set in metal frames lend additional beauty to the exterior elevation.

EARLY CENTURY with mustachioed engineer in cab of J-40 2-6-2 poses on NYC-controlled Lake Shore & Michigan Southern. NYC photo.

The first twin *Century* trains were composed of buffet, smoking, and library composite cars *Decius* and *Cyrus*; observation-compartment cars *Alroy* and *Sappho*; and new 12-section, 1-drawing-room, 1-stateroom sleeping cars *Petruchio*, *Philario*, *Gonzalo*, and *Benvolio*.

The composite and observation cars were former Wagner Palace equipment refurbished by Pullman after purchase of the Wagner enterprise. The sleepers were Pullmans built for the *Lake Shore Limited* and restenciled for the *Century*. The entire consist, in fact, appears to have been hastily assembled pending delivery of new *Century* equipment then building.

The aging Wagner and Pullman equipment was soon replaced in 1903–1904 with brand-new Pullman and New York Central cars built especially for the *Century*.

Steiner & Krueger.

K-2 PACIFIC 4834, lettered for Lake Shore & Michigan Southern, pounds through Whiting, Ind., with Twentieth Century in July 1909.

FRANCISCO, 12-section, 1-drawing-room, 1-compartment Pullman, was built for Lake Shore Limited. Sister cars rolled in first Century.

RANGER and twin Rocket were former Wagner Alroy and Sappho renamed in 1903 after withdrawal from Century. Note brass grille.

DINING CAR outshopped by Pullman for Century had five tables seating four persons, five tables seating two; was "attractively finished in Santiago mahogany. All equipment, linen, silverware, crockery were manufactured to order." Ferns flourished in wall niches.

COMPLETELY appointed barber shop in Indiana served Century's gentlemen travelers.

⤢**INDIANA**, with smoking room→, sections for card playing, library, barbershop, bathroom, and buffet, was one of series built in 1904 by Pullman for Century and Southwestern.

62

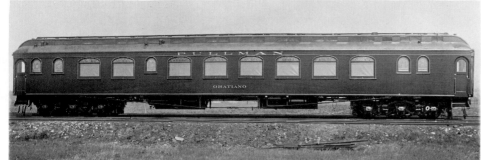

Both photos, Pullman-Standard.

↗GRATIANO featured unusual single window sash frequent in parlor cars and diners but not commonly used in sleepers until advent of air-conditioned streamline era. Car was Pullman built in 1904; had 12 sections, 1 drawing room, 1 compartment; was finished in vermilion wood→.

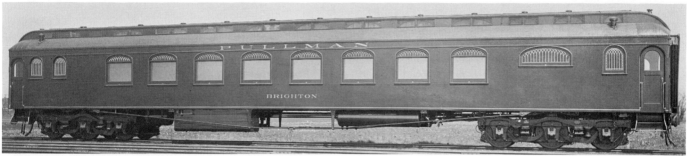

Pullman-Standard.

BRIGHTON had same single window sash as Gratiano, but contained 16 sections and was turned out by Pullman a year later.

EUDOXUS was one of four sister observation cars (others: Magnus, Proclus, and Atticus) constructed by Pullman in 1903.

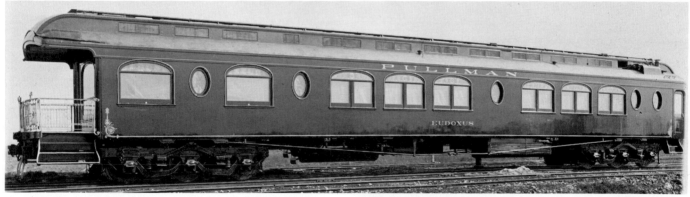

Pullman-Standard.

"The 20th Century Limited"

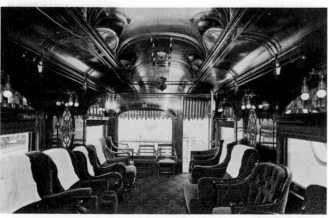

New York Central.

OBSERVATION CARS accommodated passengers in 5 compartments, 1 drawing room, and roomy-chaired observation parlor.

New York Central.

"A LARGE observation platform affords an exceptional opportunity for viewing the scenery en route" from rear of Proclus.

ABOUT the time guns of World War I boom, *Century* pulls through South Chicago, Ill., behind a 4-6-2. Observation car was withdrawn during war. A. W. Johnson.

"The 20th Century Limited"

For the Century—all-steel equipment

BETWEEN 1910 and 1912, the *Century* was newly equipped with luxurious steel equipment from the shops at Pullman. Although the typical consist of seven cars weighed 25 tons more than the wooden train of 1902, the K-2 and K-3 Pacifics continued to travel the 960 miles in 18 hours.

This magnificent train is equipped with Pullman cars of the very latest design and has all the special features which have made the New York Central service so deservedly popular. Barber, Fresh and Salt Water Baths, Valet, Ladies' Maid, Manicurist, Stock and Market Reports, Telephone at terminals, and Stenographer.

George Daniels had passed on but his spirit remained!

Collection of Herbert H. Harwood.

THROUGH Chicago sleeper and parlor-observation Vashti of B&A Century connection (replaced by New England States in 1938) follow 4-6-2 at Faneuil, Mass., in 1909.

BUFFET CAR 449's steel panels were grooved to simulate wood to quell passengers' fears of being electrocuted in severe storms.

DINING CAR 108 (Pullman 1914) was built for Boston & Albany Century connection which operated Boston-Albany 1909 to 1938.

LINDLEY carried a modification of 12-1 configuration for additional private rooms: 10 sections, 2 compartments, 1 drawing room.

HIGHLAND FALLS, built in 1914, sported unusual floor plan — 10 compartments — designed specially for NYC's de luxe service.

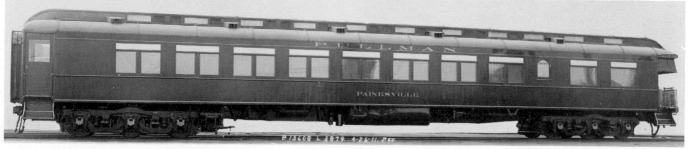

PAINESVILLE was ladies' car whose "maid in service . . . is an experienced manicurist." Included: 8 compartments, observation, lounge.

65

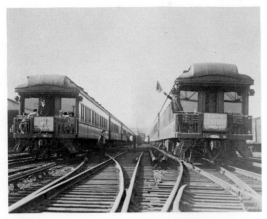

TWO sections of *Century* westbound at Harmon. NYC photo.

"The 20th Century Limited"

The acknowledged standard

"THERE are trains and trains but no train has ever received such adulation as does the *Twentieth Century Limited* from all New York Central men. It is their pet and pride. To them it symbolized their railroad." Thus wrote Franklin Snow in the *Christian Science Monitor* for November 1, 1928.

A school of enthusiasts exists which believes that the zenith of American railroading was reached with the *Century* circa 1929. Surely, this was a noble train — from its magnificent J-1 Hudson, down the line of shining olive Pullmans, to the twinkling blue lamps that spelled 20TH CENTURY LIMITED on the ob-

servation drumhead. Such was the beloved *Century* of Edward Hungerford, Christopher Morley, Lucius Beebe, and Bob Butterfield.

In 1926 when the New York Central transported more Pullman passengers than any other American railroad, the *Twentieth Century*'s gross earnings were 10 million dollars. To maintain this service required a fleet of 122 de luxe cars and 24 locomotives — all assigned exclusively to the *Century*. Rarely did the train operate without the green flags indicating additional sections. On a record January 7, 1929, seven identical trains left Chicago for the East carrying a total of 822 revenue passengers, each of whom had paid the $10 extra-fare surcharge for the privilege of riding "The Greatest Train in the World."

New York Central.

WELL-KNOWN "As the Centuries Pass in the Night" was painted by William Harnden Foster for Central's 1924 calendar.

New York Central.

ANOTHER in NYC's famous series of paintings was "A National Institution" created for '26 calendar by Walter L. Greene.

IN THE SNOW of a December day in 1924 five *Centuries* line up ready for departure from Chicago. New York Central photo.

A. W. Johnson.

CONFERENCE is held between the first and second sections of Twentieth Century Limited at Elkhart, Ind., in September 1928.

PRIDE of NYC were the handsome Hudsons named for river which parallels the main line. American Locomotive built 5297 in 1930.

VAN TWILLER had club lounge, bath, barber who practiced his art at 50 mph. Composite car, built in 1930, was one of last such cars.

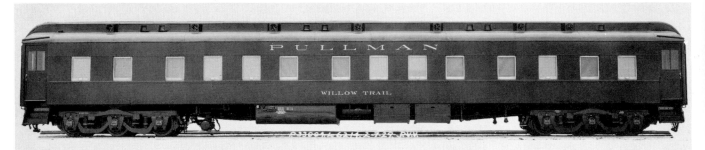

WILLOW TRAIL offered 7 drawing rooms for passengers who might spend the following night in a suite on the Aquitania or Leviathan.

"The 20th Century Limited"

ELKHART VALLEY (ladies' lounge shown) had 1 bedroom, 1 drawing room, buffet lounge. Grained walnut permanent headboards decorated 12-1 sleeper East Buffalo (of East series).

68

DINER 383 and other Century diners were staffed by expert personnel. "Feeding the trains," wrote Hungerford, "was a high art."

APTHORPE HOUSE was one of first bedroom sleepers (13 double bedrooms) in service, among last heavy steel **Pullmans** built in 1930.

CENTSTAR, with 8 sections, 2 compartments, 1 drawing room, was one of series with "Cent" prefix in New York Central operation.

CENTRAL PLAINS was an example of famous Central type (3 compartments, 2 drawing rooms) built in 1926 for NYC Limiteds.

ELKHART VALLEY and other members of Valley series replaced cars of the Central type in **Twentieth Century Limited** in 1929-1930.

69

AGAINST a background of the Board of Trade, the *Century* leaves La Salle Street Station, Chicago, in 1938. New York Central photo.

Pullman-Standard.

CENTURY INN, one of four Century-series club-lounge cars, had octagonal barber shop, lounge with cork walls, rust and gray furniture. The car was retired and dismantled in 1958.

New York Central.

New York Central.

TEN J-3a Hudsons were Dreyfuss-styled for '38 Centuries.

HUDSON model was mounted in lounge of Manhattan Island.

New York Central.

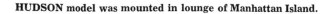

70

"The 20th Century Limited"

First all-room train for America

"FOR 36 years the *Twentieth Century Limited* has been to railroading what hallmarked silver and 18 carat gold are to those seeking superlatives of excellence," declared a 1938 New York Central brochure.

On the *Century*'s 36th anniversary, June 15, 1938, the railroad placed in operation what was purported to be "the most modern, distinctive, and luxurious equipment ever constructed for railroad service." Advertised as the "First All-Room Train in America — No Open Berth Cars," it was operated on the first regularly scheduled 16-hour run between New York and Chicago.

Sixty-two new cars built in Chicago by Pullman-Standard Car Manufacturing Company and 10 J-3a streamlined Hudsons outshopped by American Locomotive constituted four complete sections of trains which set new standards of comfort, beauty, and luxury.

Design of this new train was the combined effort of the Central's equipment engineering department and Henry Dreyfuss, New York industrial designer. No detail was overlooked from the bullet front of the streamlined Hudson to the distinctively designed drumhead seal at the rear of the observation which was repeated in the stationery, dishes, glassware, silver, railroad tickets, and even matchbook covers. The exterior color scheme was light gray with the window area painted dark gray edged in blue and set off with two silver stripes. The interior was in rust, blue, tan, and gray, using woods, metals, and leathers.

With considerable fanfare, two sections of the new train departed from New York's Grand Central Terminal westbound. One hour later two identical sections glided eastward out of La Salle Street Station in Chicago, and a new era in passenger travel was inaugurated.

Pullman-Standard.

IMPERIAL COURT was known as a "4-4-2" (4 double bedrooms, 4 compartments, 2 drawing rooms). Between 1938 and 1940 34 Imperial cars were built; 14 were refurbished by Pullman in 1949.

Pullman-Standard.

CASCADE VALLEY'S 10 roomettes, 5 double bedrooms helped to make Century one of first all-room trains. All 33 Cascade cars were sold in 1958-1959 to CP, IC, and NdeM.

Pullman-Standard.

DINING CAR 680 had unique 6-wheel trucks, was railroad owned. Car seated 38 in "atmosphere of a smart modern restaurant" with gray leather and walnut paneled walls, rust leather chairs, three-tone rust carpet. After evening meal, colored lights, rust napery, swing music took over — presto, a night club. The 680 went to NdeM in 1958.

New York Central.

Everett DeGolyer Jr.

MANHATTAN ISLAND and three sisters were observation-buffet-lounges with 1 master room, 1 bedroom. Blue leather settees, gray leather walls, gray carpet, walnut cabinetry decorated lounge. After the war, cars were assigned to second section of 1948 train. Manhattan Island was sold to NdeM in 1958, renamed Cuitzeo.

Pullman-Standard.

CENTURY CLUB: lounge of *Lake Shore* was inviting. NYC photo.

"The 20th Century Limited"

After the war, a christening

"THE favorite train of famous people," a 1948 NYC brochure said of the *Century*. No less a personage than Dwight D. Eisenhower participated in the inauguration of the postwar *Twentieth Century Limited* in Grand Central Terminal September 15, 1948. Stage actress Beatrice Lillie, assisted by the future President of the United States and the Mayor of New York City, smashed the traditional bottle on the rear of the observation car. To symbolize the railroad's "Water Level Route" slogan, the bottle was filled with a blend of waters from the Hudson and Mohawk rivers and Lakes Erie and Michigan. After two days of exhibition and ceremony in both New York City and Chicago the new streamliners went into service on Friday, September 17, on a 16-hour schedule.

Built by Pullman-Standard and Electro-Motive at a cost of more than 4 million dollars, the two trains contained many innovations including train-radio telephones, fluorescent lighting throughout, pneumatically operated doors, foam rubber mattresses, and enclosed toilets in all two-person rooms. Time-honored amenities such as the 260-foot-long maroon carpet on the platform at Grand Central, the train secretary, and the Century Club were incorporated into the new operation.

Coast-to-coast sleeping cars of the Imperial type had been inaugurated in connection with the Santa Fe *Chief* in March 1946; and for a time in the early 1940's NYC and Santa Fe seriously discussed the inauguration of a combined *Century-Super Chief* that would have been the first regularly scheduled through train from coast to coast.

Holding forth in the new full-length diners were the famed Gold Dust Twins — Stewards Tommy O'Grady and Tommy Walsh. The two Tommys made it their business to know the likes and dislikes of *Century* passengers, and with the luck of the Irish and a touch of blarney they established a national reputation. O'Grady once stated that he knew 75 per cent of the passengers on an average run and could call 15,000 people by name. Tommy Walsh's worn black notebook still indicates that Bing Crosby likes his wheatcakes piping hot at 6 a.m. and that the late Marshall Field always ordered one martini before dinner but expected to find two in the cocktail shaker.

Yet, amid all this splendor, the moving finger of destiny was writing a dramatic chapter in the history of the *Century*. Beset by the pressure of competition, management took a drastic and almost unbelievable step on Sunday, April 27, 1958. Effective that day the *Century* changed from an extra-fare, nonstop, all-Pullman showcase of rail elegance to a standard coach-and-sleeper operation.

Have patience, brother — the story has a happy ending!

ACF Industries.

7500 PIECES of mail are delivered by messenger direct to Century in New York daily, 3800 pieces in Chicago. In addition, 175,000 letters collected daily in special mail drops in Post Offices are carried for business houses not trusting of air mail. R.P.O. 5014 was constructed by ACF.

LAKE SHORE (and Atlantic Shore) contained revered "Century Club" midtrain lounge with secretary, barber valet, shower bath, lounge with bar. Cars were withdrawn from Century in 1958, sold to RI in 1959.

Pullman-Standard.

AUSABLE RIVER (all Century cars are named for shores, rivers, bays, ports, creeks on NYC) has 10 roomettes, 6 double bedrooms.

PORT CHESTER'S rooms (car has 12 double bedrooms) are arranged to open en suite. Several Port cars operate on each train.

DINER 476 has bar and lounge seating 23 persons, in addition to pantry and kitchen. The unit pairs with car 400 to form set.

DINER 400 is exclusively for dining, seats 68 persons in three sections, has piped music, is a luxurious place to take meals.

INTERIOR of 1948 diner 400 is newly refurbished in an attractive scheme.

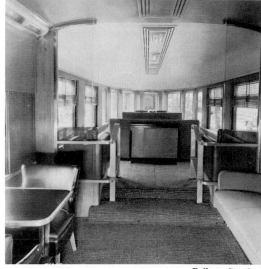

RAISED Lookout Lounge of Hickory Creek is fine spot from which to view the lovely Hudson River.

HICKORY CREEK observation-lounge car has bar and 5 double bedrooms. Two almost identical Brook-series cars protect service.

"The 20th Century Limited"

Sleepercoach streamliner

"LUXURY service at no extra cost," proclaimed a 1962 Central folder. The impending merger of the New York Central and Pennsylvania has overshadowed all other news of these roads. At this early date, however, there is little one can do other than speculate about the ultimate status of the *Century*. Nonetheless, there is a definite attempt under way to restore the train to its former glory. All of its equipment has been extensively refurbished. The dining and lounge and observation cars are newly decorated and carpeted in a manner that is warm and friendly, yet elegant.

Delicious food, new china and glassware, elaborate menus with polished black covers, stewards in dinner jackets, complimentary orchid corsages at dinnertime for lady passengers and boutonnieres at breakfast for men — all are evidence of an effort to offer the finest in train travel. Special services, described in a small folder placed in each sleeping car room, include valet and room service, the use of a typewriter and an electric shaver, and a complimentary morning newspaper placed in the shoe box.

The important passenger news from the Central, however, is the announcement of the enlarged Sleepercoach fleet in an effort to capture the rising market for low-cost sleeping car service. Ten Budd-built stainless-steel roomette sleeping cars originally designed to accommodate first-class passengers have been converted by the Budd Company at a cost in excess of 1 million dollars to all-room Sleepercoaches offering privacy with premade bed, window seat, and full toilet and washing facilities at coach fare plus a small space charge. These cars operate on the *Century** as well as on other crack Central trains.

*The following are consists of two sections of the *Century*, train No. 26, eastbound from Chicago December 20, 1963. First Section (1/26): 4058-4082 — diesel locomotives; *East River* — 10 roomettes, 6 double bedrooms; *Beaver River* — 10 roomettes, 6 double bedrooms; *Boston Harbor* — 22 roomettes; *Chagrin Valley* — 10 roomettes, 6 double bedrooms; 477 — kitchen-lounge; 400 — dining; *Chicopee River* — 10 roomettes, 6 double bedrooms; *Port of Albany* — 12 double bedrooms; *Port of New York* — 12 double bedrooms; *Port Byron* — 12 double bedrooms; *Port of Oswego* — 12 double bedrooms; *Hickory Creek* — observation, bar, lounge, 5 double bedrooms. Second Section (2/26): 4023-4046 — diesel locomotives; 4861 — mail; 5021 — baggage-mail; 8965 — baggage-dorm; 2913, 3066, 3132, 2653, 3033 — coaches; 38 — tavern-lounge; 465 — dining-grill; 10810, 10801, 10800 — Sleepercoaches; *Forest Stream* — 6 double bedrooms, buffet-lounge.

At the railroad's annual meeting in May 1964 President Alfred E. Perlman stated that the *Century* was "the most profitable passenger train in the East." With this note of optimism, the *Twentieth Century Limited* on its 62nd anniversary in 1964 entered a new era. **I**

Budd Company.

FIRST COACHES ever to run in Century consist were order of 60 85′ 7″-long identical cars seating 56 built by Budd Company in 1948.

Budd Company.

GRILL-DINING CAR 466 seats 20 in grill section, 24 in dining area. 1948 Budd-built car serves coach and Sleepercoach passengers.

74

PASSENGERS in observation-lounge car *Hickory Creek* enjoy the scenery at Cold Spring, N. Y. New York Central photo.

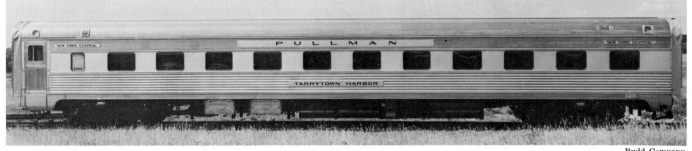

TARRYTOWN HARBOR is 22-roomette first-class sleeper turned out by Budd in 1948. Entire forward portion of Century is stainless steel.

SLEEPERCOACH 10812, rebuilt by Budd in 1962 from Harbor-type car, accommodates 36 in 10 double bedrooms, 16 single rooms.

THE BROADWAY

NEW SIGN headlining *Broadway Limited* goes up at Chicago Union Station.

PENNSYLVANIA
Nº 28
BROADWAY
LIMITED
ALL PULLMAN TRAIN
PHILADELPHIA
NEW YORK

	286
290	285
289	283
288	282
287	281
284	280
DINER	

1 EVERY EVENING at dinnertime several hundred eager travelers are welcomed aboard the Pennsylvania Railroad's *Broadway Limited* trains in New York and Chicago. Each passenger boarding these handsome twin streamliners knows that through the night the utmost in American travel luxury will be at hand.

Every modern convenience known to the carbuilder is available to the passenger on the *Broadway Limited*, which is staffed by a specially trained crew that makes personal service and passenger safety and comfort its first interest and concern.

And so it has been since June 15, 1887, when the Pennsylvania Lines placed in service the predecessor of today's

LIMITED

bled predecessors

Broadway Limited, the celebrated *Pennsylvania Limited* "composed entirely of the famous Pullman vestibuled cars." The Chicago *Times* in its editorial of the day called it "the latest triumph in catering to the traveling public," and commented soberly that "the invention of printing and the creation of the railway are the two leading events in the history of man; and the railway as an agent of civilization is not inferior to the art of printing."

The great improvement was the new vestibule. "Five cars connected with vestibuled platforms impervious to weather changes. In case of accident it is impossible for telescoping to occur."

Four trains of the vestibuled cars were placed in service. Each comprised one composite car, one dining car, and three New York-Chicago sleeping cars. A fourth sleeper, operated between New York and Cincinnati, connected with the *Limited* at Pittsburgh.

The contemporary brochure read:

"You pay for exclusive privileges and get them. You pay for strictly first-class accommodations and get them. You pay for first-class meals and get them. You pay for and receive the best service the Pullman Company and the Pennsylvania Lines can give."

PENNSYLVANIA LIMITED is drawn across Susquehanna River on iron truss bridge at Rockville, Pa., by 4-4-0 568. Structure, built in 1877, was replaced by present stone arch bridge in 1902.

 BROADWAY LIMITED

SULTAN, a vestibuled library and smoking car, was finished in English oak and contained a drawing (smoking) room, bath, buffet, and library. Its writing desk was "supplied with elegant stationery, the fine linen paper bearing the name of the train free for the use of the passengers." The barber's art was guaranteed "safe and pleasing" because of uniform train motion afforded by vestibules.

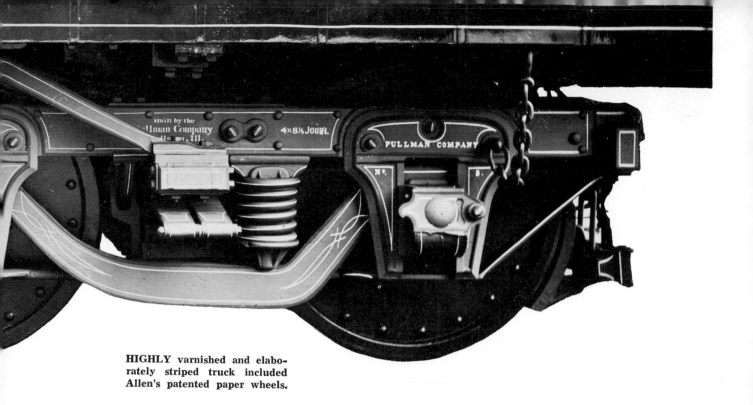

HIGHLY varnished and elaborately striped truck included Allen's patented paper wheels.

LA FAYETTE sat 40 diners for "tastefully prepared menus" featuring porterhouse steak for 75 cents; omelet with rum, 40 cents; and fancy roast oysters, 60 cents. Roomy interior was finished in French oak with myrtle green plush. Novel feature was the enclosure of two seats by rich portieres, which insured complete privacy whenever desired for small parties on the Limited.

All photos, Pullman-Standard.

When they called it the "Yellow Kid"

JANUARY 15, 1898, marked the inauguration of one of the most colorful operations ever to run on rails. Four sets of *Pennsylvania Limiteds*, each built by Pullman's Palace Car Company in Chicago, were painted in a novel color scheme which presented a striking appearance. Each car was Brewster green below the window sash rest, a creamlike yellow above, with the letterboard in red — all with a generous amount of Renaissance decoration in gold.

The livery is said to have resulted from a visit to Pullman by Pennsylvania officials on the day that the lush private cars for Don Porfirio Diaz of Mexico were outshopped from the paint and varnish sheds. The presidential cars were painted in the green, cream, and red of the Mexican flag. The brass from Philadelphia reportedly were so impressed with the scheme that they ordered it applied to the new equipment being built for their New York-Chicago trains as well as the *Congressional*. The *Limited* quickly became known as the "Yellow Kid" and is still called that affectionately by PRR old-timers.

Each train consisted of a parlor smoking and library car, dining car, three drawing room sleeping cars, and a magnificent compartment and observation car. The whole ensemble was advertised as the "newest and most complete Railway Train of this progressive age."

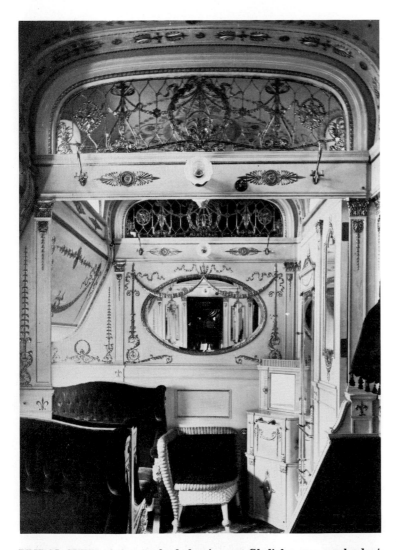

BRIDAL SUITE of the standard sleeping car Gladiolus was resplendent with white woodwork, leaded glass, gilt ornamentation, and velvet draperies with fringed tassels. Honeymooners not already overcome by such luxury could note with astonishment the innovation of electric lights.

OPEN-SECTION sleeping car London threatened to exhaust the publicists' most flowery adjectives, yet its basic 12-section, 1-drawing-room interior configuration was destined to survive for a half century in Pullman diagrams.

THE LIMITED with PFW&C 4-6-0 260; buffet *Claudius*; diner *Valentin*; Pullmans *Orleans, Gladiolus, Fort Wayne*; observation *Veritas*. Collection of A. W. Johnson.

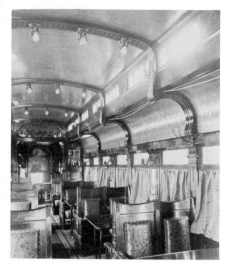

CASSIUS was the gentlemen's car, offering all the facilities of any metropolitan club. Here was the place to check the latest stock market quotations (with bourbon and branch water in hand) or discuss Dewey's capture of Manila. Barbershop and bath were near by.

DINERS Aberlin, Savarin, Magdelin, and Valentin had embossed leather chairs, curtained windows, electric lights. Lavatory of sleeper had beveled mirrors, ceramic tile floor, and padded wicker chairs.

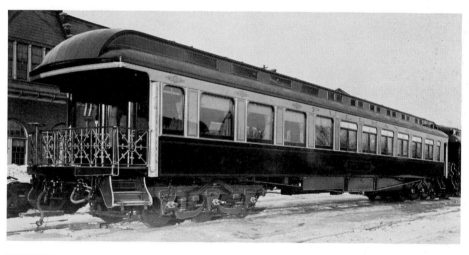

VERITAS, the compartment and observation car, was acclaimed "in high favor with bridal parties and unattended ladies." Each compartment was decorated with inlaid wood in Oriental or Louis XVI style; the finish was Circassian walnut, English oak, vermilion, rosewood, or Santiago mahogany. Observation compartment contained a writing room overhung by growing palms in handsome jardinieres, and 5-foot plate-glass windows — "largest ever placed in a car." Services of a train stenographer were available. Open platform, protected by nickel and brass guard rails, was for "enjoying the dissolving views."

BROADWAY LIMITED

The Great Speed War

THE MAIDEN RUNS of Nos. 28 and 29, the present day *Broadway Limiteds*, took place on Sunday, June 15, 1902. This was the inauguration of the fabled races with the New York Central. In an era of generally carefree living, the Great Speed War, as it was termed in blazing headlines, fired the imagination of the entire nation.

Nos. 28 and 29, originally named *Pennsylvania Special*, astonished the travel world with their 20-hour schedule at a time when the fastest regular runs took 28 hours. Resplendent in their Tuscan red, they were known locally as the *Red Ripper*.

The first 29 left Jersey City pulled by No. 1395, a high-wheeled American class D16, under command of Engineer Martin Lee, who had been personally selected for the occasion by the president of the road, Alexander Johnston Cassatt, truly a genius of a man and among the acknowledged builders of the Pennsylvania system. Twenty hours later, on the advertised, No. 29 completed its maiden run in the old Chicago Union Passenger Station.

The *Special* operated until February 1904, when it was withdrawn because of increased freight traffic and resultant congestion on the main line in the Pittsburgh area.

Then the "impossible" occurred! The New York *Daily Tribune* for Thursday, June 8, 1905, contained a bold advertisement announcing an incredible 18-hour service to Chicago via

Collection of A. W. Johnson.

82

"The Fastest Long Distance Train in the World" — the *New Pennsylvania Special*, Nos. 28 and 29. New York Central replied in kind by reducing the schedule of its *Twentieth Century Limited*, and the war was on!

On its maiden trip, June 11, 1905, No. 29 developed a hotbox 20 miles east of Mansfield, O., and lost precious minutes. Finally with a locomotive hurriedly commandeered from a freight train, the *Special* limped into Crestline and its meeting with destiny.

No. 7002 was coupled on and Engineer Jerry McCarthy en-

tered the Western Division, 26 minutes behind schedule with orders to make up as much time as possible. He covered the 131.4 miles to Fort Wayne in 115 minutes and thrilled the entire nation with his fantastic 3-mile run between AY Tower and Elida, O., at the world's record speed of 127.1 miles per hour.

A correspondent from the Chicago *Tribune* who was aboard No. 28 eastbound wrote:

> Had this been a circus train it would not have attracted any larger crowds along the way than those which have gathered to see the inauguration of the speed war between Chicago and New York. At every station, junction, and crossroads from Chicago crowds, ranging in size from a dozen to more than one thousand persons, were gathered to witness the . . . "lightning express."
>
> Farmers from the country miles around drove their biggest wagons, loaded to the guards with their wives and children and their neighbors' children, to see the 18-hour train go by. They did not see much. The cry of the whistle and a cloud of smoke warned them of its coming. Then a flash of red, and in another second their straining eyes were gazing at the spot where the train had been. It is almost as easy to mark the flight of an artillery shell as that of a train making from 85 to 100 miles an hour.
>
> At Englewood, where a stop of one minute was made, the station platform was thronged with people, and their waving handkerchiefs made it look as if a cloud of white butterflies was just settling down upon them. At Plymouth, Ind., where a stop of two minutes was made to take on water, a crowd of 200 local citizens had gathered to gaze with open mouths at this time and space annihilating monster. At Fort Wayne, which was reached two minutes ahead of schedule time, nearly 1500 curiosity seekers were on hand to watch the progress of changing engines. Many a baseball game in progress along the way was stopped while spectators and players alike gathered along the roadside to cheer the speeding train.

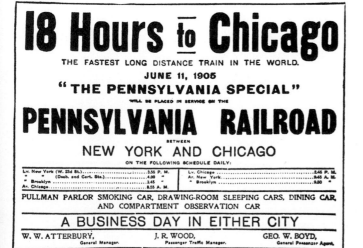

83

JAMESTOWN, the first all-steel Pullman, was named for the Jamestown Exhibition of 1907 and retitled Middletown after the fair. The sleeper was an experimental car, constructed in March 1907 as a prototype for the fireproof equipment required for operation through the Hudson River tunnels into newly opened Pennsylvania Station, which put the keystone on Manhattan.

BROADWAY LIMITED

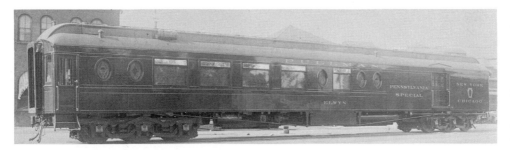

ELWYN, a buffet-smoker built by Pullman in 1905, was "really a man's Club Car. . . . Stock and market reports by wire are posted in conspicuous frames in this car. Business men are thus enabled to keep in touch with outside affairs while en route." This arrangement left the observation "free for ladies and others who prefer the beauties of scenery."

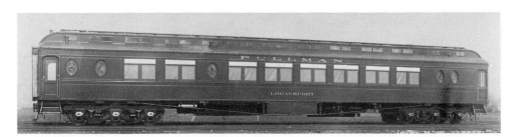

DINING CAR 4469 was Pullman-built in 1901, railroad owned.

LOGANSPORT, Pullman product of 1904, possessed orthodox 12-section, 1-drawing-room interior.

CRESHEIM included 12 sections, 1 drawing room, and 1 compartment; was built by Pullman in 1907.

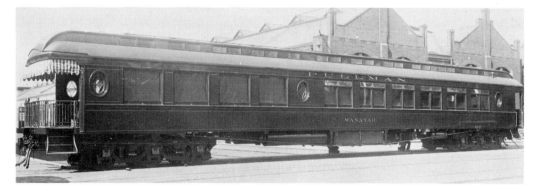

WANATAH, a 4-compartment library-observation built by Pullman in 1905, had "engraved stationery and convenient desks" at the rear, and "if one prefers an amanuensis — a stenographer (male) who occupies a desk in this car will perform this service free of charge."

BROADWAY frequently dominated the elaborate color calendars which the railroad issued each year. Typical was Grif Teller's "Spirit of America" in 1932 which depicted the Broadways hurtling past each other and included in the skyline subtle renderings of their New York and Chicago destinations.

BROADWAY LIMITED

For a splendid train, a new name

BECAUSE of the constant confusion caused by the similar titles of the road's two crack trains, *Pennsylvania Limited* and *Pennsylvania Special*, Nos. 28 and 29 were renamed on November 24, 1912, for the broad right of way over which the train operated — six tracks between New York and Philadelphia. The first advertisements indicated the name as *The Broad Way Limited*.

Regrettably, the new service was short-lived, and along with other luxury trains, was curtailed during World War I by the United States Railroad Administration. Happily, though, with the cessation of hostilities, the *Broadway* was restored, newly equipped by Pullman, and again placed in service on a 20-hour schedule.

With the public demand for heavy "all-steel" equipment and with management's desire to offer an exclusive "uncrowded" train, the *Broadway* was limited to seven or eight cars, although it was regularly operated in extra sections — all identical in consist. Special services included the club car, complete with barbershop, bath, and valet; observation car with ladies' maid, manicurist, and stenographer. The scores of athletic events and complete market reports were available by wire. Prior to departure, telephones were connected in the observation lounge, and the train was listed in New York and Chicago directories.

No detail for the passenger's comfort, however small, was overlooked. Complimentary demitasse was offered with the latest morning newspapers at breakfast; hot cinnamon buns and doughnuts were served from a special heated copper container. Fresh roses were arranged in all public spaces; there was even the renowned "Drawbridge Rule" — delaying the departure of No. 28 in Chicago at such times that traffic bound for Union Station was held up by open bridges over the Chicago River.

Through sleeping cars for Washington (via Harrisburg) were instituted and proved so popular that on May 6, 1923, the *Washington-Broadway Limiteds* were inaugurated with equipment identical to that of 28 and 29. Pennsylvania advertised the trains as "two *Broadway Limiteds*," Twin Trains, both serving the famous $1.50 *table d'hote* dinner." In 1925, when the similarity became too confusing, Nos. 58 and 59 were rechristened *Liberty Limited*.

Pennsylvania Railroad.

Pennsylvania Railroad.

AL JOLSON gives the crowd at trackside a sample of his showmanship on August 28, 1928, a few minutes before the K4 Pacific up ahead slipped the Broadway out of Chicago Union Station. Reporters in search of celebrities made Broadway departures and arrivals their beat.

↓DEPARTURE from Englewood Station, Chicago, frequently prefaced a race↖ with rival Century.

A. W. Johnson.

LIBERTY CAP — baggage-club car with 20 lounge seats and buffet — had sisters named Liberty Bell, Liberty Boys, and Liberty Park.

JAMES LOGAN, a standard 12-section, 1-drawing-room sleeper, was in series named for revolutionary figures such as Stephen Girard.

TIMES SQUARE, with 6 compartments, 3 drawing rooms, was in series containing Franklin Square, Penn Square, Washington Square.

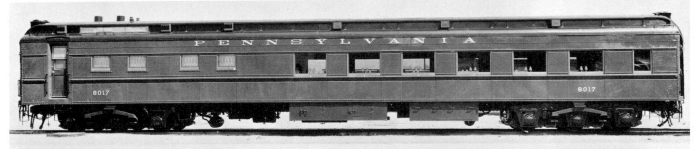

Pennsylvania Railroad.

DINING CAR 8017 was built at Altoona in 1930, retired in 1957; mahogany interior was designed by Marshall Field & Company.

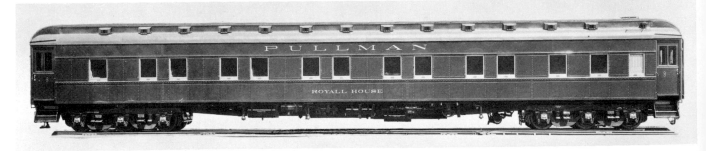

ROYALL HOUSE with 13 single rooms was successful enough to lead to decision to make 1938 streamlined Broadway an all-room train.

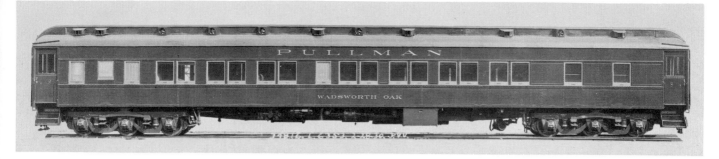

WADSWORTH OAK, an 8-section, 2-compartment, 1-drawing-room car, was built in March 1930 — one of the last heavyweight Pullmans.

ANDREW CARNEGIE, a 14-section sleeper, came out in 1930 in the twilight of heavyweight construction and open sections in the East.

 BROADWAY LIMITED

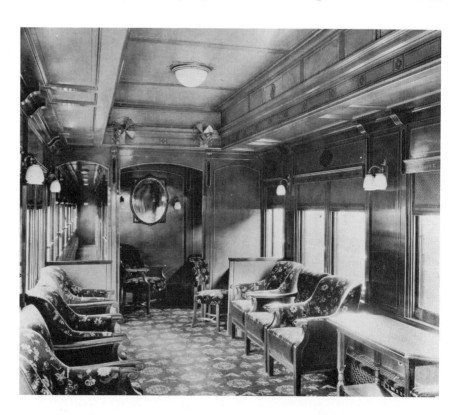

Pennsylvania Railroad.

EN SUITE look through fully compartmented Times Square. Lounge of observation Federal Hall shows globe lamps and fans that once keynoted Pullman interiors.

FEDERAL HALL contained 4 compartments and a ladies' lounge (with maid and manicurist) plus an open platform with brass railings.

BROADWAY LIMITED

LOEWY-IZED K4 3768 leaves Chicago June 15, 1938, on first eastbound revenue run of streamlined *Broadway*. PRR photo.

Pullman-Standard.

Pullman-Stand

HARBOR SPRINGS contained 2 bedrooms, bar, lounge, and facilities for bath, barber, train secretary. Decorations included steer-hide-covered walls, coppered ceilings, and mahogany paneling.

CAMBRIA COUNTY had 13 double bedrooms, included such innovations pre-made beds, folding walls between adjoining rooms, and phone service all rooms to bar and diner. Bedroom cars were named for on-line count

90

Pennsylvania Railroad.

The Fleet of Modernism

THE general business optimism of the late 1930's and the success of the streamlined train in the West prompted the famous "Fleet of Modernism — The Blue Ribbon Trains" of June 1938.

Fifty-two new sleeping and lounge cars were built by Pullman-Standard in Chicago for service on the Pennsylvania. (Similar cars were built for the New York Central.) Two railroad-owned diners were refinished in the company's shops at Altoona. All of the Pennsylvania equipment design was supervised by Raymond Loewy of New York and Paul Cret, eminent architect of Philadelphia and head of the College of Architecture, University of Pennsylvania. K4 Pacifics, including the streamlined 3768, handled the streamliner west of Harrisburg; GG1 electrics did the work under catenary to New York. Engines were green-black, cars two shades of Tuscan red.

The new Pullmans assigned to the *Broadway* included such interesting innovations of design as the master room containing the first *private-room* shower and the roomette. The new *Broadway* was first with a 16-hour schedule, and first, too, with an all-room consist, which abolished the fabled upper and lower berths.

Pennsylvania Railroad.

OBSERVATION cars Metropolitan View and Skyline View contained two master rooms (each with two beds, private shower, and radio); and the lounge at the rear↑ was done up with colored leather and cork walls, metallic curtains. Splendid for train-watchers.

Pullman-Standard.

CITY OF JOHNSTOWN bore the name of the community made famous by a flood, contained 18 roomettes — a completely private accommodation for one synonymous with the streamlined era.

Pennsylvania Railroad.

DINING CAR 4420 was built at Altoona in 1910, completely rebuilt there in 1938 for streamlined Broadway. Two separate dining compartments seated a total of 30. One section had walls of satin-finished stainless-steel squares separated by strips of brass; the other was covered with rose-colored mirrors. In addition, there were two smaller areas containing a bar and cocktail booths. Prints of old PRR engines were hung over the settee.

91

Welcome aboard the

Broadway Limited

Leader of the Fleet

New York • Philadelphia • Chicago

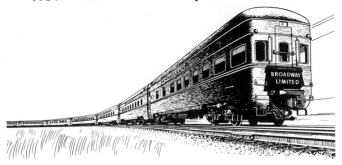

PENNSYLVANIA RAILROAD

COVER of train guide given to each *Broadway* passenger.

Today's Broadway Limited

THE *Broadway* still operates in the grand manner of the Golden Age. It is the only luxury all-Pullman room train between New York and Chicago. At a time when other passenger trains throughout the country are being withdrawn from service for lack of patronage, additional cars are frequently added to the *Broadway* and it continues to run at near capacity month after month. A principal reason is the pride of the railroad and Pullman employees who sell the service, prepare the train, operate it on time and safely, and provide the personal attention which brings so many letters of commendation. Westbound running time is 16 hours; eastbound its 15½ hours, the fastest Chicago-New York service.

One's first impression when boarding the train is that of neatness and order. Everything is shipshape. Uniformed maintenance and service supervisors ride the *Broadway* frequently, checking the cars' riding qualities, electrical accessories, carpeting, upholstery, and paint, and making sure that train crews are courteous and competent.

One of the popular services aboard the train is provided first thing in the morning when the porter slips a small mimeographed sheet under the door. This sheet contains the latest weather report for the destination.

Today's two *Broadway Limited* trains with their locomotives* represent an investment of $4,614,000 as compared with $200,000 for the 1902 operation. **I**

*Consist of the *Broadway Limited*, train No. 29, westbound, passing Pittsburgh on January 5, 1964, included: 5855A-4856A-5864A — diesel locomotives; 6582 — R.P.O.; *Chippewa Creek* — 12 duplex single rooms, 4 double bedrooms; *Clear Creek* — 12 duplex single rooms, 4 double bedrooms; *Imperial Lea* — 4-4-2; *Illinois Rapids* — 10 roomettes, 6 double bedrooms; *Swatara Rapids* — 10 roomettes, 6 double bedrooms; *Alfred E. Hunt* — 12 duplex single rooms, 4 double bedrooms; *Imperial Loch* — 4-4-2; *Harbor Rest* — lounge, 5 double bedrooms, bar (trainphone); 4622-4623 — twin-unit dining cars; *Imperial Fields* — 4-4-2; *Little Miami Rapids* — 10 roomettes, 6 double bedrooms; *Charles Lockhart* — 12 duplex single rooms, 4 double bedrooms; *Fishing Rapids* — 10 roomettes, 6 double bedrooms; *Clearfield Rapids* — 10 roomettes, 6 double bedrooms; *Tower View* — observation, 2 master rooms, 1 double bedroom, bar-lounge.

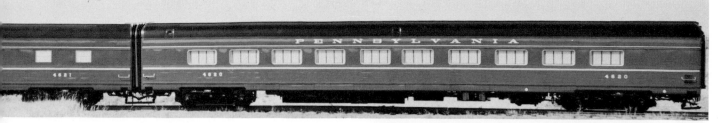

Budd.

DINING-KITCHEN CARS 4620-4621 are among the largest restaurants on rails. Car 4620 seats 68 in a clublike atmosphere (below) with soft music; twin 4621 contains stainless-steel kitchen and crew dormitory. Budd built this 165-foot set; ACF constructed a similar set, Nos. 4606-4607. Pennsylvania was one of the first roads to introduce through operation of diners, thus eliminating the adding and cutting out of such cars at intermediate points.

BROADWAY LIMITED

PRR.

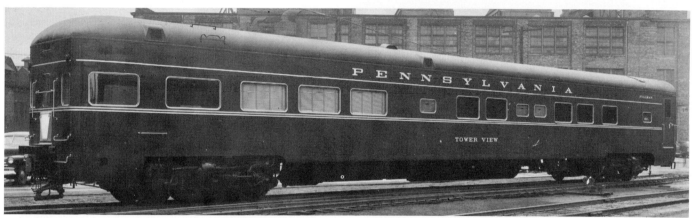

Pullman-Standard.

TOWER VIEW and its twin car Mountain View are the Broadway Limited's observations today. Built by Pullman-Standard, each includes a double bedroom and 2 master rooms as well as a buffet-lounge (below). Each master room contains two beds, roomy closets, two large windows, radio, shower, and even wood paneling.

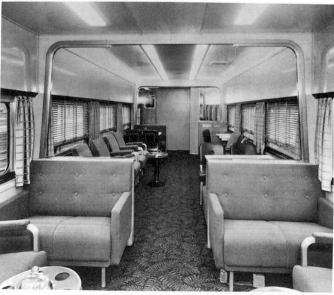

Lower photos, PRR.

RE-EQUIPPED *Broadway* of 1948 under catenary behind GG1 4902. PRR photo.

Pullman-Standard.

HARBOR REST, a 5 double bedroom-lounge, was delivered in December 1948 with a barbershop and bath. Later these facilities of mid-train lounge were replaced by a Telephone Room. Reception is excellent and costs only slightly more than a regular call for equal distance. Sign in room cautions users: "This is a Radio-Telephone . . . Federal regulations prohibit the use of profanity." Porter makes change.

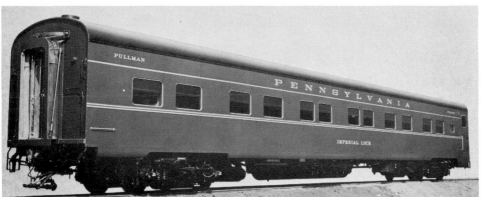

ACF.

IMPERIAL LOCH, an American Car & Foundry car, contains the larger types of space: 4 compartments, 4 double bedrooms, 2 drawing rooms. Two Imperial cars are assigned to each train. Carpeting is blue, upholstery rose and gray, walls blue-green. Sleepers were built in Berwick, Pa.

ACF.

HURON RAPIDS contains 10 roomettes as well as 6 double bedrooms with lengthwise beds (called "B" type rooms). Car was built by ACF.

94

WALTER PIDGEON confers with steward over Broadway's menu.

BROADWAY LIMITED

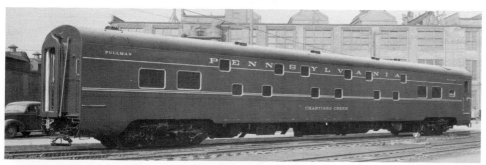

Pullman-Standard.

CHARTIERS CREEK contains 12 duplex rooms and 4 double bedrooms. Duplex room, extending across the car, is ingeniously and compactly arranged with its neighbors in alternating "upstairs" and "downstairs" rooms, each with a wide sofa bed, private lavatory, and full-length mirror. "Upstairs" rooms provide an exciting panoramic landscape view.

Pullman-Standard.

CATAWISSA RAPIDS by Pullman-Standard contains 10 roomettes and 6 double bedrooms in common with Huron Rapids on opposite page but bedroom beds are transverse to the direction of travel. Each Broadway contains two of the Rapids sleepers.

PRR.

RAILWAY POST OFFICE No. 6529, built at Altoona in February 1910 and modernized for today's Broadway, is a 70-footer of the railroad's BM70NB class. Time was when all important New York-Chicago mail was marked for Broadway or Century dispatch.

95

The
Capitol Limited
and
The George Washington

"To welcome you aboard our trains is a great pleasure"

1   ON December 31, 1962, the Interstate Commerce Commission, in a widely heralded move, approved the affiliation of the Baltimore & Ohio Railroad and the Chesapeake & Ohio Railway as a "step to merger." The new arrangement brought together two of America's oldest and greatest companies, each dating from the early days of railroading in America. Their combined lines follow routes of unsurpassed industrial, scenic, and historical interest.

Improved passenger services were among the first benefits resulting from the affiliation. Both railroads acknowledge a tradition of conscientious effort in maintaining high standards in their car equipment, and in the attentiveness and courtesy of their employees serving the public. This tradition dates from the early days of de luxe service on both the B&O Royal Blue Line (the *Royal Limited*, New York-Washington, the "Finest Daylight Train in the World"); and the C&O, "The Rhine, the Alps, and the Battlefield Line" (The Famous *F.F.V.* Vestibuled Limited — The *Fast Flying Virginian*, New York-Cincinnati).

Two of the finest trains in the land serve as standard bearers of the new affiliation — the *Capitol Limited* of the B&O and the *George Washington* of the C&O. Each has a great heritage.

96

Announcing

The
Capitol Limited
"Over the Nation's Highway"
a New All Pullman Limited Train

CHICAGO
WASHINGTON
BALTIMORE
Through Sleepers to Philadelphia and New York

Baltimore & Ohio
America's First Railroad
Established 1827

The George Washington

THE MOST WONDERFUL TRAIN
IN THE WORLD... *CREATED BY THE*

CHESAPEAKE AND OHIO

to Celebrate the

TWO HUNDREDTH BIRTHDAY ANNIVERSARY *of*
THE FATHER OF TRANSPORTATION IN AMERICA

1732
1932

OBSERVATION-lounge-sleeper *Commander in Chief*. C&O photo.

The
Capitol Limited
and
The George Washington

Two distinguished trains

THE *Capitol Limited*, B&O Nos. 5 and 6, operating between Baltimore-Washington and Chicago, is the older of the two trains. It was placed in service on May 13, 1923, "as the result of many appeals from Chicago businessmen for a later departure — after the completion of a full half-business day."

The credo for the new train was stated in the 1923 B&O inaugural brochure:

> In preparing the schedule of this train, consideration for the comfort of patrons was our constant thought — careful handling by enginemen — no excessive speed — just a comfortable, safe, dependable schedule — to meet the requirements of Chicago businessmen and women.

The *Capitol Limited* was the first all-Pullman train operated between Chicago and the nation's capital. It later became the first completely air-conditioned train on its route (1932) and the first dieselized train between Chicago and the East (1937).

Until the end of Royal Blue Line service between New York and Washington on April 26, 1958, the *Capitol* carried a New York (Jersey City)-Chicago sleeping car. (From 1923 until

1926 this car operated directly into Manhattan's Pennsylvania Station as the result of a World War I arrangement.)

In 1938 the train's all-steel equipment was thoroughly remodeled, inside and out. A new streamlined exterior included skirted sides, rounded roofs, flush vestibule closures, and a striking royal blue, gray, and gold livery. Rubber draft gear and heavy 6-wheel trucks contributed to a smooth ride.

Travelers aboard the *Capitol* have long experienced a sense of distinction. They have enjoyed its ideal businessmen's schedule, its beautiful dining cars and superb meals. They have found themselves in famous company, for the *Capitol* is a meeting place of statesmen and ambassadors, of admirals and generals, of leaders in business and industry.

The crack *George Washington*, C&O trains 1 and 2, travels overnight between Washington and Cincinnati, 599 miles (with through cars serving Louisville, Newport News, St. Louis, Chicago, Detroit, and New York).

The *George*, as it quickly became known, was placed in

MOUNTAIN ROAD concludes 1928 *Capitol*. E. L. Thompson.

A FOND FAREWELL beneath the markers of the George Washington during a conditional stop in the 1930's at West Virginia's spa.

F-17 PACIFIC 471 tows C&O's flagship under a plume of white.

service on April 24, 1932. It was created by the Chesapeake & Ohio and the Pullman Company to celebrate the 200th birthday anniversary of George Washington, "the father of transportation in America." The *George* was advertised as "The Most Wonderful Train in the World."

Reaching boldly into the future, the *George Washington* materializes a vision of the Transportation of Tomorrow; other trains are going to be like it in time.

The 1932 edition of the *George Washington* was a remarkable train. Instituted in the midst of economic depression, it catered to both Pullman and coach passengers, offering innovations in design and comfort.

The sleeping and restaurant cars were unlike any others on rails. Each one bore a name related to George Washington's part in the making of the United States. All were appropriately decorated in a colonial style with colorful paintings, prints, and architectural details of the Revolutionary period.

Coach passengers rode in the Imperial Salon cars which seated only 45 persons in near parlor-car comfort. These Salon cars exemplified the Chesapeake & Ohio policy of supplying the finest kind of transportation for the price of a coach ticket.

An outstanding feature of the *George Washington* was its air-conditioning system. On April 24, 1932, the *George* was advertised as the "world's first air-cooled and conditioned sleeping car train."* It employed the "Pullman mechanical system" of generating electricity by the revolutions of the car wheels which were connected, through their axles, to motor generators. While the train was standing in terminals, the system operated on commercial electricity. A subsequent development, the "holdover tank" charged with cold liquid, permitted continued cooling during stops without the use of auxiliary standby power.

*The B&O on April 20, 1932, advertised its *National Limited* as the "first completely air-conditioned long-distance sleeping-car train." (The first completely air-conditioned train in the world was B&O's New York-Washington all-parlor-car *Columbian*, placed in service on May 24, 1931.)

Both photos, E. L. Thompson.

THE CAPITOL of 1931 is trailed by the solarium-sleeper Capitol Square. One year later Baltimore & Ohio was to advertise the first air-conditioned long-haul sleeping-car train.

OLIVE-GREEN Pacific President Polk, one of 21 high-speed 4-6-2's B&O named for U.S. Presidents, grips sanded rail as she departs Washington Union Station with the Capitol Limited. Engine 5309, a Baldwin of 1927, also has decorative drumhead on her smokebox door.

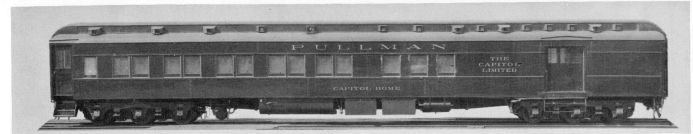

CLUB CAR Capitol Home of 1926 was finished in Pullman green with train name in gold; contained buffet, barber, bath, valet; seated patrons (below) in soft, overstuffed leather club chairs.

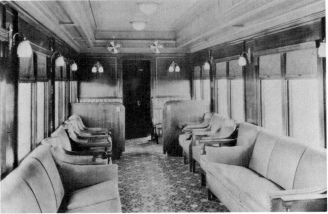

B&O.

DINER Margaret Corbin had Hepplewhite chairs (above), Georgian leaded windows, Sheraton sideboard, specially designed china.

GREEN BANK — a 12-section, 1-drawing-room heavyweight — was streamstyled in 1938; fitted with chime call bells, adjustable seats.

EMERALD BROOK — an 8-section, 4-double-bedroom car — carried 1938 blue, gray, gold colors; Capitol Limited had similar cars.

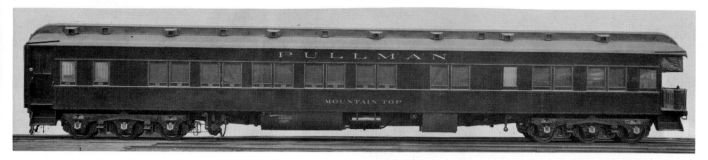

FULL-WIDTH DIAPHRAGMS, rounded roof, skirts, and retractable steps earmark rebuilt heavyweight Maryland Club, 8-section buffet-lounge car modernized in 1938 for Capitol Limited service. Capitol and National were first air-conditioned trains between East and Middle West.

MOUNTAIN TOP observation-sleeper (10 sections with a lounge) was assigned to Capitol in 1923, was replaced in 1926 by Capitol-series 10-section observations. Lounge (right) of Monte Viso (later Capitol Heights) displays restrained interior decoration.

The **Capitol Limited**

NATIONAL VIEW was one of four 3-compartment, 2-drawing-room observation cars built in 1925. Prefix names were later changed to National for service on that train. NYC's Century and Southwestern and Southern's Crescent had similar equipment.

CAPITOL CITY (3 compartments, 1 drawing room, buffet-lounge, sunroom) was built in 1929, streamlined in 1938; served until 1950.

PULLMAN   THE GEO

COMM

THE GEORGE WASHINGTON

735

COACH 735 ("Imperial Salon Car" in C&O's equipment listings) seated 45 in near parlor-car comfort. Carpeted floors (below) and 2-1 seating were luxurious innovations for 1932 coach riders.

MICHIE'S TAVERN, named for Colonial patriot rendezvous, served $1.25 Mount Vernon Dinner featuring Chesapeake Bay seafood, Colonial recipes. Inside (above) "Restaurant Car" had Colonial patterned carpet, framed prints, off-white walls, Duncan Phyfe chairs. Gadsby's Tavern and Raleigh Tavern were similar.

THE GEORGE WASHINGTON

963   MICHIE'S TAVERN   963

102

The George Washington

COMMANDER-IN-CHIEF, one of two 8-section, library-lounge cars (twin was named American Revolution), featured valet service, daily newspapers, telephone at terminals. Bust of Washington in archway (below) was gift of Washington Bicentennial Commission; framed prints were Leutze's "Washington Crossing the Delaware" and "The Signing of the Declaration of Independence." Car was sold to the NdeM in 1950 and renamed Dos de Abril.

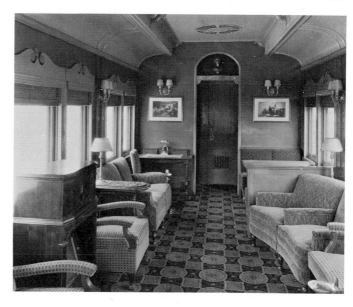

FIRST CITIZEN, an 8-section, 1-drawing-room, 2-compartment car of 1932, was finally sold to Mexico in 1950. Cooled air entered car (above) through combination grilled lighting fixture in ceiling.

BARON ROCHAMBEAU, later changed to Count de Rochambeau, was a 12-section, 1-drawing-room car of 1932 that also wound up on the National Railways of Mexico.

103

The
Capitol Limited

BOUND for Chicago, *Capitol* swings out of Washington Union Station. B&O photo.

Two of America's most modern streamliners

A WEALTH of new equipment makes both the *Capitol Limited* and the *George Washington* two of America's most modern streamliners.

Although the *Capitol* is still listed separately in the timetable as trains 5 and 6 and is shown as an all-sleeping-car train, it regularly operates with Nos. 25 and 26, the *Columbian*, which is presently a coach-Slumbercoach operation. Both trains carry the only Strata Dome service in the East. In 1963, its 40th anniversary year, the *Capitol* regularly carried near-capacity loadings. B&O officials noted evidence of a growing trend back to the rails by people rediscovering the relaxed comfort and convenience of travel on luxury passenger trains for overnight journeys.

The present-day edition of the *George Washington* is a fine, carefully maintained train. In 1950 it was completely re-equipped with diesel locomotives and the latest dining and sleeping cars. Always a popular train, it carried over 15 million passengers in its first 25 years of operation.

Although the exquisite colonial décor and many of the service features such as the barber, manicurist, and hostess have given way to the changing tastes and demands of the traveling public, the air of elegance which characterized both the

Capitol and the *George Washington* in their earlier years has remained. Courteous service is still a byword among C&O-B&O crewmen who have been trained to regard it as a tradition worthy of preservation. The same fine cuisine at prices in keeping with today's prevailing standards is offered to passengers on both trains.

One of the first visible results of the new affiliation was a stunning new Continental-flavored combined timetable of passenger services, extensively illustrated in full color with simple, easy-to-read timecards, maps, and equipment listings. On the first page appeared a friendly, straightforward expression of passenger service policy signed by Walter J. Tuohy, president, Chesapeake & Ohio; and Jervis Langdon Jr., president, Baltimore & Ohio:

There will be improvements designed to meet the needs of today's traveler who uses all modes of travel as they meet his requirements for convenience, comfort, and safety. We believe many travelers now using only the highways or airways would often prefer to take the train where rail schedules, accommodations, and service are made attractive enough. . . . Although passenger train services are a comparatively small part of total operations, they are an important way in which the public becomes aware of us and judges our performance generally.

To welcome you aboard our trains is a great pleasure. 🅘

The George Washington

STREAMLINED 4-6-4 heads *George Washington* at Richmond in 1950. C&O photo.

B&O.

CAPITOL of 1938 pauses on Potomac River bridge at Harpers Ferry, W. Va., with rebuilt sleepers behind 3600 h.p. diesel.

WESTBOUND George Washington, train No. 1, passes eastbound coal and merchandise at the passenger depot in Russell, Ky.

C&O.

105

TWIN-UNIT DINERS 1092-1093 were ordered by C&O from Pullman-Standard but were sold to NYC before completion. In a dress of stainless steel and gray they served on Commodore Vanderbilt and Detroiter from 1950 to 1957, when the team was sold to the Baltimore & Ohio for Capitol service. Unit 1092 (right) combines four-place with triangle-type table seating.

The Capitol Limited

STARLIGHT DOME, one of the only dome sleeping cars in the East, was built by Budd in 1950 for Chessie service but sold to B&O when completed.

THRUSH is one of 11 sleepers built in 1954 by Budd and named for birds. The stainless-steel car contains 16 duplex roomettes and 4 double bedrooms; features blue letterboard with gold lettering on it.

PAW PAW, one of eight cars named after rivers, was built by Pullman-Standard in 1948; contains 14 roomettes and 4 double bedrooms; is finished in blue and gray, gold trim.

NAPPANEE is one of four twins (others: Wawasee, Dana, Metcalf) built in 1950 by Pullman-Standard for C&O and acquired by B&O in 1951 for Capitol and Ambassador service. Butt-ended buffet-lounge, 5-double-bedroom cars can be operated midtrain or as observations.

Pullman-Standard.

DINING CAR Gadsby Tavern and kitchen-dormitory Gadsby Kitchen were among 14 twin-unit diners ordered by C&O. NYC bought four before completion; later sold 2 to IC, 2 to B&O.

The George Washington

Budd.

PURCHASED for Robert R. Young's stillborn Chessie, sleeper 1850 (5 roomettes, 1 single bedroom, 3 drawing rooms) was sold to B&O.

NATURAL BRIDGE, one of five identical cars built in 1950 by Pullman-Standard and now operated between New York and the posh spas at Hot Springs and White Sulphur Springs, contains 11 double bedrooms; has a black roof, yellow letterboard, blue window band, gray lower side.

Pullman-Standard.

CITY OF NEWPORT NEWS—like all 10-roomette, 6-double-bedroom cars on C&O — is named for an on-line town. Fifteen identical cars were sold by C&O to ACL, B&O, and IC.

Pullman-Standard.

ALLEGHENY CLUB was one of 13 similar cars built by Pullman-Standard for C&O in 1950. Outshopped as 5-double-bedroom observation-lounges, they were subsequently sold (four to B&O) or rebuilt as diner-lounges.

Pullman-Standard.

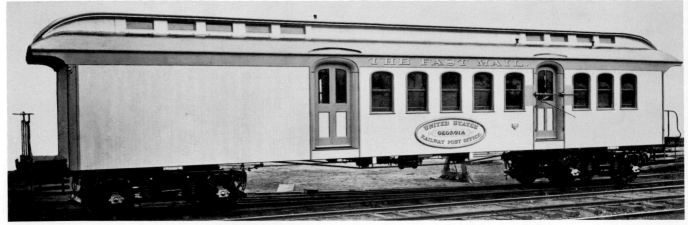

R.P.O. GEORGIA, a Jackson & Sharp car operated in New York-New Orleans service in the 1880's. Everett L. DeGolyer Jr. collection.

CRESCENT

FOUR THOUSAND horsepower rolls the *Crescent* through north Georgia. SR photo.

WASHINGTON AND
SOUTH-WESTERN VESTIBULED
LIMITED
Via RICHMOND & DANVILLE R.R.

From the "Vestibule" onward—   "a service second to none"

LIMITED

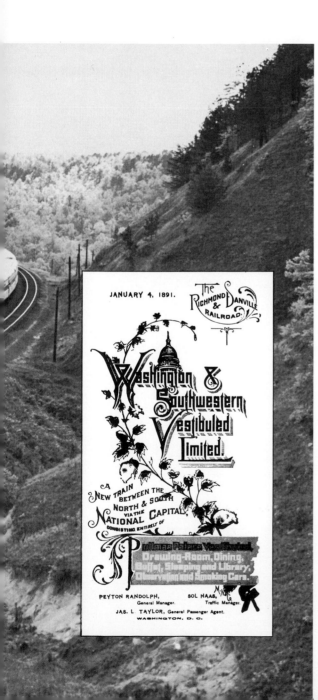

I "THE management of the leading Southern System
— The Richmond & Danville Railroad Company —
has determined to inaugurate a service second to none in
completeness and elegance of detail . . . and providing all
the latest and best facilities for the comfort and enjoy-
ment of its patrons.

"Therefore, daily, on and after the 4th of January 1891
— fitly ushering in the New Year as a new era — the
'WASHINGTON AND SOUTHWESTERN VESTIBULED LIMITED' will
start from under the shadow of the great white dome of
the National Capitol, cross the wide stream of the stately
Potomac, pass the historic spots where the best blood of
the country was poured in its great civil strife, through the
beautiful Piedmont section and in sight for hundreds of
miles of the grove-clad Blue Ridge, by cotton and tobacco
fields, forests, plantations and flourishing centers of industry; on to Atlanta, 'Queen City of the New South.'"
So declared a Richmond & Danville Railroad brochure
of 1891.

From this historic beginning in 1891 developed the
famed *Crescent* of today, operated between New York-
Washington-Atlanta-New Orleans by the Pennsylvania
Railroad-Southern Railway System-West Point Route-
Louisville & Nashville Railroad. Daily the gleaming stainless-steel *Crescent* speeds through 10 states and the District of Columbia, through an area which is important industrially, productive agriculturally, rich in history and
tradition, and unmatched for scenic beauty.

109

ABOARD the Washington & Southwestern Vestibuled Limited a man could enjoy a cigar with the boys in the smoker or join his lady for lunch, followed by an afternoon of sight-seeing from the observation car of the South's finest.

Magnificent and luxurious

THE predecessor of today's *Crescent* was one of the early luxury trains in the United States when it was inaugurated in January 1891. Originally named the *Washington & Southwestern Vestibuled Limited*, it was commonly referred to as the *R&D Limited*, Nos. 37 and 38 of the Piedmont Air Line.

The first all-year train in the South to carry vestibuled equipment, it was advertised as "a magnificent train of Pullman Vestibuled Palaces, consisting of Drawing Room, Dining, Sleeping and Library Cars of the latest, most magnificent and luxurious designs, built expressly for this service and run daily."

A so-called "extra fare" ($6 between Washington and Atlanta) included the sleeping car charge for a lower berth in the elegant new cars constructed by the Pullman Palace Car Company in Chicago.

The contract between Pullman and the Richmond & Danville dated September 30, 1890, called for equipment "to be equal in construction and design to similar cars now in service upon the New York & Chicago Limited Train of the Pennsylvania Railroad" (see page 76).

The Washington-Atlanta schedule was soon expanded to include a through Pullman to New Orleans via Montgomery and Mobile over the rails of the Atlanta & West Point, the Western Railway of Alabama, and the Louisville & Nashville. Scheduled time for the 1350-mile run from New York to New Orleans, in connection with the Pennsylvania's *Congressional Limited*, was advertised as "40 hours, Unprecedented." Because of the popularity of this service the *Washington & Southwestern Vestibuled Limited* soon became a solid train of through cars between New York and New Orleans.

Passengers soon shortened the jawbreaking title to the *Vestibule*, and many of them spent considerable time in walking from one car to another just to enjoy the then-novel experience of being able to do so without having their hats blown away. The first dining cars to run between New York and Atlanta were operated on this train.

Operation of the *Vestibule* was continued after the Southern Railway Company was incorporated in 1894 by the pur-

CRESCENT LIMITED

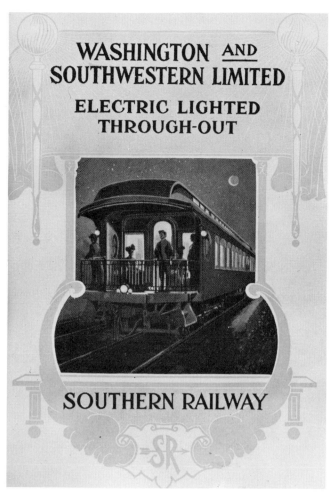

ELECTRIC lighting was praised with the enthusiasm a later generation of travelers would heap upon air conditioning.

MENUS were easy to read beneath electric lights.

chasers of the Richmond & Danville Railroad, but the train's lengthy title was shortened to *Washington & Southwestern Limited* when the vestibule became commonplace on long-distance trains.

After the turn of the century, additional through sleepers (for Tampa and Nashville) were added to the consist, and for the first time in the train's history, coaches were carried (between New York and Atlanta).

Finally, after 15 years of operation as a solid train between New York and New Orleans, Nos. 37 and 38 were renamed in 1906 as the *New York & New Orleans Limited*, and re-equipped with new observation and club cars as "a year around Exclusive Pullman car train." Coast-to-coast passengers (in connection with the Southern Pacific *Sunset Express* via New Orleans) were actively solicited.

Pullman-Standard.

IN 1906 the Pullman Works was rendered festive indeed by a lineup of new observation cars for the Southern Railway; or-nate platform railings were topped by red and white awnings. Cars were tabbed for the New York & New Orleans Limited run.

All photos, Pullman-Standard.

ACILIUS was delivered in 1890 as a combined baggage and dining car. Personnel aboard the Washington & Southwestern

Vestibuled Limited included a maid "to respond to the usual demands upon servants of this class," to quote a brochure.

MACUTA, a 12-section, 1-drawing-room sleeper delivered in August 1887 by Pullman, was as richly ornamented as one could ask.

COURTIER, one of three identical "vestibule library and observation" cars built in 1890 (others: Chevalier and Consort), exemplified what $15,992.85 would buy from Pullman in Benjamin Harrison's administration. Car contained 10 sections and a lounge, the latter complete with buffet and wicker chairs. Intricate carvings on the berth fronts alone must have consumed sizable share of car cost.

CRESCENT LIMITED

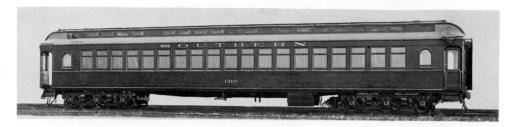

COACH 1397, delivered by Pullman in October 1909, was typical of such equipment that operated for brief periods on otherwise all-Pullman train. Vestibules had become full width but doors were still narrow.

SAXONIA possessed a unique floor plan: 8 sections, 1 drawing room, 3 staterooms. Car operated during winter season between New York and Aiken, S. C., the Newport of the South, in consist of posh Palm Limited.

DEERCOURT of 1906 was a 10-section observation; sister cars in this series were named Greensboro, Manassas, and Spartanburg.

NO. 1454, an elegant example of a wooden club car, was built in 1910 for service on New York, Atlanta & New Orleans Limited.

REPLACEMENT for car above was all-steel club car 2107 built in 1917. Car weighed 132,500 pounds, was 70 feet long over-all.

CRESCENT LIMITED

CRESCENT of 1929 poses near Easley, S. C., behind Ps-4 1394 for famed timetable cover photo.

No finer train than this

> CRESCENT LIMITED. The New De Luxe Train Between New York and New Orleans. Keeping pace with the development of the South, the railroads whose lines form the most expeditious route between New York and New Orleans unite in offering this *new and distinctive service.* The schedules assure the quickest and best travel accommodations ever offered between North and South, and the trains are provided with every modern comfort and convenience. — *Crescent Limited* brochure, 1925.

ON APRIL 26, 1925, a new No. 38 of the Louisville & Nashville departed from Canal Street Station in New Orleans at 10 p.m., northbound for New York City via Montgomery, Atlanta, and Washington over the L&N, West Point Route, Southern, and Pennsylvania railroads. The new service, named to honor the Crescent City of New Orleans, consisted of five complete sets of cars and locomotives valued at approximately 2 million dollars. Each train included an observation car, sleeping cars, dining car, and club car.

The operation of each train required 5 engine and train servicemen, 9 sleeping car attendants, and a dining car crew of 12 — a total of 26 for each train, or 130 for the five.

The new *Crescent* was the first bona fide excess-fare train operated in the South. The Louisville & Nashville modestly announced in its folder that "a reasonable extra fare ($5 New Orleans-New York) will be charged on this train in view of the superior facilities."

These superior facilities included a valet and a maid who "is in constant attendance to wait on ladies throughout the train. She will go to any section or room of any woman passenger for such service as may be desired."

And yet all this was not the last word. The Southern Railway *News Bulletin* of June 1925, describing the first *Crescent*, stated:

> Additional comforts will be offered about September 1st when the entirely new trains which are being built by the Pullman Company especially for the *Crescent Limited* are substituted for the cars now in service.

In conjunction with the newly speeded-up schedule (37 hours 50 minutes), Train Speed Tables listing seconds per mile and miles per hour were furnished to passengers for train-clocking. A footnote to the table cautioned that "although there are approximately 30 telegraph poles to a mile, they are *not* accurately spaced to indicate distance."

After July 1926 the *Crescent* was hauled between Atlanta

FANFARE attended debut of new Crescent April 26, 1925.

114

and Washington by the Southern's new Virginia-green and gold heavy Pacific locomotives, each decorated with a gold crescent on the cylinders and the train's name emblazoned on the tender. There is general agreement among locomotive fanciers that these handsome iron horses rank among the most beautiful of all time.

LADIES' MAID was feature of new train.

In October 1929 new Pullmans supplemented the 1925 equipment. All of the 1929 cars, together with some of the 1925 models, were newly painted in a green and gold livery to match the locomotives. Altogether, 35 Pullmans were decorated in the new colors.

The car side plates below the belt rail, letterboard, and doors were painted Virginia green, a shade described as being the color of burnished gold. The piers and mullions between windows were a lighter sylvan green. All lettering and a stripe near the bottom of the side plate were genuine gold leaf.

All of the Pullman cars on the *Limited* were named to

"THERE is no finer train than this," claimed Crescent Limited's publicists.

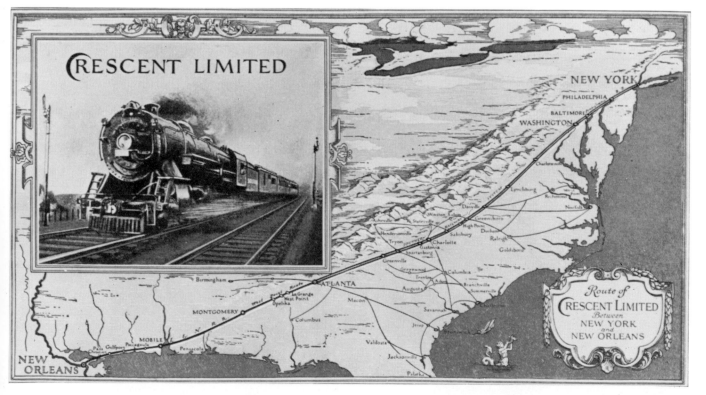

CRESCENT of 1925 apparently followed a gradeless route from New York to New Orleans judging by this map issued at the time.

SPECIALLY lettered Ps-4 Pacifics headed the Crescent. Great green and gold engines had 73-inch drivers, exerted 47,500 pounds tractive effort, were lovingly cared for by roundhouse forces. Sister 1401 is now on permanent display at Smithsonian.

WILLIAM MOULTRIE, club car of 1925 named for an early governor of South Carolina, was painted Pullman green, contained movable chairs (below) in its lounge. Overhead fans were standard equipment at that time.

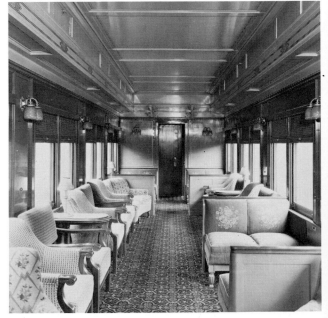

"honour the memories" of distinguished citizens of the Southern states through which the train traveled. At the request of the Southern Railway, the governors of these states nominated the "statesmen, soldiers, jurists, and publicists" for whom the cars were to be designated.

Between 1932 and 1939, bedroom and private-section (enclosed) Pullman cars were added. In order to perpetuate such prominent Southern names as P. G. T. Beauregard and Henry W. Grady, the newer cars on the Crescent were constantly being renamed in a manner to confound the student of such esoteric matters.

On April 30, 1938, the train's name was officially shortened to the Crescent; in 1941 the train's first diesel power was received. Strikingly attired in green and white, the new 4000 h.p. General Motors units hauled the train between Atlanta and Washington, where Pennsylvania GG1 electrics continued the trip to New York. Steam locomotive enthusiasts were saddened at the passing of the great Pacifics, but happily, one has been preserved, courtesy of the Southern and the Smithsonian Institution, in the nation's capital.

At the start of World War II there were 49 U. S. Military posts and camps located on Southern Railway lines. Each generated an enormous amount of wartime traffic. Throughout the emergency the Crescent performed heroically.

DINING CAR NO. 3159, Pullman built in 1924, specialized in Southern cuisine. Car was proudly advertised as being "of Oriental Limited type."

116

FRANCOIS XAVIER MARTIN, named for famous Louisiana jurist, contained 10 sections and 2 drawing rooms; weighed 166,500 pounds. Car was completed for Crescent Limited on November 2, 1925, and was renamed W. W. Finley October 30, 1929.

ROBERT F. HOKE, 10-section, 2-drawing-room car of 1929, is shown in famous Virginia green and gold livery which train displayed from Ps-4 Pacific to observation car. Sleeper was named in honor of Maj. Gen. Robert F. Hoke of the Confederate States Army.

CRESCENT LIMITED

HENRY W. GRADY, esteemed editor of the Atlanta Constitution and prophet of the "New South," was paid homage by 14-section Pullman delivered in 1929. "Pullman" was relegated to car ends as words "Crescent Limited" dominated central letterboard position.

All car photos, Pullman-Standard.

WILLIAM RUFUS KING, with 8 sections, 1 drawing room, and 2 compartments, honored early U. S. Vice-President who was born in South Carolina. Sleeper was built in 1929 expressly for new edition of Crescent of that year and painted Virginia green and gold.

JOEL CHANDLER HARRIS, named for author of Uncle Remus stories, was built in 1925, refurbished for 1929 Crescent Limited. The observation-sleeper held 3 compartments, 2 drawing rooms, observation lounge (right), and a ladies' lounge with bath and maid attendant. Clearly the grandest car in a grand train.

CRESCENT LIMITED

BIG Lima Pacific 290 of the Atlanta & West Point brings No. 37, the *Crescent Limited*, through East Point, Ga., in 1939. R. E. Prince photo.

SOUTH of Montgomery, Ala., in 1941 the Crescent Limited covers ground behind the tank of light U.S.R.A. Mountain-type 412 of the Louisville & Nashville. Baldwin-built L-1 has her cylinder heads and running boards silvered for the occasion.

RACING for Atlanta, the Crescent Limited is in charge of Western Railway of Alabama Pacific 190 on steel any roadmaster could take pride in. Lima 4-6-2 features a sawtooth stack with a light bulb affixed in front to ascertain density of smoke.

CRESCENT near Seneca, S. C. SR photo.

CRESCENT LIMITED

Grand new train with a grand old name

A SHINING stainless-steel *Crescent* was delivered by Pullman-Standard in 1949. Each of the roads that operated the train contributed equipment from an 11.5-million-dollar order for 141 cars to streamline and renew the *Crescent*, the *Southerner*, the *Tennessean*, and the *Royal Palm*.

From diesel to private-room Pullman, this fine streamliner provides the latest in modern, comfortable, safe all-weather transportation. A worthy successor to its famed predecessors, the present train offers accommodations to meet every travel need. Five kinds of private rooms are available — roomettes; bedrooms (singly and *en suite*); drawing rooms; and the only master room in the South, complete with private shower and radio. De luxe reclining-seat coaches are operated between Washington-Charlotte and Atlanta-New Orleans.

The *Crescent* is equipped with all the comforts of home. A beautifully decorated buffet-lounge car is clublike and friendly — the perfect place to read, chat, or listen to the radio.

Round-end observation-lounge cars, similar to the type built for the *Twentieth Century Limited*, have been rebuilt into 11-bedroom cars which operate between New York and Atlanta. Altogether, four different types of Pullmans are operated in the train.

Southern cuisine and service combine to make dining en route a memorable experience. In addition, all passengers aboard the northbound *Crescent* are cordially invited to the hospitality hour in the dining car every day between 3 and 4 p.m. Complimentary orange juice or coffee is served.

The Washington-Sunset Route, coast-to-coast through the deep South and the romantic Southwest, via the *Crescent* and Southern Pacific *Sunset*, is advertised as "the most interesting Transcontinental Route."

Passengers are delighted with the new *Crescent* — streamlined, stainless steel on the outside, and soft upholstery, thick carpets, and subdued colors on the inside. Persons along the line call it "a grand new train with a grand old name." ⚏

SOUTH of Mobile, Ala., 4000 h.p. rolls the *Crescent* through scrub pine terrain on Louisville & Nashville. L&N photo.

ROLLING past waterplugs it no longer requires, eastbound Crescent slows for a stop at CofG crossing in Opelika, Ala., while running on Western Railway of Alabama rails. The dieselized streamliner was photographed on July 12, 1952, at 11:30 a.m.

ROYAL ARCH is one of seven Royal cars built for Crescent and New Royal Palm service and owned by SR, L&N, NYC, and West Point Route. They contained raised-end "Lookout Lounges." Three of the observations have been rebuilt into 11-bedroom cars.

DINING CAR NO. 3306, built by Budd entirely of stainless steel (and identified as such by fluted roof), seats 44 at its tables.

121

Pullman-Standard.

ROANOKE VALLEY, with 14 roomettes and 4 double bedrooms, is one of 11 P-S-built Valley-series cars owned by the Southern.

Pullman-Standard.

ENOREE RIVER contains 10 roomettes and 6 double bedrooms; River-series cars are owned by SR, West Point Route, L&N, PRR.

(RESCENT LIMITED

SR.

CRESCENT CITY is a buffet-lounge with 2 drawing rooms as well as a master room with shower. Sister cars: Crescent Harbor, Crescent Moon, and Crescent Shores. Lounge (right) has race mural.

Pullman-Standard.

SR.

"LOOKOUT LOUNGE" type of raised observation end is depicted in scene of Crescent racing away from camera behind diesel power.

L&N.

PRIOR to its installation into revenue service, streamlined Crescent Limited stands on exhibition in New Orleans Union Passenger Terminal. En route to New York, train operates behind diesels and electrics over L&N, West Point Route, Southern, and PRR.

OIL-BURNING 4-8-2 447 parallels palms with the Florida Special on the Florida East Coast. FEC photo.

ATLANTIC COAST LINE
VESTIBULED TRAIN TO FLORIDA
MDCCCLXXXVII

THE 1887 announcement of New York and Florida Special.

Florida SPECIAL

Second only to the Century in the number of sections operated

1 THE New York *Daily Tribune* of January 1, 1888, carried the first announcement of the *New York and Florida Special*:

"Composed of Pullman Vestibule Sleeping, Dining, and Smoking Cars, heated by steam. The 1074-mile trip to Jacksonville scheduled for 30 hours. This train leaving New York every Monday, Wednesday, and Friday at 9:30 a.m."

The route of the new seasonal operation was Pennsylvania Railroad-Richmond, Fredericksburg & Potomac-Atlantic Coast Line-Florida East Coast via Washington, Richmond, Charleston, Savannah, Jacksonville, and St. Augustine.

No part of the American continent appealed more strongly to the northern tourist of the 1880's — and none provided a more delightful haven from the rigors of the northern winter — than the East Coast of Florida, the land of flowers and sunshine.

The modern streamlined *Florida Special*, advertised as the "Aristocrat of Winter Trains," combines the experience and tradition of an illustrious past with the modern convenience of today. Since its successful 75th anniversary season, the *Special* has continued to provide the winter vacationer with luxurious and dependable service.

1896 MARCH was composed by the director of the United States Marine Band, F. Fanciulli.

A train de luxe

This train is an eminent example of what the French call a "train de luxe," and it may be declared with all truth that the world has not yet produced its equal. — *The New York and Florida Special*, brochure, 1888.

IN January of 1888 two events occurred which greatly affected the history of Florida. The magnificent Hotel Ponce de Leon at St. Augustine was completed and officially opened. And for this occasion on January 10, 1888, the all-Pullman *New York and Florida Special* was inaugurated. Both the hotel and the train were to become important in the development of Florida as a winter resort.

Builder of the Ponce de Leon and President of the Florida East Coast Railway was Henry Morrison Flagler who had amassed a fortune as one of the founders of the Standard Oil Company. Charmed with the climate and beauty of St. Augustine, Flagler became convinced that wealthy Americans could be induced to forsake the Mediterranean Riviera for

TURN-OF-CENTURY advertising: a purple, white, and gold brochure sold Special to Florida, Cuba.

All illustration, ACL.

"ONE continuous car" was the way period brochure described the effect of vestibules on the Special. The train was a "series of apartments" between which the traveler passed as easily as from one room of a house to another. Vestibules were carpeted, lighted.

126

PRESIDENTIAL SPECIAL
EN ROUTE TO THOMASVILLE, GA.,
Via, the Atlantic Coast Line
and Plant System.
PULLMAN DINING CAR SERVICE.

Luncheon.

BOUILLON

RAW TOMATOES   PIM-OLAS

BROILED SALMON STEAK
STRING POTATOES

ROAST PHILADELPHIA CAPON

BOILED POTATOES   BOILED ONIONS   SPINACH

ROAST BEEF

TONGUE

HAM

SARDINES

LOBSTER SALAD, MAYONNAISE

ICE CREAM   CAKE

PRESERVED FRUITS   GOLDEN GATE FRUITS

ENGLISH AND GRAHAM WAFERS

APPLE PIE

FRUIT

ROQUEFORT, CANADIAN AND EDAM CHEESE

BENT,S WATER CRACKERS

BAILEY'S BEATEN BISCUIT

COFFEE   TEA

EN ROUTE, MARCH 14, 1899

AN EMBOSSED EAGLE raised its wings over special menu for President McKinley in March 1899.

Pullman Dining Car "Alhambra."

DINNER.
NEW YORK, JANUARY 18, 1888.

Mock Turtle, a l'Anglaise   Consomme, Victoria

Salmon, a la Chamborg
Parisienne Potatoes

Boiled Beef Tongue   Boiled Chicken, Egg Sauce

Roast Beef, with Browned Potatoes
Roast Leg of South Down Mutton, Currant Jelly
Young Turkey, Cranberry Sauce

Fricandeau of Veal, a la Richelieu
Salmi of Duck, a la Jardiniere
Banana Fritters, Port Wine Sauce

Roast Saddle of Antelope, with Currant Jelly.

Lobster, Mayonaise   Lettuce Salad
Spanish Olives.   Celery.
Chow Chow.   Pickled Onions.   Girkins

Boiled Potatoes   Mashed Potatoes   Baked Sweet Potatoes
Stewed Tomatoes   Squash
French Peas   Succotash

Mince Pie   Apple Pie
Cocoanut Pudding, Hard Sauce

Fruit.
Ice Cream.   Assorted Cake.   Preserved Fruits
Marmalade.   Figs   Dry Canton Ginger.   Raisins
English, Graham and Oatmeal Wafers.

Roquefort and Edam Cheese.   Bent's Crackers
Cafe Noir.

MEALS, ONE DOLLAR.
Table Water from the Silurian Springs, Waukesha.

SPRING water from Waukesha, Wis., accompanied
dollar meals served aboard the diner Alhambra.

Florida SPECIAL

Florida if proper accommodation could be provided for them.

The Hotel Ponce de Leon was decorated and furnished in a Spanish style designed to rival the splendor of the Alhambra, fabled Moorish palace of Granada.

No less effort was expended on the Pullman equipment which made up the *New York and Florida Special*. Two sets, each composed of six cars, were furnished by George Pullman.

Two baggage cars (equipped with electric dynamo), combination smoking cars *Alroy* and *Aladdin*, and Pullman dining cars *Alhambra* and *Alcazar* were built in Chicago in December 1887. Six sleepers *Amphion, Charmion, Ixion, Ilion, Pelion,* and *Phocion* were outshopped in Pullman's Detroit works early in January 1888.

On January 9, the great Flyer, the first electrically lighted, vestibuled train ever operated in the United States, departed from Jersey City. At 9:30 a.m. Conductor Ralph Myercks pulled the bell cord, and amid many farewells, the six-car train rapidly pulled out of the terminal. A reporter from the Jacksonville *News-Herald* on that first southward trip noted that the conductor and his crew "resembled Prussian officers, so gaudy and gorgeous were their uniforms." One of the 70 passengers on board was George M. Pullman traveling to make certain that everything about his elegant cars was in apple-pie order. Mr. Pullman, who had financed the construction of the cars, was quoted as saying, "It is in all respects the most complete train yet constructed."

During the night run between Richmond and Charleston, bonfires were lighted at many stations and the train was greeted with the hurrahs of delighted onlookers.

ALHAMBRA interior was "furnished in rare taste with Nile green silk plush" and chandeliers with opaque glass globes.

At first the famous vestibule train could not be operated through to St. Augustine. At Jacksonville passengers had to transfer to a ferry across St. Johns River. This procedure was continued until January 1890 when the first large steel railroad bridge in the South was completed by Henry Flagler.

Announcing the arrival of the first run in Jacksonville, the Florida *Times-Union* of January 11, 1888, reported:

The Pioneer trip was made exactly on time. A large assemblage had gathered at the station to welcome 'The Aristocrat of Winter Trains' from the Winterbound North.

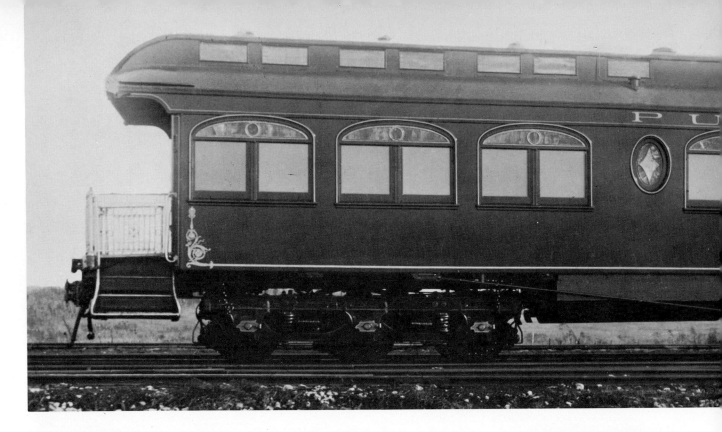

Florida SPECIAL

LIFFEY — ACL owned but Pullman maintained — cost $16,230 to build in December 1895; contained 12 sections, drawing room, buffet. Its interior was finished ornately in vermilion wood.

ACL.

ALTHOUGH not the first locomotives of their wheel arrangement, five Baldwin 4-4-2's delivered to the Coast Line in late 1894 were first to be christened the Atlantic type. One of them ran 1.4 million miles.

PETERSBURG baggage car, No. 414, ran through from New York to Florida; it contained the dynamo of 85-volt power (driven by an axle belt) which generated electricity for the Special's 120 lamps. Open-platform wood car was built in December 1896.

128

All photos Pullman-Standard unless otherwise credited.

JACKSONVILLE, a Pullman observation containing 8 sections, buffet, and observation parlor, was one of the early cars with round arched windows. As you'd surmise, Jacksonville's interior counted heavily upon mahogany to place its passengers at ease.

 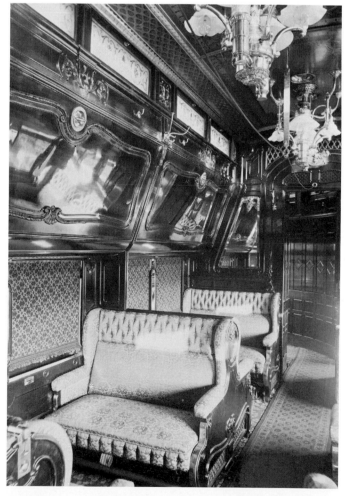

ALROY'S smoker contained "chairs of light cane manufacture covered with cherry plush." Patrons were promised "book cases filled with the latest publications" as well as a writing desk.

"BERTHS or sections finished in bird's-eye maple burnished to the smoothness of glass which reflects all objects like a plate mirror" — so read a description of combination smoking car Alroy.

Florida SPECIAL

FOUR sections of the *Special* ready to depart Miami. FEC photo.

FEC.

OBSERVATION platform of January 3, 1937, Golden Jubilee Special was crammed with girls, palm fronds, 50-candle cake.

SEVEN SECTIONS: that was the record established by the Florida Special, No. 87, on February 29, 1936. Each train was complete with every advertised de luxe feature. During the 1936 season, incidentally, the Special ran south over the FEC in two sections on 44 days, three on 23 days, four on 12 days, five on 2 days, and six on 4 days. And all this during the depression!

All steel, and a golden anniversary

THE FIRST *New York and Florida Special* was an immediate success, and for succeeding winter seasons the operation was continued. As Florida travel became more and more popular the triweekly *Special* was changed to a daily service. The train's purple, white, and gold brochure was a tradition in hotel timetable racks after the turn of the century.

After January 22, 1912, the *Special* operated cars through to Key West via Henry Flagler's remarkable 128-mile "overseas railroad" completed at a cost of 20 million dollars — a line traveling from island to island over concrete and steel viaducts some several miles in length.

Florida became an established winter haven for thousands of people from the North. The grand hotels continued to operate, but after World War I the quiet elegance of more gracious times was replaced with the hustle and bustle of the great Florida boom. Travel to Cuba and Nassau, via Florida and connecting P&O steamships, became increasingly popular.

In the early 1920's the *Special*, trains 87 and 88, was given a thorough modernization which included a shorter name (*Florida Special*), faster schedule (40 hours 40 minutes, New

NO. 87 at WN Tower, south end of Pee Dee River Bridge, S. C.

ACL.

NO. 88 thunders north on double track iron at Monteith, Ga.

ACL.

FEC.

OVERSEAS LIMITED (with Florida Special Pullmans) discharges passengers onto 1200-foot Key West pier for transfer to the P&O vessel S.S. Governor Cobb. A 6-hour sail over the Spanish main and the vacationists will be setting foot in Havana.

York-Miami), new heavy steel equipment, and an enlarged all-Pullman consist which included through cars for Belleair and St. Petersburg on Florida's west coast.

During the wild years of the prohibition era the *Special* was frequently swelled with extra sleepers, and in 1926 the country's first recreation cars were furnished by the Pullman Company. Three 12-1 sleepers were stripped and completely rebuilt as the *Coliseum, Lyceum,* and *Trocadero.* They were decorated with potted palm trees, bridge tables, horse-racing games, and gaily colored curtains. A hostess and small orchestra for dancing completed the ensemble.

Until the market crash and resultant depression, the train daily carried a unique hotel supply car between Jacksonville and West Palm Beach. This car was used to stock the distinguished Flagler System hotels.

January 2, 1937, marked the beginning of the golden anniversary season. Festivities included birthday cakes, beautiful girls, decorations galore, and voluminous speech-making.

The winter season of 1939-1940 marked the high point of the *Florida Special* in the Age of Steam. Three sections operated every day from Pennsylvania Station in New York during the height of the season (26¼ hours to Miami, 25½ hours to St. Petersburg).

Extra No. 87 (East Coast section) departed at 1:40 p.m. with 11 Pullmans, 2 dining cars, and a recreation car. (A "Super De Luxe" coach was added at Washington.)

Ten minutes later, at 1:50 p.m., *Regular No. 87* (East Coast section) pulled out with 15 Pullmans, 2 dining cars, and a recreation car.

Finally, at 2:05 p.m., *No. 187* (West Coast section) departed with 8 Pullmans, 2 dining cars, recreation car, and 2 coaches.

Except for the glory days of the *Twentieth Century Limited* no such *regular* operation had ever before occurred on American rails.

FEC.

131

THROUGHOUT the '20's Pacifics were the mainstay of ACL's locomotive roster. The 1546 was of light U.S.R.A. specification.

BUILT to haul 20 cars at 100 mph, Coast Line's 1800-series R-1 4-8-4's of 1938 were Baldwin's answer to rival Seaboard Air Line's new diesels. But the 447-ton (engine and tender) machines were hard on track.

BAGGAGE CAR 493, Pullman built in 1926, carried delicate lettering of Florida East Coast together with the "Flagler System" slogan.

FLORENCE was a Florida East Coast diner built by Pullman in 1918. Flagler System diners were named after Florida towns and hotels.

DINING CAR 10 was one of 14 diners built and owned by Pullman in 1925, later leased and finally bought by ACL. It seated 36.

ST. AUGUSTINE dining car of FEC was beautifully decorated.

Florida SPECIAL

RECREATION CARS (former sleepers refurbished by Pullman and railroad staffed) livened up the journey with music and contract bridge. Hostess and accordionist anticipated Mitch Miller.

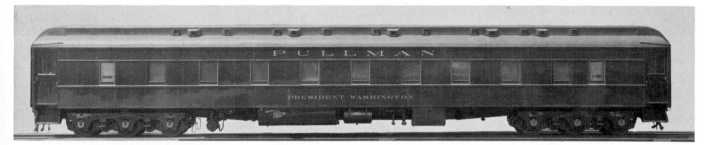

PRESIDENT WASHINGTON, one of celebrated President series of 1923, contained solely rooms: 7 compartments, 2 drawing rooms.

SKYLAND, section sleeper of 1913, was among 10 identical cars named for such Southern travel destinations as Bahama, Nassau, and so on.

PALM SPRINGS, "four poster" (for safety) observation, contained 10 sections and lounge. Sister cars included Key West, Fort Pierce.

A new streamliner, and a diamond jubilee

IN the emergency years of World War II the *Special* ceased operation; however, with the return of peace it was reinstated.

For its 61st season in 1949, the *New Florida Special* was re-equipped as Florida's first lightweight diesel-powered all-room Pullman streamliner. The postwar train set new standards for beauty, styling, and comfort. All sleeping cars were air conditioned and equipped with private lavatory and toilet facilities. Each room contained circulating ice water, full-length mirrors, and combination radio and recorded music. The new train carried 12 regularly assigned Pullmans, 2 luxurious bedroom-lounge cars, and 2 dining cars. The 1949-model *New Florida Special* operated between New York and Miami on a 25-hour 10-minute schedule connecting at Miami with the P&O steamship *Florida* for the overnight "trip abroad" to Havana.

The 1962-1963 season marked the 75th anniversary of the *Florida Special*. In commemoration of the diamond jubilee, a new extra-fine, extra-fare ($5 Pullman, $2.50 coach) streamliner went on a 24-hour New York-Miami schedule. Coast Line President W. Thomas Rice, an enthusiastic supporter of prosperous long-haul passenger trains, arranged for a stage-production train to rival the original *Florida Special* of 1888. Included in the luxuries are pert train hostesses; dinner reser-

BLACK AND YELLOW diesels lead stainless-steel Florida Special of 1963 around curve in a palm-tree-bordered publicity photo.

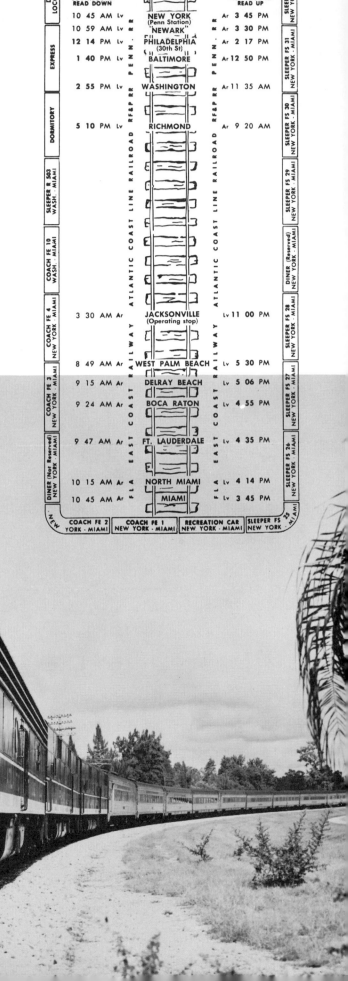

FLORIDA SPECIAL
Schedule and Equipment

SOUTHBOUND READ DOWN	STATION	NORTHBOUND READ UP
10 45 AM Lv	NEW YORK (Penn Station)	Ar 3 45 PM
10 59 AM Lv	NEWARK	Ar 3 30 PM
12 14 PM Lv	PHILADELPHIA (30th St)	Ar 2 17 PM
1 40 PM Lv	BALTIMORE	Ar 12 50 PM
2 55 PM Lv	WASHINGTON	Ar 11 35 AM
5 10 PM Lv	RICHMOND	Ar 9 20 AM
3 30 AM Ar	JACKSONVILLE (Operating stop)	Lv 11 00 PM
8 49 AM Ar	WEST PALM BEACH	Lv 5 30 PM
9 15 AM Ar	DELRAY BEACH	Lv 5 06 PM
9 24 AM Ar	BOCA RATON	Lv 4 55 PM
9 47 AM Ar	FT. LAUDERDALE	Lv 4 35 PM
10 15 AM Ar	NORTH MIAMI	Lv 4 14 PM
10 45 AM Ar	MIAMI	Lv 3 45 PM

Railroads: PENN. RR — RF&P RR — ATLANTIC COAST LINE RAILWAY — FLA EAST COAST RAILWAY

Equipment (left, southbound side): DIESEL LOCOMOTIVES; EXPRESS; DORMITORY; SLEEPER R 503 WASH.-MIAMI; COACH FE 10 WASH.-MIAMI; COACH FE 4 NEW YORK-MIAMI; COACH FE 3 NEW YORK-MIAMI; DINER (Not Reserved) NEW YORK-MIAMI

Equipment (right, northbound side): SLEEPER FS 32 NEW YORK-MIAMI; SLEEPER FS 31 NEW YORK-MIAMI; SLEEPER FS 30 NEW YORK-MIAMI; SLEEPER FS 29 NEW YORK-MIAMI; DINER (Reserved) NEW YORK-MIAMI; SLEEPER FS 28 NEW YORK-MIAMI; SLEEPER FS 27 NEW YORK-MIAMI; SLEEPER FS 26 NEW YORK-MIAMI; SLEEPER FS 25 NEW YORK

Equipment (bottom): COACH FE 2 NEW YORK-MIAMI; COACH FE 1 NEW YORK-MIAMI; RECREATION CAR NEW YORK-MIAMI; SLEEPER FS 25 NEW YORK

TELEPHONE in lounge car was popular innovation of the Special's diamond jubilee season.

STEWARD displays buffet tables of cold hors d'oeuvres awaiting Special's passengers.

All photos, ACL.

Florida

vations and complimentary champagne; recreation car with movies, fashion shows, and games; long-distance telephone service.

ACL happily reports that during its diamond jubilee season the train did "amazingly well," with loadings well ahead of the previous season and more compliments than any other train the road had ever operated. Everything about the diamond jubilee *Special* has been tremendously successful. Passengers are enthusiastic about the new recreation car which is filled to standing-room capacity during group singing.

The week of January 6, 1963, was proclaimed *Florida Special* Week by the Mayor of Miami Beach. On January 9, a ribbon-cutting ceremony was held in Miami to commemorate the 75th anniversary of the arrival of the first *Florida Special* in the Sunshine State.

The success of the 1963 season helped establish modern rail travel as the most dependable, enjoyable transportation available. ⏚

ANOTHER view of the 1963 Florida Special rolling through tropical surroundings behind three diesel units worth 6250 h.p.

TAMPA, a Budd-built diner of ACL ownership, serves meals without reservations at front end of the train.

Budd.

EDISTO ISLAND, a 21-roomette sleeper destined for a Florida Special assignment, poses for its official photo outside the Pullman plant on September 21, 1949. Letterboards added purple touch to a car otherwise sheathed in stainless steel.

Pullman-Standard.

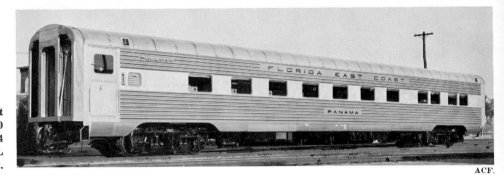

PANAMA, assigned to FEC, was built by American Car & Foundry in 1950 for Florida Special, contained 14 roomettes and 2 drawing rooms. ACL and RF&P bought similar equipment.

ACF.

ACF.

Florida SPECIAL

ASHLEY RIVER, named for a South Carolina stream, was built in February 1950 as a 14-roomette, 2-drawing-room car. Six such cars were rebuilt in 1961, exchanging their roomettes for 7 double bedrooms, and were renamed for birds. Surf Bird (below) is a rebuild.

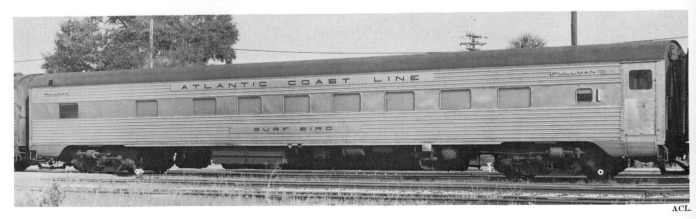

ACL.

COLONIAL BEACH, a 6-double-bed-room-lounge, is one of nine cars built by American Car & Foundry in 1949-1950 for ACL, FEC, and RF&P and operated as midtrain lounges.

ACF.

Pullman-Standard.

MOULTRIE diner was built for ACL by Pullman-Standard on March 14, 1950; has 36 staggered seats for reservation dining.

ACL.

"I'VE been working on the Coast Line" — group singing aboard one of three diners (e.g., Port Tampa) used as recreation cars.

ACL.

Pullman-Standard.

NORTHAMPTON COUNTY, a 10-roomette, 6-double-bedroom Pullman, is one of six County series carried in each Florida Special consist.

ACL.

CAPE FEAR RIVER is representative of six Special sleepers which have the newest interior configuration but the greatest seniority on the seasonal train. They were built in 1938 for the 20th Century as 4-double-bedroom, 4-compartment, 2-drawing-room Imperial-series cars; were rebuilt by Pullman in 1962 as 4-compartment, 4-drawing-room cars for ACL, named for Southern rivers.

137

The Panama Limited

MAILBOX and telephone in observation parlor were features of *Capricorn* on rear of de luxe, all-sleeping-car 1916 *Panama Limited*. IC photo.

All Pullman and very de luxe

1   ONE of the most brilliant chapters in the annals of American commerce is the history of the Illinois Central Railroad. The Main Line of Mid-America today continues an enviable record of never having been in receivership; of never having undergone reorganization; and of never having defaulted on one dollar of bonded debt.

The builders and leaders of the Illinois Central include many of the country's greatest names: Abraham Lincoln, Stephen A. Douglas, and Jefferson Davis; P. G. T. Beauregard and George B. McClellan; Judah P. Benjamin and Grenville M. Dodge; Collis P. Huntington, Sir William Van Horne, and Edward H. Harriman; Mark Twain and Casey Jones. All played important parts in the Illinois Central story.

The IC line from Chicago south to Cairo, Ill., was completed in the spring of 1856. In July of that year the road placed in service the first sleeping cars west of the Alleghenies on the overnight to Cairo. At this important town, the confluence of the Ohio and Mississippi rivers, connections were made with the famous Blue Line packet steamers for New Orleans. Flying the Blue Line house flag were such famous boats as the *Robert E. Lee* and the *Great Republic*. This rail-water arrangement continued until all-rail service from Chicago to New Orleans was effected in 1873 via the IC and "The Great Jackson Route" comprised of the Mississippi Central and the New Orleans, Jackson & Great Northern railroads. At Cairo the transfer steamer *H. C. McComb* ferried the trains across the Ohio River.

In 1882 "The Great Jackson Route" was absorbed by the Illinois Central, and on October 29, 1889, the remarkable 4-mile-long Cairo Bridge was completed. For the first time Illinois Central trains ran through by rail from Chicago to New Orleans.

Built for *Chicago & New Orleans Limited* in 1890. IC photo.

EARLY *Panama* pauses on outskirts of Chicago southbound behind Brooks 4-6-2.

The Panama Limited

The first Panama

The Panama Canal is the greatest engineering project of all history. . . . Men of all nations concede it without question, and felicitate the United States upon the remarkable success with which it has been carried out. — Frederic J. Haskin, 1913.

DURING the good years which preceded World War I, the United States was emerging as a world power. Under the leadership of Theodore Roosevelt Americans were experiencing an intense feeling of national pride. One of the greatest symbols of this pride was the Panama Canal which was finally constructed under the American flag after years of heartbreak and failure on the part of Europeans. The major gateway to the enormous undertaking at Panama was the Port of New Orleans, the southern terminal of the Illinois Central Railroad — the Main Line of Mid-America.

On April 10, 1904, the Stars and Stripes were first raised over the Canal Zone. Slowly at first the work progressed. As the years passed and the construction continued it became apparent that the canal was to become an incredible success. The name Panama symbolized the maturity of the United States.

In honor of the mighty work at the Canal Zone, the Illinois Central on February 4, 1911, renamed its premier train. There-

after the *Chicago & New Orleans Limited*, Nos. 3 and 4, was known as the *Panama Limited*.

The earliest *Panama* consisted of a high-wheeled Pacific and wooden cars. From Chicago and St. Louis to Memphis it carried only first class passengers, but between Memphis and

gold eagle on the Pacific. IC photo.

New Orleans coaches were added. The 921-mile trip via Fulton, Memphis, and Jackson, Miss., took 25 hours. Through sleepers destined for Hot Springs (via Rock Island) and both San Antonio and San Francisco (via Southern Pacific) were carried.

With the ever-increasing traffic to the Crescent City, the *Panama* was thoroughly refurbished early in 1912. New equipment built by Pullman replaced the wooden cars and the train became "all steel, electric lighted" from Chicago and St. Louis through to New Orleans.

141

PACIFIC 1056 had 75-inch drivers, weighed 224,000 pounds, exerted tractive force of 31,327 pounds, was built by Brooks in 1910.

BAGGAGE AND EXPRESS 639 was 61 feet long and was illuminated by Pintsch gas and oil light. Lettering was crescent shaped.

BUFFET-LIBRARY 4055 was IC owned, measured 70 feet in length. Inside electrically lighted car were 25 club seats and a buffet.

LEANDER, built by Pullman in 1908 at cost of $17,233, contained 12 sections, drawing room. Car was dismantled in May 1937.

DINING CAR 3963 was 70 feet long, seated 30 persons. Electric lights and Baker heater were incorporated. Weight: 128,100 pounds.

142

CRESCENT CITY (twin of Mound City) was rebuilt in 1901 with frame of earlier sleeper; had 8 sections, buffet, library, observation.

DINER 3976 (above), built by **Pullman** in 1911, was all steel and seated 30. Note Harriman arched roof. Interior of another diner (below) shows sparkling silverware, linen, and flowers.

The Panama Limited

SUN-PARLOR OBSERVATION 3851 (below), one of earliest enclosed sun-parlor cars (1911), was especially designed for viewing northern part of Panama's journey in wintertime. Mahogany (above) contrasted with cream ceiling, green carpet and upholstery.

143

The Panama Limited

"An impressive, perfect, modern train"

ON November 15, 1916, the *Panama* became a de luxe all-sleeping-car train. Special newly designed equipment was placed in service on a 23-hour schedule after on-line ceremonies and exhibitions.

Invitations engraved in flowing script went to dignitaries inviting their inspection of the train. The new train, Nos. 7 and 8, was operated in addition to the former *Panama*, Nos. 3 and 4, which continued to run and later was named the *Louisiane*.

The *Panama* grew up during the Roaring '20's. Many of her passengers were discriminating Easterners who preferred to travel to New Orleans by way of Chicago in connection with the *Century* or the *Broadway*. But no passengers were more important than those she carried on a run in March 1925 after a terrible tornado had torn across southern Illinois. In answer to a call for help, the *Panama*, already made up for her run, was detained until 130 doctors and 40 nurses with medical supplies and food could be loaded aboard. Engineer J. V. Fogarty opened the throttle of engine 1109 and raced southward on the mission of mercy.

Chancellor T. P. Guyton of the Sixth Mississippi District located at Vaiden recessed his court 5 minutes every session for 12 years so that everybody could watch the *Panama* roll through town.

The Rev. Thomas J. S. McGrath, S.J., a Jesuit missionary, made the *Panama*'s remarkable punctuality the subject of a sermon at Bogalusa, La., in 1930. Father McGrath credited the train's precise operation "not to mere chance, but to intelligence of planning." So near perfect was the record that the Illinois Central paid passengers a refund on their tickets if the train was over an hour late.

The Illinois Central Railroad Co. extends to you a cordial invitation to inspect their new all steel
Panama Limited
New Orleans train, the latest product of the car builders' art, which will be on private exhibition at Van Buren Street Station platform south of viaduct (Stairway from viaduct) from 10:30 A.M. to 12:00 noon on Tuesday, November 14th, and for the public from 12:00 noon to 2:00 P.M.

This handsome new train will make its initial trip from Chicago on Wednesday, November 15th 1916, and continue in service daily thereafter, leaving from Central Station at 12:30 P.M. and arriving New Orleans 11:30 A.M. the next day.

An impressive, perfect, modern train

May 28, 1932, was a sad day for the *Panama*. The lean years of depression and a resultant dearth of passengers caused the train to be discontinued. The Memphis *Commercial Appeal* editorialized sadly:

> The *Panama Limited* ceases to run! Gone, but we hope not forever, is the pride of the great Illinois Central Railroad Company — that magnificent train that raced with time to and from Chicago and New Orleans.

After 2½ years retirement ended on December 2, 1934. In the presence of the Governor of Illinois, the Mayor of Chicago, opera star Ruth Lyon, and an orchestra, the mayor's 8-year-old daughter broke over the engine's pilot a bottle of water taken from Lake Michigan, the Mississippi River, and the Gulf of Mexico. The *Panama* was back — air conditioned and on a new 18-hour schedule. Towns along the route turned out with brass bands to welcome her back.

AT HEAD END of same 1916 *Panama Limited* whose tail was being held down by *Capricorn* in photograph on page 138 was Brooks 4-6-2 No. 1158. IC photo.

PAUSE TO POSE came for *Panama* behind another of IC's group of Pacifics with Walschaerts gear built by Brooks in 1916 and 1918. IC photo.

SPECIALLY STRIPED 4-8-2 2411, turned out by Alco's Schenectady Works in 1923, poses before site of Chicago World's Fair while awaiting first run of the new Panama Limited in 1934. Such power also handled famous MS-1, onetime world's fastest freight train.

BUFFET CAR 4074, "a club for men while en route," was constructed by Pullman in 1916. It boasted barber (trimming of beard cost gentlemen 35 cents), shower bath, valet, and buffet stocked with cigars, cigarettes, playing cards, and mineral water.

The Panama Limited

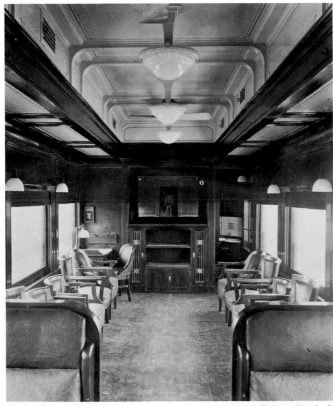

INTERIOR of buffet car 4074 combined rich mahogany paneling and leather chairs. Note camera reflected in large mirror.

DINER 3990 offered a la carte menu listing 22 entrees, delicacies supplied daily from markets of Chicago and New Orleans.

146

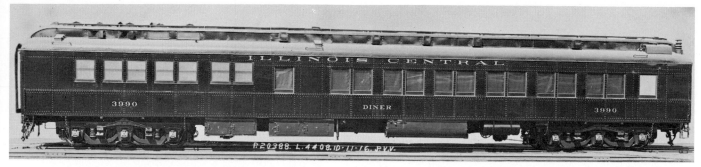

Pullman-Standard.

DINER 3990, built by Pullman in 1916, seated 36, was served by crew which consisted of a chef and steward, six waiters, four cooks.

Pullman-Standard.

LAKE WINTHROP'S (Pullman 1926) 10 sections, drawing room, 2 compartments were "in harmony with the refined taste of the day."

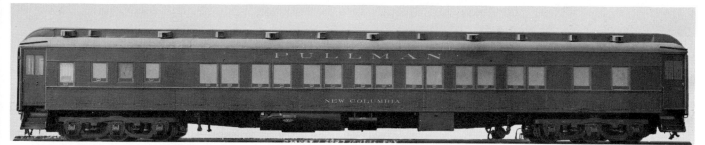

Pullman-Standard.

NEW COLUMBIA was delivered by Pullman in 1926. The 14-section car was sister of New Arcadie, New Midway, and New Orleans.

Pullman-Standard.

ORCHARD DALE was 1930 Pullman product, contained 8 sections and 5 chambrettes (single bedrooms). Illinois Central was one of first roads to use bedroom cars and assigned them to both Panama Limited and Night Diamond (between Chicago and St. Louis).

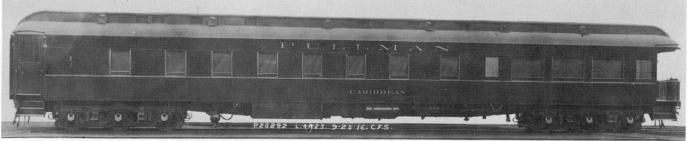

Pullman-Standard.

CARIBBEAN (others in 1916 Pullman series: Campeche, Capricorn, Cordillera) had 4 compartments, 2 drawing rooms, observation parlor equipped with mailbox, telephone. Ladies' maid was "at the service of passengers, especially ladies traveling alone, or with children."

147

The Panama Limited

War-born beauty

ON May 1, 1942, a superb new diesel-powered streamlined *Panama* was placed in service — the last of the great prewar lightweight trains. The 12-month period required for construction included a temporary stop order imposed by the War Production Board shortly after Pearl Harbor. Resplendent in a new yellow-orange-brown livery, the 18-hour *Panama* inaugurated a new era in train travel to the Gulf.

Like the new streamliners in the East and West, the outstanding feature of the equipment was the beauty of its interior design. Faithfully authentic details of coloring and materials were taken from New Orleans, the Deep South, Mexico, Central and South America.

Special features included two-way telephone service con-

GULFPORT displayed yellow neon sign. IC photo.

necting all sleeping cars with the dining and lounge cars, and portable radios available for passengers in private rooms. All who paid the *Panama*'s extra service charge were served an elegant evening meal in the dining car without charge.

Notwithstanding this delightful equipment designed for care-free living, the new train quickly entered into a more serious job. War was upon the land and the *Panama* performed yeoman service during the somber times.

Illinois Central.

LAKE PONTCHARTRAIN (IC 1902) accommodated baggage, dormitory for crew; sported IC diamond insigne and train name. Car was rebuilt in 1942 from heavyweight buffet car 4074 [page 146], was twin of Lake Michigan — No. 1901 rebuilt from the 4073.

Pullman-Standard.

GENERAL BEAUREGARD (and General Jackson) had 3 double bedrooms, 1 drawing room, 1 compartment-lounge. Bar (below) was faithful reproduction of New Orleans courtyard, even to potted ivy.

Illinois Central.

Illinois Central.

VIEUX CARRE diner seated 32 in main room, 16 in two cocktail booths. Photo murals were of Southern ante-bellum mansions.

AT CHICAGO in the 1940's a shiny EMD E6 headed the *Panama Limited*. IC photo.

Pullman-Standard.

MAGNOLIA STATE (of 6-6-4 configuration) was one of 12 cars with such names as Land o' Strawberries, Banana Road, King Cotton.

Pullman-Standard.

CITY OF JACKSON (18 roomettes) and City of New Orleans were the last of prewar City series built by Pullman-Standard.

Pullman-Standard.

VIEUX CARRE, named for New Orleans' Old Quarter, was counterpart of diner Evangeline. Cars were Pullman-Standard built.

Pullman-Standard.

ST. LOUISAN and Chicagoland sleeping accommodations (4 double bedrooms, 4 compartments, 2 drawing rooms) were done in pastels.

Illinois Central.

Pullman-Standard.

GULFPORT and Memphis observation-lounge cars provided 2 double bedrooms, 1 drawing room, 2 compartments. Gulfport lounge (left) was accented with print draperies; car exterior carried unique yellow neon Panama Limited sign.

Passengers relax in lounge of *Mardi Gras*. IC photo.

Golden Anniversary Panama

THE present day 16½-hour Golden Anniversary *Panama* ranks in the select group of four remaining all-Pullman trains in North America.*

Indeed, the *Panama* is a first-rate operation.† The sleeping cars are maintained in the finest Pullman Company tradition; the lounge and dining cars are operated by the Illinois Central. The IC Dining Service Department, which in 1961 served over 1 million meals, maintains a special school for teaching such subjects as cooking, serving, courtesy, sanitation, and safety. The department on four separate occasions has been given a special citation, awarded by the United States Public Health Service.

A newly introduced King's Dinner provides an epicurean experience in the grand tradition of another day. The $9.85 repast includes cocktail, fresh shrimp or crab, fish course, broiled steak accompanied by a bottle of imported wine, apple pie with cheese, coffee, and a choice of liqueur. Since 1954 it has been customary to place on every table at mealtime cards containing a devout thought for the day written by Illinois Central President Wayne Johnston, together with three original prayers submitted by Catholic, Protestant, and Jewish clergymen from towns along the IC.

While some railroad executives grumble loudly about the cost of passenger modernization, most concede that good passenger service builds up good will that cannot be measured in mere dollars and cents.

Top-notch railroader Wayne Johnston says candidly: "The *Panama Limited* is the standard bearer of the Illinois Central fleet. It provides a service between Chicago and New Orleans passengers can't obtain anywhere else. It is a good will builder for the Main Line of Mid-America and keeps the Illinois Central name before the public." 1

*The other three are the *Broadway Limited* and the *Pittsburgher* of the Pennsylvania, and *El Tapatio* of the National Railways of Mexico.

†A typical winter 1963 consist of the *Panama* on a southbound run: Electro-Motive diesels 4026 and 4017; 1821 — mail and express (Illinois Central); *Fort Dodge* — 22 roomettes (Pullman); *Clifton* — 10 roomettes, 6 double bedrooms (Pullman); *Champaign* — 10 roomettes, 6 double bedrooms (Pullman); *Bloomington* — 11 double bedrooms (Pullman); 3309 — club lounge (rebuilt Illinois Central); 4126 and 4126A — twin unit diner (Pullman); *Hattiesburg* — 4 double bedrooms, 2 drawing rooms, 4 compartments (Pullman); *Carbondale* — 10 roomettes, 6 double bedrooms (Pullman); *Mardi Gras*, 3351 — parlor car (rebuilt Illinois Central); *Memphis* — drawing room, 2 compartments, 2 double bedrooms, lounge-observation (Pullman).

The Panama Limited

Illinois Central.

TWIN DINER UNIT is 170-foot-long set built by P-S in 1950 with restaurant (above) for 56 diners in one car, cooking and dormitory accommodations in other — including shower for crew.

BLOOMINGTON is 11-double-bedroom sleeping car — the type of sleeper most popular with patrons of the IC's Panama Limited.

CARBONDALE is "C" series car with 10 roomettes, 6 double bedrooms. Thirteen "C" series cars (Covington, Cairo, etc.) and six "B" series cars (Baton Rouge, Belleville, etc.) are assigned to Panama and City of Miami. They are among the latest Pullman cars and incorporate such modern features as foam rubber mattresses, enclosed toilets in all two-person rooms.

PANAMA LIMITED steps across bridge over Pass Manchac, La. IC photo.

CLUB-LOUNGE 3309, rebuilt in 1952 from heavyweight coach 2187, has bar and lounge (left) seating 42 in two areas. Car runs through Chicago-New Orleans.

ILLINI (above), parlor car 3350 — rebuilt from parlor car 3150 — operated Chicago-Carbondale; was replaced by Mardi Gras (right), parlor car 3351 rebuilt in 1948 from heavyweight coach 2176, remodeled with Mardi Gras decor in 1959.

FULTON is one of four 22-roomette "F" series cars purchased in 1959 from New York Central which labeled them Bay series, operated them on 20th Century Limited.

ON display in Chicago in 1924. A. W. Johnson photo.

There is no better train on any railway. There is no passenger train affording service between Chicago and St. Louis on a better schedule. Further, there is no train on any railway affording so many new and distinctive features of travel luxury. — The New Alton Limited, 1924.

1 DURING the era of the lightweight streamliners, it was an exceptional train that was not attired in a bright and fanciful livery. This was not the case in the period from the turn of the century until the end of the great depression of the 1930's. In those decades of the standard heavyweight train, olive green was the rule. Of the thousands of passenger cars in service, only a relatively small number were brightly painted.

THE HANDSOMEST TI

The greatest C&A train of all cost over a million dollars

Notable exceptions were found on the Chicago-St. Louis speedway known as the Rainbow Run. Three railroads which were major contenders for this business operated trains the likes of which have rarely been seen before or since.

The Illinois Central entry was a fine operation called the *Daylight Special*. Advertised as a "handsome train," it was a two-tone affair painted black-brown below the window sill and bright green above, all generously trimmed and lettered with gold leaf. Travelers called it the "green train."

Not to be outdone, the Wabash repainted its crack *Banner Limited* a royal blue with gold striping and renamed

the new train *Banner Blue Limited*. It was popularly known as the "blue train."

It remained for the Chicago & Alton to place in service on September 28, 1924, what it termed with little regard for modesty, "the handsomest train in the world — the great new *Alton Limited*, the Red Train."

Always a fine railroad, the Chicago & Alton was also a pioneer. The road, one of the earliest built from Chicago, was the first to furnish through service between Chicago and St. Louis. It was the first railroad to employ George Pullman to remodel day coaches into sleeping cars in 1858. It was the first to place in service, in 1865, an all-new Pullman sleeper, the *Pioneer*, the realization of George

BRAND-NEW Alco Pacific 659 heads display train alongside uncompleted Chicago Union Station in 1924. A. W. Johnson photo.

AIN IN THE WORLD

Pullman's life ambition. Again, the Chicago & Alton was the first road to operate a full-fledged dining (not hotel) car, the *Delmonico*, built by Pullman and placed in service in 1868.

Always concerned with the passenger's welfare, the C&A in 1869 printed the poetry of Robert Browning in its public timetables when Alton's general passenger agent became annoyed with the run-of-the-mill traveling salesman jokes then printed in C&A folders (in the best practice of the day).

In 1899 and 1902, Pullman built new *Alton Limited* trains — fine wooden red trains, to be sure — but the greatest C&A train of all was the model of 1924. New from locomotive to observation platform, it represented an in-

vestment of over 1 million dollars. The interiors were finished in rosewood, the exterior was rich maroon with red doors and pier panels. Silver roof, black underframe, gold lettering and lining completed the beautiful effect. Each car was 84 feet in length (the observation car was 90 feet over all — at the time, the largest cars ever built in Pullman's shops).

The cars in the two trains bore names featuring the states of Illinois and Missouri, the cities of Chicago and St. Louis and their suburbs, and prominent presidents of the United States. After exhibition at Chicago and St. Louis, twin *Alton Limiteds* departed on their respective 6½-hour trips from the still uncompleted Chicago Union Station and the St. Louis Union Passenger Station.

MISSOURI, combination baggage-smoker, provided leather reclining seats with foot-rests for 48 passengers. In common with all coach and parlor cars of the new Alton Limited, the Missouri contained a sanitary drinking fountain for thirsty travelers.

ARMSTRONG Railway Post Office was emblazoned with a very decorative U.S. Mails insigne. Car was named for Colonel G. G. Armstrong, railway mail service founder.

All photos, Pullman-Standard.

THE HANDSOMEST TRAIN IN THE WORLD

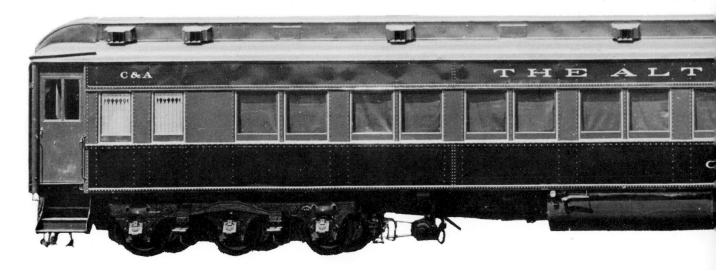

WEBSTER GROVES was one of two chair cars in consist of each train, seated 84 in reclining seats upholstered in green plush.

BLOOMINGTON dining car seated 36, was finished in South American rosewood and equipped with many candelabra and deck chandeliers, served famous "Alton Standard" meals. In competitive Chicago-St. Louis market, a menu could mean much.

WILSON parlor car possessed chairs for 36 plus a drawing room accommodating 5. Each Alton Limited carried three such parlors, all of them named for United States presidents.

CHICAGO observation car was defined as "the most novel and luxurious feature of this new and most luxurious train." Kimono-clad Japanese maid waited on ladies in a separate tearoom.

RIGHT and left (below) sides of the Wagner-built *New North Western Limited* of 1896 — with Schenectady 4-4-0 No. 91; C&NW buffet 576; sleepers *Regal, Bombay*

North Western Limited

Euclid; dining car *Illinois*; and a C&NW coach. Both photos, South collection of Everett L. DeGolyer Jr.

"The Best of Everything"

I   IN its 14th fiscal year, 1872-1873, the Chicago & North Western Railway arranged a through car line with the newly completed West Wisconsin Railway to form the "Elroy Route" between Chicago and St. Paul-Minneapolis. The new routing provided for an overnight service complete with sleeping and dining cars and was advertised as:

"The Pullman Palace Car Route between St. Paul and Chicago. . . . These cars are specially made and adapted to the trade of the Northwest, and families and ladies traveling alone will appreciate the advantages and comforts offered by this line. Gentlemanly CONDUCTORS and PORTERS accompany each car through from St. Paul to Chicago, who are hired for the purpose of waiting on passengers, and especially to render every assistance in their power to LADIES AND CHILDREN, THE AGED AND INFIRM."

CHICAGO-Twin Cities in 12½ hours in 1886.

North Western Limited

Electric-lighted elegance

The most comfortable, convenient, unique, and beautiful trains ever placed in service between Chicago, Milwaukee, Minneapolis, and St. Paul. — *The North Western Limited,* brochure, 1905.

IN 1881 F. K. Vanderbilt became a director of the Chicago & North Western when the road came into the Vanderbilt sphere of influence. One year later, Wagner sleeping cars of the Vanderbilt-owned New York Central Sleeping Car Co. replaced Pullmans on every North Western line except the Overland Route. Also during 1882 the C&NW purchased a controlling interest in the Chicago, St. Paul, Minneapolis & Omaha Railway (successor to the West Wisconsin); and for the first time, the C&NW Twin Cities service, advertised as the "Royal Route," operated under one ownership.

Following the lead of the progressive Eastern railroads, the North Western Line in 1888 ordered a new *Vestibuled Limited*. Viator, reporting in the Chicago *Tribune* of May 15, 1888, stated:

> By process of natural selection, that class of travelers who demand the best service, and do not hesitate to pay for it, are concentrating upon the vestibuled trains of the Chicago & North Western Railway.

On July 26, 1896, elegant new cars fresh from Wagner's Buffalo shops were placed in service on the *Limited*. Two years later, in March 1898, this entire train was completely redecorated and remodeled with electric lights. The St. Paul *Pioneer Press* on March 13, 1898, commented:

> The Aladdin of the North Western Line has rubbed his lamp again and set to work the 19th century genii of mechanics, electricity, and art. Their work far surpasses even the wonders of the Arabian Nights, for they have produced the new *North Western Limited* by which one may dream himself to and from Chicago while in a bed that has all the comforts of home.

A reporter from the Minneapolis *Journal* was overwhelmed by the train. Commenting about the compartment car *Regal,* he wrote:

> It is in the compartment sleeper that the richest artistic effects are worked out. The world has been ransacked for

costly woods; designers, carvers, upholsterers, and metal workers have apparently been given carte blanche in working out their ideas with no limit placed on the cost of materials. Silken tapestries of oriental richness, European refinement, and pleasing variety adorn the walls of the various rooms. Each compartment has its special scheme of color, upholstering, and decoration. Circassian walnut, San Domingo mahogany, English oak, pymirna, vermilion wood, bird's-eye maple, and rosewood, richly inlaid and highly polished, delight the eye.

Competition on the Chicago-Twin Cities run after the turn of the century was intense, and in 1905 the *Limited* was again re-equipped. Because of the purchase of the Wagner enterprise by Pullman, the new train was built by the successor company at its Pullman (Ill.) shops, thus ending the Wagner era on the North Western Line.

BUFFET CAR 2826, wherein "electric lights glow softly through art glass of delicate tints." Cigars were available for the men.

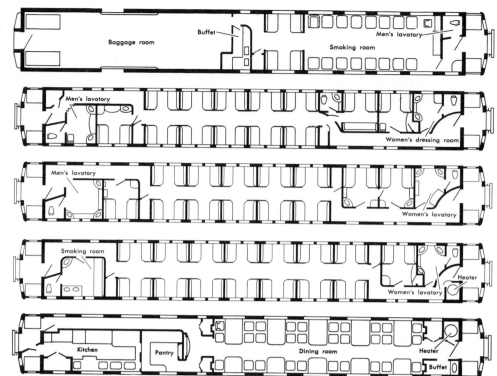

DEEPLY upholstered leather chairs placed the gentlemen at their ease in the buffet-smoker and library car.

CHICAGO-Minneapolis sleeping car contained a drawing room and 2 compartments and upper and lower berths.

ANOTHER Chicago-Minneapolis sleeping car had 3 "private compartments" along with 10 traditional sections.

SET-OUT car for Milwaukee from Minneapolis contained a single compartment together with 14 sections.

BASIC interior configuration of the dining car has changed little from that day to this — as attest C&NW's car.

All plans, author's collection.

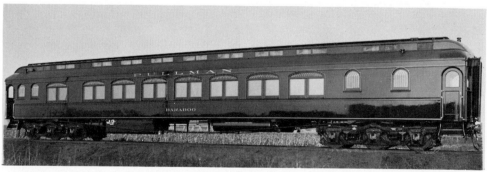

MILLSTON, a 10-section, 3-compartment Pullman, exemplified intent of North Western, which was to abolish all-room sleepers in favor of providing private rooms in each car.

Pullman-Standard.

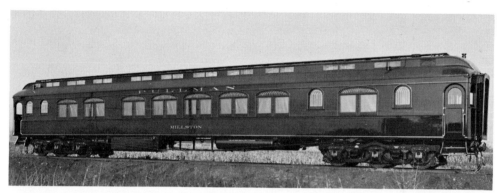

BARABOO, the Milwaukee-Minneapolis car, was named for Wisconsin birthplace of the Ringling Brothers of circus fame, contained the unusual floor plan of 14 sections and 1 compartment, was delivered in 1905.

Pullman-Standard.

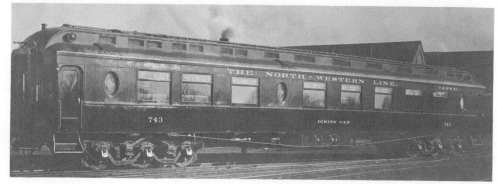

DINING CAR 743, a Pullman creation, seated 30 in the green and gold surroundings of the train. The upholstery was done in olive green plush.

Author's collection.

THREE generations of Middle West businessmen admired and rode aboard the classic twins of lounge cars, Nos. 7300 and 7301. Aboard 7300 they found (above) a soda fountain as well as (right) traditional overstuffed chairs.

ILLUMINATED tailgate sign brought up the rear.

The best of everything

> A superb train of quality, affording the acme of travel comfort, convenience, safety — and service. — *The New North Western Limited*, brochure, 1912.

FEW TRAINS have equaled the beauty of the *New North Western Limited* of 1912. Standing in the trainshed, the yellow and green cars and glistening black Pacific were a sight to behold. The shaded silver lettering on the steel cars and the new illuminated C&NW trademark on the brass railing of the observation car were details that set the *Limited* apart from other trains in the depot.

The North Western's new Chicago passenger terminal stationed many pedigreed trains — the *Overland Limited*, *North Coast Limited*, *Centennial State Special*, *China and Japan Fast Mail*, *Los Angeles Limited*, *Colorado Special* — all were listed daily on the arrival and departure boards. But the *New North Western Limited* was different. It operated over C&NW rails exclusively and was the pride and joy of North Western men.

It was a stunning train to be sure. Marvin Hughitt made certain of that. The onetime Illinois Central telegrapher who had worked 36 hours straight at his dispatcher's desk in Centralia making sure that the Union Army got through to Vicksburg in 1862 was now the highly respected president of the Chicago & North Western. The C&NW offered "The Best of Everything," and in 1912 the best of everything meant the *New North Western Limited*.

160

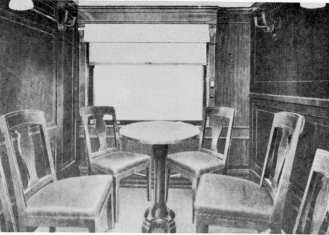

Author's collection.

SMALL table and straight-backed chairs furnished the conference room aboard the famous lounge 7300 constructed in 1912.

North Western Limited

THOSE dining aboard the North Western Limited were greeted with (left) snowy napery and fresh flowers in cut glass. On Christmas Day the menu (below) tempted those away from home to whet appetites on bisque of pigeon before the main course of venison cutlets. An accompanying individual of Old Fitzgerald or Canadian Club set one back just 20 cents. Oh, yes, the steward would provide recipes for any especially appealing dishes.

THE NORTH-WESTERN LIMITED

CHICAGO-ST. PAUL-MINNEAPOLIS

VIA

THE NORTH-WESTERN LINE

DINNER

CANAPE CAVIAR

BLUE POINTS
CELERY

BISQUE OF PIGEON, A LA HOTELIERE   CONSOMME, NIVERNAISE
PICKLED WALNUTS   SALTED ALMONDS   OLIVES

COLUMBIA RIVER SALMON, SUPREME
POTATOES, HOLLANDAISE   CUCUMBERS

LOBSTER A LA NEWBURG, EN CASSEROLE

TOMATO FRITTERS

SNOWBALL PUFF

PRIME ROAST BEEF, YORKSHIRE PUDDING
NEW POTATOES IN CREAM   BRUSSELS SPROUTS, BECHAMEL

ROAST TURKEY, CRANBERRIES
CANDIED YAMS   ARTICHOKES FARCIE   FLAGEOLETS

FROZEN EGG-NOG

VENISON CUTLETS, CURRANT JELLY
OLD VIRGINIA CORN RELISH

ENDIVE SALAD

HOME-MADE PLUM PUDDING, HARD OR BRANDY SAUCE

INDIVIDUAL MINCE PIE

MAPLE MOUSSE   ASSORTED CAKES

HICKORY NUTS AND SWEET CIDER

ROQUEFORT   WAUKESHA CREAM AND CAMEMBERT CHEESE

BAR-LE-DUC

COFFEE

CREAM DE MENTHE   BON BONS

Author's collection.

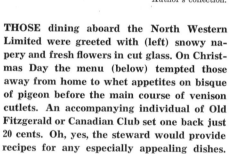

WINE LIST

		QUARTS	PINTS
Champagnes	MOET & CHANDON (WHITE SEAL)	$2.00	
	POMMERY SEC	2.00	
	G. H. MUMM'S (EXTRA DRY)	2.00	
	VEUVE CLICQUOT (YELLOW LABEL)	2.00	
	RUINART, VIN BRUT	2.00	
	IMPERIAL (COOK'S)	1.25	
California Red Wines	ST. JULIEN (CALIFORNIA) (CRESTA BLANCA)	.75	.40
	ST. JULIEN (CALIFORNIA) (GOLD MEDAL, CORDOVA) .25	.75	.40
	TIPO CHIANTI (ITALIAN SWISS COLONY)		.50
	MEDOC TYPE (ALTA VISTA)		.50
	CHATEAU MARGAUX TYPE " "		.75
	CHATEAU LAFITE TYPE " "		.75
Imported Red Wines	ST. JULIEN (CRUSE & FILS FRERES)		.75
	PONTET CANET " "		1.00
	CHATEAU LAROSE " "		1.75
	ST. JULIEN (BORSHAMER, LEON & CO.)		.75
	PONTET CANET "		1.00
California White Wines	SAUTERNE (CALIFORNIA) (CRESTA BLANCA)	.75	.40
	SAUTERNE (CALIFORNIA) (GOLD MEDAL, CORDOVA) .25	.75	.40
	TIPO CHIANTI (ITALIAN SWISS COLONY)		.50
	SAUTERNE TYPE (ALTA VISTA)		.50
	CHIANTI TYPE "		.60
	MOSELLE TYPE "		.50
Imported White Wines	SAUTERNE (CRUSE & FILS FRERES)		.75
	CHATEAU LATOUR BLANCHE " "		1.50
	RUEDESHEIMER (CARL ACKER)		1.00
California Sparkling Wines	BURGUNDY TYPE (ALTA VISTA)		1.00
	SAUTERNE TYPE " "		1.00
	MOSELLE TYPE " "		1.00
Imported Sparkling Wines	SPARKLING CHAMBERTIN, RED (B. L. & CO.)		1.50
	SPARKLING CHABLIS, WHITE (B. L. & CO.)		1.50
Waters	HIAWATHA LITHIA SPLITS, .15		.25
	CLUB SODA		.25
	CONGRESS OR HATHORN		.25
	UNCHARGED WATER SPLITS, .10		.15
	WHITE ROCK LITHIA .15		.25
	APOLLINARIS "		.25
	HUNYADI WATER PER GLASS, .15		.35
	LONDONDERRY LITHIA SPLITS, .15		.25
	RED RAVEN		.15
Beers	PABST'S "BLUE RIBBON"		.15
	SCHLITZ' "PALE"		.15
	BLATZ' "WIENER"		.15
	MILLER'S "HIGH LIFE"		.15
Whiskies	OLD FITZGERALD RYE OR BOURBON - INDIVIDUALS, .20		
	NATIONAL CLUB BOURBON " .20		
	SCOTCH OR CANADIAN CLUB " .20		
	WESTMORELAND RYE " .20		
	KING WILLIAM SCOTCH " .35		
	RYE OR BOURBON, FLASKS, 50c AND 75c		
Miscellaneous	COCKTAILS:		
	WHISKY, MARTINI OR MANHATTAN, INDIVIDUALS, .20		
	HENNESSY BRANDY " .35		
	AMONTILLADO SHERRY " .20		
	BASS' ALE, WHITE LABEL OR DOG'S HEAD		.30
	GUINNESS' DUBLIN PORTER		.30
	BELFAST GINGER ALE		.25
	WHITE ROCK GINGER ALE		.15
	OLD TOM GIN INDIVIDUALS, .20		
	CREME DE MENTHE " .20		
	BENEDICTINE " .20		
	EFFERVESCENT BROMO SELTZER " .10		
	HORLICK'S MALTED MILK " .15		

IMPORTED AND DOMESTIC CIGARS, 10c, TWO FOR 25c, 15c AND 25c

E-CLASS Pacific 1560, built by Alco's Schenectady Works in 1911, rode on 75-inch drivers; exerted 33,700 pounds tractive effort; like all C&NW engines, dispensed with illuminated numbers on headlight sides. White-shirted official posed in cab.

North Western
Limited

DINING CAR 6914, an 82-footer from the shops of Pullman, sported "C&NW Ry" in Gothic-style silver lettering shaded with black. Car was not withdrawn from service finally until 1956.

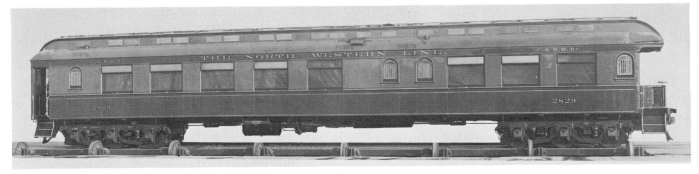

CABARET (or lounging) car 2829 was built by Pullman in 1910 with observation platform, was rebuilt in 1912 (see plan) as 7301 with vestibule.

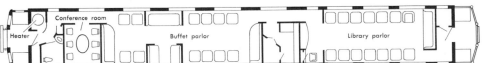

OBSERVATION-LOUNGE 7107 was built by Pullman in 1915 to provide North Western Limited with full-length lounge on markers end.

162

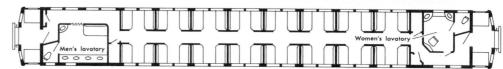

WINNETKA, a 16-section car named for a Chicago suburb, was finished in green and yellow livery of C&NW.

GARDEN CITY contained 10 sections, 1 drawing room, and 2 compartments.

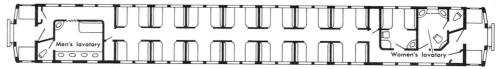

BELLE PLAINE — Milwaukee-Minneapolis sleeper with 14 sections and 1 compartment — is remembered today for its unorthodox floor plan.

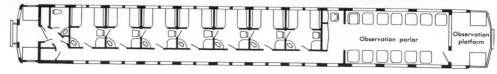

LAKE GENEVA, sister car of Lake Forest, had 7 compartments and observation lounge. When replaced by full-length lounges in 1924, the cars became San Lucas, San Ardo on SP.

THE *Limited* threads its way through the commuter rush entering Chicago in 1949. C&NW photo.

A smart train

THE *North Western* was the first train on the fiercely competitive Chicago-Twin Cities run to be refurnished after World War I. In the early 1920's new cars and locomotives were placed in operation. The stately 1912-model lounging cars, richly fitted with hand-rubbed panels and Spanish leather club chairs, were retained along with the dining car.

Improved E-2 4-6-2 locomotives and the latest types of Pullman-Standard sleeping cars were installed in 1923 on "the shortest route to St. Paul and Minneapolis" — via the beautiful North Shore suburbs, Milwaukee, and Eau Claire. Automatic electric block signals protected the train for the entire

distance over a rock-ballasted double-tracked roadbed that was renowned for ensuring restful sleep.

Again, in August 1928, another upgrading was effected. The newest Pullmans finished in Spanish design and containing the latest-style bedrooms were placed in service. Once again the classic lounging cars and diners remained — by polite demand of the train's prominent patrons, many of whom enjoyed the convenience of entraining in their North Shore home towns.

Duluth and Superior, the Twin Ports, were served by the *Limited* throughout its history except during the operation of the *North American* (1915-1931). North of Eau Claire the Duluth car operated in the *Duluth-Superior Limited*.

A feature of the *Limited* was its extraordinary dining-car

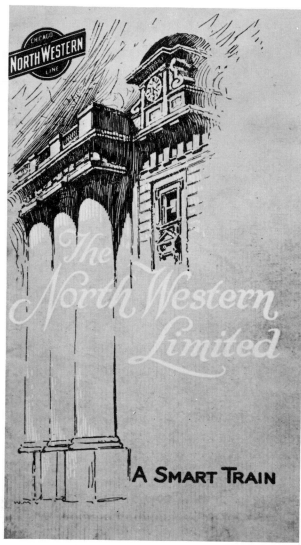

THREE words said it all in 1923 . . . "A Smart Train."

Author's collection.

North Western Limited

cuisine. Joseph Verona, present manager of C&NW dining cars, recounts nostalgically the sumptuous repasts of bygone years.

Although the depression and highway competition cut deeply into the train's earnings, traditional *North Western Limited* service was maintained until World War II forced drastic changes. Compliance with a Federal order banning sleeping cars on runs of less than 450 miles practically destroyed the de luxe operation.*

The postwar edition of the *Limited* carried new streamlined

*Complying with the same order, the New Haven equipped its famous *Owl* (all-sleeping-car overnight between Boston and New York) as an all-parlor-car "sleeper" train with special cars for ladies and extra pillows for sleeping in parlor-car chairs.

sleeping cars of the *Northern* series along with prewar heavy-weight equipment. It was an interesting and well-run train.

After the unfortunate end of Overland Route operation on the C&NW in October 1955, the road had a surplus of stream-lined cars, and for the first time Nos. 405 and 406 were advertised as the *Streamliner North Western Limited*.

In 1956 the North Western, beset on all sides by economic difficulties, received a change of management. The new leadership of the road was outspoken in its pessimism about the future of passenger train operation — the tide had turned for the once great limited. Nos. 405 and 406 started on their last runs on June 14, 1959. After that fateful day "The Best of Everything" in "The Best of the West" was no more. ‡

RAILWAY POST OFFICE 9436, built by American Car & Foundry in 1921, was a beautifully lettered example of carbuilder's art.

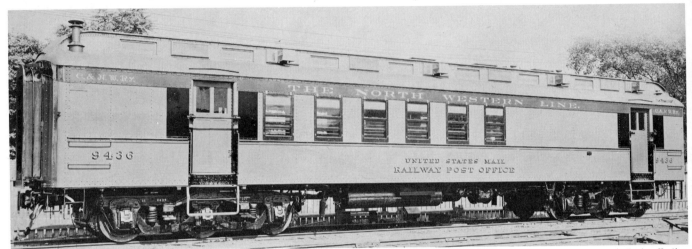

CHAFFEE measured 73 feet 6 inches over sills, contained 12 sections and 1 drawing room. Green and yellow vanished in 1928.

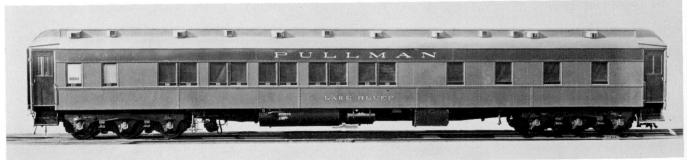

LAKE BLUFF had 10 sections, 2 compartments, 1 drawing room. Green and yellow livery — out in 1928 — was restored during 1939.

E-2 PACIFIC 2910, outshopped by Alco in 1923, typified final evolution of the 4-6-2 wheel arrangement on Chicago & North Western. As built, the engine had 75-inch drivers, exerted 45,000 pounds tractive effort, weighed 292,000 pounds. Certain E-2's were later rebuilt and fitted for oil to haul 400 in 1935.

Author's collection.

Pullman-Standard.

MT. FORAKER, a 10-section lounge-observation, was sold in 1954 to become a Fort Dodge, Des Moines & Southern office car.

North Western Limited

FORT DEARBORN, twin of the gloriously named Cadwallader C. Washburn, was built in 1928 as a solarium-lounge with 6 single bedrooms, but 2 extra rooms were added later. Special aluminum paint was added in 1935; interior was trimmed in carved walnut.

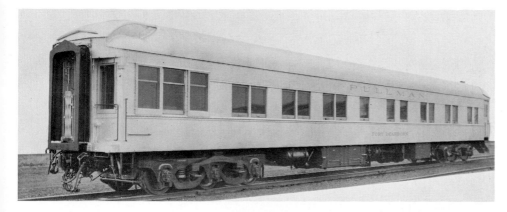

Both photos, Pullman-Standard.

NORTHERN FORESTS helped streamline the Limited after World War II; possessed 1 compartment, 3 double bedrooms, and 16 duplex roomettes. A duplex roomette afforded private room comfort for a mere 35 cents more than lower berth. In the spring of 1964 Northern Forests was sold south of the border to the NdeM. It's now named Lago Aral.

Pullman-Standard.

167

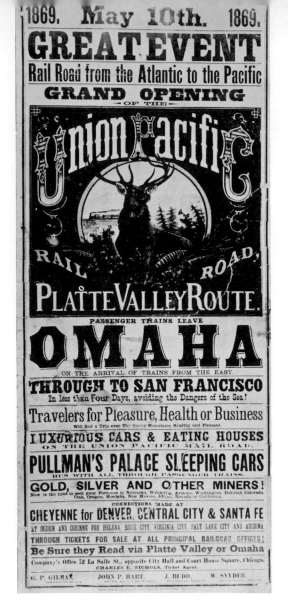

UP TRAINS avoided "dangers of the sea!" UP collection.

WEST of Cheyenne on Dale Creek Bridge in 1876. Author's collection.

THE OVERLAND

1 ON February 7, 1849, Sen. Thomas Hart Benton of Missouri rose in the United States Senate chamber in the national capitol and declared:

"The road I propose is necessary to us — and now. The title to Oregon is settled, and a government established there. California is acquired, people are there, and a government must follow. We own the country from sea to sea, from the Atlantic to the Pacific, upon a breadth equal to the length of the Mississippi, and embracing the whole temperate zone. We can run a road through and through, the whole distance, under our flag and under our laws."

Senator Benton spoke with foresight and wisdom when

he proposed the Overland Route. Even as he was orating in the capitol, hundreds of weary gold-seekers were going West, wending their way by foot, oxen, and wagon train through a country filled with hostile Indians and wild animals. Over paths worn by these pioneers were laid the shining rails on which the great rolling palaces of the Overland Route later traveled: *Golden Gate Special, Overland Limited, Pacific Limited, China and Japan Fast Mail, Gold Coast Limited, Continental Limited, Los Angeles Limited, Columbine, Portland Rose, Forty Niner, Treasure Island Special,* and finally the famed fleet of yellow *City* streamliners and domeliners.

On that crisp December day in 1863 when the first sod

UNCLE SAM picks a transcontinental. C&NW collection.

ROUTE

Classic trains of the original way West

was turned for the Union Pacific at Omaha, there was scarcely a house west of the Elkhorn River, 20 miles from town. But thanks to the courage and determination of such men as Sidney Dillon, Jack Casement, Grenville Dodge, the Ames brothers, and the "Big Four" of the Central Pacific — Crocker, Huntington, Hopkins, and Stanford — the Overland Route was completed.

Few events of American history will outrank the memorable occasion on May 10, 1869, when under a blazing sun the golden Last Spike of the Union Pacific and Central Pacific was driven. The little telegraph instrument at Promontory, Utah, flashed word that the Atlantic and the Pacific were wedded for the ages.

UP.

"WHAT was it the engines said?" The joining of the rails on May 10, 1869, created America's original transcontinental route.

169

PULLMANS *Golden Gate, Aladdin, Alhambra,* and *Feronia* at Pullman, Ill., in August 1888 prior to *Special* service.

Finest train in the world

THROUGH passenger trains began operating on the new Overland Route five days after the driving of the Golden Spike in 1869. "Palace Day and Sleeping Coaches" departed daily from Omaha and Sacramento via the Union Pacific and Central Pacific. Running time for the 1773-mile trip was 5 days 7 hours. Through service to Oakland began later, in November 1869.

The first transcontinental trains were known simply as the *Express.* In 1875, Nos. 1 and 2 on the Central Pacific and connecting Nos. 3 and 4 on the Union Pacific were titled *Atlantic & Pacific Express.* They were a colorful operation equipped with Pullman cars on the UP and company-owned Silver Palace sleepers on the CP.

Noting the success of the new luxury trains in the East, the Overland Route placed the *Golden Gate Special* in operation on December 5, 1888. It was one of the earliest de luxe trains in regular service in North America.

The *Special* contained five unique electric-lighted vestibuled Pullman cars painted umber with red and gold trim: *Golden Gate, Casa Monica, Khiva, Rahula,* and *Aladdin. Golden Gate* was a baggage car with barbershop and gentlemen's bathroom. The electric light apparatus was located in the baggage compartment. *Casa Monica,* the dining car, was owned and operated by the Pullman Company. "The fact that the cuisine is under the immediate supervision of the Pullman Commissary Department is a sufficient guarantee of delicious meals and perfect service," states the brochure. *Khiva* and *Rahula* contained sleeping apartments and consisted of 12 sections, drawing room, and ladies' bathroom. The interiors of these elegant cars were finished in mahogany with carpets, upholstery, and draperies all selected to harmonize. *Aladdin,* listed as a "composite car" (observation-sleeper), was rebuilt in November 1888 from the smoking car of the same name originally built one year earlier for the *New York & Florida Special* (described

The *Golden Gate Special*

The Golden Gate Special.	Miles.	STATIONS.	Miles.	The Golden Gate Special.
8.00 AM	0	Lv...COUNCIL BLUFFS ..Ar.	1867	9.00 AM
8.15 "	3	" ....OMAHA.......... "	1864	8.45 "
1.00 PM	156	" ....GRAND ISLAND.... "	1711	4.20 "
4.10 "	294	" ....NORTH PLATTE..... "	1573	12.35 "
7.40 "	417	" ....SIDNEY........ "	1450	8.20 PM
10.45 "	519	" ......CHEYENNE....... "	1348	5.35 "
1 10 AM	576	" ......LARAMIE .. .... "	1291	3.10 "
5.30 "	712	" ......RAWLINS........ "	1155	10 50 AM
9.55 "	848	" ....GREEN RIVER..... "	1019	6.25 "
1.15 PM	958	" ....EVANSTON .... "	909	3.05 "
2 45 "	1034	" ....OGDEN .... "	833	12.15 "
9.45 "	1253	" ....WELLS........ "	614	3.45 PM
12.30 AM	1333	" .....CARLIN .... "	534	1.00 "
....	1342	" ....PALISADE..... "	525	....
4.15 "	1453	" .....WINNEMUCCA... "	414	9.00 AM
8.40 "	1589	" ..... WADSWORTH..... "	278	4 50 "
9.50 "	1623	" ....RENO .... "	244	3.20 "
11.30 "	1658	" ....TRUCKEE........ "	209	2.00 "
3.40 PM	1723	" ....COLFAX .... "	144	9.15 PM
6.15 "	1777	" ......SACRAMENTO..... "	90	5.50 "
9.45 PM	1867	Ar....SAN FRANCISCO....Lv	0	2.00 PM

—THIS IS—
THE FINEST TRAIN IN THE WORLD.

SP.

SILVER PALACE sleeping car, built by Jackson & Sharp for Central Pacific Railroad of California, posed for photo outside the carbuilders' Wilmington (Del.) works. In 1883 the open-platform vehicle was transferred to the custodianship of Pullman.

170

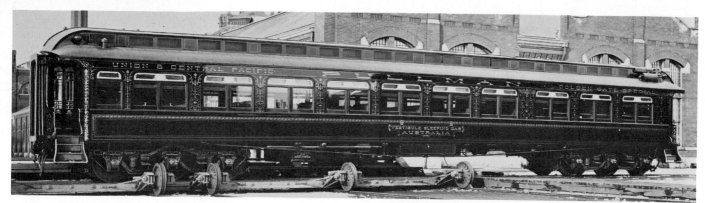

on page 127). *Aladdin* was, in fact, one of the first observation cars built. The train brochure states:

> The Composite Car *Aladdin*, the last car, deserves especial mention, having several new features. This car is divided into compartments; the first contains six luxurious sleeping sections; the second contains a buffet; the third, a large open room furnished with easy chairs, contains a Library, with writing materials, and will be used for smoking, but more particularly as an observation room. The end windows are very large, extending from the top of the car to within 15 inches of the floor, and afford a full view of the magnificent scenery en route.

The *Golden Gate* operated between Council Bluffs and San Francisco, leaving the Iowa city every Wednesday at 8 a.m. and arriving San Francisco 9:45 p.m. the following Friday. Eastbound, the train left San Francisco at 2 p.m. every Saturday and arrived Council Bluffs 9 a.m. Tuesday. The entire cost of the one-way trip was $100 — $60 for rail transportation and $40 for the extra-fare surcharge with meals included. Baggage of 150 pounds was carried free, but passengers were cautioned that personal services were extra: shave 25 cents; haircut and shampoo each 50 cents; and bath 75 cents. Accommodations were limited, and reservations not paid for 30 minutes before train time were canceled and sold to other applicants.

Despite all this grandeur, the *Special* was not a success and was discontinued in May 1889.

THE OVERLAND ROUTE

AUSTRALIA (sister of New Zealand and China) was delivered in March 1889; cost $20,463; contained 12 sections, a drawing room, and stateroom; coddled its patrons with flowered upholstery and mahogany paneling.

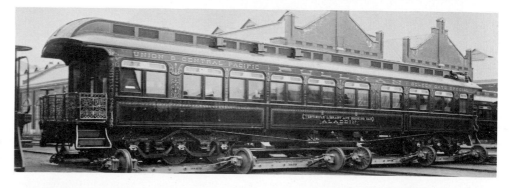

ALADDIN, original observation car of Golden Gate and one of the first brass-railed cars, was rebuilt in 1888.

SYBARIS, an 8-section observation, was completed in 1889 and replaced Aladdin in consist of Golden Gate.

IN 1909 Baldwin compound 4-4-2 No. 22 heads the *Overland* on the Lane Cutoff. UP photo.

Most luxurious and fastest
daily cross-continent train

THE *Overland Limited* was as revered in the West as its counterpart, the *Twentieth Century Limited*, was in the East. Aboard the *Overland* for nearly a half century rode the celebrities of the world — great men and women of the arts and letters, presidents of the United States, and men of finance. Among the *Overland's* passengers were such luminaries as Ethel Barrymore, Enrico Caruso, J. P. Morgan, William McKinley. A toy train coveted by boys of the early 1900's was named *Overland*, and the well-known Boston grocer S. S. Pierce has for many years purveyed an Overland cigar. One of the first extra-fare trains in the West ($10 Chicago-San Francisco), the *Overland Limited* was the pride of the Overland Route.

The *Overland Flyer*, Nos. 1 and 2, was inaugurated by the Union Pacific on November 13, 1887. After the *Golden Gate Special* was withdrawn in 1889, the *Flyer* succeeded as the crack train of the line. It carried free reclining chair cars, sleepers, and a dining car from Chicago (and also Kansas City) to San Francisco via Chicago & North Western-Union Pacific-Southern Pacific.

In the early 1890's, when UP controlled the Texas Panhandle Route (Fort Worth & Denver City and Union Pacific, Denver & Gulf), connections were made at Denver with the *Texas Panhandle-No. 2* which carried a Pullman from New Orleans via the Texas & Pacific. With only one change of cars it was possible to travel in sleeping-car comfort from New Orleans to the West and the Northwest.

In 1896 Nos. 1 and 2 became the *Overland Limited*. Grandly the Union Pacific proclaimed:

THE ORIGINAL OVERLAND ROUTE
IT WAS THE ROUTE IN '49!
IT IS THE ROUTE TODAY, AND
WILL BE FOR ALL TIME TO COME

The average reader does not stop to think what the saving of a whole day between Chicago and San Francisco means to the busy, bustling public of America, but we will tell one and all that it means time and money, and it is

172

THE place is Cheyenne, the train is the *Los Angeles Limited*, the engine is Pacific 116, the photographer J. E. Stimson. Collection of Everett L. DeGolyer Jr.

proper to ask who is there among you who is not doing his best to win out on both propositions? Messengers from the frozen North and alkali deserts of the South will sing soft songs of the beauties of their routes to the coast, but would-be visitors should remember that there is only one line in the temperate zone — one line that is not harassed by the stifling alkali dust at all seasons of the year; nor by snowslides and icebergs for six months out of twelve. In fact, a line that is all that it should be in every particular, and one that is in reality 'The World's Pictorial Line.'

In 1899 the Southern Pacific finally conceded the existence of the name *Overland Limited* for trains 1 and 2 and joined with C&NW and UP to operate "the most luxurious and fastest (73 hours) daily train across the continent."

For the refurbishing of the *Overland* of 1902, Pullman de-

THE OVERLAND ROUTE

ATLANTIC 1023 (Schenectady 1901) leads the *Overland* across the Kate Shelley Bridge over the Des Moines River at Boone, Ia. C&NW photo.

livered 2 million dollars' worth of new wooden cars. Each was built on a steel frame covered with "a new material known as monolith." The term was an early name for concrete, and this method of construction prevailed to the end of the heavy-weight era.

Advertised as the most novel feature of the 1902 equipment was the telephone, "the adaptation of which to railway trains is entirely original and absolutely unique." It was located in the observation lounge and was in the custody of a special uniformed attendant.

From 1905 until 1914, two separate *Overland Limiteds* operated daily between Chicago and the UP Transfer near Council Bluffs, each with through West Coast cars. One ran via the Chicago & North Western line; the other operated over Chicago, Milwaukee & St. Paul rails. The latter was the precursor of the Milwaukee Road-Overland Route service which was to become effective in October 1955, a half century later.

On December 15, 1905, the *Los Angeles Limited* was instituted between Chicago and Los Angeles via the C&NW–UP–Salt Lake Route (San Pedro, Los Angeles & Salt Lake). It was described as "a palatial train for particular people. . . . The trip between Chicago and the Coast by the *Los Angeles Limited* is an exposition of what the West stands for — socially, commercially, and from an agricultural standpoint."

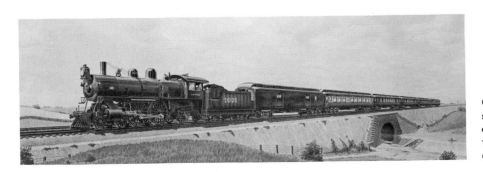

CLASS D Atlantic 1021 displays a clean stack in painting of the Overland by Chicago artist-photographer Alfred W. Johnson whose art was published on C&NW calendars. Schenectady built the 4-4-2 in 1901.

174

Life aboard the Pullmans in those leisurely days was described in a 1906 Overland Route folder:

The day contains no dull moments. Much time is spent in the composite car, where, from the observation parlor, or from comfortable campchairs in the broad recesses of the brass-railed, rubber-tiled observation platform, the great panorama of the West is watched as it unfolds in fast-receding miles.

At evening the ladies read and chat, the children play, the older members of the company sink comfortably into the big armchairs of the library, and the men gather in the smoking room, a delightful group in which tourists from all nations, army officers, and diplomats, men of affairs and their families, forget the outside world in the comradeship of travel.

Social life on the *Overland Limited* during this journey of 70 hours is not unlike that on an ocean steamer, where a congenial company finds rest and recreation amid surroundings that include all the luxuries of twentieth century travel.

THE OVERLAND ROUTE

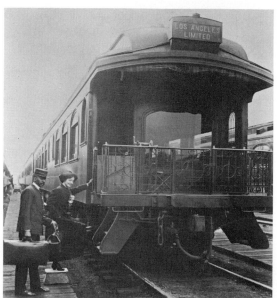

UP.

THE lady grips her parasol, smiles demurely, ascends the steps of Los Angeles Limited's observation car.

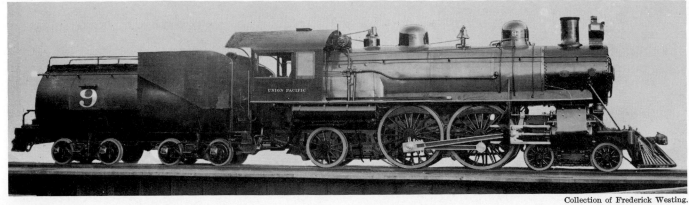

SPEEDSTER No. 9, a standard Harriman Atlantic, was constructed by Baldwin in 1904, rode on 81-inch drivers, developed 23,500 pounds tractive force, weighed approximately 323,000 pounds with tender, could part the breeze at a rapid gait.

BUFFET CAR 711, built by Pullman in 1902, contained electric lights equal in illumination to "350 sixteen-candlepower lamps."

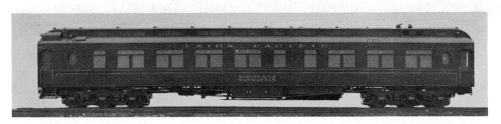

MANHATTAN, UP diner outshopped by Pullman in 1900, was acclaimed by proud owner in these words: "As perfect as every accessory to elegance can make it." Two vestibules and more or less conventional window pattern make kitchen hard to locate.

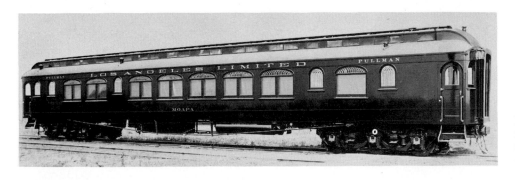

MOAPA was built in 1905; contained 10 sections, 2 compartments, 1 drawing room; was lettered in gold leaf for Los Angeles Limited service.

BERNARDINO, a 10-section, 2-compartment, 1-drawing-room sleeper of 1905, boasted lavatories with white-tiled walls and a "dainty little heater for ladies' curling irons." This car, too, was Pullman green with lettering in gold leaf.

GLENVIEW, Milwaukee Road-owned 10-section, 2-compartment, 1-drawing-room sleeper, bespeaks 1905 CM&StP Overland participation.

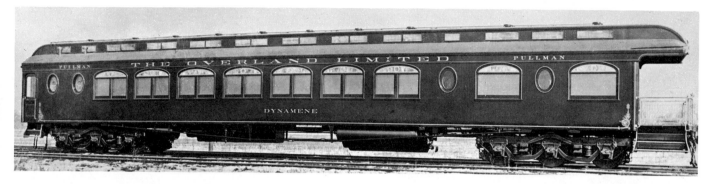

DYNAMENE, Pullman-built observation of 1902 with 6 compartments and drawing room, kept its riders informed when they weren't occupied with passing prairies and sagebrush. Its lounge contained a library furnished by Booklovers of Philadelphia. (Below) Dynamene on the Overland Limited in Chicago.

THE OVERLAND ROUTE

C&NW.

Both photos, UP.

OBSERVATION 726 typifies identical equipment ordered by UP and SP for the Overland and Los Angeles Limiteds. Smoking room (above) was mahogany paneled with leaded window sashes.

H-CLASS 4-8-4's 3016 and 3027, in fresh from Omaha, bracket a smaller Pacific in North Western's Chicago station. C&NW photo.

Finest and fastest

The air of quiet luxury and the spirit of ready service have made this train noted throughout the world. The richness of carpets, upholstery, and finishings makes you imagine you are at a fine hotel or at your club. — Overland Route, brochure, 1926.

DURING the era of World War I and the 1920's the *Overland* was advertised as the finest and fastest train between Chicago and the Golden Gate. Its handsome "all-Pullman" equipment consisted of a buffet-club car at the forward end of the train, luxurious drawing room-compartment sleeping cars, library-observation car, and the famous Overland Route dining-car service. Other amenities included clothes pressing and a drinking fountain. Train attendants, carefully selected for their experience and efficiency, included a maid, manicurist, hairdresser, barber, and valet. The ladies' maid was noted as an expert "in intimate attentions to women and children, and always at the service of patrons."

A special representative who accompanied each train furnished information regarding points of interest and "other services of worth and convenience to passengers. He will stenograph, typewrite, and attend to mailing letters, free of charge." A bulletin board in the club car chronicled world-wide happenings of the day, posted stock quotations, sporting news, and "other things we think we must know."

The dining car ran through between Chicago and San Francisco. Stewards, cooks, and waiters were picked from the best in the regular employ of the Overland Route companies. The menu represented the choice of markets in Chicago, San Francisco, and intermediate cities. Genuine Irish linen, gleaming silver, sparkling glassware, and deftness of service created

San Francisco
Overland
Limited
Extra Fare

FINEST
AND
FASTEST

*Only 63-hour Train
between*
**Chicago and
San Francisco**

**CHICAGO & NORTH WESTERN
UNION PACIFIC
SOUTHERN PACIFIC**
The Overland Route

SP.

EAGLE ad praised 63-hour Overland schedule.

178

SECOND, third, and fourth sections of No. 28, the *Gold Coast Limited*, eastbound at Los Angeles April 22, 1929. UP photo.

an atmosphere rivaling that of world famous dining salons.

Effective June 1, 1930, the schedule of the westbound *Overland* was cut from 58 hours to 56 hours, and the fastest train between Chicago and San Francisco, the aristocrat of the Overland Route, became even faster.

THE OVERLAND ROUTE

A. W. Johnson.

FLAGMAN examines his Hamilton at 8:20 a.m. July 13, 1934, as the eastbound San Francisco Overland Limited makes an un-scheduled stop at Oak Park, Ill., in the suburban territory of Chicago & North Western. Operation is left-handed, of course.

Homer O. Frohardt.

OBSERVATION platform of Forrest Lake is well patronized on the morning of July 3, 1921, as the California-bound Overland pauses at Council Bluffs, Ia. Congressional resolution declaring peace with Germany and Austria was signed July 2 by Harding.

C&NW.

COACH RIDERS eye the photographer as Chicago & North Western No. 3, the Los Angeles-bound China and Japan Mail rumbles over the Kate Shelley Bridge at Boone, Ia., behind a trimly proportioned Pacific constructed by Schenectady in the year 1911.

A. W. Johnson.

CRYSTAL-SERIES Pullman observation carries red drumhead of the air-conditioned San Francisco Overland Limited as train runs southpaw through Geneva, Ill., in 1934.

THE OVERLAND ROUTE

FAMOUS SP publicity shot of the Overland "at sea" crossing Great Salt Lake.

A. W. Johnson.

OVERLAND flashes through Oak Park, Ill., at 9:13 a.m. August 6, 1916, behind a North Western D-class Atlantic, No. 399, fitted with rotary valves. Behind buffet and diner are Pullmans Elkington and Portslade. Pullman observation Cedar Point carries markers.

DINNER

Canape of Anchovies, 25

Cotuits on Deep Shell, (Overland Style) 40

Clear Green Turtle, 25   Consomme in Cup, 20

Celery, 25   Melon Mangoes, 20   Olives, 20   Salted Almonds, 20

Mountain Trout, Meuniere, 65

Cucumbers, 25

Oyster Patties, 50   Stuffed Green Peppers, 35

Roast Young Turkey, Cranberries, 65   Suckling Pig, Baked Apples, 65
Ribs of Prime Western Beef, 60

Boiled Potatoes, 10   Mashed Potatoes, 15   Candied Sweet Potatoes, 20
Stringless Beans, 15

OVERLAND PUNCH (WITH OUR COMPLIMENTS)

Broiled Philadelphia Squab, 65   Broiled Teal Duck, 65
Roast Mallard Duck (Special to Order), $1.25

Brussels Sprouts, 20   Asparagus, 30

Tomato and Lettuce Salad, 30   Fresh Coast Crab Salad, 50

English Plum Pudding, 25   Hot Mince Pie, Brandy Sauce, 15
Ice Cream, 15   Assorted Cake, 10
Assorted Fresh Fruit, 20
Roquefort or Imperial Cheese with Toasted Crackers, 25
Camembert Cheese with Toasted Crackers, 30
Bar-le-duc, 30

Japan, Ceylon, English Breakfast, Formosa Oolong, or Blend Tea, per pot 10
Special Blend of India and Ceylon Tea, per pot, 15
Special Bottled Milk, 15
Coffee, pot for one, 15; for two, 25; cup, 10

EN ROUTE, DECEMBER 25, 1913
UNION PACIFIC RAILROAD

Author's collection.

YULE menu from 1913 features free Overland punch.

C&NW.

CHIC SALE, of outdoor plumbing fame, chats with Columbine hogger Alex McGraw during celebrity's cab ride May 21, 1930.

UP.

LIGHT gray boiler and cylinder jacketing, Delta trailing truck, coal pusher, and vestibule Vanderbilt tank were earmarks of Pacific 2901, built by Baldwin for UP in 1920. She weighed 461,200 pounds with tender, exerted 38,636 pounds tractive force.

BUFFET 2833, a Harriman-roof C&NW car built in 1913 for Overland Limited service, provided head-end power (below) with dynamo.

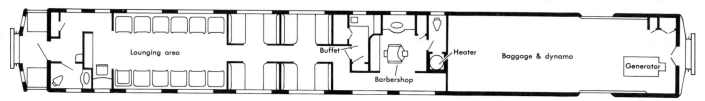

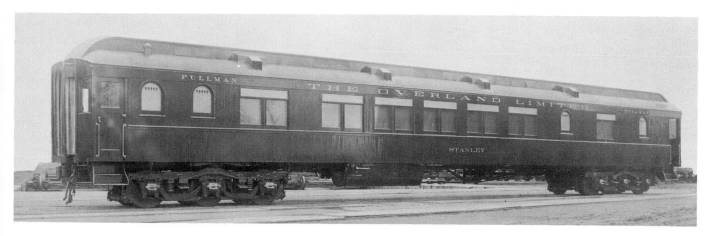

STANLEY — a 10-section, 2-compartment, 1-drawing-room car — survived for more than a quarter century. The Pullman product was built in 1909 for Overland, remained in extra service until 1935.

THE OVERLAND ROUTE

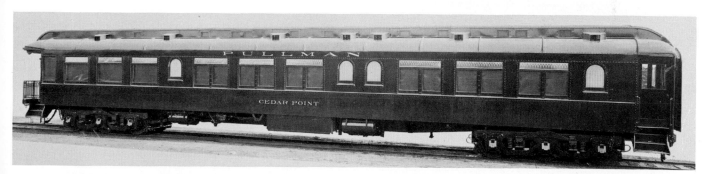

CEDAR POINT was built in 1913 as 2-drawing-room, 4-compartment observation, later had a compartment removed to increase lounge.

OBSERVATION-LOUNGE 553 built by Pullman in 1913 for Union Pacific (OWRR&N) was a handsome Harriman-roof car assigned to Chicago-to-Portland Oregon-Washington Limited — a flyer to Pacific Northwest which was billed then as "A High Class Train."

"LARGEST dual-service locomotive in the world" was claim for North Western's $120,000 85 mph H-class 4-8-4 of 1929. C&NW proudly said that the Baldwin-built H could "maintain an even speed uphill and downhill" and "eliminate jerky starts and stops."

PRAIRIE RACER: Union Pacific 7869, built by Alco in July 1924, weighed 585,800 pounds with tender, exerted 54,838 pounds tractive force, burned oil. Union Pacific began buying 4-8-2's in 1921, acquired a fleet of 60, and did not scrap the last until 1956.

DEUEL, a Pullman club car of 1927, was one of 16 named for on-line counties and divided equally between Overland and Golden State service. Interior (below) provided space for lounge, buffet, barber, and bath as well as dining-car crew dormitory.

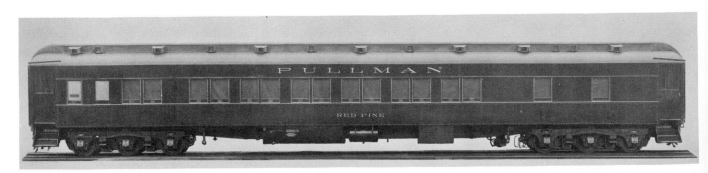

RED PINE contained Pullman's most traditional configuration: 12 sections, 1 drawing room. In 1930 many such Red-prefix cars were renamed after famous roses for service on Chicago & North Western-Union Pacific Chicago-Portland limited, the Portland Rose.

184

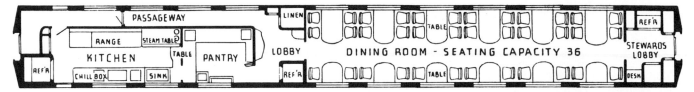

DINER 328 was built by Pullman for UP in 1929. It seated 36, possessed cuisine equal to that of the finest metropolitan hotels.

THE OVERLAND ROUTE

GLEN ALLEN typified the most luxurious sleeping-car equipment of the Overland Limited during Hoover's administration. The all-room car of 1928 — 6 compartments and 3 drawing rooms — forecast an impending era that would sidetrack the open section.

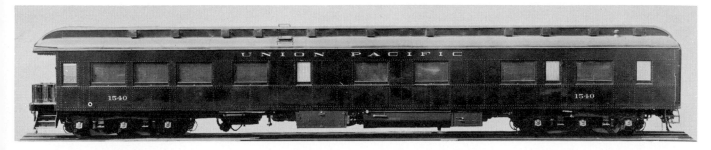

OBSERVATION-LOUNGE 1540, constructed by Pullman in 1925 for Overland Route service, afforded UP patrons a lounge, buffet, private smoking apartments, a women's lounge, a barbershop, and bath. Hardier travelers held down chairs on the open platform.

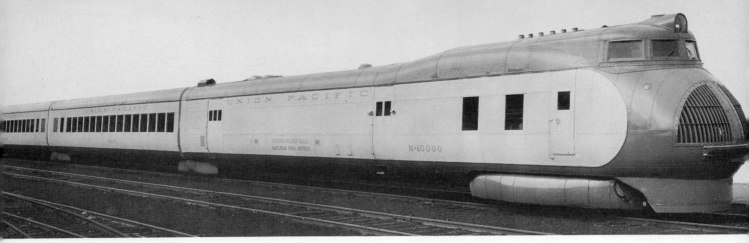

M-10000, later the *City of Salina*, was introduced in 1934 as "Tomorrow's Train Today." Pullman-Standard photo.

A radically different type of equipment

The executive officers of the Union Pacific several months ago reached the conclusion that to save and restore passenger business to the rails would necessitate the development of a radically different type of passenger equipment. — *W. A. Harriman, Chairman of the Board, Union Pacific Railroad, May 23, 1933.*

UNION PACIFIC'S first streamliner, *M-10000*, was completed at Pullman during February 1934. The revolutionary new train consisted of three "stream-lined" articulated cars, 204 feet long from rounded nose to finlike tail. It was built of aluminum alloy and painted Armour yellow (for visibility) and trimmed with brown and scarlet. GM's Winton Division developed the 600 h.p. V-type motor. Cost of the *M-10000* was $200,000.

During the spring of 1934, *M-10000* made a 12,625-mile coast-to-coast test and exhibition trip. It was displayed in 68 cities in which 1,195,609 persons inspected every feature. Number 1 visitor was President Franklin D. Roosevelt. In the course of this historic trip the train experienced every kind of climatic condition and operated over every type of roadbed — all without difficulty. During a special test run, the speed of 111 mph was attained (in the face of a 32 mph head wind).

On January 31, 1935, after a successful exhibition at Chicago's 1934 Century of Progress, where it was inspected by 2 million persons, *M-10000* went into revenue service between Salina, Kans., and Kansas City as the *City of Salina*, first of the famous *City* fleet. The Union Pacific annual report for 1935 happily stated that with a total of 116 seats available, the

new train averaged 280 passengers each day for the entire year.

With great expectations the Union Pacific ordered *M-10001*, a six-car train similar in design to *M-10000* but with the addition of streamlined Pullman sleeping cars — the first articulated Pullmans built. (Each berth was equipped with a unique collapsible lavatory.)

On an exhibition run from Los Angeles to New York, *M-10001* shattered every speed record for cross-continent train

Streamliner
CITY OF SAN FRANCISCO

travel. It departed from Los Angeles at 10 p.m. October 22, 1934; attained a maximum speed of 120 mph; traveled 508 continuous miles at an 84 mph average; arrived Chicago in 38 hours 52 minutes, New York City in 56 hours 55 minutes.

Following this heroic performance, the new train was christened the *Streamliner City of Portland* and placed in service on June 6, 1935, between Chicago and the Rose City. The distance of 2272 miles was scheduled in 39¾ hours. Averaging

THE OVERLAND ROUTE

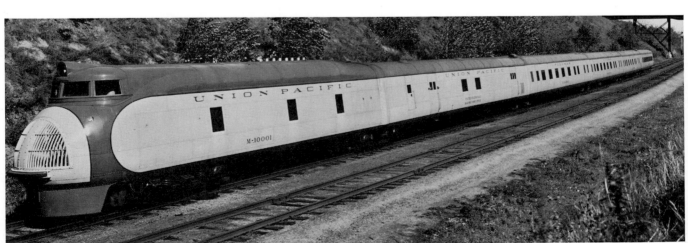

M-10001 rides double track during 1935 exhibition run with following consist: power unit M-10001; R.P.O.-baggage 12200; Pull-mans E. H. Harriman, Abraham Lincoln, and Oregon Trail (first regularly assigned articulated sleepers); chair car-buffet 10402.

THE High Sierra was a favorite locale for publicity poses; two-year-old 17-car City of San Francisco pauses there in 1939.

57 mph, the *City of Portland* slashed 18 hours from the fastest regularly scheduled run.

In 1935 when passenger service was being curtailed on many railroads, the Union Pacific introduced its unique *Challenger*—the only all-coach-and-tourist-sleeping-car train in America.* Equipped with steam power and air-conditioned conventional cars, the new train operated on a fast schedule as the second section of the crack *Los Angeles Limited*. The *Challenger* provided the utmost in luxurious travel comfort at lowest possible prices: three table d'hote meals per day for only 90 cents total, the first railroad stewardess-nurse service, free pillows for coach passengers, special coaches reserved for women and children, and attractive tourist sleeping cars. An immediate success, the service was soon expanded with the addition of a *San Francisco Challenger*.

Favorable response to the first streamliners prompted the order for two 11-car trains — the *City of Los Angeles* and the *City of San Francisco* — with details of construction similar to the earlier UP models. The 11-car trains were completed by Pullman and placed in service in May and June 1936.

Averell Harriman's prediction was borne out by the performance of the radically new trains. Passenger revenues on the UP for 1936 increased 34.5 per cent over the previous year — the largest advance of any major railroad. The Union Pacific annual report noted:

The popularity of these (streamlined) trains has been so great that it has frequently been impossible to accommo-

*Similar service was later offered by the Santa Fe and Rock Island-Southern Pacific.

date all who wished to ride them. An order was therefore placed late in the year (1936) for two new streamliners of 17 cars each with 40 per cent greater passenger-carrying capacity!

The year 1936 also marked the inauguration of the fifth and sixth streamliners, twin 12-car trains named the *City of Denver*, which were placed in service June 18 between Chicago and Denver, 1048 miles, on the fastest long-distance schedule in the country. Total elapsed time of 16 hours included eight stops, and the average speed was 65 mph.

The major improvement of the *City of Denver* and the 17-car West Coast equipment was the use of a wider cross-section, with straight instead of tapered car sides.

The interior designs of the club cars of both the Denver and Los Angeles streamliners were unique. The *City of Denver* featured the "Frontier Shack," replica of a frontier tavern. Corresponding car on the *City of Los Angeles* was the "Little Nugget," reproduction of a late Victorian salon. Both rooms were designed and furnished by Walt Kuhn, the noted artist.

To ease the strain for accommodations on the San Francisco streamliners, the Overland Route in conjunction with the Pullman Company assembled a train consisting of steam power and a single consist of eight unique Pullmans. The new train was appropriately titled the *Forty Niner*. Each car was named to honor California and the Gold Rush of '49. The *Forty Niner* went into service on July 8, 1937, almost 50 years after the first run of the *Golden Gate Special*, and continued to operate until 1941.

The 17-car trains were placed in service during the winter

RIVIEW (no population) is a passing track in Wyoming on the Green River. Streamliner immortalized it with this picture.

187

SECOND DAY out on its inaugural run, Forty Niner stands in Evanston, Wyo., July 9, 1937, behind tank of 4-8-2 7002, which Omaha shops placed beneath brown-and-yellow inverted bathtub shroud. She contrasted sharply with Model T beyond pilot beam.

of 1937-1938. The *City of Los Angeles* (owned jointly by the Chicago & North Western and the Union Pacific) commenced operation on December 22, 1937; and the *City of San Francisco* (owned by the C&NW-UP-Southern Pacific) "sailed" westward on January 2, 1938. Each train featured a registered nurse-stewardess and full-length observation-lounge car with barber-valet and bath.

Increased travel to the Golden Gate International Exposition on San Francisco's Treasure Island prompted another

LITTLE NUGGET, one of the most elegant railroad cars ever, served as club for 1937 City of Los Angeles, seated 35 in replica of bonanza hostelry. Decorative treatment embraced star-studded deep blue ceiling, red velvet draperies, marble-topped tables, blue-flowered wallpaper, lace curtains, photographs of some old-time footlight favorites, and gas chandeliers. There was even a mechanical "bird in a gilded cage" (located at the right of the bar) that warbled!

FRONTIER SHACK, class of 1936 tap car of City of Denver, seated 32 in replica of Western barroom. Walls and ceiling were fashioned of unfinished, unmatched white pine boards which held period photos, posters, lamps, guns.

188

HAWAII, an early model articulated sleeping car which contained 11 sections and featured upper-berth windows, was built in 1936 for 11-car City of San Francisco. The Hawaii remained in service until 1951.

Pullman-Standard.

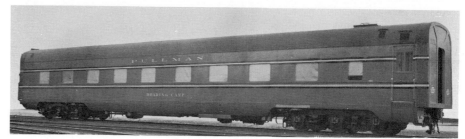

ROARING CAMP, originally the Pullman club car Eagle Rock, was rebuilt for the 1938 season as a 17-roomette sleeper, ran on the Forty Niner in gold-trimmed gray.

Pullman-Standard.

LOUNGE 7331 began life in pre-World War I days as a Pullman, was converted years later into full-length lounge, and sold to C&NW in 1937 for San Francisco Challenger.

Pullman-Standard.

GEORGE M. PULLMAN, shown as specially painted for Treasure Island Special service, was built in 1933 (page 409). The observation and room car was the first all-aluminum Pullman. Its original 4-wheel type A804 cast-aluminum trucks were replaced with the standard 6-wheel trucks illustrated.

Pullman-Standard.

UP.

DINING CAR of Forty Niner, owned by Pullman, possessed unique round tables, was formerly Pullman special dining-room car D-100. Kitchen was located in an adjacent car.

THE OVERLAND ROUTE

unique single-consist steam operation named the *Treasure Island Special*, which ran during the summers of 1939 and 1940 alternating on the timecard with the *Forty Niner*. Originally composed of conventional heavyweight de luxe equipment, the extra-fare all-Pullman *Treasure Island Special* was re-equipped in 1940 with streamlined *Imperial* and *Cascade* sleepers. On the rear was the first lightweight Pullman car, *George M. Pullman*.

Crowning achievement of the pre-World War II era was the delivery of stunning new equipment from Pullman-Standard in mid-1941. The new cars permitted establishment of streamliner service every third day for both Los Angeles and San Francisco (the latter supplanting the *Forty Niner*). Jointly equipped by the C&NW-UP-SP, the new trains offered the acme of travel comfort.

World War II ended the glory days on the Overland Route. One by one the luxury services were eliminated and the de luxe cars stored until the return of peace. World conflict brought to a close one of the most colorful chapters in the history of passenger transportation.

189

SOUTH PLATTE, an all-room car built in 1939 for the City of Denver, contained 4 roomettes, 3 compartments, 1 drawing room, and 4 bedrooms. It was the last of the low-silhouette cars (12 feet 8 inches to top of car, a foot under standard).

Unless otherwise credited, all photos Pullman-Standard.

HOLLYWOOD served as City of Los Angeles' full-length lounge; included 30-seat lounge, bar, barber and valet, showers. Interior (below) employed plastics and synthetics exclusively for decoration. Gray and white walls were Formica; scarlet upholstery was Nylon and Saran; porthole windows were glazed with glare-eliminating Polaroid. In 1941 such trade names were fresh, unfamiliar.

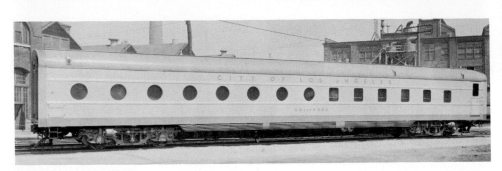

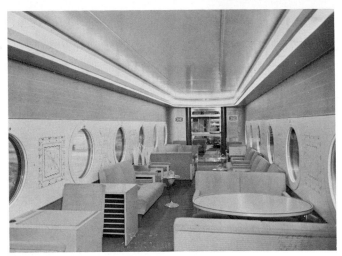

TWIN-UNIT diner-kitchen (below) stretched 144 feet; Fort Mason contained kitchen and 32-seat coffee shop while adjacent St. Francis Woods was main dining room with seats for 64. Woods (above) was furnished in tones of blue with rust-color chairs, had fluorescent lighting. Team ran on the City of San Francisco.

BILTMORE main diner of City of Los Angeles (twin of Ambassador) was named for plush L.A. hotel. The 56-seat car served a dinner described by road as a "Chef's masterpiece."

190

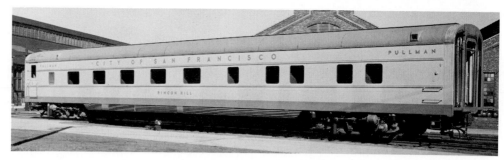

RINCON HILL was assigned to City of San Francisco, had 10 roomettes and 5 double bedrooms, provided patrons with every known convenience.

TWIN PEAKS—de luxe all-room car —was one of 19 duplicates assigned to both the City of Los Angeles and the City of San Francisco. It contained 4 double bedrooms, 4 compartments, 2 drawing rooms; was built June 1941.

EMBARCADERO, City of San Francisco's dormitory-club car, contained 28 lounge chairs, bar, natural wood walls, mural under bar.

THE OVERLAND ROUTE

C&NW.

BALDY MOUNTAIN observation-lounge had 4 double bedrooms, buffet. Twin Russian Hill (left), named for San Francisco peak, was renamed Hoover Dam in 1951 during McCarthy era.

191

MILWAUKEE ROAD E9's lead *City of Portland* through Idaho near Pocatello. UP photo.

Astra Domes and a new link

DURING World War II the enormous West Coast traffic on the Overland Route demanded peak performance. Long trains rolled eastward and westward day and night for the duration. Finally, with cease fire in the Pacific, railroad operation slowly returned to normal. Many luxuries withdrawn during the emergency were reinstated, and large orders were placed with locomotive and car builders for modern equipment.

In 1946 the age-old dream of traveling from coast-to-coast in a regularly scheduled railroad car came true. Through Pullman service was instituted over lines between New York-Los Angeles and New York-San Francisco (via New York Central and Pennsylvania); and Washington-San Francisco (via Baltimore & Ohio and Pennsylvania). West of Chicago the trans-

C&NW.

MORE than 9 million dollars' worth of streamliners were parked at C&NW's California Avenue yard in Chicago October 22, 1947: (left to right) City of Portland inbound on the main; C&NW and UP diesels; two C&NW passenger units; City of Denver; Twin Cities 400 on wash track; City of Los Angeles; and City of San Francisco. Not a single one of these named trains is serviced there now.

"ROOF GARDEN" dining is the phrase publicists justly use to describe Union Pacific's ACF-built dome diners. They're the only diners in the land which permit a passenger to dine on trout or steak yet keep an eye on signals and otherwise backseat-drive.

THE OVERLAND ROUTE

continental Pullmans were carried in traditional Overland trains, although for a brief period during 1946 the C&NW-UP operated a short-lived but appropriately named train, the *Transcon,* between Chicago and Los Angeles.

Another new train, the *City of St. Louis,* was initiated in June 1946. Routed via the Wabash between St. Louis-Kansas

STAR boards the City of Los Angeles: Rosalind Russell of stage and screen.

City, it transferred through cars at Cheyenne to other trains for Los Angeles, San Francisco, and Portland.

As additional new postwar cars arrived, the *City* trains were placed in daily service. By the end of 1947 the entire West Coast streamliner fleet was operating with daily departures.

October 29, 1955, was a historic date for the Overland Route. On that day the Union Pacific terminated its 66-year-old

formal agreement with C&NW for Chicago-Council Bluffs operation of through trains. The following day all of the *City* trains and the *Challenger* were routed over the CMStP&P, and once again the Milwaukee Road became the eastern link in the Overland Route.

Service during 1964 features the yellow and scarlet Domeliners operating between Los Angeles-San Francisco-Portland-St. Louis-Chicago via the Union Pacific-Southern Pacific-Milwaukee Road-Wabash.

There have been, of necessity, some regrettable changes in the transportation pattern. Gone from the Overland trains are the luxuries of the barber, shower bath, and stewardess. Gone, also, are the coast-to-coast Pullmans which ceased operating in 1958 with the last New York-Los Angeles car via the New York Central. Nonetheless, the Overland Route during 1964 offered real luxury transportation with some of the finest and most modern railroad equipment in existence.

Dome dining cars featuring "roof garden" eating in a picture-window setting were introduced to the West on the *City* trains. Beautiful dome lounge cars containing the comforts and luxuries of a fine private club are equipped with cocktail lounge, card room, and radio or recorded music.

Southern California is served by the *City of Los Angeles* and the *City of St. Louis* which provide two-nights-out service to the East. Both trains are equipped with luxurious Astra Dome lounge cars, dining cars, and coaches.

The *City of Portland* to the Pacific Northwest also features Astra Domes for the thrilling ride through the evergreen empire, covering nearly 200 miles along the Columbia River.

Serving San Francisco is the *City of San Francisco,* lone survivor on the original line of the Overland Route. Dome lounge cars and private-room sleeping cars operate between Chicago and the Golden Gate. At Ogden the connecting sleeper from St. Louis is attached to the train for the overnight run via the 103-mile Salt Lake Cutoff and the Sierra Nevada.

The *City of Denver* offers dome dining between Chicago and Denver. A dome lounge car, modern Pullmans, and dome coach provide relaxation and all-night comfort on the modern successor to the 12-car streamliners of 1936.

As Western travel becomes increasingly popular, more and more people choose the Domeliners for the new and luxurious accommodations which they offer.

Union Pacific Railroad President A. E. Stoddard, commenting on the future of passenger business, stated recently:

Currently this railroad is operating some of the most modern passenger equipment in the country and more new equipment is on order. As long as our friends support our efforts we will do our best to offer safe, dependable passenger service. ⚡

AMERICAN FORUM, a 6-section, 6-roomette, 4-double-bedroom car of 1942, was repainted for Overland in 1946; is now SP's 9152.

NO. 9041 of Southern Pacific was built in 1950 for City of San Francisco and contains 10 sections and 6 double bedrooms.

PACIFIC BEAUTY, a 6-bedroom, 10-roomette Budd Company product of 1950, is one of 49 sleepers of this configuration in UP's ownership, all of them bearing the prefix "Pacific." Pacific Beauty is all stainless steel in construction but is painted over.

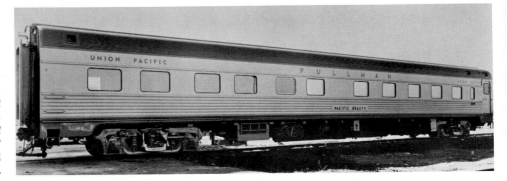

WESTERN VIEW, a 4-bedroom, 12-roomette car delivered to Wabash by ACF's St. Charles (Mo.) plant in January 1950, is usually operated between St. Louis and the West Coast.

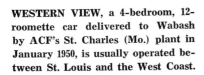

LOUP RIVER lost its name to a number in 1950. ACF built the club-lounge car for Union Pacific streamliner service in 1949.

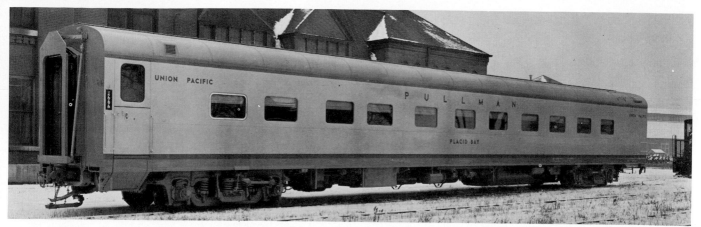

Pullman-Standard.

PLACID BAY, one of 10 Placid-prefix sleepers built for UP in 1956, has 11 double bedrooms. Door has lighted number panel.

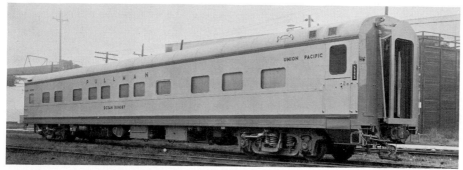

Pullman-Standard.

OCEAN SUNSET (above) and Ocean View furnish an interesting comparison between two cars by different builders with identical floor plans (5 double bedrooms, 2 compartments, 2 drawing rooms). Sunset is a Pullman product of 1956; ACF built the View in 1954.

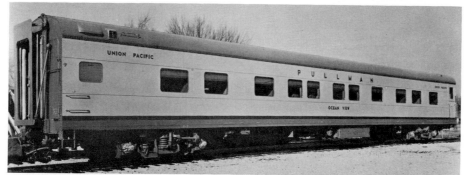

ACF.

Pullman-Standard.

DINER 10209 was constructed by Pullman-Standard for Southern Pacific in 1949 and assigned to Overland Route service. The car seats 48 beside Venetian-blinded windows, rides on roller bearings, and — in current SP tradition — bears no name on it.

THE OVERLAND ROUTE

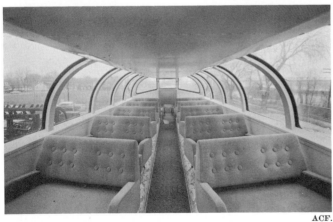

ACF.

DOME features angled love seats in 9000-series cars by ACF; downstairs (below), lounge chairs are arranged with back to aisle.

UP.

DOME-OBSERVATION 9002, one of 15 steel-aluminum lounges built by ACF, was delivered with neon train sign (below) but has since been rebuilt for midtrain operation next to diner.

ACF.

DOME DINERS are 85 feet long; stand 15 feet 10 inches over the dome; seat 18 on main floor, 18 under glass, 10 under dome in Gold Room; and feature pink tablecloths and flowers on tables.

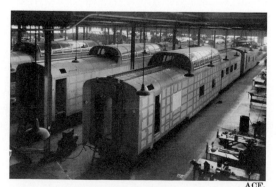

ACF.

DOMES under construction at St. Charles, Mo.

UP.

THE OVERLAND ROUTE

"On downy beds of ease"

Sunset Limited

A transcontinental train for travelers of discrimination. — The Sunset Limited, *Southern Pacific brochure.*

I   IN 1894 the Southern Pacific placed in service its first *Sunset Limited*, a brand-new thoroughly equipped edition de luxe of American travel. It was a solid Pullman limited, operating on a once-a-week schedule between New Orleans and San Francisco. Time in transit for the 2500-mile trip was 75 hours (58 hours to Los Angeles), "the shortest possible limit consistent with safety."

Transcontinental travelers were cautioned not to "take a line that will carry you into the heart of the Rockies, and leave you there a week or more, snowbound." Passengers "not anxious for Alpine experiences," seeking instead the "quickest, safest, and pleasantest route to the coast," were advised to take the *Sunset*, the fastest scheduled rail service from New York to San Francisco via New Orleans in connection with the Sunset Route.

For more leisurely travelers the Southern Pacific instituted a fleet of palatial steamers which offered a delightful five-day ocean voyage between New York and New Orleans advertised as "100 Golden Hours at Sea." By steamer and limited, it was possible to travel Southern Pacific from coast to coast. Between New Orleans

and San Francisco the train journeyed through country rich in historical association and picturesque landscape, from the bayou region of Louisiana and the vast high plains of Texas, past the painted mesas of New Mexico and Arizona, to the orange groves and missions of California.

In its inaugural season of 1894-1895 the *Sunset* was a once-a-week train, but the following season, 1895-1896, it operated twice weekly leaving New Orleans Monday and Thursday and departing from San Francisco on Tuesday and Saturday. During the winter season of 1897-1898 (October to April) the *Sunset* operated twice weekly between San Francisco and Chicago.

"The magnetic power that drew the Columbian Exposition to Chicago is well able to disturb pathways of pleasure or of commerce. Notably this has been so in the advent of Southern Pacific Company's famous *Sunset Limited*." The unusual routing from San Francisco was via SP to El Paso; Texas & Pacific to Texarkana; St. Louis, Iron Mountain & Southern to St. Louis; Chicago & Alton to Chicago. An annex train was operated from El Paso to New Orleans.

In the early 1900's the *Sunset* operated on weekly, biweekly, and triweekly schedules, but between 1904 and 1911 not at all. Finally, on November 16, 1913, it became a daily train. The daily schedule has been continued to the present.

There have been varied *Sunset Limiteds*. Over the years the train has grown from five wooden cars (drawn by a "great engine, patterned after the Columbian Exposition flyer and guaranteed to do 100 miles an hour"). Today the *Sunset Limited* is a fine stainless-steel and orange streamliner built in 1950 by the Budd Company. However splendid the modern train, it could hardly be more romantic than the 1896 edition which is described in an

198

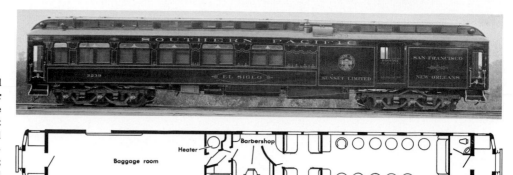

EL SIGLO was one of three identical cars built by Pullman in 1888 for Pennsylvania Limited service [see page 78]. It was completely rebuilt with wide vestibules in 1895 and sold to Southern Pacific. The combine embraced a barbershop, bath, and buffet; was trimmed in polished oak; sported upholstery of fawn-colored plush.

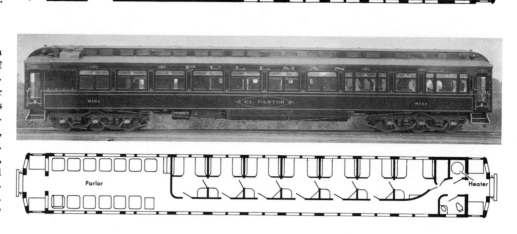

EL PASTOR, built by Pullman in 1895 for $15,975.84, was "The pride of the Limited" and was dubbed a combined parlor and drawing-room car for ladies. Its seven drawing rooms were finished in mahogany, vermilion, and walnut and contained olive, blue, and maroon plush upholstery. "In the apartment at the forward end, the ladies, for the first time, find themselves supplied with all the comforts and conveniences that the gentlemen enjoy in their smoking room."

EL ORO contained 10 sections and 2 drawing rooms, cost $16,123.39 when new in 1895. Two such cars were carried in each train. The open sections were finished in vermilion with fawn-colored plush; drawing rooms were white mahogany with red upholstery.

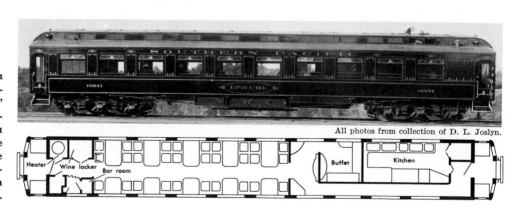

All photos from collection of D. L. Joslyn.

EPICURE, the diner, was last car in the train. Its quartered oak woodwork was stained to a "fine color." Artistic alcoves along the sides contained potted plants. And the menu delighted in "viands peculiar to the lands and climate traversed by the Sunset Limited." Breakfast specialties: oysters, shrimp, biscuits, corn cakes prepared by a Southern cook.

early SP brochure from which the following is quoted: ". . . The Whistle blows and we are off, soon crossing the Brazos on a fine steel bridge and passing through mammoth sugar plantations, prairies, and stock ranges. A smoke in the smoking room, a game of whist, and to bed. Stranger, didst ever, after a day of weary toil, repose thy weary limbs more blissfully than on this luxurious couch? Didst ever compose thyself to slumber on downy beds of ease more wholly restful? There is a certain sense of complete happiness experienced in this triumph over circumstance that is experienced nowhere but in a Pullman Palace Sleeper of the *Sunset Limited*."

ALL-PULLMAN *Shasta* was Shasta Route's flagship until advent of *Cascade* in 1927. SP photo.

De luxe on the
Shasta Route

1 OVER each of its traditional four great scenic routes — Sunset, Golden State, Overland, and Shasta — the Southern Pacific Company operates a premier train. Standard bearer on the Shasta Route between San Francisco and Portland is the *Cascade*, SP Nos. 11 and 12. The present streamlined *Cascade* continues the daily de luxe service inaugurated in 1899 when the original Nos. 11 and 12 were instituted as the *Shasta Express*.

The modern *Cascade* is a sophisticated train which provides "a world of quiet luxury on wheels." Its consist in-

"THE Scenic Line of the Pacific Coast"— 1893 claim.

THROUGH CAR SERVICE

Trains 12 and 11. SHASTA LIMITED DE LUXE.
Electric Lighted—Daily Extra Fare Train.

Through Standard Pullman Sleepers: One car drawing-room, two compartments, and sections San Francisco, Portland, Tacoma and Seattle.
One car, sections only San Francisco and Portland.

Drawing Room Compartment Sleeper: Los Angeles and Seattle via Coast Line to San Jose and Oakland Pier for Portland, Tacoma, Seattle.

Observation Car: Library, parlor, clubroom, writing-desk, newspapers free. magazine and periodicals, observation rotunda, shower bath, barber shop.
San Francisco, Portland, Tacoma, Seattle.

Dining Car:
Oakland, Cal., and Portland, Tacoma, Seattle.

Complement: Stenographer, barber, ladies' maid, hairdresser, manicure. Valet who will press ladies' and gentlemen's garments.

Telephone Connections in Observation Cars for thirty minutes before departure; at Oakland Pier, Cal., "Lakeside 1420"; Portland, Ore., "Broadway 802"; Seattle, Wash., "Main 6933".

Transportation Honored: First-class full fare tickets only when presented with Pullman Sleeper ticket and extra fare ticket.

Extra Fare: An extra fare charge of $5.00 is made between San Francisco and Portland, and intermediate stations. No extra fare tickets required between Portland and Seattle.

Coach:
Portland and Seattle.

Equipment list from 1915 Southern Pacific timetable.

718 miles of bay, valley, canyon, forest, mountain

cludes an articulated triple-unit dining-lounge set known as the *Cascade Club*. This vehicle ranks among the longest and most elegant rolling stock ever built.

Daily the luxurious streamliner *Cascade* offers swift overnight service on one of the world's most magnificent scenic routes — 718 miles of bay, valley, canyon, forest, mountain, lake, and river.

SHASTA pauses at Shasta Springs at turn of the century to allow sampling of the crystal water at ornate spring house. SP photo.

Shasta *and* Cascade

Road of a thousand wonders

THE first Southern Pacific trains between San Francisco and Portland operated on the original Siskiyou line of the Shasta Route which was completed in 1887 through the Siskiyou Mountains of southern Oregon. Daily the trains chuffed over what was later known as the Road of a Thousand Wonders via the Sacramento Valley, Shasta Springs, the canyons of the Siskiyou Range, and the fertile valleys of the Rogue and Willamette rivers. In October 1899 the *Shasta Express*, Nos. 11 and 12, was inaugurated. It was named for the majestic mountain of the Shasta Route.

Frequent and interesting changes in the operation of the *Shasta* occurred during the era which preceded World War I. In June 1909 Nos. 11 and 12 were renamed *Shasta Limited*. On January 1, 1910, the new Oregon & Washington Railway, the Harriman Line between Portland and Seattle, was opened for traffic. Operation of the *Shasta Limited* was then extended to Seattle with all cars going through.

New equipment arrived for the renowned *Shasta Limited De Luxe* on January 3, 1913. This electric-lighted extra-fare ($5) train continued to operate solid through from San Francisco to Seattle in 36 hours 40 minutes.

During the Panama-Pacific International Exposition at San

SP.

TEN-WHEELERS doublehead across a steel bridge in the Siskiyous at Milepost 413 with a considerable train behind them.

Francisco in 1915 the *Shasta Limited De Luxe* traveled with capacity loadings on a new 33-hour schedule. The Southern Pacific (the Exposition Line) added a through Seattle-Los Angeles Pullman which operated to Los Angeles via the Coast Line to Oakland and San Jose pier (southbound in the *Lark*, northbound in the *Seashore Express*).

From July 1, 1918, until November 14, 1920, during the period of Federal control, the *Shasta Limited* was discontinued. Like many another institution catering to luxurious service, the train was temporarily withdrawn during World War I.

Pullman-Standard.

DINING CAR 10057 (twin of No. 10056) was built by Pullman in 1904 for Oregon & California service, possessed vestibules at both ends and highly polished handrails.

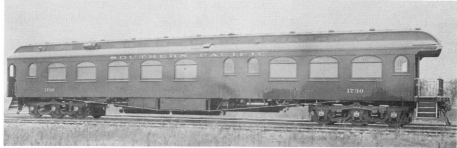

Pullman-Standard.

OBSERVATION CAR 1730, built by Pullman in 1907, contained "Library, Parlor, Club-room, Shower Bath, Barber Shop, Observation Rotunda," was similar to UP car (page 177).

Pullman-Standard.

SHASTA, a 10-section, 2-drawing-room sleeper, was one of eight identical cars built in 1899 for the SP Association. Inside (below) vermilion and mahogany held full sway.

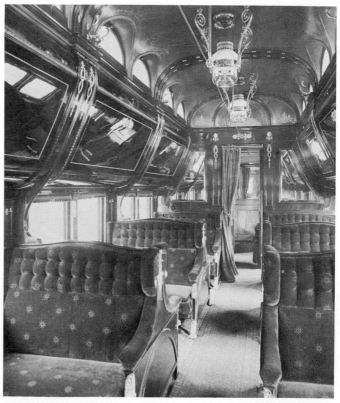

UP.

HARRIMAN-ERA photo of Shasta's brass railing and drumhead.

Pullman-Standard.

WHITE deck and black stacks: the *Santa Clara* plies San Francisco Bay. SP photo.

Cascade—Southern Pacific extra-fare flyer

ON April 17, 1927, the 4:40 p.m. Southern Pacific ferry glided away from the pier at the foot of San Francisco's Market Street. Aboard were passengers bound for the venerable Oakland Mole. In that cavernous terminal across San Francisco Bay a brand-new all-Pullman flyer, the de luxe *Cascade* (Nos. 17 and 18), stood waiting to load for its inaugural departure at 5:05 p.m. for Portland and Seattle.

Occasion for the new extra-fare train was the completion of Southern Pacific's Cascade Short Line of the Shasta Route. The scenic new road offered a thrilling journey through towering pine forests and along lakes between Black Butte, Calif., and Eugene, Ore., via Klamath Falls and the Cascade Range.

The *Cascade* (extra fare $3) was equipped with the finest appointments: barber, valet, ladies' maid, shower baths for men and women, observation car, club car, dining car, and intercar telephone service. The new schedule of 23 hours 20 minutes (San Francisco-Portland) shaved 3½ hours and was the fastest time ever announced for the run.

Economic depression soon brought hard times to the *Cascade* and in 1933 the extra fare was abolished. The following year coaches were added to the once-proud flyer, then Nos. 19 and 20.

Four years later, Southern Pacific's familiar blue timetable effective June 13, 1937, announced with poetic license:

> Another New S.P. train!
> *Cascade* becomes all Pullman
> train on Faster Schedule.

Newly re-equipped with the latest sleeping accommodations, the *Cascade* (now numbered 23 and 24) was again established as all Pullman on a 19-hour 40-minute schedule (San Francisco-Portland). This general arrangement prevailed for nearly a decade which included the Golden Gate International Exposition and World War II.

During the wartime emergency the *Cascade* was consolidated with the *Beaver*, an economy-class train. The *Cascade* operated with head-end and first-class-Pullman cars. The *Beaver* ran as second section with tourist Pullmans and coaches.

204

Shasta *and* Cascade

RIDERS rim the railings of the 3-compartment, 2-drawing-room observation Jacques Cartier below Mt. Shasta on the 1927 Cascade.

EASTBOUND passengers riding across the Bay on an SP ferry saw Oakland Pier like this. Stained-glass emblem was over the exitway.

WESTBOUND *Cascade*, train No. 11, is hurried into Oakland by Lima GS-4 4-8-4 4431. SP photo.

SP.

IT'S sunlight and snow for those braving the outdoors of the westbound Cascade's observation (radio, valet) during the 1930's.

"FASTEST train in history to California": No. 19 hits 65 mph behind GS-1 4-8-4 4404 in a splendid 1934 panorama of the Cascade in Oregon.

206

Author's collection.

"LEAVE after business hours," stated ad for 1937 speedup.

Shasta *and* Cascade

INSIDE the Oakland Mole at 8:30 p.m. January 27, 1952, as No. 74, the Oakland Lark, accepts passengers for Los Angeles. Observation car, SP No. 9500, gained fame when, as the American Milemaster, it was exhibited by Pullman at 1939 New York Fair.

J. Foster Adams, collection of Everett L. DeGolyer Jr.

Fred H. Matthews Jr.

Shasta *and* Cascade

FIRST No. 11 westbound for Oakland comes off the Martinez Bridge behind 6000 h.p. worth of Alco-GE units. Bridge replaced train ferry operations.

STREAMLINED Cascade, First No. 12, stands at 16th Street station, Oakland, before inaugural run August 13, 1950. Pilot plows are needed in the mountains ahead.

IN SP parlance, trains to San Francisco are westbound, away eastbound. Hence Cascade No. 11, running south, is "westbound."

An all-streamlined Cascade

ON August 13, 1950, an all-new diesel-powered *New Cascade* commenced operation on a swift 16½-hour overnight schedule for the 718 miles between San Francisco and Portland. The sleek all-private-room *Streamliner Cascade*, renumbered 11 and 12 and attired in the smart two-tone gray livery of the prewar *Lark*, offered at no extra fare a choice of roomettes, bedrooms, compartments, and drawing rooms — all with private enclosed washrooms, foam-rubber seating, premade beds, non-glare fluorescent lighting, and circulating ice water. Public telephone service added in 1956 was a short-lived innovation.

The greatest attraction of the *New Cascade* was the wonderful expanse of pleasure-on-wheels known as the *Cascade Club* — a triple-unit articulated lounge-diner-kitchen measuring 203 feet 10 inches over couplers. The dining and lounge rooms were two full cars, 130 feet in length. Cleverly concealed articulation between the cars made it appear to be one large area. Interior design was inspired by the Northwest — blue carpet, silver-blue and cedar drapes, blue or cedar upholstery.

During the 1960's, Nos. 11 and 12 continue as one of the premier trains of the Southern Pacific. After the advent of triweekly service by the *Shasta Daylight*, the *Cascade* remained as the sole year-around luxury train to operate daily over the Shasta Route. **I**

Pullman-Standard.

BLUNT-END "10-and-6" SP sleeper No. 9054.

209

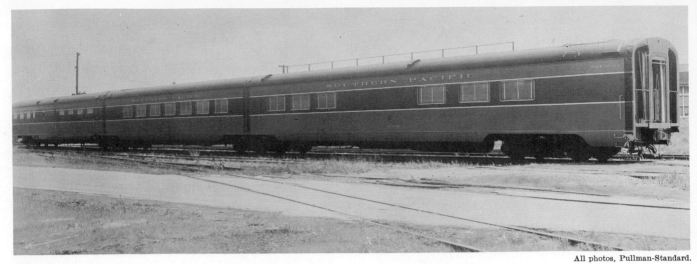

All photos, Pullman-Standard.

CASCADE CLUB — 203 feet 10 inches of dining-lounge space. Left to right: dormitory-kitchen No. 10283; dining section 10284; and lounge 10285. Pullman-Standard constructed the triple-unit and articulated masterpiece of carbuilding for SP in 1949.

Kitchen occupies this next car.

The Diner, a full car length.

"Hidden" articulation of two cars here.

Lounge and Bar, a full car length.

"Cascade Club" DINER & LOUNGE

SP.

INSIDE Cascade Club full-width car connections lend the impression of one continuous room rather than a triple-unit car.

 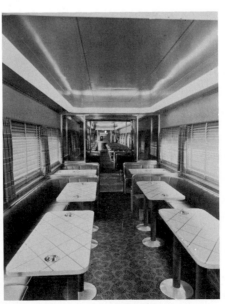 

DINING CAR has light tan ceiling, blue walls; dark blue carpet; blue or cedar chairs; and drapes done in silver blue with cedar.

VIEW from lounge into dining room over point of articulation illustrates unique continuous room effect of the interior design.

LOUNGE is finished in tones of blue and cedar; bar section is done in gold, silver and blue with gold-tone mirrorwork accents.

SP 9300, a 22-roomette sleeper. Each 1950 edition of the Cascade contained two streamlined Pullmans of this all-room configuration.

SP 9401, bearing Cascade emblem on flanks, contains 12 double bedrooms. Each Cascade contained one car of this type in consist.

Shasta and Cascade

SP 9119 — the de luxe sleeper of the Cascade — contained 4 double bedrooms, 4 compartments, 2 drawing rooms. Each train had one.

NP 364 with 10 roomettes, 6 double bedrooms — one of two Cascade cars furnished by NP for Seattle-San Francisco service.

SP 9054 contains 10 roomettes, 6 double bedrooms, was constructed with blunt end (see page 209) for operation at the end of train.

1937 DES MOINES ROCKET: diesel 603; baggage-dinette *Norman Judd*; chair cars *Henry Farnam, Grenville Dodge*; parlor-observation **L. M. Allen.** Photo: RI, Richie.

. . . and the strange tale of

BUDD-BUILT *Centennial.*

"A promise of luxurious travel"

ﾉ ON October 10, 1852, the *Rocket*, a gaily painted 4-4-0 built by Rogers, pulled six new yellow coaches from Chicago to nearby Joliet. That was the first train of the Chicago & Rock Island Railroad. From that humble beginning the present Chicago, Rock Island & Pacific Railroad has grown to a progressive system which operates nearly 8000 miles of road in 14 states of the midcontinent.

In the fall of 1936 while American business was stunned by the impact of the depression, the Rock Island Lines ordered six new diesel-powered streamlined *Rockets* for service on five Midwestern routes. Guiding force behind this impressive order was Rock Island's John Dow Farrington whose doctrine of "planned progress" transformed the railroad from bankruptcy to a sound, rehabilitated property.

The new semi-articulated *Rocket* streamliners were Budd-built of stainless steel and powered by red and silver customized 1200 h.p. units from Electro-Motive. They arrived from the builders in fall of 1937 and were placed in revenue service. During their first year of operation they carried a half million passengers with an enviable record of on-time performance.

Most extraordinary of all the *Rockets* was the fabled *Golden Rocket.* Planned for postwar service on the Rock Island-Southern Pacific Golden State Route, the luxury streamliner was beautifully designed and highly publicized. But the *Golden Rocket* never ran one mile. The story of this train is one of the curious tales of American railroading.

The GOLDEN ROCKET

Route of THE ROCKETS

TRANSCONTINENTAL flagship: Rock Island's *Golden State Limited* of 1929 behind burnished Alco Mountain-type 4011. RI photo.

THE *Golden State* pauses in the sage country of New Mexico in January 1925. RI photo.

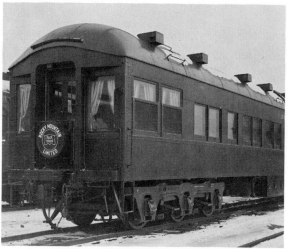

BRAND-NEW in 1929 for Rocky Mountain Limited: sun parlor-observation Cheyenne Mountain (sister cars: Estes Park, Grand Lake, San Isabel) with lounge, ladies' parlor, barbershop, soda fountain. Army bought car in 1943.

An early de luxe limited

If, as is said, "the apparel doth oft proclaim the man," so the equipment of a modern railway may be said to voice its desire to please the traveler, and by well-adapted catering to the wants of the public in the essentials of luxurious accommodations and fast train service, to prove its title to the high benefits of popularity. The *Rocky Mountain Limited*, just added to the regular Colorado service of the Chicago, Rock Island & Pacific Railway, embodies to the fullest extent these essential features. — *Rocky Mountain Limited* brochure, 1898.

THE first *Rocky Mountain Limited*, Nos. 41 and 42, was inaugurated in 1898 by the Great Rock Island Route. An early de luxe limited, it quickly became one of the most popular trains operated in the West. Scheduled time from Chicago to both Denver and Colorado Springs (via Limon) was 28 hours 30 minutes, through Des Moines and Omaha.

Equipment built by the Pullman Company included buffet library cars, standard Palace sleeping cars, chair cars, and new 64-foot dining cars which featured Rock Island's famed 75-cent meals.

At the turn of the century the *Rocky Mountain* was displaced as the premier train on the Colorado run by train No. 5, curiously titled the *Big Five*. It was described in a Rock Island brochure of the period as being built "expressly for the Colorado service . . . charming in superb appointments and richly elegant furnishings, the evidence and a promise of luxurious travel."

With the summer schedule of May 1902, the *Rocky Mountain* (Nos. 41 and 42) was reinstated as the Rock Island standard bearer to Colorado. Later, in May 1907, during another reshuffling of the timetable, the *Rocky Mountain* received its present numbers (7 and 8) during the hectic period when the Reid-Moore Syndicate secured control of the Rock Island Lines. The bizarre financial manipulations of this syndicate resulted in bankruptcy and tribulation for the once-great railroad. Only after years of careful and patient rebuilding was the company again financially sound.

Prosperity returned to the Rock Island with the boom of the 1920's, and the road embarked on a program of upgrading its main passenger trains. In the general rebuilding during 1929, the *Golden State Limited* (63 hours Chicago-Los Angeles), the *Iowa-Nebraska Limited,* and the *Rocky Mountain Limited* were thoroughly re-equipped. Brand new rolling stock from Pullman consisted of sun-parlor lounge cars, diners, and Pullman sleepers, some of which contained the first upper-berth windows. Mountain-type engines built by American Locomotive Company between 1920 and 1923 furnished the power. Once again Rock Island Lines passenger service ranked among the great in the land.

215

ROCK-ISLAND ROUTE buffet-library car 1095 was built by Pullman in 1898, dismantled in 1920. Pullman-Standard photo.

IN 1929 Pullman built 20 Rock-series and 15 Island-series sleepers for new Rock Island limiteds. Inside, cars seemed orthodox enough, but exterior (below) of 10-section, 1-drawing-room, 1-compartment Island Rose reveals experimental upper-berth windows.

QUEEN of the silent screen, Pola Negri, is given an escorted tour of RI parlor car.

216

Route of **THE ROCKETS**

GOLDEN GATE, a 3-compartment, 2-drawing-room observation-lounge, re-created old Spain in carved walnut, green and gold walls.

"MEALS — the Best on Wheels" were served in a Spanish decor aboard dining car 8030, constructed by Pullman Company in 1929.

PARLOR of Cheyenne Mountain sported electric clock over door, parchment-shaded lamps, and—of course—traditional electric fan.

Pullman-Standard.

IN 1939 *Rocky Mountain Rocket* posed for publicity near Joliet, Ill.

GARDEN OF THE GODS, an 8-section, 2-double-bedroom, 2-compartment Pullman-Standard car, featured semi-private sections (above) with upper-berth windows, air-conditioning vents.

CENTENNIAL—"Diner That's Finer" — seated 32 at tables, another 14 in leather-upholstered cocktail divans.

Budd.

218

Route of THE ROCKETS

Stainless-steel works of art

The Rock Island Lines proudly presents its new Rocky Mountain Rockets. They are the most sensational examples of the modern train builders' art. No expense has been overlooked to make these trains outstanding in every respect. — Rock Island brochure, 1939.

OPERATING over the direct route to the Colorado Springs-Pikes Peak region, the new addition to the *Rocket* fleet was placed in service on November 12, 1939, on a 19½-hour schedule (between Chicago and Denver). Unlike the six earlier *Rockets* in service throughout the midcontinent, the new *Rocky Mountain* offered sleeping accommodations.

Each new *Rocky Mountain Rocket* was composed of seven cars in addition to the 2000 h.p. diesel-electric locomotive. The trains were completely streamlined, with stainless-steel cars and the distinctive red and maroon color scheme on the power unit. An unusual consist contained cars built by Budd and Pullman-Standard.

The decorative treatment of the interiors carried unity of color throughout all cars. Walls were tinted in tan, pearl, and gray. Carpets were co-ordinated in tones of brown, tan, and beige. Exotic wood veneers enriched the observation car.

Sleeping cars offered roomettes, double bedrooms, compartments, and open sections with windows in upper berths — a Rock Island innovation developed for the 1929 trains.

"A Diner That's Finer" contained tables for dining as well as a "modernistically appointed cocktail lounge . . . containing curving divans and small intimate tables."

Reclining-seat chair cars, appointed with sponge rubber seats and extra-wide windows, offered luxury coach service. Combined coach-mail cars serving Colorado Springs were later rebuilt to club diners offering meal service west of Limon, Colo., the junction point where the train was divided for Denver and Colorado Springs.

The new train continued the traditions established by the venerable *Rocky Mountain Limited* — courteous attendants, competent chefs and waiters, and the "best meals on wheels." Stewardess-nurses catered particularly to elderly people and children.

A favorite of experienced travelers between Chicago and the Rocky Mountains, the *Rocky Mountain Rocket* offered a pleasant afternoon and overnight journey across a vast country rich in historic lore, a country agriculturally and industrially abundant.

ACTUALLY, Rocky Mountain Rocket never rolled as close to its namesake peaks as it appears in this superimposed publicity shot.

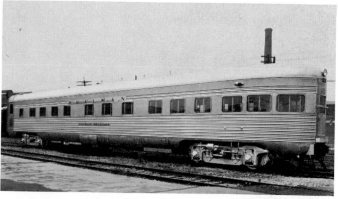

Pullman-Standard.

THUNDER MOUNTAIN, twin of Phantom Valley, was built by Pullman-Standard as 5-double-bedroom observation-lounge; its observation room, finished in wood veneer, contained 25 chairs, radio speaker, chimes for meal announcements. In 1956 car was remodeled into full lounge with butt end for midtrain operation.

All photos Rock Island unless otherwise credited.

ON THE WAY! Another magnificent Rock Island streamlined train-the "Golden Rocket" — still faster, more beautiful and more comfortable — will offer 39¾-hour service between Chicago and Los Angeles. Be on the lookout!

Strange tale of a train

IN February 1946 Rock Island and Southern Pacific officials concluded arrangements for an exciting custom-built luxury train to be called the *Golden Rocket*. The new multi-million-dollar streamliner was planned for operation on a triweekly 39¾-hour schedule over the traditional Golden State Route to Los Angeles via Kansas City, Tucumcari, and El Paso. A tentative timecard called for evening departures from Chicago and Los Angeles Sunday-Tuesday-Friday and morning arrivals Tuesday-Thursday-Sunday.

Two 11-car trains were ordered from Pullman-Standard for delivery early in 1947. One was to be purchased by the Rock Island, the other by the Southern Pacific. The two consists employed the latest postwar techniques in car architecture and engineering. Pullman-Standard Engineer of Color and Design Ralph Haman designed furnishings on a Mexican theme with wood and metal artwork to be executed by famed Mexican craftsman Jesus Torres. Exterior was to be SP red with RI stainless steel. Names appropriate to the Mexican theme were chosen for the cars:

Car	RI set	SP set
Baggage-dorm	No. 820	--
Chair car	Valle Verde	Valle Rio Grande
Chair car	Valle Vista	Valle del Sol
Chair car	Valle Mar	Valle Imperial
Coffee shop-lounge	El Cafe	El Cafe Frontero
Dining car	El Comedor	La Fonda
4-4-2 sleeper	La Quinta	Monte Chiricahua
22 rmt. sleeper	La Costa	Monte Santa Rita
12 DBR sleeper	La Jolla	Monte San Jacinto
12 DBR sleeper	La Palma	Monte Santa Catalina
Observation-sleeper	La Mirada	La Galeria

Pullman-Standard.

LA MIRADA observation displays train sign in June 1948 at Pullman shops for a famous streamliner that never ran a mile.

Pullman-Standard.

INSIDE La Mirada's observation lounge bright red upholstery complemented gray carpeting and walls and a yellow ceiling. Potted Sansevieria plants completed Southern California color scheme.

Blueprints and artists' drawings were approved, and in 1947 Pullman-Standard began work on the Rock Island equipment under Lot 6761. So unique were the plans for the new cars that many of their features were incorporated into the Pullman blueprints for the 1948 *Twentieth Century Limited.*

While construction of the cars proceeded at Chicago's Pullman Car Works, other arrangements were being formulated by the publicity offices of Carl Byoir & Associates. Plans for a spectacular introduction of the *Golden Rocket* in Chicago included inaugural dinners and a public dedication to be attended by nationally renowned personages.

Southern Pacific public relations personnel in Los Angeles were equally busy. The Hollywood *Reporter* of April 18, 1947, carried a story describing hush-hush plans for a mid-July Hollywood launching of the *Golden Rocket* on its maiden eastbound run from the corner of Hollywood and Vine streets via the Pacific Electric Hollywood Boulevard tracks to Sawtelle. The story predicted that the new train would be filled with movie stars for the occasion. This announcement created an enormous stir in Hollywood where representatives from the newsreels, press, and radio clamored for space on the first run.

Pacific Electric and Southern Pacific engineers actually surveyed the possibility of the Hollywood stunt and were preparing to adjust the track curvature at several points on the trolley line to permit the *Golden Rocket*'s diesels to negotiate the line.

Suddenly the Southern Pacific brass reconsidered the entire *Golden Rocket* proposition. The irrevocable decision at 65 Market Street in San Francisco was to cancel the SP equipment order. In November 1947 a terse announcement in a Rock Island brochure stated that "operation of the *Golden Rocket* is being postponed because of delays in production of some of the equipment necessary for its inauguration." That was the last public notice of the *Golden Rocket.*

During late 1947 and spring of 1948 the Rock Island consist was completed at Pullman. Each car's nameboard was inscribed *Golden Rocket* as originally designed and the rolling palaces were delivered for service. However, there was no *Golden Rocket* to receive them. They were assigned instead to the *Golden State,* successor as the premier train of the RI-SP route, and the splendid *Golden Rocket* became only a rare memory. 1

Rock Island.

EL CAFE, the coffee shop-lounge, was showpiece of stillborn Golden Rocket, featured red and yellow canopy, red leather upholstery, hand-carved wood trim. It was on display at 1949 Railroad Fair.

Route of THE ROCKETS

Rock Island.

EL COMEDOR dining car seated 36 in sheer luxury: hammered copper masks, grilles, and window trim by Jesus Torres; dark turquoise carpet, medium turquoise walls, light turquoise ceiling; gold upholstered chairs.

Pullman-Standard.

CORRIDOR of 12-bedroom sleeper, with tan walls and ceiling, rust-colored carpeting and window shades.

221

Arriving soon...Rock Island's new super-luxury Rocket

The GOLDEN ROCKET

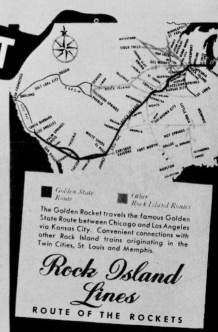

In only 39¾ hours this magnificent, million dollar train will whisk you between Chicago and Los Angeles!

'Most any day now, America's most beautiful new Diesel-electric train, the Golden Rocket, will begin 39¾-hour, super-de luxe service between Chicago and Los Angeles over the scenic Rock Island-Southern Pacific Golden State Route.

Riding the Golden Rocket will be a thrilling adventure; its decorations capture the picturesque beauty of the Southwest—the grandeur of its mountains, deserts and canyons—the inspiring colors of its flowers, minerals and native costumes.

The Golden Rocket strikes a high note in comfort and convenience. *Coach Passengers* enjoy deep-cushioned, form-fitting reclining seats with individual, full-length leg-rests. *The Fiesta Car*—gay meet-

Rock Island

ing place for all passengers—has a refreshment bar, a coffee shop lounge, and a dining section serving delicious meals at modest prices. *The Diner* offers full-meal service comparable to that of the finest restaurants. *Sleeping cars* are all-room cars with roomettes, bedrooms, compartments and drawing rooms. *The Observation* has a fine lounge with buffet and beverage service, barber shop and valet.

For the utmost in travel luxury at modest extra fare, ride the Golden Rocket. Ask your local Rock Island Passenger Agent for full facts—or write: A. D. Martin, Passenger Traffic Manager, Rock Island Lines, 723 La Salle Street Station, Chicago 5, Illinois.

■ *Golden State Route* ■ *Other Rock Island Routes*

The Golden Rocket travels the famous Golden State Route between Chicago and Los Angeles via Kansas City. Convenient connections with other Rock Island trains originating in the Twin Cities, St. Louis and Memphis.

Rock Island Lines
ROUTE OF THE ROCKETS

FULL-PAGE, full-color advertisement for the streamliner that never appeared was scheduled for the August 1947 issue of Holiday.

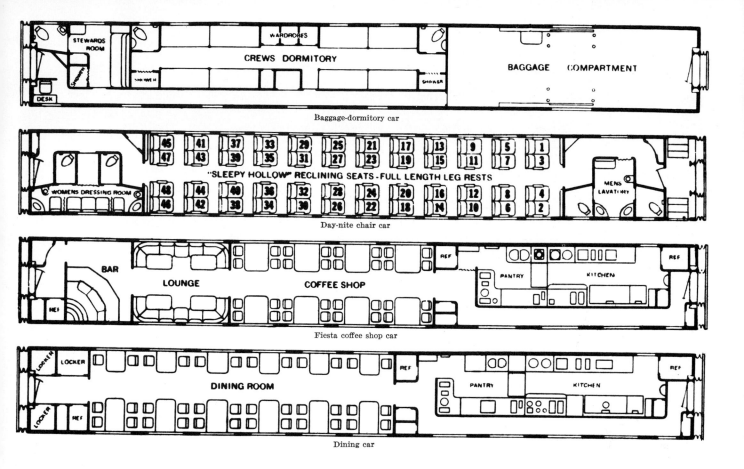

Baggage-dormitory car

STEWARDS ROOM
WARDROBES
CREWS DORMITORY
BAGGAGE COMPARTMENT
SHOWER
SHOWER
DESK

Day-nite chair car

WOMENS DRESSING ROOM
"SLEEPY HOLLOW" RECLINING SEATS - FULL LENGTH LEG RESTS
MENS LAVATORY

45 41 37 33 29 25 21 17 13 9 5 1
47 43 39 35 31 27 23 19 15 11 7 3
48 44 40 36 32 28 24 20 16 12 8 4
46 42 38 34 30 26 22 18 14 10 6 2

Fiesta coffee shop car

BAR
LOUNGE
COFFEE SHOP
REF
PANTRY
KITCHEN
REF
REF

Dining car

LOCKER LOCKER
DINING ROOM
REF
PANTRY
KITCHEN
REF
LOCKER
REF

Route of THE ROCKETS

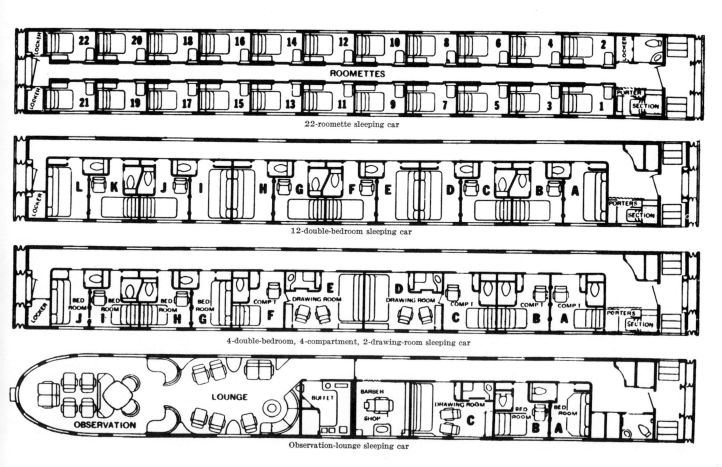

22-roomette sleeping car

LOCKER
LOCKER
22 20 18 16 14 12 10 8 6 4 2
ROOMETTES
21 19 17 15 13 11 9 7 5 3 1
PORTER
SECTION

12-double-bedroom sleeping car

LOCKER
L K J I H G F E D C B A
PORTERS SECTION

4-double-bedroom, 4-compartment, 2-drawing-room sleeping car

LOCKER
BED ROOM J I H G F
COMP'T
DRAWING ROOM E
DRAWING ROOM D
COMP'T C B A COMP'T COMP'T
PORTERS SECTION

Observation-lounge sleeping car

OBSERVATION
LOUNGE
BUFFET
BARBER SHOP
DRAWING ROOM C
BED ROOM B
BED ROOM A

223

BAGGAGE-DORMITORY car No. 820, completed in 1947, contained baggage compartment and a crew dormitory with bunks and showers.

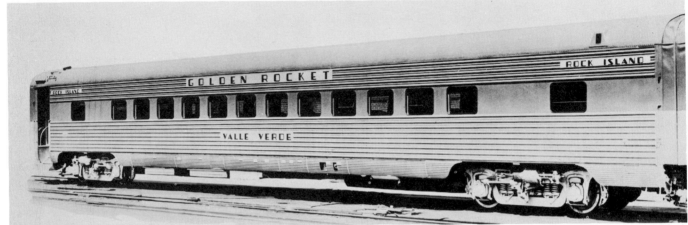

Rock Island.

VALLE VERDE (green valley) contained 48 Sleepy Hollow reclining seats and flesh-tinted mirrors in oak frames by Jesus Torres.

WHETHER one desired a ham sandwich and coffee in El Cafe (left) or a full-course dinner in El Comedor (right), the surroundings were elegant. Credit Jesus Torres for the Adobe Bar, grillwork, and hammered copperwork.

Route of **THE ROCKETS**

Rock Island.

LA COSTA (the coast) was a red and silver 22-roomette sleeper. Similar cars were later constructed for the New York Central.

224

LA PALMA (the palm) and twin car La Jolla (the jewel) contained 12 double bedrooms and served as prototype for the Port-series Pullmans of postwar 20th Century Limited.

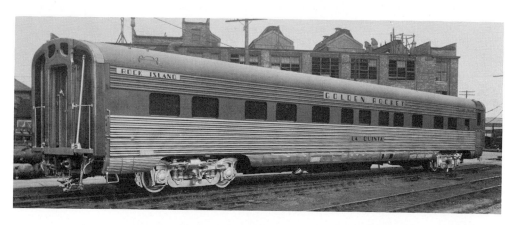

LA QUINTA (the country home) was the de luxe sleeper of the would-be Golden Rocket. Car had 4 double bedrooms, 4 compartments, 2 drawing rooms, and red and silver finish.

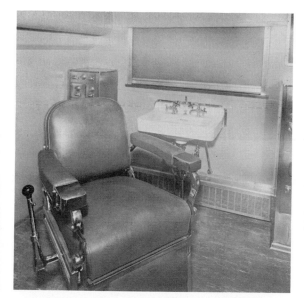

LA MIRADA (the view), twin of La Galeria (the veranda), possessed high windows for viewing, a card table for relaxation, barbershop for grooming.

the Santa Fe

"All the comforts, plus the luxuries"

1 THE Santa Fe system is known as the railroad that built an empire—an empire that includes the southwestern United States from the Mississippi and Missouri rivers to the Pacific Coast, from the Rockies to the Gulf.

On October 30, 1868, Col. Cyrus K. Holliday turned the first spade for the road at Topeka, Kans. From that beginning, the Atchison, Topeka & Santa Fe has grown into the largest railway system in the West. It was built by tough men through rugged country. Westward the iron was laid to Dodge City, La Junta, over the Raton Pass, on to Albuquerque, across Arizona, and in 1887, into Los Angeles.

Where slow-moving oxen once pulled the covered wagons of westbound pioneers, the great Santa Fe streamliners of today roll smoothly along at 80 or 90 mph. From a comfortable seat in a dome car of the *Super Chief* or the *El Capitan*, one can see rich farmlands where once endless herds of buffaloes and Indians in war paint terrified the weary traveler.

Santa Fe.

TIMETABLE of 1881 was triumphant.

Santa Fe.

FROM left to right in a prewar photo at Chicago: El Capitan, Super Chief, Chief, and El Capitan in a mix of Budd and Pullman.

de-Luxe

FAMOUS Super Chief of 1937 pauses in Illinois for a company publicity photo.

THE *California Limited* in Los Angeles behind Southern California Railway 4-6-0 No. 53, built by Baldwin in 1887. Santa Fe photo.

The king of the limiteds

"TWENTY years ago (1892) the Santa Fe put on the first limited train ever run from Southern California. That train is in service yet, every day in the year. It is called the *California Limited*. It is exclusively for first-class travel and is the king of the limiteds." So proclaimed a 1912 Santa Fe brochure.

The Santa Fe inaugurated its first *California Limited* on November 27, 1892, as a sleeping-car and coach train from Chicago to Los Angeles and San Diego (with a St. Louis Pullman via the Frisco Lines). A Fred Harvey dining car was carried from Fort Madison, Ia., to Kansas City, but meals for the remainder of the trip were served at the renowned Harvey House dining rooms en route. This train ran until May 3, 1896, when it was discontinued.

For the winter season of 1896-1897 the Santa Fe introduced the new *California Limited* — a biweekly luxury train which left Chicago every Wednesday and Saturday at 6 p.m. and arrived in Los Angeles at 6 p.m. the third day. The run of 2265 miles, scheduled in 72 hours, was advertised as being "faster than the celebrated *Orient Express*, Paris to Constantinople, or *P&O Express*, Calais to Brindisi." Eastbound, the train left Los Angeles at 8 p.m. Mondays and Thursdays, and arrived Chicago at 9:43 a.m. the fourth day.

This new de luxe *California Limited* carried three Pullman palace sleeping cars (10 sections, double drawing room), a through dining car, and buffet-smoking car, "vestibuled throughout and brilliantly lighted by Pintsch gas." Two of

Collection of Everett L. DeGolyer Jr.

WHEN Mallets were on the point: California Limited pauses in open country so that 4-4-6-2 No. 1398, outshopped by Baldwin in 1909, can take on a tank of water. When built, such engines were heralded as the largest passenger locomotives in the world.

de -Luxe

the three sleepers ran between Chicago and Los Angeles. The third operated from St. Louis to Los Angeles (via the Wabash Railroad and Kansas City). The dining car was "always attached," immediately ahead of the sleeping cars, but the buffet-smoking car was operated only between Kansas City and Los Angeles.

A flower boy met the train near the California state border and presented each lady passenger with a "boutonniere of choice roses, lilies, carnations, violets, or other characteristic flowers." Souvenir alligator wallets were presented to men passengers.

The Santa Fe proudly described its customers: "On a long journey it is pleasant to know that no over-crowding is permitted, and one's traveling companions are of a desirable class. Persons you like to meet — successful men of affairs,

authors, musicians, journalists, 'globe trotters,' pretty and and witty women and happy children — these constitute the patrons of the CALIFORNIA LIMITED."

The train was de luxe in every detail of equipment. Reportedly, it combined the "three requisites of safety, speed, and comfort" and was "confidently recommended to the patronage of a discriminating public as affording the best accommodations en route to or from Southern California."

THE first *California Limited* to enter Los Angeles knocks off the miles behind Ten-Wheeler 54. Santa Fe photo.

NAMED as well as numbered was the 1307, Pullman-built buffet-smoking car — with vestibule at one end — that bore name San Rafael.

Santa Fe.

LONG-LEGGED balanced compound, four-cylinder 79-inch-drivered Atlantic No. 1443 drove on first driving axle; was built by Baldwin in 1907; was finally scrapped at Topeka January 19, 1927.

GILSEY, Pullman-built diner of 1887, was under the management of Fred Harvey — which "should render further comment superfluous," according to a suitably impressed company publicist.

de·luxe

Fred Harvey
set a standard of
excellence

"When that name appears the traveling public expect much. It may be out in Arizona, but if it is a Fred Harvey meal you get every good thing that you can find at the best places in New York or Chicago"

wrote "Fra Elbertus" in the Philistine

Fred Harvey — Santa Fe — Meal Service

The meal service on the Santa Fe is managed by Fred Harvey.
It is the best in the world.

It comprises dining-cars, dining-rooms, lunch-rooms and sumptuous hotels like the Cardenas (Trini-dad), Castañeda (Las Vegas), Alvarado (Albu-querque), Escalante (Ash Fork) and El Tovar (Grand Canyon).

On request will mail you a leaflet containing the full text of Elbert Hubbard's remarks about Fred Harvey.
Also pamphlets describing Alvarado and El Tovar hotels.

Passenger Dept., A. T. & S. F. Ry. System, 1117 Railway Exchange, Chicago.

SANTA FE was anything but reluctant to praise Harvey.

OLD MISSION IN CALIFORNIA --------

ASSORTED FRUIT, 20
STEWED PRUNES, 20   ORANGE MARMALADE, 20
PRESERVED FIGS, 25

SHREDDED WHEAT BISCUIT WITH CREAM, 25
ROLLED OATS WITH CREAM, 25

OYSTERS
FRIED, 40   BROILED, 40   MILK STEW, 35   CREAM STEW, 50

BROILED LAKE TROUT, 45

TENDERLOIN OR SIRLOIN STEAK, 80
WITH MUSHROOMS OR FRENCH PEAS, 95   WITH BACON, 90
WITH BORDELAISE OR BEARNAISE SAUCE, 1.00

EXTRA SIRLOIN STEAK (FOR TWO), 1.50
WITH BACON, 1.75   WITH MUSHROOMS OR FRENCH PEAS, 1.75
WITH BORDELAISE OR BEARNAISE SAUCE, 1.75

MUTTON CHOPS, 60; WITH BACON OR TOMATO SAUCE, 70

BROILED OR FRIED BACON, 40   BROILED OR FRIED HAM, 40
BACON AND EGGS, 50   HAM AND EGGS, 50
VEAL CUTLET, PLAIN OR BREADED, 45
CALF'S LIVER AND BACON, 45
LITTLE PIG SAUSAGE WITH FRIED APPLE, 45

BOILED, FRIED, SCRAMBLED, OR SHIRRED EGGS, 25
POACHED EGGS ON TOAST, 40
PLAIN OMELETTE, 30; WITH HAM, CHEESE, OR JELLY, 40
SPANISH OR MUSHROOM OMELETTE, 40

POTATOES, BAKED, 10, FRENCH FRIED, 15
HASHED BROWNED, OR LYONNAISE, 15   AU GRATIN, 25

HOT ROLLS, 10   CORN MUFFINS, 10
WHEAT CAKES WITH MAPLE SYRUP, 20
DRY TOAST, 10   BUTTERED TOAST, 10
MILK TOAST, 20   CREAM TOAST 30

COFFEE, PER POT, FOR ONE, 15; PER POT, FOR TWO, 25
COCOA OR CHOCOLATE WITH WHIPPED CREAM, PER CUP, 15

TEA—CEYLON, YOUNG HYSON, ENGLISH BREAKFAST, OR SPECIAL
BLEND, PER POT, FOR ONE, 15; PER POT, FOR TWO, 25
MILK, PER GLASS, 10   CREAM, PER GLASS, 20

MALTED MILK, PER CUP, 15

GUESTS WILL PLEASE CALL FOR CHECK BEFORE PAYING AND COMPARE AMOUNTS CHARGED

A CHARGE OF 25 CENTS IS MADE FOR EACH EXTRA PERSON
SERVED FROM A SINGLE MEAT OR FISH ORDER

SANTA FE DINING CAR SERVICE
BY FRED HARVEY

SIRLOIN steak for two cost a mere $1.50 long ago.

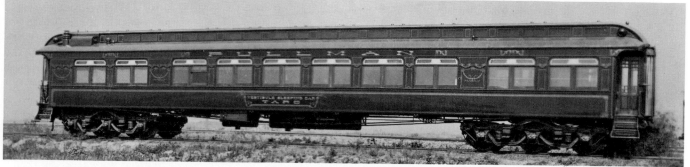

Car photos, Pullman-Standard.

TARO — a narrow vestibuled 12-section, 1-drawing-room sleeper with elaborate striping — was built by Pullman in September 1890.

IOWA, one of a dozen cars named for on-line states, contained 10 compartments. Cars were built by Pullman in 1902 for assigned service on Santa Fe, Monon, and Chicago Great Western. Horizontal stripe along bottom of carbody finished in scroll flourishes.

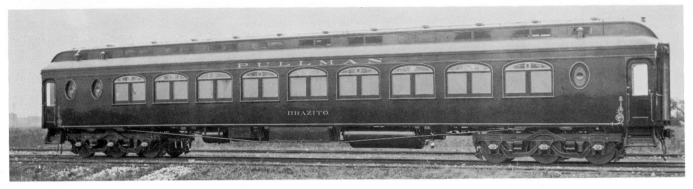

BRAZITO, a de luxe car with 7 compartments and 2 drawing rooms, was one of 20 such sleepers constructed in 1902. Half the cars were assigned to Atchison, Topeka & Santa Fe limiteds; the balance of the equipment went to Rock Island's Golden State.

BEN AVON was representative of one of the earliest groups of Pullmans to be named in a series (mates included Ben Lomond, Ben Vorlich, Ben Wyvis, etc.). Built in November 1899, the 12-wheel observation contained 10 sections as well as a lounge at rear.

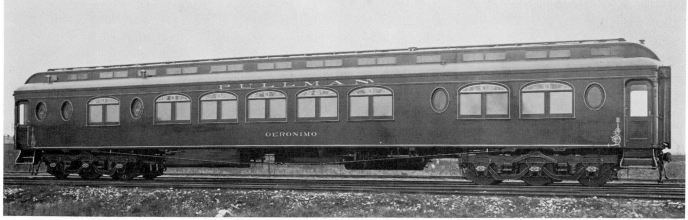

GERONIMO, built by Pullman in 1902, had 10 sections and 2 drawing rooms; was known as a "double drawing room" car. Ten such cars were constructed and, again, order was divided equally between Santa Fe and rivals Rock Island-SP for Golden State.

de -Luxe

de-Luxe

SANTA FE 4-4-2 529 speeds down a knife-edged right of way with the *De-Luxe* in 1911. Collection of Everett L. DeGolyer Jr.

The Santa Fe de-Luxe

Many travelers are satisfied with getting to their destination comfortably. They only want good cars, good food, and pleasant surroundings. But others are more particular. They like all the comforts plus the luxuries. They are in somewhat of a hurry. They like, too, to be a bit exclusive. Thus, the "Extra Fast — Extra Fine — Extra Fare" train has been evolved.

A de-luxe train should denote quality. Not how fast, but how fine, is the new interpretation, first put in effect by the Santa Fe. Hence, last season (1911) the Santa Fe put on the first extra-fare train ever run from Chicago to California — the *Santa Fe de-Luxe. — The Santa Fe de-Luxe*, brochure, 1912.

THE superb *De-Luxe*, one of America's truly great railway trains, commenced operation in December 1911 on a once-a-week schedule continuing until the spring and the end of the winter season. Westbound departure from Chicago was 8 p.m. every Tuesday, arrival in Los Angeles 9 a.m. every Friday.

Author's collection.

THIS was the scene at Dearborn Station, Chicago, minutes before the Santa Fe de-Luxe departed for Los Angeles.

Eastbound the train left Los Angeles 6:10 p.m. Tuesdays and arrived in Chicago 11:10 a.m. Fridays. Scheduled time was 63 hours en route. Extra fare was $25.

The all-steel cars were newly built by Pullman from special designs for artistic interiors of the most expensive mahogany and rosewood. The dining car included "an air-cooling and air-washing device" and the "indirect system of lighting whereby the entire room is flooded as if with sunlight." All this in 1911.

World War I marked the end of an era of leisure and elegance. Grand hotels and trains de luxe disappeared when the lights went out all over Europe. The *Santa Fe de-Luxe* was no more.

Collection of Everett L. DeGolyer Jr.

ABOUT 1916 the De-Luxe fogs it up while hitting at least 60 per.

234

Santa Fe de-Luxe

_to Chicago Kansas City and a quick way to New York

_tuesdays

Limited to sixty people extra fare twenty-five dollars

NOSE-IN-AIR butler on Santa Fe poster captured the tone of a train that ran once a week for 60 people at extra fare.

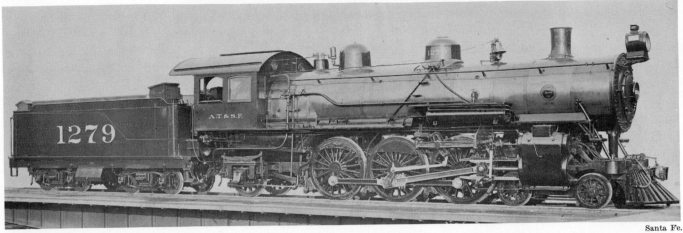

Santa Fe.

ONCE the superheater killed compounding, Santa Fe power became more orthodox — along the lines of Baldwin-built Pacific type 1279.

SAN GABRIEL carried a barber, ladies' maid, manicurist, and stenographer. In it one could bathe, read books or market reports, or (below) post letters in the locked mailbox at the end.

de -Luxe

DINING CAR 1434, built in 1911, presented fresh flowers to all lady passengers; featured (above) elegant "indirect lighting" bounced off a highly polished ceiling.

PIUTE contained 7 drawing rooms and was closely patterned after the famous "brass-bed" cars of the New Haven, illustrated on page 399 of this volume. There were two all-drawing-room cars of this description assigned to each weekly extra-fare De-Luxe.

TEHACHAPI had a configuration of 7 compartments and 2 drawing rooms, but in spite of such de luxe space, eschewed fancy striping.

EL NARVAEZ, a 10-section observation, possessed end posts on its platform. Such cars were dubbed "four posters" by railroaders.

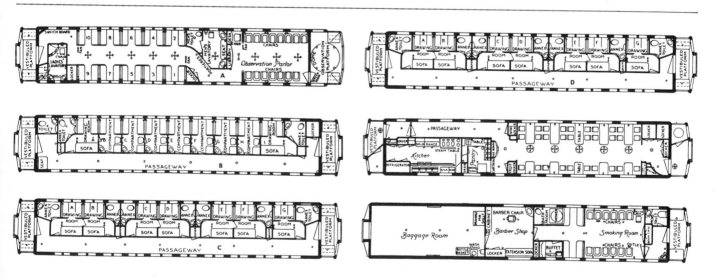

FLOOR PLANS of the entire De-Luxe, reading from the back to the front of the train: "A" — all-steel observation with 10 sections in forward half plus observation room and platform "for all passengers"; "B" — all-steel compartment car, with 7 compartments and 2 drawing rooms but "no sections"; "C" — all-steel, all-drawing-room car with 7 drawing rooms but — to quote the brochure again — "no sections"; "D" — sister all-steel, all-drawing-room car; dining car — "built expressly for this service" with indirect lighting, electric fans, "recently invented air-cooling device," steel underframe; and club car — with baggage compartment in forward end, "buffet, barbershop, bath, and smoking and reading room for gentlemen," steel underframe. Railway Age Gazette was enthusiastic over extra fare of the De-Luxe, editorialized that it was time U. S. roads charged more for extra speed and comfort.

SEVEN sections of the *California Limited* await departure from Los Angeles in the early 1920's. Santa Fe photo.

The Santa Fe Chief

As a befitting conveyance to and from the new America and the old, the Santa Fe Railway has installed the *Chief*, the most commodious and luxurious train on rails. . . . Those who remember the *Santa Fe de-Luxe* of prewar days will appreciate the *Chief*. Far more commodious and luxurious than the *de-Luxe*, the *Chief* leaves daily instead of weekly and costs less than half of the old extra fare. — *The Chief — Extra Fast, Extra Fine, Extra Fare*, brochure, 1926.

WITH the country's return to normalcy after World War I, the Santa Fe passenger department determined the need for additional train service to Southern California to supplement the hard-pressed *California Limited*. On November 14, 1926, the *Chief* made its maiden run. Placed in service on a 63-hour schedule with a $10 extra fare, the *Chief* was "frankly designed for people who want the best."

The new train quickly became the favorite of Hollywood screen actors and visiting celebrities. Travelers of the late 1920's and early 1930's achieved status by announcing that they had "*Chiefed*" to or from "L.A."

The new train was made up of seven cars: four sleepers

Santa Fe.

BALDWIN Pacific 3448 and a California Limited with an early model air-conditioned dining car splicing its 10-car consist at Morris, Kans.

238

(including a through San Diego car); Harvey-operated club car; dining car; and the traditional brass-railed observation lounge car with two drawing rooms, three compartments, and ladies' lounge with shower. Fred Harvey's epicurean delights, refreshing showers in the heat of the Southwest, fresh-cut flowers, an expert barber who also attended "to such important trifles as the correct creasing of trousers"—all were available on the Santa Fe way to California in the Roaring '20's.

On July 7, 1929, an interesting but short-lived service was inaugurated when Col. Charles A. Lindbergh pushed a button in California and coast-to-coast rail-air service became a reality. Travel time between New York and Los Angeles was slashed from 100 to 80 hours by utilizing the Pennsylvania and Santa Fe railroads at night and flying Ford Tri-Motor aircraft by day.

The new service, under the direction of Colonel Lindbergh, was named Transcontinental Air Transport and was jointly sponsored by the Santa Fe, Pennsylvania, and Curtiss Aero-

plane Company. Routing was New York to Columbus overnight via Pennsylvania Railroad; Transcontinental Air Transport to St. Louis, Kansas City, and Waynoka, Okla.; Santa Fe overnight on the *Grand Canyon* to Clovis, N. Mex.; and Transcontinental Air Transport to Los Angeles. The first flight, with Colonel Lindbergh at the controls and passenger Amelia Earhart, landed triumphantly on the coast and a new era was born.

A. W. Johnson.

"FOUR POSTER" observation car carries markers of California Limited as it cants to a curve at Forest View, Ill., July 13, 1924.

239

SANTA FE acquired its first 4-8-2 in 1918, owned 51 3700-class engines by 1924. Baldwin constructed 69-inch-drivered 3740 in 1923.

SAN VINCENTE (No. 1348), a buffet-library car built in March 1923, was subsequently remodeled (below) with a white enameled club room which contained bar, locked mailbox, and easy chairs.

de -Luxe

DINING CAR 1464 was built in 1925, subsequently was air-conditioned (above) for re-equipped Chief. Waiters-at-attention shot was made in 1934. Car had AT&SF-type channel underframe.

240

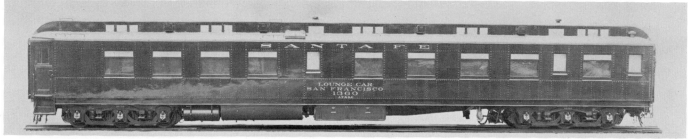

SAN FRANCISCO (No. 1360) was built for service on the California Limited in 1925 but later saw service on the Chief, too.

WILLOW RANGE contained 7 drawing rooms. All of the Willow-series sleepers were specially built for service on de luxe limit- eds of Santa Fe and New York Central. In 1929 one could sleep in such a car at night, fly during day in joint air-rail service.

GENERAL CROOK, a 10-section lounge car constructed in 1930, was assigned to midtrain service on Santa Fe's finest — the Chief.

SILVER SPRINGS observation contained 3 compartments and 2 drawing rooms as well as a ladies' lounge with maid and bath. It was one of nine identical cars built for Santa Fe service in 1924 — the year Lenin died and two women became U. S. governors.

CRYSTAL BAY — a 3-compartment, 2-drawing-room observation — was one of the new Crystal-series cars which replaced Silver- series equipment on the Chief in 1929. Similar cars were as- signed to UP's Overland Limited just before "Black Friday."

241

THE 1937 *Super Chief* with baggage car 3400, sleepers *Isleta, Taos*; lounge *Acoma*; diner *Cochiti*; and sleepers *Oraibi, Laguna, Navajo*. Santa Fe photo.

America's first

IN a special issue dated May 22, 1937, *Railway Age* described the re-equipping of the *Super Chief* by the Budd Company and Electro-Motive. Working closely with the manufacturers was a team composed of architects Paul Cret and John Harbeson of Philadelphia; designer S. B. McDonald of Chicago;

and Santa Fe advertising manager Roger Birdseye, a specialist in Southwest Indian lore. America's first all-Pullman diesel-powered streamliner, the 1937 *Super Chief*, was the result of this collaboration.

Santa Fe had always been plagued with the problem of supplying water to its mammoth steam locomotives in the arid deserts of New Mexico and Arizona. During the depression days of the 1930's officers at the company headquarters in

HEAVYWEIGHT Super Chief of 1936 drones through the Western desert behind Mutt and Jeff, the celebrated 3600 h.p. diesel team numbered 1 and 1A delivered by Electro-Motive and St. Louis Car the preceding year. They cut 15¼ hours off the Chief's time.

Both photos, Otto C. Perry.

TRAIN 17, the Super Chief, nears La Junta, Colo., with Prairie type 1105 on the point ahead of Electro-Motive diesels 1 and 1A.

ON its maiden trip west, the streamlined Super Chief tackles Raton Pass with 2-10-2 925 giving an assist to box-cab diesels.

Chicago's Railway Exchange Building took a long hard look at the diesel locomotive, and made the decision that was to spell finis to steam operations on the line.

Upgrading of the *Chief* into a *Super Chief* was to be a two-step operation. While the brand-new streamliner was being designed and built, a diesel-powered train composed of refurbished heavyweight *Chief* cars was placed in service on May 12, 1936. This interim operation, which cut 15¼ hours from the running time of the *Chief*, was made possible by extensive improvements to right of way and motive power. The now-famous blunt-nosed diesel locomotives, Mutt and Jeff, Nos. 1 and 1A, were delivered by St. Louis Car and Electro-Motive

in 1935. They spent the following months trial running over the entire route.

One month before the heavyweight train was placed in service, work was commenced in Philadelphia on the light-weight streamliner which was to be the permanent *Super Chief*. Nine stainless-steel cars, superbly trimmed, were completed by the Budd Company in early 1937. They were powered by a new, improved 3600 h.p. two-unit streamlined locomotive built by Electro-Motive at La Grange.

The Budd cars rank among the most luxurious rolling stock built in modern times. Stan Repp, well-known railroad artist and biographer of the *Super Chief*, has described them as a masterwork. Not since the turn of the century was such lavish use made of exotic wood for interior design.

On May 18, 1937, at 7:15 p.m., after ceremony and excitement rivaled only by that lavished on the *Scott Special* of 1905, the new *Super Chief* began a twice-weekly operation from Chicago.

With the Budd train regularly carrying capacity loads, the Santa Fe ordered a second train. The new equipment furnished mainly by Pullman-Standard and placed in service on February 22, 1938, was less flamboyant than that built by Budd. Nonetheless, it permitted the Santa Fe to advertise the only pair of all-first-class diesel-powered streamliners in America.

de·Luxe

Both photos, Santa Fe.

ITS streamlined 1800 h.p. diesel units wearing the dust of the long desert miles, the Super Chief bores through mountain terrain while it is holding to its prewar twice-weekly schedule.

PURPLE drumhead sign on the Budd-built Navajo brings up the rear of the 1937 edition of the Super Chief. Train registered such instant popularity that a second train was installed in 1938.

DESIGNED and powered by Electro-Motive, built by St. Louis Car Company: Santa Fe 1800 h.p. units 1 and 1A . . . "Mutt and Jeff."

FORWARD — 8 sections, 2 double bedrooms, 2 compartments — was pioneer nonarticulated lightweight Pullman of 1936 (see page 410).

DINING CAR Cochiti was presided over by the genial Peter Tausch, Fred Harvey steward of long standing. Car was finished in warm tones of burnt orange, brick red, and brown; served mountain trout, raisin pie, English Cheshire cheese, other specialties.

THE Super CHIEF

Santa Fe

- DINNER -

ROMANOFF FRESH MALOSSOL CAVIAR 1.75

ANTIPASTO 75   HEARTS OF CALIFORNIA ARTICHOKES 35
Hearts of Celery 30   Salted Almonds 30   Colossal Ripe Olives 25
NEPTUNE COCKTAIL 50   AVOCADO 40
GRAPEFRUIT, ORANGE AND RAISINS 40

CHICKEN OKRA, LOUISIANNAISE IN CUP 20; TUREEN 30
Consomme, Hot or Jellied 25   Clam Broth 20

SWORDFISH STEAK SAUTE, MEUNIERE WITH CAPERS 75
POACHED TRANCHE OF SALMON, AU VIN BLANC 70

FRESH MUSHROOMS SAUTE, AU FINES HERBES, AND BACON 75
OLD FASHIONED BONELESS CHICKEN PIE, AMERICAINE 85
POACHED EGGS ON FRIED FRESH TOMATO, SAUCE HOLLANDAISE 65
SPAGHETTI WITH JULIENNE OF VIRGINIA HAM, MADAME GALLI 65
ROAST LARDED TENDERLOIN OF BEEF, SAUCE MADERE 95
Small Sirloin Steak a la Minute 1.25
Sirloin Steak for one 1.60   Sirloin Steak for two 2.75
Calf's Liver and Bacon 70   Lamb Chop, Extra Thick (1) 80
(to order—20 minutes)
Bacon 65; Half Portion 40   Ham 70; Half Portion 40
Bacon and Eggs 70   Ham and Eggs 70

FRESH ASPARAGUS, DRAWN BUTTER 30
NEW CORN ON COB 25   NEW LIMA BEANS 20
NEW POTATOES, PERSILLADE 15   MASHED 15   COTTAGE FRIED 25

COLD
ASSORTED MEATS, POTATO SALAD 90   BRISKET OF CORNED BEEF 70
TOMATO STUFFED WITH LOBSTER SALAD 60
CHEF'S SPECIAL COMBINATION SALAD, PLATE 30
ROMAINE, COTTAGE CHEESE AND RAISIN SALAD, PLATE 30
Lettuce Salad 35   Potato 25   Chicken (White Meat) 80
Rye Bread and Dinner Rolls with Butter, per person 10   Dry or Buttered Toast 15
Melba Toast 15   Milk Toast 30 Boston Brown, Raisin or Whole Wheat 10; Toasted 15

OLD FASHIONED FRESH STRAWBERRY SHORTCAKE WITH WHIPPED CREAM 30
CANTALOUPE 20   RAISIN PIE 20   APRICOT PARFAIT 35
VANILLA ICE CREAM 25; WITH ASSORTED CAKE 35
ENGLISH CHESHIRE CHEESE WITH PRESERVED GUAVA 50
Roquefort 35   Petit Gruyere 35
Coffee, per Pot 25   Demi Tasse 15   Kaffee Hag Coffee, per Pot 25
Cocoa or Chocolate, Whipped Cream, per Pot 20   Tea, per Pot 20

PRICES SHOWN ON THIS MENU ARE SUBJECT TO VARIOUS STATE SALES TAXES
Guests will please call for checks before paying and compare amounts charged
An extra charge of twenty-five cents each will be made for all meals served outside of Dining Car

SANTA FE DINING CAR SERVICE
Fred Harvey
Santa Fe.

MENU of Super's inaugural run on May 12, 1936.

de-Luxe

ACOMA lounge also had dormitory and barbershop.

Santa Fe.

DRAWING ROOM finished in golden ribbon-striped satinwood from Ceylon. Both public and private rooms of the streamlined Super Chief were paneled with such romantic veneers as African rosewood, English sycamore, American holly, Macassar ebony, bird's-eye cypress, and Burma teak — all in all, an ad man's dream.

Santa Fe.

Santa Fe.

NAVAJO observation was rich in Indian artifacts: hand-hammered silver fittings; colorful blanket upholstery; and beauteous Indian sand paintings.

Author's collection.

Pullman-Standard.

ORAIBI — a 2-drawing-room, 2-compartment, 6-double-bedroom car built by Budd in 1937 for first lightweight Super Chief — was lettered for Santa Fe. Yampai, Pullman-built in late 1937 for second new Super, had 8 sections, 2 compartments, 2 double bedrooms.

245

WESTBOUND *Super Chief* overhauls a freight train and meets UP's *Los Angeles Limited* at Summit, Calif., atop Cajon Pass. Photo by Robert Hale.

Santa Fe.

ROUND-END observation was squared off.

de - Luxe

Great train of a great railroad

THE daily 39½-hour extra-fare *Super Chief* between Chicago and Los Angeles is the flag-bearer of the Santa Fe streamlined fleet. It is the most famous of the Santa Fe trains that provide transcontinental passengers with the utmost in rail comfort.

The *Super*, as it is affectionately termed by Santa Fe personnel, provides all-private-room service offering modern sleeping accommodations in the newest style Pullman cars. Luxury features include the elaborately decorated Turquoise Room-Pleasure Dome lounge car. Push-button radio and recorded musical programs are available through special speakers in every room.

Car equipment assigned to the *Super Chief* is always the finest. Several of the first orders of passenger cars produced by Pullman-Standard after the end of World War II were delivered to the Santa Fe for the initiation of daily *Super Chief* service on February 29, 1948.

In 1950 and 1951 the train was again re-equipped. Sleeping cars were delivered by ACF and Budd. Dining and dome-lounge cars were furnished by Pullman-Standard. This equipment was thoroughly refurbished and redecorated in 1958.

Santa Fe made passenger train news in 1964. Twelve 11-bedroom sleeping cars, fresh from the Pullman Company's Calumet shops, arrived in time for the summer season. Originally 24-duplex-roomette cars, they were stripped down to the shell and completely rebuilt at a cost of over 1 million dollars. All toilet facilities were enclosed, and 10 of the bedrooms easily convert into 5-bedroom suites by folding dividing partitions.

Fine food is a feature of the *Super Chief*. Fred Harvey meals, pleasing to the most discriminating gourmet, are courteously served. An innovation in railroad dining is the *Super Chief* Champagne Dinner. Complimentary service of fine champagne accompanies a superb dinner for $6.50.

The Pleasure Dome, "top of the *Super*, next to the stars," contains individual rotating seats. In the thickly carpeted main lounge, traditional Santa Fe Indian décor is preserved by two authentic Navajo sand paintings which adorn the walls. Zuni Indians in New Mexico hand fashioned the sterling silver medallion inlaid with specially selected turquoise that is mounted in the Turquoise Room.

Regrettably, the barbershop and shower bath have been eliminated. Gone also are the round-end observation cars and the coast-to-coast Pullmans (which operated between New York and Chicago via the *Broadway* and the *Century*). Notwithstanding these changes, the *Super Chief* of 1964 is a stunning train and must be ranked as one of America's best. Beautifully appointed, superbly maintained, and impeccably staffed, it continues as a great train on a great railroad. **I**

DINING CAR 601, constructed by Pullman-Standard in 1950, serves Harvey meals, features 2- and 4-place tables for customers.

PLEASURE DOME 501, built by Pullman in 1950, includes Turquoise Room (below). Outside swing hanger trucks added in 1958.

VISTA VALLEY, a 4-compartment, 1-double-bedroom lounge-observation, has had round end squared off for midtrain operation.

248

PINE BEACH, one of the 10-roomette, 6-double-bedroom Pine-series cars of all-stainless-steel constructed by Budd in 1949.

Budd.

de-Luxe

INDIAN SQUAW, 11-bedroom car, was completely rebuilt by Pullman in 1964 from a 24-duplex-roomette car built by P-S in 1947.

REGAL COURT, with 4 bedrooms, 2 drawing rooms, and 4 compartments, was constructed in ACF's St. Charles plant in 1950.

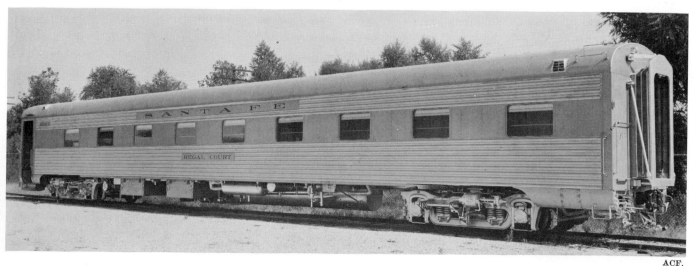

ACF.

THE PIONEER LIMITED

EAGLE accented Pacific on 1927 *Pioneer*.

1 THERE are still old-timers in Deerfield who remember the Pioneer—during the Golden Age. Twilight of a hot summer day, the cool of the night falling over the peaceful Illinois prairie. The first indication of impending importance was always the click of the depot semaphore arm as it locked into place — straight up — all clear! Next there was the mournful wail from the south — the whistle for County Line Road crossing. No. 1 was on the way. From around the curve at Elm Street came the ear-splitting roar and the pounding of drivers. A flash of golden yellow cars, then quickly off to the north as the

The train they called the "Rolls-Royce of American Railroading!"

red-and-white striped awning valance and the red illuminated drum sign of the observation car disappeared in a swirl of dust. Seconds more and she was a tiny speck off in the distance.

Things will not be quite like that again — ever.

For nearly 100 years Milwaukee Road trains No. 1 and

ALCO F-7's of 1938 were built for the *Hi's* but took turns on trains 1 and 4.

PIONEER LIMITED

4, the *Pioneer Limiteds*, have faithfully transported travelers between Chicago and the Twin Cities through the rich valleys of the Wisconsin and Mississippi rivers. Night after night, year after year, in fair weather and foul, they have departed and arrived with clockwork precision. True *Pioneers* (the name was selected in an 1898 contest), they were the first through trains connecting Chicago and St. Paul-Minneapolis. They were awarded the first Government mail contract to the Northwest. Indeed, for years the "St. Paul Road"* advertised itself as "The Great National Route Carrying the U. S. Mail."

The *Pioneer* included the north country's first sleeping cars. It was also first with the Westinghouse air brake, and first with steam-heated and electrically lighted equipment. Nos. 1 and 4, running in opposite directions each evening between Chicago and the Twin Cities, were piloted initially by 4-4-0's. Later they were powered by

"MABEL, it's President Harding!" Earphone magic.

4-4-2's, 4-6-0's, 4-6-2's, 4-6-4's, and today . . . diesels. On at least one occasion the *Pioneer Limited* was headed by Lima Locomotive Works' famous Super-Power demonstrator of 1925, 2-8-4 A-1.

Rounding out their first century, Nos. 1 and 4 meet at New Lisbon, Wis., in the summer of 1964, where they arrive at 2:30 and 2:15 a.m., respectively, while the passengers are comfortably asleep in hushed Pullmans.

*Not until 1927 did the Chicago, Milwaukee & St. Paul advertise itself as "The Milwaukee Road."

251

TYPICAL Chicago, Milwaukee & St. Paul flyer of 1889 poses smartly in Union Depot, Milwaukee, behind the drawbar of 4-4-0 723, an H-6 class American. Train is Chicago bound, about to round curve on which present-day No. 1 is standing in the nighttime illustration reproduced on page 261.

In the beginning they were

simply Nos. 1 and 4

IN January 1872 the present route of the *Pioneer* between Chicago and the Twin Cities via La Crosse and Portage was conveyed to the Milwaukee Road and the first through service without change of cars was inaugurated. The public timetable for March 1880 provides much enchanting reading about Nos. 1 and 4 and their operator. For example, running time from Chicago to the Twin Cities was 21 hours 10 minutes (allowing 21 minutes difference between Chicago and St. Paul clocks during the era prior to standard time zones). Sleeping cars were available ($2 for a double berth), and they were noted as being "wider and higher than any other cars in the country." Of even greater interest was the following notice: "Compose yourself to sleep and never mind your pocketbook. Each sleeper contains an iron safe. The only Iron-Safe Sleeping Car Line in the Country." Parlor cars were carried between Chicago and Milwaukee, but diners did not make an appearance until 1882.

A severe note printed in red in the 1880 table admonished the traveler to "please read":

This Company owns its entire line from Chicago to St. Paul and Minneapolis and is the only Company which does. It has not manufactured a title to deceive the public, and catch business. Those wishing tickets by this route will have to be careful to see that the name MILWAUKEE is

the second in the title of the Road. This caution is necessary to protect people against the fraudulent attempt of another line to benefit itself by the prestige of the Chicago, Milwaukee & St. Paul Railway Company, by a close imitation of its name; and which now, with sublime cheek, cautions the public against the line it has thus attempted to defraud.

Even the accompanying map bore a stern warning:

Travelers — please note the information contained in this folder. It is true in every particular. THE MAP IS NOT DISFIGURED WITH FRAUDULENT STRAIGHT LINES to deceive the uninitiated. . . .

An interesting travel journal entitled *A Reconnaissance of the Golden Northwest* published in 1883 stated this:

We forwarded ourselves to the capacious and commodious new Chicago Union Passenger Station. . . . Arriving there we discovered royally magnificent coaches, sleeping, parlor, and dining cars with the legend "Chicago, Milwaukee & St. Paul" emblazoned in letters of gold on their sides.

We reached the rear car of the long train and found ourselves in the most resplendent and comfortable *salon* on wheels which had ever met our vision. Fearing we had trespassed upon the private car of some railway magnate, whose lightest breath might shake Wall Street, we turned appealingly to a smiling son of Africa in livery, and asked whose private car we had invaded, and he answered, "No one in particular"; that there were no "reserved seats," and that 35 cents per chair was all the charge to Milwaukee. "Why," said he, "this is one of our ordinary parlor cars."

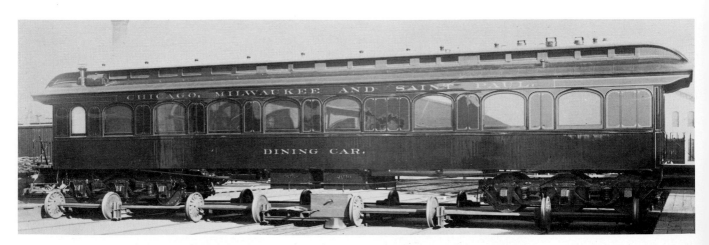

DINING CAR C (early Milwaukee diners were lettered instead of numbered) was built in Wilmington, Del., by Harlan & Hol- lingsworth in 1882. Open-platform 12-wheeler weighed 86,000 pounds, had an over-all length over couplers of 70 feet 3 inches.

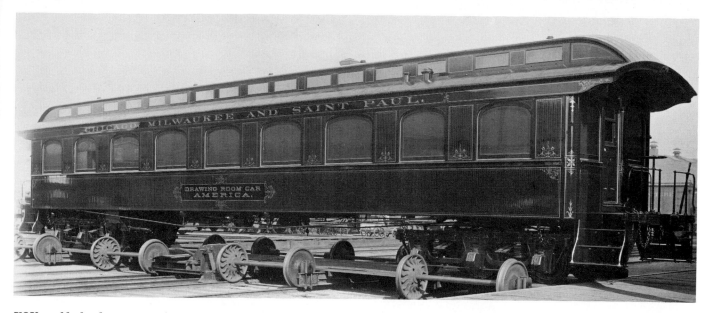

YOU could clearly see your face in the shining exterior of the "Drawing Room Car" America, one of six 68-foot, 12-wheel parlors built by Barney & Smith of Dayton, O., in 1879-1881 which included luxury of individual upholstered footstools.

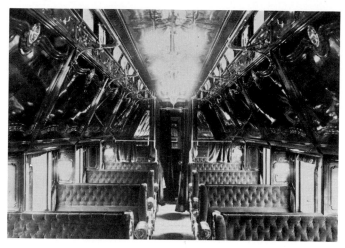

SLEEPER Marion (Harlan & Hollingsworth, 1881) contained 10 sections in an interior of crimson plush, Brussels carpet, and "highly polished" French black walnut panels. "Not a particle of varnish has been used in the finish," exclaimed the press.

PRINCE HENRY of Prussia traveled in a special section of the *Pioneer* on his U. S. tour of 1902; engine, car, and depot lights were only illumination for this shot.

Pioneer of 1898:

"$250,000 worth of gorgeousness"

THE year 1898 was a special one for the *Pioneer Limited*: the train received its name and superb new cars from Barney & Smith. Motive power was Vauclain compound Atlantics from Baldwin (one of which — No. 840 — ran off 74 miles in 67 minutes with 13 cars).

A contemporary brochure described the newly re-equipped limited of 1898:

A veritable *edition de luxe*, bound in covers of yellow and gold. . . . Many who pay the small sum requisite to possess all this $250,000 worth of gorgeousness for the 13 hours journey between Chicago, St. Paul, and Minneapolis never before lived for that length of time in such harmonious surroundings.

In the sweet was and was, when rails were made of iron and bridges of wood, and trains were *not* constructed on the principles of "sugar and spice and all that's nice," we were to associate traveling with three d's — dirt, discomfort and disgust — and linen dusters and "any old thing" as a traveling suit; but now time hath wrought changes. Mademoiselle emerges from her magnificent silk-lined compartment . . . spreads her pretty white wings and disappears, while Monsieur le Papa may proceed to his office in immaculate and groomed shape.

Chances are that Mama stayed in her compartment when Papa visited Buffet Car No. 270 [photo next page] built in July 1893 by Barney & Smith.

The library and smoking room is a dream of smoke wreathes which mingle tints with the St. Jago mahogany that looks down upon you from the walls and ceilings, with its rich carvings and inlaid marquetry. . . . Here you may read and smoke the hours away, while the clinking ice in the glass at your elbow distracts your attention at times from My Lady Nicotine.

But the Barney & Smith elegance on the *Pioneer* was short lived. It was soon replaced during the early 1900's with the even more luxurious Pullman-built cars illustrated. All were among the last wooden cars built for the limited.

The famous rode Nos. 1 and 4. The spectacular night photo above, taken in Milwaukee, depicts First No. 1, a special for the conveyance of H.R.H. Prince Henry of Prussia on his American visit in 1902. A Baldwin booklet of the period said in awe, "It will be noted that the photograph was taken at night. The only illumination being furnished by the electric lights in the station and cars, and by the headlights of the locomotives in the vicinity."

THE PIONEER LIMITED

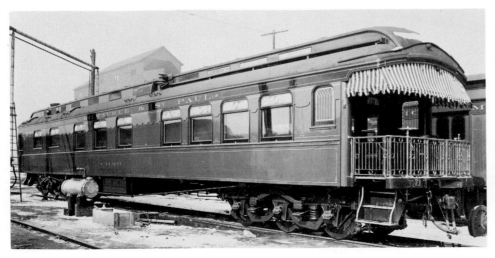

CAFE-OBSERVATION Como boasted ga

ST. JAGO mahogany was lavishly employed inside buffet No. 270, a Barney & Smith combine of 1893 whose narrow but enclosed vestibules were dusted by cinders of 4-4-2's.

PULLMAN built 4500-series diner in 1908 and it was among the last wooden cars constructed for the St. Paul's Pioneer Limited.

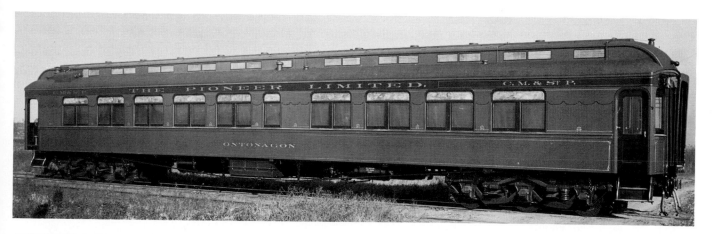

ALL-ROOM de luxe sleeping car Ontonagon, built by Pullman in 1905, clearly identified its mission in life on the letterboard.

ped awning over its brass railing. Parlor Juneau, built in 1907, combined wicker and plush in its long row of aisle-facing chairs.

WOODROW WILSON rode Pioneer Limited in 1912.

ROOM SLEEPER Wyandotte was one of two "honeymoon cars."

On the eve of World War 1—
an all-steel Pioneer

THE years preceding World War I brought sweeping changes to the Chicago, Milwaukee & St. Paul Railway. Maps of the road depicted the Western extension steadily closing the gap toward the Pacific Northwest until May 28, 1911, when the *Olympian* and *Columbian* made their maiden runs from Chicago to Seattle-Tacoma. New steel equipment was built by both Pullman and Barney & Smith for the de luxe trains throughout the St. Paul system. By 1914 the *Pioneer* had been completely refurbished with fine new cars offering a multitude of accommodations.

Competition on the Twin Cities run was as keen as on any route in the country. Every evening of the week during the dinner hour seven trains left Chicago for St. Paul and Minneapolis over seven *competing* rail routes. They were the North Western's *North Western Limited* . . . Burlington's *Minnesota Limited* ("dynamo electric lighted") . . . Chicago Great Western's *Great Western Limited* ("Dining Car serves dinner à la carte on leaving Chicago") . . . Rock Island's *Chicago-Twin Cities Express* . . . Minneapolis & St. Louis-Illinois Central's *Twin City-Chicago Limited* ("Newest and best electric-lighted sleepers") . . . and Soo's *Twin Cities, Chicago, Milwaukee Express* ("All Cars Vacuum Cleaned"). Each was a de luxe named train composed of buffet-club, dining, and sleeping cars. All seven would arrive in the Twin Cities the

THE PIONEER LIMITED

following morning in time for an early breakfast. With such extraordinary competition, it was necessary for the CM&StP to provide the ultimate in service.

The *Pioneer* of 1914 ran daily northbound in two sections which left Chicago 5 minutes apart. No. 1 carried head-end mail cars and coaches. No. 101, the following train, was advertised as "the *only* solid sleeping-car train from Chicago to St. Paul-Minneapolis." Regularly it ran with 14 heavy steel sleeping cars.

For many years the St. Paul owned and operated its own sleeping cars, one of the few U. S. roads to do so. At one time, 1926, there were over 200 such cars on the company's equipment register. Railroad operation of sleeping cars began in the early 1870's. Commencing in 1882 the service was actually operated by the Pullman Palace Car Company. In 1890, however, the railroad once again became the sole operator and continued the service until 1927, when the premier trains of the road became Pullman equipped. Thereafter only local services were company operated.

BUILT by Pullman in 1911 but operated by the railroad was the all-steel 10-section, 1-drawing-room, 1-compartment Oneida.

THE Pioneer Limited's all-sleeper section in 1914 carried as many as 14 cars; Westport contained 2 drawing rooms, 7 compartments.

1927 . . . Pioneer by Pullman

"THE Greatest Achievement of the Golden Age of American Transportation" — in such terms was the roller-bearing *Pioneer* of 1927 advertised. During May of that year the Pullman Company delivered 18 special new sleeping cars to the Milwaukee Road; at the same time shopmen at the West Milwaukee Shops were putting the finishing touches to complementary Pacifics, club and dining cars. Fortunately for posterity, the able photographers of Kaufmann & Fabry, Chicago, set up their cameras along the right of way and recorded the exhibition train — hence these extraordinary pictures of "The Rolls-Royce of American Railroading!"

LOCOMOTIVE 6109

F-3 CLASS Pacific 6109 was built by Alco in 1910, souped up for Pioneer Limited service with Milwaukee orange and dark-maroon trim and Automatic Train Stop equipment. The 79-inch-drivered engine bore a cast eagle atop smokebox, "Safety First" on cylinders. Years later some F-3's were painted orange again for the Chippewa Hiawatha, pending streamlining of sisters for that train.

BAGGAGE CAR 1032

THIS 72-foot baggage car was built by Standard Steel Car Company in 1919, rebuilt with roller bearings by the railroad in 1927.

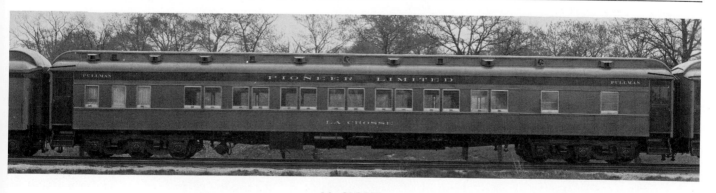

LA CROSSE

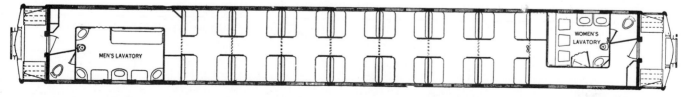

FOURTEEN-section sleeper, one of three such 83-footers built for each train, had a Spanish motif interior created with headboards and arches. These formed semiprivate sections in attempt to eliminate the tunnel-like effect of standard Pullman aisle.

257

NAGAWICKA

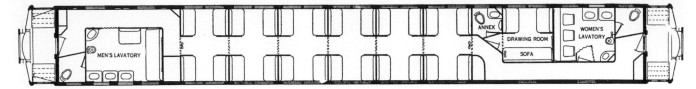

THREE 12-section, 1-drawing-room sleepers were available for each train. Warm tan contrasted with blue upholstery in interior scheme.

CHICAGO

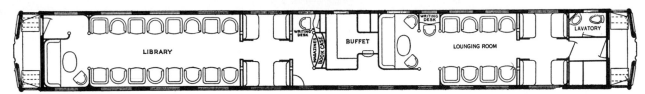

THE PIONEER LIMITED

LIBRARY-CLUB CAR was built by Barney & Smith in 1909, subsequently refurbished and steel-plated by railroad. It had brown leather chairs for 32, leaded glass windows, sections for card playing, a 32 x 49-inch tapestry, ivory-tinted ceiling, cuspidors.

DAN HEALEY

DINING CAR was 72 feet long, seated 36, was finished in mahogany, contained first electrical refrigeration in U.S. rail dining service. It was named for Dan Healey, who was the oldest dining car steward in the country at the time of his death in 1922. He'd served nine different presidents of the country, inspired columnist Frances Boardman of the St. Paul Daily News to write: "You probably know Dan Healey. And you doubtless feel confident that Dan Healey knows you. Maybe he does. If he doesn't you'll never know or find it out, for he'll contrive to keep you thinking that he and your father were bosom friends, and that you've inherited his devotion to the family. He'll confirm your belief in this personal attachment by such substantial attentions as a plate of perfect griddle cakes (that you didn't order and won't be asked to pay for) served at the psychological moment when he feels that your breakfast on the Pioneer Limited calls for just that addition. For it's on the Pioneer that Dan Healey practices the art of hospitality and diplomacy." No wonder, therefore, that the employer of the late "Mr. Dan" respectfully named in his honor the dining car of the new Pioneer Limited of 1927. Like the club car, it was operated by the railroad.

258

FRONTENAC

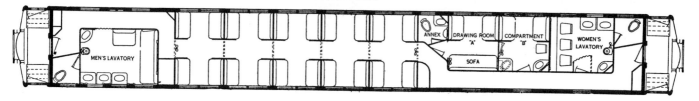

ON each Pioneer there was a 10-section, 1-drawing-room, 1-compartment Pullman operating between Milwaukee and Minneapolis.

Frontenac boasted brass window sash, bronze lights, and "fluted pilasters in polychrome and gold with Moorish arches."

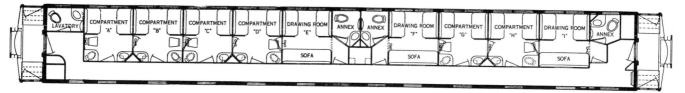

OCONOMOWOC

THERE was one 6-compartment, 3-drawing-room Pullman on each train (the other was named Okauchee) and the road termed

the type one "so much appreciated by families, and parties of friends." Each room had a clock, electric fan, door knocker.

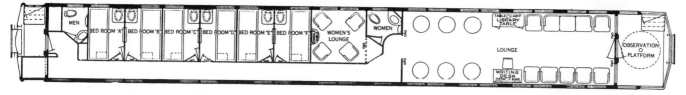

MINNEHAHA

"REAL BEDS" were a feature of the 6-single-bedroom observation lounges that trailed each Pioneer. "Each room is designed for occupancy by one person and contains a single bed almost 6½ feet long — a real bed with deep box spring, thick comfortable

mattress, and a silk spread." So read the brochure, which described such bedrooms as "an amazing novelty for overnight travel." There were 140 miles of Mississippi River to be seen from lounge. Or the hardy could set up a camp chair on the platform.

259

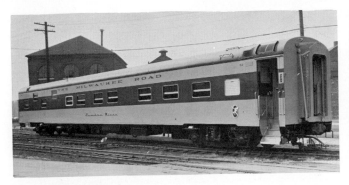

CHIPPEWA RIVER has 8 duplex roomettes, 6 roomettes, 4 DBR's.

THE PIONEER LIMITED

THE *Pioneer Limited* remains one of America's finest trains. But the leisurely travel of other years has given way to the pace of today. The old dinnertime departure has been moved back many hours, thus allowing a free evening before train time. Dan Healey's diner of another age has been replaced by a comfortable lounge-diner offering satisfying fare for the evening hours and a club breakfast before the early morning arrival. The fusty palace sleeping cars have been supplanted by the latest products of Pullman-Standard which offer luxuries undreamed of in the bygone era of silk and brocade.

Nos. 1 and 4 acquired streamlined all-room sleeping cars for the first time November 15, 1948; latest-model streamlined coaches, diner-lounges, and dormitory-baggage cars had been introduced earlier that year. At that time there was even thought of calling the limited the *Pioneer-Hiawatha* (and one ad appeared with that name), but fortunately common sense prevailed. Technically, Nos. 1 and 4 ceased to exist for a while during the mid-1950's when the *Pioneer* was consolidated with the *Columbian* and acquired the latter's numbers, 17 and 18 (even though the public timetable retained Nos. 1 and 4 and the distinguished *Pioneer* name); with the total demise of the *Olympian*'s old running mate west of Minneapolis, the old numbers 1 and 4 were restored.

The splendid morale of the Milwaukee Road personnel who contribute to the operation of the train is obvious to the traveler. For this reason, more than any other, the *Pioneer* is well patronized and is a moneymaker for the road.

Everyone on the Milwaukee, from President Quinn on down the line, has a soft spot in his heart for this grand train.* I

*A typical operation out of Milwaukee en route from Chicago to St. Paul-Minneapolis on May 29, 1964, included 2400 h.p. EMD E9 33A, 1500 h.p. EMD F7's 96B and 103A; 5222 — storage-mail car; 1605 — PRR high-speed box car; 7564 — REA Express storage mail-refrigerator car; 2150 — Railway Post Office; 1317 — baggage car; 1107 — working baggage car; 453 — coach-dormitory car; 658, 612, 619 — coaches; *Union Grove*, 182 — cafe-lounge; *Madison River*, 19 — Pullman sleeping car; *Rodney*, 30 — Pullman sleeping car; *Gallatin River*, 22 — Pullman sleeping car; 487 — coach (special group); 482 — coach (special group); 486 — coach (special group); *River Grove*, 184 — cafe-lounge; 485 — coach; 1109 — express car; 1957 — storage-mail car.

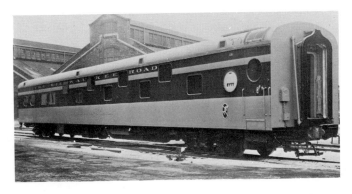

WISCONSIN DELLS contains 16 duplex roomettes, 4 DBR's.

SPRING EVENING in 1961 finds today's Pioneer Limited, dressed in Union Pacific yellow, pausing on curve into Milwaukee station.

TALL-STACKED CB&Q 4-4-0 78 and the famed Chicago-Omaha *White Mail*. CB&Q photo.

CRACK LIMITEDS OF THE

ON last lap into Chicago, *Chicago-Nebraska Limited* — an early predecessor of *Denver Zephyr* — passes through La Vergne, Ill., September 3, 1916. A. W. Johnson photo.

BURLINGTON

Passengers are "guests"

1 THE Burlington Lines celebrated its 100th anniversary on February 12, 1949. One century earlier a charter had been granted for the construction of the Aurora Branch Railroad to connect with the Galena & Chicago Union, the only railway then serving Chicago. During the 1850's the little Aurora line, under the direction of Boston capitalist John Murray Forbes, pushed westward to the Mississippi River.

On February 11, 1855, the company became the Chicago, Burlington & Quincy Railroad, and by 1859 it was providing through service to the Missouri River at St. Joseph by connecting with the Hannibal & St. Joseph Railroad by means of ferry service on the Mississippi between Quincy and Hannibal. The main Burlington line across Iowa reached Council Bluffs in 1870 where it connected with the Union Pacific to form one of the earliest transcontinental routes.

In 1901, when the Burlington was purchased by Great Northern and Northern Pacific, it operated almost 8000 miles of track including lines to Denver, St. Paul-Minneapolis, and northward to Billings, Mont., where it connected with the Northern Pacific. During 1908, the Burlington acquired both the Colorado & Southern and the Fort Worth & Denver City roads, linking Texas and

IN the 1870's: "only route" with 16-wheel sleepers.

the Rockies. Today passengers and shippers alike know the Burlington to be a progressive, modern railroad operating nearly 11,000 miles in 14 states.

263

BALDWIN Vauclain compound 4-4-2 1592 on the eastbound *Fast Mail* near Mendota, Ill., in 1899. CB&Q photo.

Burlington's Number 1

There are several railroads reaching from Eastern territory to Colorado, but none has the many advantages of the Burlington route. This road operates over its own tracks from Chicago, Peoria, and St. Louis to Denver, and it has a world-wide reputation from the excellence of its equipment, the high standard of its dining car service, and the regularity with which its trains make schedule time. — *The Burlington's Number One*, brochure, 1901.

THE PRIDE of the Burlington at the turn of the century was its celebrated No. 1, Chicago-Denver Express. It departed from Chicago in the late afternoon and arrived in Denver the following evening. No. 6, the companion train, operated eastbound on the same schedule. The consist included a mail car,

smoking car, reclining-seat chair car, dining car, 12-and-1 Pullman sleeper, and observation-lounge sleeping car with 10 sections. The exterior of the train was uniformly of the standard Pullman color — umber body, red doors and sash, gold lining and lettering. In 1901, when Pullman changed to Brewster green, the Burlington repainted No. 1 accordingly.

In the early years of the 20th century, the Burlington also operated daytime and overnight service between Chicago and the Twin Cities. The morning train, Nos. 51 and 52, the *Minnesota Day Limited*, carried an open-platform observa-

CRACK LIMITEDS

TYPICAL Burlington train during Wilson's administration: Atlantic 2942 at Clyde, Ill., September 3, 1916. A. W. Johnson photo.

BALANCED COMPOUND No. 2700 was built by Baldwin in 1904 and simpled in 1928 (and renumbered 2583); served during World War II.

S-2 PACIFIC 2939, constructed by Baldwin in 1910 and rebuilt in 1929, was typical of Burlington's first-generation 4-6-2's.

EARLY 20th century coach construction: CB&Q 1701, built by the American Car & Foundry plant located in Jeffersonville, Ind.

ANGELO, de luxe sleeping car with 7 staterooms and 2 drawing rooms, was built for Chicago-Twin Cities service by Pullman in 1897.

LOUNGE NO. 201 — one of the earliest solarium cars built — contained library, buffet, smoking and observation sunroom (above and right). The big 12-wheel vehicle was turned out by Pullman in August 1909. The car was first operated on the Minnesota Limited, trains 47 and 48, but its range was subsequently extended with its assignment to Burlington's crack Colorado Limited to Denver.

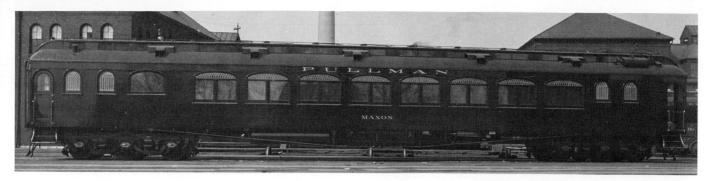

MAXON, a 16-section sleeper built in 1907 by Pullman, is representative of the 16-section series cars nicknamed "battleships."

CRACK LIMITEDS

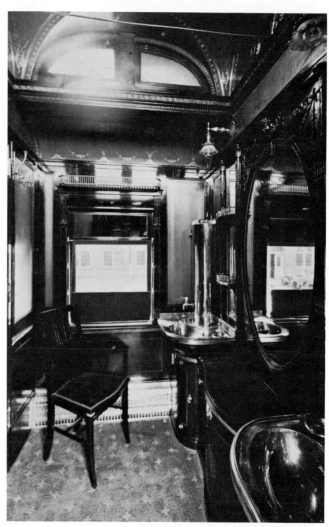

tion-parlor car for viewing the beautiful sights along the Mississippi River Scenic Line. The overnight, Nos. 47 and 48, was advertised as "the finest train in all the world." It was first known as the *Commercial Limited*, then was later named the *Blackhawk*. The last car of this train was a classic wood buffet, smoking, and lounge car containing what is probably the first enclosed sun parlor or solarium ever built.

After the purchase of the Burlington by the Great Northern and Northern Pacific during 1901, many of the great Pacific Coast-Twin Cities trains were routed into Chicago over the CB&Q, inaugurating the through car arrangements which continue to the present as the *Empire Builder, Western Star, North Coast Limited,* and *Mainstreeter.*

The Burlington was one of George Pullman's first customers. Sleeping cars in CB&Q service have always been of the latest and most modern design. When electricity was first adapted to railroad cars, No. 1 was among the first trains so equipped. Thus ran a description in a CB&Q brochure in 1901:

> At each end of each section is an electric light fitted to an ornate metal shield. To extinguish the light, the passenger has only to press the shield in against the wall; to restore it, he merely presses a button. Seven electroliers of four lights are suspended from the ceiling of each car. . . . Special features of the women's dressing rooms include four electric lighted mirrors and electric curling irons.

Elbert Hubbard, the original Philistine, said: "On the Burlington I heard an old word used with a new application. The conductor referred to his passengers as his 'guests.' Your welfare is guarded, your privacy respected, your wishes anticipated, and the servants seem to have been hired just for you."

All photos, Pullman-Standard.

INTRICATE woodwork designs and bright metal adorn ladies' dressing room of the 16-section sleeping car Parthenon of 1897.

NORSEMAN, a 10-section observation, was built by Pullman in 1908 for service in the Chicago to Kansas City Missouri Limited.

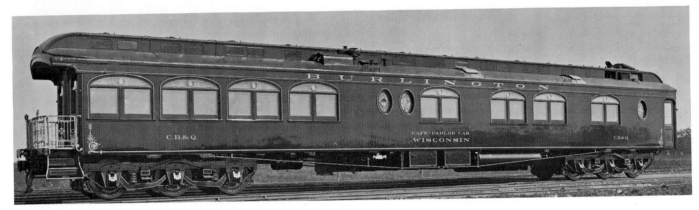

WISCONSIN (sister cars: Illinois, Iowa, Minnesota, and Nebraska), a cafe-parlor-observation built in 1901. Brass-railed beauty subsequently lost some of its esthetic appeal when the car was sheathed in steel for greater safety and reduced maintenance.

UNDER a signal bridge at Riverside, Ill., rolls the *Minnesota Day Limited* on August 31, 1924. A. W. Johnson photo.

268

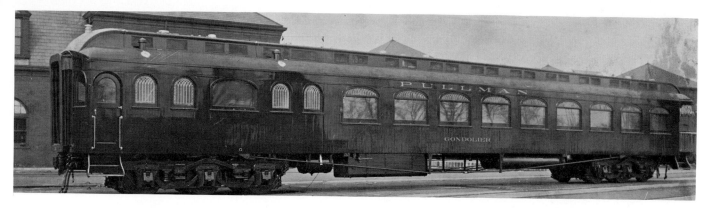

GONDOLIER, an observation-parlor car constructed by Pullman in 1906 for first-class passengers of the Minnesota Day Limited.

DINING CAR NO. 149, turned out by Pullman in July 1909, served the meals that built a national reputation for the CB&Q.

CRACK LIMITEDS

C.B & Q. DINING CAR

BURLINGTON ROUTE
PASSENGERS MUST HAVE 'EM
NO WONDER THEY THINK OUR MEALS
ARE CHEAP AT 75¢

Author's collection.

TRADE CARD of 1880's promoted CB&Q meals.

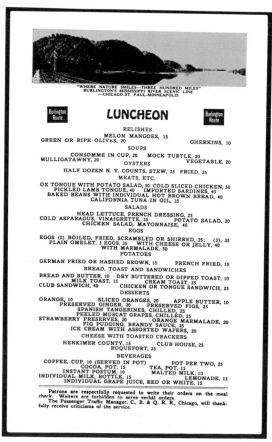

"WHERE NATURE SMILES—THREE HUNDRED MILES"
BURLINGTON'S MISSISSIPPI RIVER SCENIC LINE
—CHICAGO-ST. PAUL-MINNEAPOLIS

LUNCHEON

RELISHES
MELON MANGOES, 15
GREEN OR RIPE OLIVES, 20   GHERKINS, 10
SOUPS
CONSOMME IN CUP, 20   MOCK TURTLE, 20
MULLIGATAWNY, 20   VEGETABLE, 20
OYSTERS
HALF DOZEN N. Y. COUNTS, STEW, 35   FRIED, 35
MEATS, ETC.
OX TONGUE WITH POTATO SALAD, 50   COLD SLICED CHICKEN, 50
PICKLED LAMB TONGUE, 40   IMPORTED SARDINES, 40
BAKED BEANS WITH INDIVIDUAL HOT BROWN BREAD, 40
CALIFORNIA TUNA IN OIL, 35
SALADS
HEAD LETTUCE, FRENCH DRESSING, 25
COLD ASPARAGUS, VINAIGRETTE, 35   POTATO SALAD, 20
CHICKEN SALAD, MAYONNAISE, 40
EGGS
EGGS (2) BOILED, FRIED, SCRAMBLED OR SHIRRED, 25;   (3), 35
PLAIN OMELET, 3 EGGS, 35   WITH CHEESE OR JELLY, 40
WITH MARMALADE, 50
POTATOES
GERMAN FRIED OR HASHED BROWN, 15   FRENCH FRIED, 15
BREAD, TOAST AND SANDWICHES
BREAD AND BUTTER, 10   DRY BUTTERED OR DIPPED TOAST, 10
MILK TOAST, 15   CREAM TOAST, 25
CLUB SANDWICH, 40   CHICKEN OR TONGUE SANDWICH, 25
DESSERTS
ORANGE, 10   SLICED ORANGES, 20   APPLE BUTTER, 10
PRESERVED GINGER, 20   PRESERVED FIGS, 25
SPANISH TANGERINES, CHILLED, 25
PEELED MUSCAT GRAPES, CHILLED, 25
STRAWBERRY PRESERVES, 20   ORANGE MARMALADE, 20
FIG PUDDING, BRANDY SAUCE, 25
ICE CREAM WITH ASSORTED WAFERS, 20
CHEESE WITH TOASTED CRACKERS
HERKIMER COUNTY, 15   CLUB HOUSE, 25
ROQUEFORT, 25
BEVERAGES
COFFEE, CUP, 10 (SERVED IN POT)   POT PER TWO, 25
COCOA, POT, 15   TEA, POT, 15
INSTANT POSTUM, 10   MALTED MILK, 10
INDIVIDUAL MILK, BOTTLE, 15   LEMONADE, 15
INDIVIDUAL GRAPE JUICE, RED OR WHITE, 15

Patrons are respectfully requested to write their orders on the meal check. Waiters are forbidden to serve verbal orders. The Passenger Traffic Manager, C. B. & Q. R. R., Chicago, will thankfully receive criticisms of the service.

CB&Q.

LUNCHEON menu of Minnesota Day Limited in 1916.

"BURLINGTON HOUR" at the CHICAGO UNION STATION

5.15 P.M.! The busiest moment of the fullest hour in the pulsating life of the splendid Chicago Union Station presents the striking spectacle of four great Burlington trains drawn up on contiguous tracks—steam up—personnel on the qui vive!

It is doubtful that such a galaxy of crack trains is gathered together at one moment on any other railroad anywhere else in America. Every one of the four is a distinguished, de luxe train—a thorobred stripped for action.

At 5:30 the great DENVER LIMITED moves, and in another minute is gone from view on its 1,000-mile flight to Denver and the Rocky Mountains. At 6:00 the MISSOURI LIMITED silently pulls away—headed for Kansas City and St. Joseph. With machine-like precision the NEBRASKA LIMITED departs at 6:15 for Omaha and Lincoln, followed at exactly 6:30 by the peerless BLACK HAWK for St. Paul, Minneapolis and Northwest.

Thus, *in one hour*, the Burlington starts 800 people—on business, on pleasure, on every sort of errand—to distant places which the genius of American railroading has brought close together.

And this is less than half the story of the Burlington's Chicago service.

10:30 this morning witnessed the departure of the COLORADO LIMITED. Five minutes later the great NORTH COAST LIMITED left for St. Paul, Minneapolis, Spokane, Seattle, Tacoma and Portland, with the YELLOWSTONE PARK COMET wheeling out at the same moment. At 8:45 p.m. the COMMERCIAL LIMITED (newest Burlington train) leaves on its swift flight to St. Paul and Minneapolis. At 11:00 p.m. the famous ORIENTAL LIMITED pulls out for St. Paul, Minneapolis, Glacier National Park and all the Pacific Northwest, followed at 11:30 by the OVERLAND EXPRESS for Denver, the Royal Gorge, Salt Lake City and California.

* * *

And so in the thirteen hours from 10:30 a.m. to 11:30 p.m., *ten great flyers* go out of the Chicago Union Station over the Burlington Route—headed West, Northwest, Southwest, *EVERYWHERE WEST.*

Every train is really several trains. That is—the same *Oriental Limited* which leaves Chicago tonight for Seattle and Portland, makes its next start from here seven days later, and meantime another *Oriental Limited* leaves Chicago every night for seven days.

It is the same with the *North Coast Limited.* Eight editions of this train always on the road between Chicago and the North Pacific Coast.

When the de luxe *Denver Limited* was installed in June this year, four *Denver Limiteds* were born. There are four editions of the *Colorado Limited* and four of the *Denver Overland Express;* two *Nebraska Limiteds*, two *Missouri Limiteds*, two *Black Hawks*, two *Commercial Limiteds*, five *Yellowstone Comets.*

The ten peerless flyers are really *forty-one* separate and distinct trains carrying more than 500 cars which are on the go every day—all the time, constituting the Burlington's regular Chicago service to and from Omaha, Lincoln, Denver, Kansas City, St. Joseph, St. Paul, Minneapolis, Yellowstone Park, Glacier National Park, the North Pacific Coast, California—West, Northwest, Southwest—*EVERYWHERE WEST.*

FROM 1927 timetable: "four great Burlington trains drawn up on contiguous tracks — steam up." Author's collection.

The anniversary fleet

> *How smoothly the trains run beyond the Missouri;*
> *Even in my sleep I know when I have crossed the river.*
> — Going Home, *Willa Cather.*

IN 1930 the Burlington celebrated its 80th anniversary. To commemorate the event, the road re-equipped three of its crack limiteds. For the overnight run from Chicago to Omaha and Lincoln, Nebr., a new train, the *Ak-Sar-Ben*, was instituted. On the Denver line, via Omaha and Lincoln, the road refurbished its *Colorado-Chicago Limited* and renamed it the *Aristocrat.* The *New Blackhawk*, continuing a "felicitous service already well known," received brand-new equipment for the Twin Cities overnight service.

These three peerless flyers represented an investment of 3 million dollars and more than a year's labor on the part of the master craftsmen at Pullman. Each new consist contained

HUDSON 3000, world's heaviest and most powerful 4-6-4 when built by Baldwin in 1930. CB&Q photo.

several types of matched Pullmans, "lounging" cars (as they were called on the Burlington), dining cars, reclining-chair car, and head-end equipment. Motive power for all trains was the fine new S-4 Hudsons built by Baldwin. The anniversary trains and their specially selected personnel reflected the rich traditions and proud achievements of the Burlington Route's serving of the West.

The *Ak-Sar-Ben* honored the famed Nebraska organization whose high ideals and fine traditions have contributed to the development of the great Cornhusker commonwealth. *Ak-Sar-Ben* spelled backwards reveals the name of the state.

The *Aristocrat* was considered by the Burlington as a patrician among trains, befitting its line of distinguished ancestry as one of America's oldest de luxe operations and dating from 1888.

The *New Blackhawk*, on its night flight to and from the Twin Cities, flashed across the ancient domain and historic battle-ground of the Sac and Fox warrior. The train's tailgate symbol appropriately contained a reproduction of Lorado Taft's towering Black Hawk statue which stands in dignity on a promontory overlooking the Rock River near Oregon, Ill.

The Pullmans for these three services were matched cars, permanently assigned to their respective trains. Each car's interiors were highly lacquered in tones of gray and light green. Semi-compartmented sections contained winged seats patterned after colonial fireside armchairs. Upholstery and carpet were pearl green with rose undertone in Oriental patterns. Oversized dressing rooms contained individual shaving mirrors for men, and "quaint Jeffersonian prinking seats for women."

The *Ak-Sar-Ben* and the *Blackhawk* carried unique salon-club cars with 4 single bedrooms, 1 drawing room, 2 compartments, and an intimate club room with walls finished in handsome old walnut paneling rubbed to a velvet sheen.

The dining cars — decorated in old ivory, blue, and dull gold — perpetuated the traditions of the Burlington's famed cuisine and were enhanced, "if you please, by music from a famous orchestra transmitted by wireless."

On the rear of all three trains was one of the road's stunning

CB&Q.

PRESIDENT Franklin D. Roosevelt rides the Q, October 1936.

new full-length lounging cars. Each of these cars contained card nooks, restful chairs, a special room for ladies, radio, buffet, and a glass-enclosed solarium.

All of the sleeping and lounging cars of each train were appropriately named to compliment the states, people, and clubs along the route.

THE *Mississippi Riverview*, a *Zephyr* predecessor, at Sugar Grove, Ill., in 1935. A. W. Johnson photo.

CRACK LIMITEDS

S-4 HUDSON No. 3000 was one of a dozen huge, booster-equipped 4-6-4's built by Baldwin in 1930 for Burlington's Anniversary Fleet.

MINNESOTA CLUB, a salon-club sleeper with 4 single rooms, 1 drawing room, 2 compartments, and lounge, was one of a series named for on-line clubs when built in 1930 as well as one of the last orthodox heavyweight Pullmans constructed. Have a seat (below) in a cozy corner of sister-car Lancaster Club.

DINING CAR 178 seated 36 (above) at staggered tables in surroundings painted ivory, blue, and old gold. Such cars were operated on Burlington's Aristocrat and Blackhawk limiteds.

Pullman-Standard.

CYRUS NORTHROP, built in 1930, contained 8 sections, 2 compartments, 1 drawing room, and was lettered for service on the Blackhawk.

Pullman-Standard.

PEPIN, with 12 sections and a drawing room, was assigned to Ak-Sar-Ben. Below is typical interior of matched Pullmans.

CRACK LIMITEDS

CB&Q.

CB&Q.

MINNEAPOLIS, a solarium-lounging car built in 1928, seated its passengers in typical American decor (above) during administration of Calvin Coolidge.

Pullman-Standard.

273

RALPH BUDD

The first diesel-powered streamlined train

Trim as a sail-boat; speed king of the rails — the ZEPHYR strikes the most advanced note in up-to-date transport methods, and writes a colorful, interesting, and significant chapter into American railroad history. — *Burlington Zephyr*, CB&Q brochure, 1933.

ON November 11, 1934, the Burlington placed its *Pioneer Zephyr*, the first diesel-powered streamlined train in America, in regular service between Lincoln, Omaha, St. Joseph, and Kansas City. The outstanding success of this venture marked the beginning of the widespread use of diesel power and lightweight equipment in the transportation of passengers.

The *Pioneer Zephyr,* preserved for posterity at Chicago's Museum of Science and Industry, was already well known when it made its first run in revenue service as train Nos. 20 and 21. Millions of visitors to the 1934 Century of Progress Exposition in Chicago had walked through the train, awed by its many innovations. Thousands more had lined the tracks and shouted their approval as the glistening streamliner flashed by on its record-breaking exhibition runs.*

Named for the Greek personification of the West Wind by Burlington President Ralph Budd, the revolutionary motor train first incorporated many features now commonplace in carbuilding. Electric shot-welding, stainless-steel siding, electropneumatic brakes, shatterproof glass, round-end solarium — all were innovations when the *Pioneer Zephyr* was outshopped at the Edward G. Budd plant in Philadelphia in April 1934.

The combination of diesel power and durable lightweight car construction made faster schedules possible and paved the way for the high-speed passenger-train service enjoyed throughout the world today. The popularity of the *Pioneer Zephyr*, and its extraordinary record of on-time performance, resulted in the construction of additional Burlington *Zephyr* trains.

April 21, 1935, brought the first *Twin Zephyrs* trains, Nos. 23 and 24, between Chicago and the Twin Cities. Later, in October 1935, the *Mark Twain Zephyr* was placed in service between St. Louis and Burlington, Ia.

In December 1936, the second *Twin Zephyrs* started operation between Chicago and the Twin Cities at which time the original Twin Cities trains began traveling between Fort Worth and Houston as the *Sam Houston Zephyr.*

Two of the most famous of all *Zephyrs,* the original twin 12-car *Denver Zephyrs,* were placed in service on November 8, 1936. After christening by Buffalo Bill Cody's granddaughter — Miss June Garlow — mounted on her pinto pony, the twin trains went into daily 16-hour overnight service, clipping almost 10 hours from the schedule of the fastest steam-powered train.

Designed by the eminent Paul Cret and built by the Budd Company, they contained features never before used on a railroad train such as 110-volt electrical outlets in dressing rooms

*On its celebrated "Gentlemen Adventurers" dawn-to-dusk trip of October 23, 1936, the *Denver Zephyr* streaked from Chicago to Denver 1017 miles nonstop in 12 hours 12 minutes, averaging 83.69 mph. Between Akron and Brush, Colo., the train hit 116 mph.

for the new electric razor. Also new were tightlock couplers, electric brakes, blue night lights in berths, and extra-long 6-feet 8-inch berths for tall passengers. "Invisible dry nitrogen between double panes of safety glass" prevented fogging or frosting and assured clear windows.

Each train consisted of a two-unit power car, a combined generator-R.P.O.-baggage car, lounge-dormitory car with baggage compartment, two coaches, dining car, three open-section Pullmans, an all-room sleeper, and finally an observation-lounge car. Continuing an established practice, the Burlington named each car with the prefix "Silver" as a reflection of the silvery, stainless steel with which the trains were constructed. Lavish use of rare woods, for which architect Cret

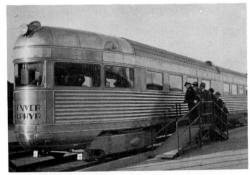

DENVERITES inspect new *Zephyr.*

was famous, was apparent throughout the interior design. Colorful modern fabrics with pastel trim created a warm, bright atmosphere. Newly developed foam-rubber seats in the coaches were covered in leather. Pillows and continuous porter service were available, and all seats were assigned at the time tickets were purchased.

In 1939 the *General Pershing Zephyr* was placed in service

CRACK LIMITEDS

"SYMPHONY in Stainless Steel": the original *Denver Zephyr*.

AMERICA'S first stainless-steel diesel-powered streamliner: *Pioneer Zephyr* of 1934.

between St. Louis and Kansas City. This train was followed in 1940 by the *Silver Streak Zephyr* running from Kansas City to Lincoln. In August 1940, the first *Texas Zephyrs* were introduced between Denver and Dallas, using stainless-steel cars and refurbished heavyweight sleeping cars.

January 1941 marked the initiation of the last of the prewar *Zephyr* trains, the *Zephyr-Rocket*. This train, which operated overnight between St. Louis and Minneapolis, consisted of lightweight cars owned by both Burlington and Rock Island plus rebuilt heavyweight sleeping cars supplied by the Pullman Company.

World War II interrupted the expansion of the *Zephyr* service, but after the end of the conflict, the trend was continued as quickly as materials for carbuilding became available.

275

Everett L. DeGolyer Jr.

SILVER LINING, ex-Denver Zephyr dormitory-bar-lounge shown as relettered for its present train assignment: **Texas Zephyr.**

Everett L. DeGolyer Jr.

SILVER CITY, one of the multi-million-mile articulated chair car veterans of the 1936 Denver Zephyr, now running to Texas.

Everett L. DeGolyer Jr.

SILVER SCREEN, 12-section articulated sleeping car as built (below) with truck covers for 1936 Denver Zephyr, and as pres- ently lettered and equipped (above) with new trucks for operation on Denver-Dallas Texas Zephyr of subsidiaries C&S and FW&D.

CB&Q.

Everett L. DeGolyer Jr.

SILVER SIDES, an all-room articulated sleeper with 6 bedrooms, 3 compartments, and 1 drawing room — now in the **Texas Zephyr.**

SILVER GRILL, another articulated, seated 40 (right) for mealtimes that were a festive occasion in a dignified and beautifully decorated room. In common with all other cars shown on these pages, Grill has been running since November 8, 1936.

CRACK LIMITEDS

SILVER FLASH observation-lounge contained (above) seats for 26 in lounge plus revolving parlor chairs for 8 and was equipped with soda fountain and radio-phonograph. Car carries on today (below) in consist of C&S-FW&D Texas Zephyr.

CLOSE-UP of Zephyr articulation equipment.

CRACK LIMITEDS

The Denver Zephyr, a great train

What a great train the Denver Zephyr has proved to be. — Letter from Ralph Budd, November 22, 1961.

IN 1945 the Burlington introduced the country's first Vista-Dome car. This innovation proved so popular that 40 additional cars were immediately ordered. By 1947 enough Vista-Domes had been received to equip two brand-new *Twin Zephyrs* for the scenic run to the Twin Cities, thus releasing the original trains for Chicago-Omaha-Lincoln service as the new *Nebraska Zephyrs*. In 1949 the luxurious Vista-Dome *California Zephyrs* extended *Zephyr* service to San Francisco through the heart of the Rocky Mountains and the Feather River Canyon in California via the Denver & Rio Grande Western-Western Pacific route.

In 1953 the new Brookfield-Kansas City Shortline was completed. Thirty-four new streamlined cars of 10 types were delivered by Budd. Ten of these cars were used to establish a daytime train — the *Kansas City Zephyr* — made possible by the shorter route. The overnight *American Royal* acquired new lightweight Pullman sleepers and became the *American Royal Zephyr*. Similar treatment was given both the *Ak-Sar-Ben* and the *Black Hawk* which received the remainder of the Budd order.

On Sunday, October 28, 1956, a pair of new Vista-Dome *Denver Zephyrs* entered service between Chicago-Omaha-Denver with a new through car serving Colorado Springs. Powered by a 4800 h.p. Electro-Motive diesel, each train consisted of 14 Budd stainless-steel cars designed and built to embody the most modern techniques of car architecture and construction.

In an era when passenger service in the East was being curtailed, President Harry Murphy of the Burlington invested 6.5 million dollars for the new *Denver Zephyrs*. Thoughtfully designed to serve the growing Colorado trade, the new train is a joy to ride. It has colorful interiors and is exquisite in every detail. Each consist has three Vista-Dome cars, an authentic Western buffet car called the Chuck Wagon, the first regularly assigned Slumbercoaches in America, and the glamorous Colorado Room in the rear dome observation car. Train architects created a masterpiece. The blues, greens, and warm browns of Colorado combined with original watercolor paintings, murals, and wood carvings make the train a thing of beauty.

The popularity of these trains has made the Vista-Dome *Denver Zephyr* trains a profitable operation. During their first five years they netted a 9.1-million-dollar operating profit on gross revenues of 22.7 million dollars.

In answer to a question about the future of passenger trains, Harry Murphy stated:

We believe the new Vista-Dome *Denver Zephyr* is one of the most modern trains in the world today. It is something more, too — it is a multimillion-dollar investment in the future of passenger business. It is a sound investment by private enterprise without benefit of subsidy of any kind. This new *Zephyr* is a tangible demonstration of our belief that the traveling public will appreciate good transportation, will patronize it, and will reward the railroads which in their own special manner do their utmost not only to hold but to attract new business — and that is as it should be. I

278

SILVER POUCH, Budd-built stainless-steel baggage-mail Railway Post Office, was assigned to one of the Denver Zephyrs built in 1956.

SILVER HALTER, "flat-top" coach, seats 56 passengers in de luxe stretch-out reclining chairs with leg rests for overnight run.

SILVER KETTLE, the famed Chuck Wagon car, contains (below) lunch counter serving economy meals as well as 19-seat coffee shop — both in Old West decor of copper fixtures, saddle leather.

CRACK LIMITEDS

SILVER SLUMBER, Budd's famous Slumbercoach design, accommodates 40 passengers in 24 single rooms and 8 double rooms at economy fares. Each train carries two such cars.

SILVER GLADIOLA contains a mix of accommodations (6 roomettes, 4 double bedrooms, 6 sections) for American Royal and Blackhawk.

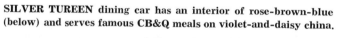

SILVER TUREEN dining car has an interior of rose-brown-blue (below) and serves famous CB&Q meals on violet-and-daisy china.

SILVER VERANDA parlor-observation lounge has reserved parlor chairs in forward section as well as a drawing room seating 5. Beneath dome is beautifully decorated Colorado Room cocktail lounge. At end of butt-ended car is the Zephyr's observation.

A train that was

QUIETLY filed away in library stacks are the yellowing pages of old *Official Railway Guides* which contain the timetables and equipment listings of exotic trains that long ago faded from memory.

Such a train was the *Soo-Pacific Train De-Luxe* which operated from St. Paul, Minn., to Spokane, Wash., and Portland, Ore., via the Soo Line and the Canadian Pacific. The July 1907 *Official Guide* contains a full page describing the "de luxe service between the Unsalted Seas and the Inland Empire":

"The trains used in this service will be composed of the finest of Day Coaches, Tourist Sleeping Cars, Dining Cars,

"the finest money can buy"

TWIN train signs decorated solarium-lounge of 1929 all-sleeping-car *Mountaineer*. Soo Line photo.

first-class Sleepers, Compartment Cars, and Buffet Library Observation Cars that money can buy, even in this age of luxurious rolling stock. Trains will be solidly vestibuled throughout and will be electric lighted."

Commencing July 1, 1907, the elegant new dark red equipment, fresh from the Dayton (O.) works of Barney & Smith was placed in service. The new train was routed via Soo Line to Portal, on the border of North Dakota and Assiniboia (now Saskatchewan); Canadian Pacific via the Crow's Nest Pass through the Kootenay to Kingsgate on the boundary; thence over the Spokane International

Railway with through cars to Portland routed via the Oregon Railway & Navigation Co. from Spokane. The 1912-mile trip was scheduled in 59½ hours. Passengers were also carried in other through cars for Vancouver and Seattle; the latter operated via the Seattle & International Railway, a subsidiary of the Northern Pacific.

Although the Spokane-Portland service was not an outstanding success, the Soo-Canadian Pacific operation to Vancouver and Seattle grew to become a renowned international train. Later, as the *Mountaineer*, it ranked among the great limiteds of North American railroading.

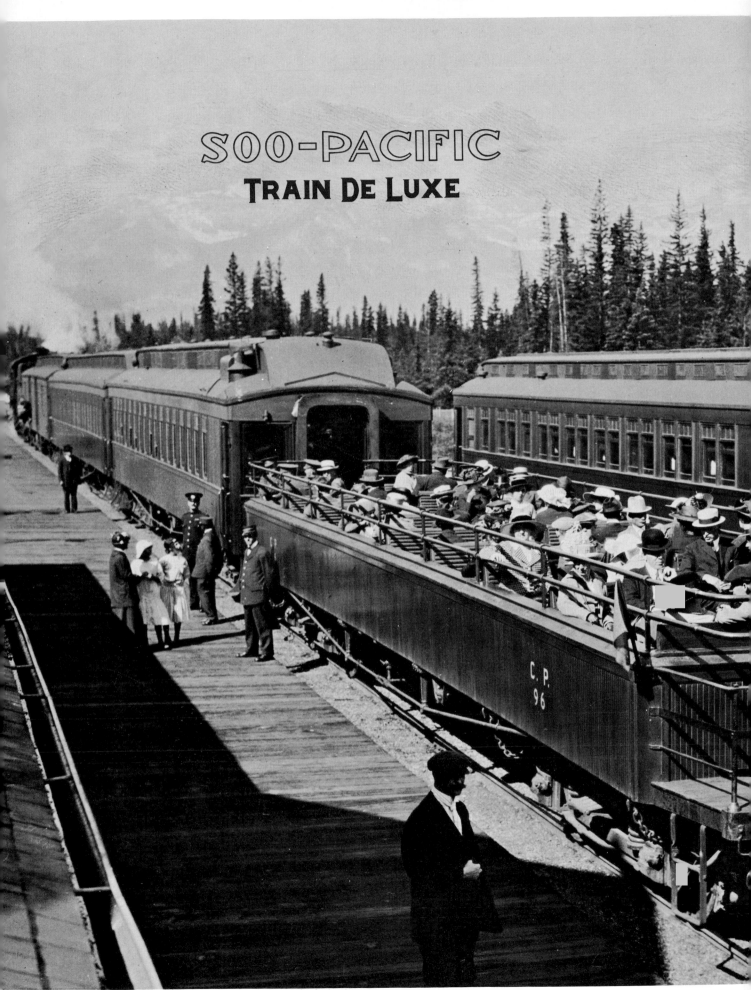

SOO-PACIFIC
TRAIN DE LUXE

OPEN observation car 96 fills up with passengers for daylight ride on CP through Canadian Rockies. Soo Line photo.

CAPACITY crowd on the observation.

The Soo-Pacific de luxe train

THE *Soo-Pacific* was a beautiful train inside and out. Equipment jointly furnished by the Soo Line and the CPR had been extravagantly built in an era of splendor. Interior trim was mahogany and Circassian walnut. Seats were upholstered in silk plush, with headrests covered by pure white linen anti-macassars embroidered with the railroad insigne. The railroad-owned Barney & Smith sleeping cars were slightly larger than standard Pullmans, and the *Soo-Pacific* advertised "higher and wider berths." Table linen, silverware, and the entire table service were produced expressly for the new dining cars. Smoking rooms were upholstered in black leather. Lavatory fittings were nickel and bronze. The train ended magnificently with a stunning observation car, complete with illuminated drumhead sign and brass-railed platform — a splendid place to view the breath-taking scenery along the "Canyon Route to the Inland Empire."

Unfortunately, the Soo-Spokane-Portland train was not successful, and with the coming of World War I to Canada in 1914, it was discontinued. Although another Soo Line-CPR *Express* continued the operation through the Canadian Rockies to Banff, Lake Louise, Seattle, and Vancouver, never again would the shining rails from Kingsgate to Spokane and Portland sing with the passage of the de luxe *Soo-Pacific* flyer.

SOO-PACIFIC of 1909 heavily promoted its Barney & Smith sleeping cars, which featured "higher and wider berths" than Pullmans.

EARLY Soo Line Pacific No. 703 was classified H-1; completed at the Schenectady Works of the American Locomotive Company in 1904. Lanky 4-6-2 rolled on 69-inch drivers, and weighed in at 195,000 pounds.

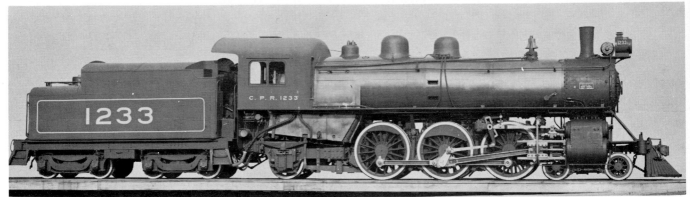

PACIFIC 1233, built by American Locomotive Company in 1906, exerted 30,400 pounds tractive effort, endured on CP into dieselization.

RAILWAY Post Office No. 557 was constructed by Barney & Smith Car Company of Dayton, O., for the Minneapolis, Saint Paul & Sault Sainte Marie (Soo Line). Also famous for its traction products, Barney & Smith was in business from 1849 to 1921.

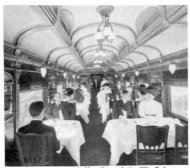

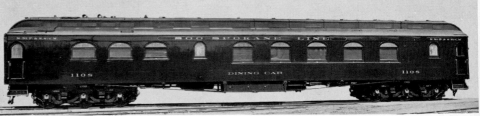

DINING CAR No. 1108, a Barney & Smith product, is lettered for "Soo-Spokane Line" in this rare builder's print. Inside (left) patrons found that "not a single comfort has been forgotten."

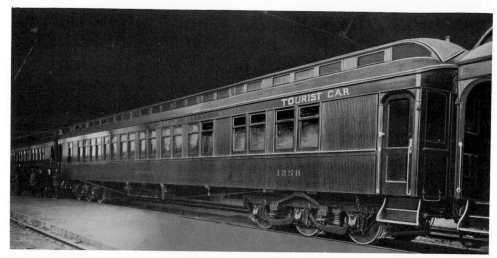

Soo Line.

TOURIST car No. 1258, a big wooden 12-wheeler, was photographed under a trainshed. Barney & Smith constructed this economy sleeper as well as similar cars for Canadian Pacific.

Barney & Smith, courtesy Soo Line.

SPOKANE, built by Barney & Smith for CP in May 1907, had 4 compartments, drawing room, buffet, lounge. Soo owned sister Curzon (above).

CP.

FERNIE, a sister of Curzon, was built by Barney & Smith in 1907 for Soo and assigned to Soo-Pacific. In 1926 car was rebuilt and repainted for use on Boston-Montreal Redwing service.

CP.

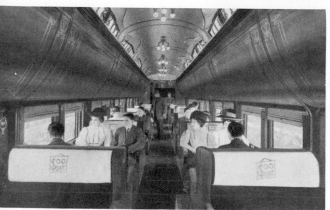

Collection of A. W. Johnson.

SOO-PACIFIC
TRAIN DE LUXE

"NO expense has been spared in making these sleepers perfect" — so read brochure illustrating Soo-Pacific's very large sleepers.

287

SOO-PACIFIC
TRAIN DE LUXE

CP.

TYPICAL of the classic train in Canadian Pacific's timetable of the 1920's was the Trans-Canada Limited, shown in Montreal.

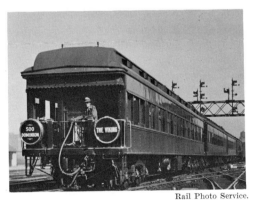

Rail Photo Service.

DUAL drumheads at C&NW station, Chicago.

The Mountaineer

TO SUPPLEMENT the year-around Pacific Coast service, the Soo Line and Canadian Pacific on June 10, 1923, inaugurated a new transcontinental train scheduled for summer-only operation from June until September. The new train, appropriately titled the *Mountaineer*, was routed from Chicago to Vancouver via the Twin Cities and the Canadian Rockies resorts at Banff and Lake Louise. Canadian Pacific *Princess* steamers for Victoria and Seattle connected with the train at Vancouver.

Except for the wooden observation cars and tourist sleepers built for the 1907 service, all of the consist was new heavyweight steel. The Soo Line equipment was built at the St. Charles (Mo.) plant of American Car & Foundry. CPR cars were erected in the company shops at Montreal. All were painted the familiar Soo dark red. The American and Canadian joint operation imparted a truly international flavor to the train.

The *Mountaineer* traveled with capacity loads during the prosperous years of the late 1920's. For the 1928 season it be-

came an all-sleeping-car operation and the brochure indicated in small italics that the train would handle neither "*extra nor special cars . . . nor coach passengers.*"

This restricted de luxe service proved very successful and was scheduled again in 1929 when it was newly equipped. Elegant solarium-lounge cars with men's and women's baths and valet and maid service were outshopped by Pullman together with the first Pullman-operated sleeping cars to run in regular service over the Canadian Pacific Railway.

After several profitable seasons, the devastating economic depression of the 1930's settled upon the land. It was decided not to run the *Mountaineer* during the 1932 season, and the *Soo-Dominion* continued service throughout that summer.

Starting in 1933 the Chicago & North Western operated the Soo-CPR cars between Chicago and St. Paul as part of the *Viking*, C&NW's predecessor of the famous *400*. The new three-road arrangement proved to be popular and was continued for many years. During the summer the train ran through from Chicago to Vancouver as the *Mountaineer*. In the winter it was known as the *Soo-Dominion* and made close connections at St. Paul with the *Viking* and later with the *400* for service to and from Chicago.

Through the years of peace and war (which came to Canada in 1939) the *Soo-Dominion* and the *Mountaineer* continued their regular year-around pattern. On August 28, 1949, the last through car from Chicago to Vancouver was operated. Henceforth no regular through car service was available south of St. Paul.

The *Mountaineer* departed from the Twin Cities on its westbound trip of August 23, 1960, for what was to be the last run of that great train. The following summer the St. Paul-Vancouver train was named *Soo-Dominion*.

The present summer-only service, via Winnipeg and the *Winnipeger* (Soo Line 9 and 10), was introduced on June 29, 1962. A new route to the North Pacific Coast, it features traditional Soo-Canadian Pacific comfort. Between the Manitoba capital and Vancouver the through sleeping cars are carried in the CPR's crack *Dominion*. Formerly one of the last lines of heavyweight Pullmans, it is now operated with streamlined cars equipped with modern bedrooms and roomettes.

West of Winnipeg the train contains splendid new Budd-

MOUNTAINEER bridges Des Plaines River near Chicago behind Soo Line Pacific 2722, its speed enhanced by air flow lines of artist.

SOO-DOMINION heads west through River Forest, Ill., under a plume of white behind Soo 4-6-2 2721 on a very cold November 21, 1932.

MORE vintage Soo Line action: Pacific 2709 heads an express at Forest Park, Ill., July 6, 1921, in a rare Johnson photograph.

The Mountaineer

built stainless-steel equipment. Famous Canadian Pacific meals are served in the elegant de luxe dining car which offers such delicacies as soupe aux pois, Saskatchewan turkey, prime Western beef, Winnipeg goldeyes, and Oka cheese — all prepared from exclusive Canadian recipes.

Glare-proof glass makes the Scenic Dome ideal for the daylight ride through the Canadian Rockies with their spectacular white peaks, beautiful lakes, foaming torrents, and pine forests. 1

289

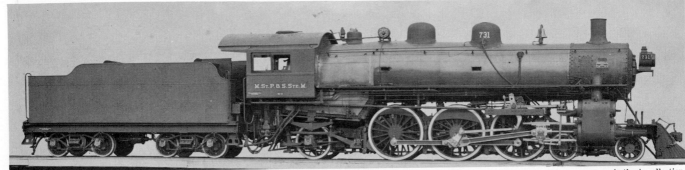

H-3 CLASS 4-6-2 No. 731 of the Soo was built by Alco, developed 33,200 pounds tractive effort, could set a gait on 75-inch drivers.

THE PACIFIC type was a favorite with Canadian Pacific until dieselization. Example 2322 was built by Montreal in July 1923.

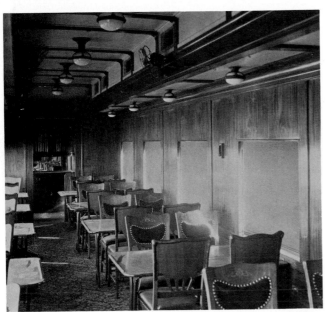

DINING CAR No. 1111 was built for Soo Line by American Car & Foundry's St. Charles (Mo.) plant in 1921; seated 48.

BEHIND diesels, combined Soo-Dominion and Winnipeger arrive in Minneapolis May 4, 1958, during a famous train's twilight years.

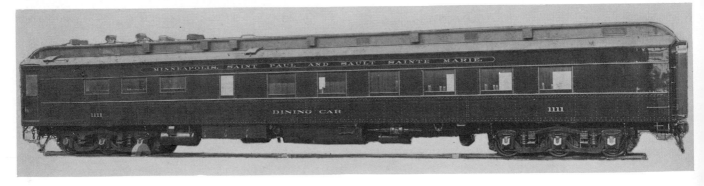

ACF.

NARAMATA, a handsome dark red Canadian Pacific sleeper built in 1921, contained 12 sections, 1 drawing room; weighed 184,000 pounds.

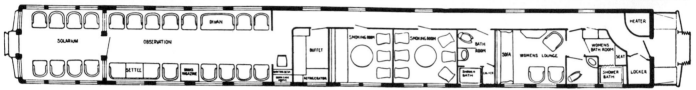

The Mountaineer

WISCONSIN RIVER, a Soo Line solarium-lounge built by Pullman in 1929, weighed 175,800 pounds. Sister cars were named Chippewa River, St. Croix River, and Mississippi River. Each contained women's lounge and bath, men's bath, smoking rooms, buffet and observation-lounge (below); offered valet service, maid service, library, magazines. They became U. S. Army hospital cars in 1943.

THE MOUNTAINEER

TABLE D'HOTE DINNERS

$1.00

CONSOMME, CLEAR   CREAM OF TOMATO
BAKED SPRING SALMON, CELERY SAUCE
COD STEAK, PARSLEY BUTTER
STEAK AND KIDNEY SAUTE   SAVORY OMELET
ASSORTED COLD MEATS
NEW POTATOES IN CREAM   NEW PEAS OR SPINACH

SALAD BOWL

DIPLOMAT PUDDING   CHERRY PIE
CANADIAN CHEDDAR CHEESE WITH CRACKERS
PINEAPPLE SUNDAE
ASSORTED BREADS   HOT CORN BREAD
TEA   COFFEE   MILK

$1.25

CELERY AND RADISHES OR GRAPEFRUIT COCKTAIL
CONSOMME, MACEDOINE   CREAM OF TOMATO
CHICKEN FRICASSEE   EGGS MEYERBEER
"RED BRAND" ROAST RIBS OF BEEF AU JUS
STEAMED NEW POTATOES
NEW BEANS OR NEW ASPARAGUS

SALAD BOWL

FRUIT JELLY   STRAWBERRY SHORTCAKE
CANADIAN CHEDDAR CHEESE WITH CRACKERS
PEACH MELBA
ASSORTED BREADS   HOT BISCUIT
TEA   COFFEE   MILK

I T will be a great aid to the service and avoid any possibility of mistakes, if passengers will kindly ask for meal order blanks, and upon them write their orders, because stewards and waiters are not allowed to serve any food without a meal check.

T. M. McKEOWN, Manager, Sleeping, Dining and Parlor Cars;
Restaurants and News Service, Montreal.

2 D.E. V-12

STAINLESS-STEEL and dome-equipped *Canadian* negotiates curves along the Bow River near Lake Louise, Alta. CP photo.

292

SOO-PACIFIC
TRAIN DE LUXE

THE ORIENTAL

No. 1.   **FIRST DIVISION**   No. 1.

ST. PAUL & PACIFIC R. R.

TIME CARD.

Into Effect July 2nd, 1862.

ST. ANTHONY AND MINNEAPOLIS TRAINS.

LEAVE.	A. M.	ARRIVE.	A. M.	LEAVE.	P. M.	ARRIVE.	P. M.
St. Paul	8:00	St. Anthony	8:45	St. Anthony	12:20	St. Paul	1:00
St Anthony	8:50	St. Paul	9:40	St. Paul	3:45	St. Anthony	4:30
St. Paul	11:30	St. Anthony	12:15	St. Anthony	4:35	St. Paul	5:20

Extra trains will meet all Steamboats for the accommodation of Passengers living in St. Anthony.

Special trains will be run on Sunday and Evenings by special arrangement.

No Engines allowed on the road except on order of the Superintendent or Master Mechanic.

Irregular Trains slow on curves, and look out for Section men.

In case of doubt, follow the safe course.

SIGNALS

1. A red flag by day—a red light by night, when swung upon the track; the absence of lights or flags at places where usually shown; and all signals given, are signals of danger. On perceiving either, the Engineer must bring the Train to a dead stop; nor shall he receive any information from any person as to the cause of the signal, until the Train is brought to a stand.

2. A white flag or a white light indicates that the track is all right for Trains to pass.

3. One sound of the whistle is signal to apply brakes. Two sounds of the whistle is signal to let go the brakes. Three sounds of the whistle is signal to back the Train. Four sounds of the whistle is signal for changing a switch. Five or more rapid sounds of the whistle is the signal for the flag or signal-men who have been sent out to guard train, to come in. A long continued sound of the whistle is signal for approaching a Station or Road Crossing.

4. One Stroke of the bell signifies stop. Two strokes of the bell—go ahead. Three strokes—back.

5. A lantern swung across the track is a signal for stopping. Raised and lowered perpendicularly—the signal for the Train to go ahead. Swung in a circle—for the Train to back.

6. One large white head-light on the front of the Engine, and a red light on the rear of the Train, must always be exhibited by all regular trains upon the road after dark.

7. A red flag by day or a red light by night, when placed upon the front of an Engine, indicates that the Engine or Train is to be followed by another, which is to be considered a part of the signal Train; and no Train will move out of sidings until the Train has passed.

8. Signal Cords shall be used on all Passenger Trains, and shall extend from the rear car to the whistle or signal bell of the engine

TIMETABLE No. 1 of the St. Paul & Pacific. Courtesy G N.

Pride of the Empire Builder

I JAMES JEROME HILL was secure in his role as an empire builder when he died in 1916. The story of his life is the story of the development of the American and the Canadian Northwest. The idol of Jim Hill's boyhood was Marco Polo, and the dream of this Ontario-born lad was to be a sea captain in Oriental commerce. Pursuing that dream, he arrived, at the age of 18, in the frontier river town of St. Paul, en route to the Canadian West Coast. Here he was stranded by transportation difficulties, an event which not only altered his immediate plans but, paradoxically, shaped transportation history. The year was 1856, and St. Paul was to be Jim Hill's home for the remainder of his life.

Twenty-two years later Hill, by that time a successful young businessman, embarked on the mainstream of his transportation career. With a group of friends, including Norman Kittson of St. Paul, Donald Smith of the Canadian Hudson's Bay Company, and George Stephen who was president of the Bank of Montreal, he acquired control of the struggling St. Paul & Pacific Railroad in 1878. Under Hill's leadership the small railroad was extended northward through the rich Red River Valley and across the border to Winnipeg, Man.

In 1879 the St. Paul & Pacific became the St. Paul, Minneapolis & Manitoba, and Hill, his eye still on the Orient,

LIMITED

ORIENTAL LIMITED of 1912 bridges Mississippi between St. Paul and Minneapolis on famous Stone Arch Bridge. GN photo.

announced his intention to build his railroad to Puget Sound. Without benefit of subsidy, the Manitoba was pushed westward along the banks of 10 great rivers, across the Great Plains of Minnesota and North Dakota, through the majestic Montana and Idaho Rockies, and thence over the Cascade Mountains to Seattle, Wash. The last spike was driven high in the Cascades on January 6, 1893. Meanwhile, in 1890, the St. Paul, Minneapolis & Manitoba had become the Great Northern Railway.

The nation's northernmost railway, serving a sparsely populated territory and labeled "Hill's Folly" by the disbelievers, was an immediate success. Every component of the new Great Northern was first rate. The longest tangents, easiest curves, heaviest rail, and finest equipment — Jim Hill would tolerate nothing less. Great Northern's advertising proudly proclaimed: "To have opened a new way across America is in itself a great achievement and it becomes doubly so when it is coupled with the fact that that way is the shortest, the easiest, the most interesting route across the continent. This is the case of the youngest and already one of the greatest transcontinental lines, the Great Northern Railway."

ORIENTAL LIMITED

BALDWIN Pacific 1443 escorts *Oriental Limited* along Puget Sound in 1909. GN photo.

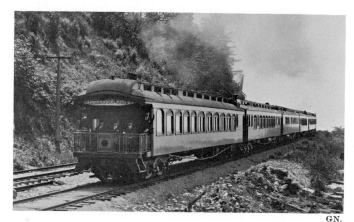

GN.

SCARLET tailgate sign on the Oriental in 1909 publicity pose.

The first Oriental

It is no exaggeration to state that the Oriental Limited is the fulfillment of inventive genius in train equipment. Few people appreciate the necessary thought that is embodied, the care bestowed, and the complicated and smoothly working mechanism which makes the whole a thing of beauty and perfection in the art of transportation. — Oriental Limited brochure, 1909.

JIM HILL'S boyhood dreams of the Orient were realized on January 23, 1905. On that date the fine new Great Northern steamship *Minnesota*, a 20,000-ton liner, commenced her maiden voyage from Seattle to Japan and China. Henceforth it was possible to travel in Great Northern luxury between St. Paul and the Far East.

In an era when the traveling public was presented almost daily with announcements of new trains, the Great Northern introduced its de luxe transcontinental, the *Oriental Limited*, trains 1 and 2, in December 1905. Scheduled time from St. Paul to Seattle was 58 hours for the 1829 miles.*

One of the tangible remainders of the first *Oriental Limited* is an elaborate brochure prepared for the Seattle World's Fair of 1909. This oversize booklet, an outstanding example of the printer's art, describes in detail and illustrates with magnificent colored lithographs the equipment used in the train which became a through operation Chicago to Seattle, 2259 miles, on May 23, 1909, via the Burlington on a 72-hour schedule.

Luxurious in appointment, well-nigh perfect in mechanical construction, complete in every detail from the head-light to the rear-end lantern, this train fulfills every requirement. The operating force will at once appeal to the passenger, for the selection of the attachés from conductor to porter is made with a view to their adaptability. In all, the train is a triumph of car architecture.

*On November 1, 1911, a special Great Northern train of eight cars loaded with silk made a record run from Seattle to St. Paul in 45 hours 16 minutes en route to New York City.

Author's collection.

BELPAIRE-BOILERED Pacific 1463 heads the Oriental Limited.

FANCY railroad herald adorns tank of Pacific 1461, one of 25 H4-class engines constructed by Lima Locomotive Works in 1914.

COACH No. 3710, built by American Car & Foundry in 1913, seated 76 passengers in surroundings paneled in birch and mahogany woods.

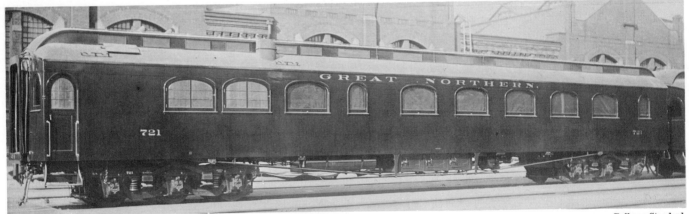

DINING CAR 721, built by Pullman in 1905, reproduced atmosphere of an English pub (left) with overhead beams, leather-covered chairs, and — to quote the publicists — "enclosed cathedral globes."

ORIENTAL LIMITED

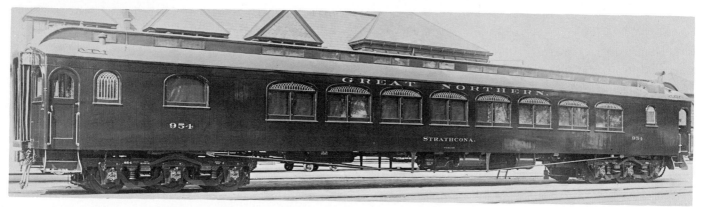

All car photos, Pullman-Standard.

STRATHCONA, a 16-section, 82-foot car built by Pullman in 1905, was — like all GN sleepers — railroad owned and operated until 1922.

TUMWATER contained 12 sections, a drawing room, and a smoking room; was built by Pullman in 1906. Barney & Smith delivered 30 identical cars in 1910 which bore such Oriental names as Tokio, Fujiyama, Yokohama, Manila, not to mention Foochou!

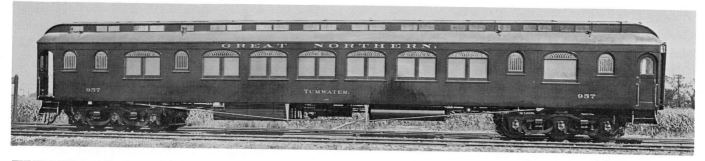

COMPARTMENT-observation-library car No. 760 (built by Pullman in 1905) contained 4 compartments, 1 drawing room, buffet and card room, library and lounge. Rooms (below right) were fitted in mahogany, coco, tonkin, vermilion; upholstered in olive, rose, green. Vacuum cleaning (below left) was widely advertised extra. The car was sold to Alaska Railroad in 1923.

Interior scenes, GN.

NEW ORIENTAL LIMITED was displayed at Chicago Union Station behind GN's own 4-8-2 2527 in 1924. A. W. Johnson photo.

IN August 1928 *Oriental Limited* inched through downtown La Crosse, Wis., on the Burlington. A. W. Johnson photo.

ORIENTAL was trailed by steel-sheathed observation about 1922.

ORIENTAL LIMITED

Collection of Everett L. DeGolyer Jr.
"SILK EXPRESS" of Great Northern with 4-8-2 2517 up front.

Beyond the reach of princes

One contemplating travel between Chicago, St. Paul, Minneapolis, Glacier National Park, Spokane, Seattle, Tacoma, and Portland may confidently look forward to the journey on the *New Oriental Limited*. He will be surrounded while aboard the train, by comforts and luxuries which, a few decades ago, were beyond the reach of princes. — *Great Northern brochure*, 1924.

FROM May 26, 1918, through May 30, 1920, the *Oriental* operated only between St. Paul and the Pacific Coast by Government order during the wartime period of Federal control of the railroads.

With the ending of Government operation and return of control to St. Paul, plans were made to refurbish the *Oriental*. Pullman operation of sleeping cars on the *Oriental* was instituted in 1922. It proved so successful that an agreement was signed by which Pullman furnished new equipment for the entire train.

June 1, 1924, was the initiation date for the new 68-hour service. Seven sets of dark green cars were turned out of the Pullman shops and were delivered to the Burlington. Special features of the *New Oriental* included a barber and valet shop with adjacent bath. Barbers were recruited from the best metropolitan shops. A tastefully decorated women's lounge and bath with ladies' maid-manicurist were located in the observation car. Maids on the *Oriental* were given a thorough training course by the Pullman Company before they entered regular train service.

Dinner hour was announced by the traditional melodious chimes. Fresh cut flowers from Great Northern gardens and greenhouses decorated each table. Food specialties included berries and vegetables from the Northwest, prize-winning Minnesota butter, and North Dakota beef. Breakfast featured special GN Health Griddle Cakes. Every afternoon at 4, tea was served in the observation lounge by a waiter from the diner. Close behind followed the maid with platters of dainty cakes.

301

WASHINGTON, 1924 Pullman-built dining car No. 7006, had gray-green interior; was named (as were all diners) for Northwest states.

ORIENTAL LIMITED

TACOMA, a 12-section, 1-drawing-room Pullman of traditional internal configuration, was built in 1924; possessed an interior "painted the color of a beech grove in spring": gray-green with jewel-like designs in black and gold, vermilion and blue.

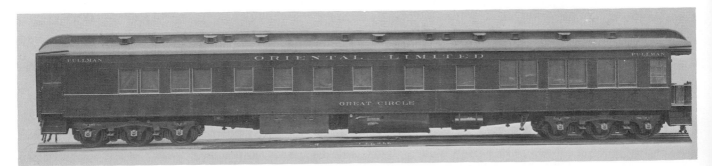

GREAT CIRCLE, one of seven identical cars with prefix "Great," had 2 compartments, a drawing room, lounge facilities, and a deeply recessed platform. Built in 1924, Great Circle had new high lounge windows for better viewing of mountain terrain.

302

PRIMARY reason for Great Northern's purchase of 28 P2-class 4-8-2's from Baldwin in 1923 was to handle the Oriental Limited.

TOURIST CAR No. 1728 was unique. Originally a GN-owned 12-section, 1-drawing-room car, it was rebuilt in 1924 with barbershop and bath located in former men's room and its drawing room rebuilt for use as a men's room. Twelve sections were retained.

CHICKEN PIE specialty sold for just 75 cents.

ALSO for 75 cents: baked ham with GN's own sauce.

EMPIRE BUILDER bridging Mississippi in 1929 was headed by 4-8-2 No. 2517 named Marathon for feat of completing a fast 3600-mile round trip between Seattle and St. Paul in 1925 without requiring mechanical attention at any time while en route.

WESTBOUND Builder enters Cascade Tunnel.

EMPIRE BUILDER on 2100-foot Stone Arch Bridge built in 1883 — the only structure on Great Northern on which James J. Hill allowed his name to be inscribed.

304

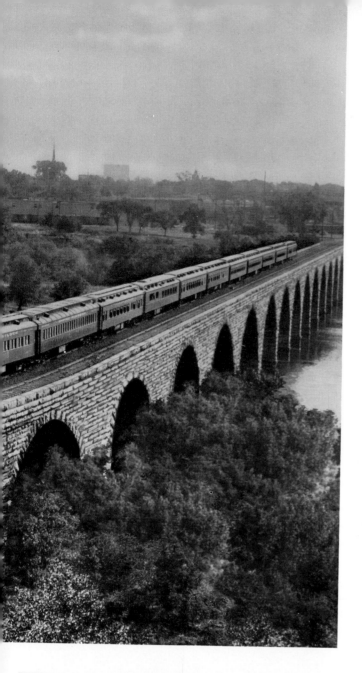

EMPIRE BUILDER

The Empire Builder

> Now, as an ambassador of good will, the *Empire Builder* represents the fruition of years of constructive study of railroading in the Northwest. — *The Empire Builder*, Great Northern brochure, 1929.

BECAUSE of his role in helping transform the vast fertile Northwest into a rich productive country, James J. Hill became known as the "Empire Builder." When Great Northern's directors authorized the refurbishing of the road's premier train in 1929, they agreed that Nos. 1 and 2 should be renamed *Empire Builder* to pay tribute to the memory and achievements of the Great Northern founder.

The new train — with each car bearing the name *Empire Builder* — began operating on June 10, 1929, between Chicago and Tacoma. Schedule was 63 hours westbound, 61½ hours eastbound. The old *Oriental Limited*, renumbered 3 and 4, continued in service until March 29, 1931, when the name was dropped.

Most elegant car in the new *Empire Builder* consist was the Pullman observation-lounge. Seven identical cars — each named for a builder of the Great Northern — contained lounging rooms, buffet, barbershop, and shower baths. Décor throughout was characteristically Tudor with carved walnut, old gold, candelabrum side lights, and parchment shaded lamps. Special features included radio, stock market reports, and 4 o'clock tea "served daily as an expression of courtesy and hospitality by the dining car steward." One major innovation was particularly pointed out in the train's descriptive brochure: "A sunroom furnished with gayly upholstered wicker chairs replaces the conventional observation platform and sets a new note in travel appointment."

The Cascade Tunnel — 7.79 miles long between Berne and Scenic in the state of Washington — is described by Great Northern as a "straight-as-a-rifle bore." When built it was the longest tunnel in the Western Hemisphere and was regarded as an engineering marvel. The new tunnel replaced 43 miles of tortuous mountain railway with 34 miles of easier electrified line. Maximum elevation was reduced from 3383 to 2881 feet above sea level. The 25-million-dollar undertaking was completed in a record time of three years. An impressive ceremony on January 12, 1929, at the tunnel opening included President-elect Herbert Hoover speaking from Washington over one of the first radio networks. Completion of the important project made possible the inauguration of the new *Empire Builder*.

Z1-CLASS ELECTRIC B5004, built by Baldwin-Westinghouse for Cascade Division service, is tied in ahead of train's 4-8-2.

305

RAILWAY POST OFFICE and baggage No. 60, 70-footer of all-steel construction, was outshopped in 1918 by American Car & Foundry.

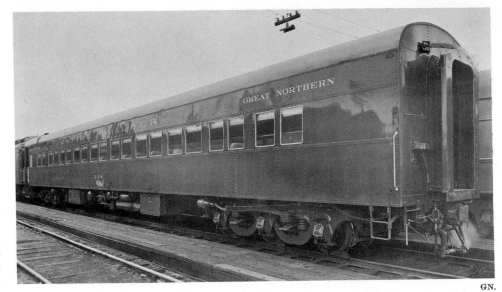

COACH NO. 938, too smoothly contoured to be termed conventional yet not quite streamlined either, was built by Pullman-Standard in 1937 — a decade before Great Northern fully embraced modernism. Car seated 58; contained a ladies' lounge as well as a smoker for the men.

COACH NO. 955 was delivered by Barney & Smith in 1914, was 81 feet long, rode on 12 wheels, and seated 78 on its walkover seats.

EMPIRE BUILDER

JOHN MILLER was one of six 14-section sleepers built in 1930; all were rebuilt in 1935 with 6 sections, 6 double bedrooms.

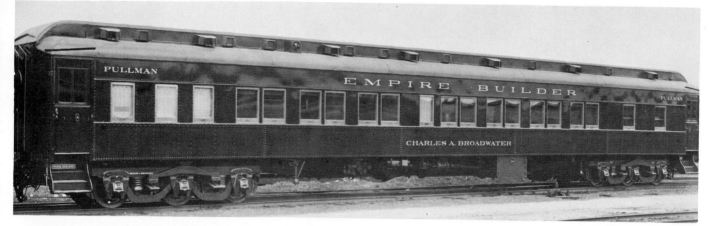

CHARLES A. BROADWATER was built in 1929; had 8 sections, 2 compartments, 1 drawing room. Rooms could be arranged en suite.

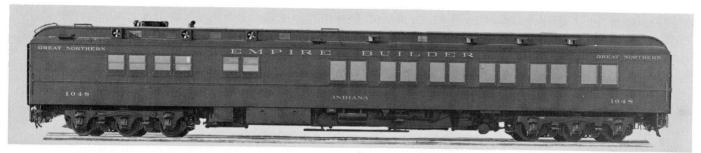

INDIANA, a 36-seat diner delivered in 1929, was staffed by a steward, six waiters, a chef and two assistants. Menu readers (below) could find a steak dinner with all the trimmings for $1.25.

JAMES J. HILL was one of seven solarium-observation-lounge cars built by Pullman in 1929 and named for GN builders. The lady standing in the aisle (above) is perusing a copy of Redbook.

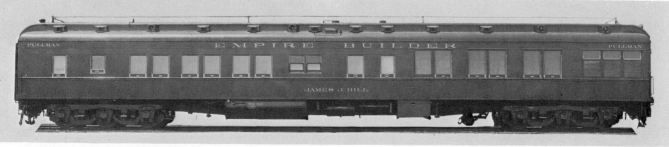

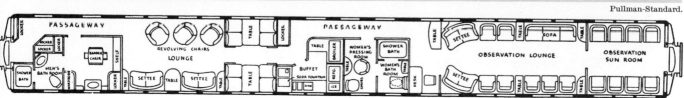

THE 1947 edition of the Empire Builder
bores out of morning fog in a GN photo.

GN.

TRANSITION from conventional to streamlined dress for the Empire Builder began in 1942 when 4050 h.p. Electro-Motive diesel gave an assist to 4-8-4 road engine over the Continental Divide.

EMPIRE BUILDER

Streamlined Empire Builders

FIVE new streamlined *Empire Builders*, built at a cost of 7 million dollars, entered service on February 23, 1947. These trains were the first to be ordered by any railroad for postwar delivery (the contract had been awarded to Pullman-Standard on November 4, 1943, during the height of World War II). The sleeping cars were the first to be built in the nation since passenger-car construction had been halted by war in 1943. Four of the consists were owned by the Great Northern; the fifth belonged to the Burlington Lines. The new trains inaugurated the first 45-hour schedule between Chicago and the Pacific Northwest, trimming 13½ hours from the timecard.

The entire train was thoughtfully created. Engineers, designers, artists, and historians worked closely with Great Northern operating personnel. "With the end of the war, the world is coming out of uniform," said Ralph Haman, engineer of color and design for Pullman-Standard. "We are ready for gaiety and beauty, and the new *Empire Builder* will have these qualities." Exterior coloring consisted of alternating bands of green and orange separated by narrow stripes of gold. Interior design featured the blues and greens of the lakes of Glacier Park combined with tans and greens of the Cascade and Rocky mountains. The colorful motif of the Blackfoot Indians was echoed throughout the cars. Murals by Winold Reiss and reproductions of water colors by cowboy-artist Charlie Russell graced the bulkheads.

When the streamlined *Empire Builder* went into service the *Oriental Limited* name was revived and was applied to the heavyweight fleet which formerly had been the *Empire Builder*. These heavyweight trains continued in service between Chicago-Seattle-Portland as Nos. 3 and 4.

On June 3, 1951, Great Northern initiated five new *Mid-Century Empire Builder* trains. The luxury fleet cost 12 million

dollars exclusive of locomotives and comprised five identical 15-car streamliners similar in design and décor to the 1947 model. Included in each 1951 consist was the Ranch Car, a unique coffee shop serving delicious and inexpensive meals. The entire car was decorated in authentic Western style, patterned after a rustic ranch house with oakboard walls, branding irons, and pinto leather seats.

Concurrent with the inauguration of the *Mid-Century Empire Builder*, a new train named the *Western Star* joined the GN streamliner galaxy. The *Western Star* fleet was made up of the five original *Empire Builder* streamliners plus one additional all-new train, making a total of six consists. Introduction of the *Western Star* as trains 3 and 4 brought retirement of the *Oriental Limited* name.

The addition of 22 completely new dome cars in 1955 marked the third re-equipping of the postwar streamliner. Six-full-length Great Dome lounge cars and 16 individual dome coaches represented an investment of 6 million dollars in passenger progress on the Great Northern; Burlington; and Spokane, Portland & Seattle.

Empire Builder is a name which has become synonymous with excellence in transportation throughout America. Operating as Nos. 31 and 32*, it offers de luxe equipment, polite and competent employees, and good food. John Budd, Great Northern president, once stated: "The world judges the railways by their passenger services. If this is the window through which we are viewed, we must wash it and shine it, or else cover it up with a dark shade." Needless to mention, the *Empire Builder* is a clean-window train. ⚟

*A typical heavy summer run consist of the *Empire Builder*, No. 32, eastbound out of Spokane, Wash., July 4, 1963, was: diesels 366-A, 370-B, 350-B, 351-C; 37 — R.P.O.; 276 — storage-mail car; 1200 — dormitory car; 1212 — flat top coach; 1330, 1320 — dome coaches; *Running Crane Lake*, 1241 — ranch car; 1224, 1221 — flat top coaches; 1331 — dome coach; *Hart Pass*, 1376 — sleeper; *Suiattle Pass*, 1380 — sleeper; *Lake Wenatchee*, 1251 — diner; *Prairie View*, 1394 — dome lounge; *Skykomish River*, 1260 — sleeper; *Park Creek Pass*, 1374 — sleeper; *Corral Coulee*, 1192 — sleeper-lounge.

SIX THOUSAND horsepower rolls the 1955 edition of the Empire Builder over Marias Pass under a backdrop of Montana Rockies.

IN western Montana the 1947 edition of the Empire Builder is forwarded by a pair of Electro-Motive 2000 h.p. E7-model cab units.

APPEKUNNY MOUNTAIN seats 36, contains 2 roomettes, and features high-window lounge with beverage service. ACF constructed it in 1951.

CORRAL COULEE is one of six observations (with drawing room and 2 double bedrooms) built by Pullman-Standard. After purchase of "Great Domes" in 1955, 6 roomettes were added to each Coulee-series car, replacing Mountain-series (above).

310

EMPIRE BUILDER

MID-CENTURY Empire Builder rides along the Wenatchee River near Wenatchee, Wash., behind 5000 h.p. GE-built electric 5018. GN eliminated its electrified mountain zone in 1956.

DOME coach No. 1322 is a Budd stainless-steel car, seats 46 on its lower level (below right) and 24 upstairs (below left).

POPLAR RIVER contains 1 compartment, 3 double bedrooms, 7 duplex roomettes, 4 open sections; carries train name on its letterboard.

EMPIRE BUILDER

MOUNT ST. HELENS, SP&S-owned sleeping-club-lounge car, contains 6 roomettes, 3 double bedrooms, and 25 lounge seats; operates on-line only between Portland, Ore., and Spokane, Wash.

CROSSLEY LAKE, unique "Ranch Car" built by ACF, contains coffee shop-lounge (below) in Western decor. "G Bar N" brand is officially registered with the Montana Livestock Association.

LAKE OF THE ISLES, ACF-built 36-seat dining car, features beautiful carved-glass partitions (above), 2- and 4-place tables.

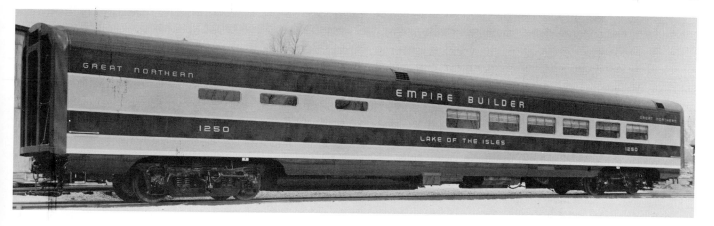

GLACIER VIEW, full-length Great Dome lounge built by Budd, rides on 12 wheels, is 85 feet long, cost $325,000, weighs 94 tons, features beverage lounge below and seats 75 upstairs.

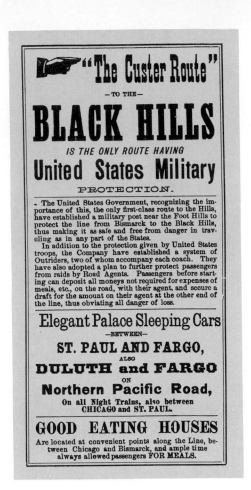

North Coast Limited

A venerable name provides the finest in service

1 THE story of the Northern Pacific, the first of the northern transcontinentals, is the story of the American Northwest. Rich in romance and adventure, it is the tale of the opening and development of a vast wilderness stretching from Lake Superior to the Columbia River and Puget Sound.

On July 2, 1864, President Abraham Lincoln signed the Act of Congress which created the Northern Pacific. The road was to be built from Carlton, Minn., near Duluth, westward nearly 2000 miles to the Pacific Coast by way of the valleys of the Yellowstone and Columbia rivers, following closely the explorations of the Lewis and Clark Expedition of 1804. Of the new railroad Gen. William T. Sherman once said, "The Northern Pacific must be built, both as an economic and military necessity. The West can never be settled, nor protected, without the railroad."

NORTH COAST LIMITED enters Rocky Canyon east of Bozeman, Mont., circa 1925.

314

LAST spike is driven at Gold Creek, Mont., in 1883. NP photo.

In a rugged country filled with unfriendly Indians and road agents, protecting the railroad was a full-time job for the U. S. Army. The NP timetable for 1879 prominently advertised that this was the "only route having United States Military protection."

The railroad survived the Great Panic of 1873 and the failure of Jay Cooke & Company, the railroad's bankers; and construction progressed. Fifteen thousand Chinese laborers and 10,000 American workers pressed forward from opposite ends of the line until the last spike was driven on September 8, 1883, at Gold Creek, Mont., in an extravagant ceremony attended by 3000 persons, including Ulysses S. Grant; Joseph Pulitzer; and Henry Villard, the Northern Pacific's colorful president.

Within seven years of the completion of the road, the entire tier of territories from the Dakotas to Washington had sufficient population to join the Union as states. The growth and prosperity of the Northwest was reflected by the Northern Pacific. Always a leader in progressive railroading, NP was the first road to offer sleeping and dining cars to the Pacific Northwest. With the great increase in traffic at the end of the 19th century the company decided to offer a de luxe service. Since its inauguration in 1900, the *North Coast Limited* — one of the oldest named trains in the land — has consistently ranked among the finest trains in North America.

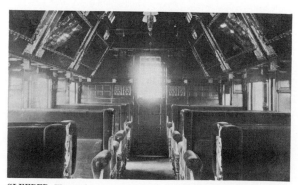

SLEEPER *Wynooche* was constructed by Barney & Smith in 1888.

Northern Pacific.

315

NORTH COAST LIMITED

The first North Coast—a notable train

ON April 29, 1900, trains 1 and 2, the *North Coast Limited*, made the inaugural run between St. Paul and Seattle. Scheduled time was 62 hours 30 minutes. This new train, the pride of the Northern Pacific, became the talk of the West. Ten sets of eight cars each were required to complete the line. The aggregate represented an investment of $800,000. For this princely sum the Pullman Company furnished equipment containing features never before seen in the Northwest except in private cars.

Each train, pulled by a Schenectady Ten-Wheeler, contained a mail car; one 70-foot combined dynamo and baggage car (complete with electrician to tend the train's 300 Mazda lamps); combined second-class coach and smoking car; first-class coach; 16-section tourist sleeper; through dining car; 12-section, 1-drawing-room sleeper; and observation car.

The observation car was devoted exclusively to purposes of lounging and recreation, one of the very first cars of this type to be built. With justifiable pride, it was widely advertised by the Northern Pacific:

> The crowning feature of this train is the Observation Car. By common consent it outranks anything of the sort in the entire country. It is the notable car of a notable train. The first 40 feet of the car contain a gentlemen's toilet room; two smoking and card rooms each with six wicker chairs; buffet; barber shop; bath room; and a ladies' toilet room, all opening on a side corridor. Then follows a space containing a library of 140 volumes and the current magazines; a writing desk and *North Coast Limited* stationery free; two open-seated sections; and lastly the ladies' parlor and observation room. . . . The rear platform is 6½ x 9 feet in dimensions. It is surrounded by an ornamental brass railing and is partially enclosed by the extended sides of the car. At the rear of this car is attached a large trademark of the road which is electrically illuminated at night.*

*The Northern Pacific trademark depicts the monad, a mystic symbol of eternal life represented by darkness and light. It was devised in 1017 A.D. by Chinese scholar Chow Lien Ki to illustrate the philosophy established by Fuh Hi about 3000 B.C. This philosophy divides the entire universe into equal parts representing darkness and light, good and bad, male and female, and so on. In the author's research, this is the earliest mention (1900) of the once-famous tail sign.

THIS was NP's first timetable announcing *North Coast Limited*.

INAUGURAL run of North Coast Limited behind Schenectady Ten-Wheeler 271 is shown in NP photo taken in April 1900.

E5 Ten-Wheeler 300 (Schenectady 1893), renumbered from 620 in 1900, was among 4-6-0's that hauled first North Coast Limited.

R.P.O. 150, Pullman built in 1903, was 63 feet long. Note monad emblem of Northern Pacific Express Co., onetime NP banking operation.

TOURIST CAR 540 (Barney & Smith 1904) boasted storm windows, smoking room, kitchen, 16 sections upholstered in green leather.

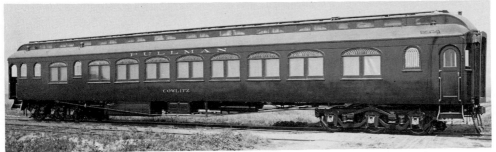

COWLITZ, built in 1905, had 14 sections, 1 drawing room; went to Mexico as Cruz Blanca in 1928.

SAHWA contained 12 sections, 1 drawing room. Until 1917, NP sleepers were owned jointly with Pullman, were maintained by latter.

Pullman-Standard.

Pullman-Standard.

DINING CAR 1034 seated 30, was 78 feet long. Food came from NP-owned farms, dairies, and bakeries. NP fruit cake won Grand Prix at 1889 Paris Exposition. Celebrated "Big Baked Potato" debuted in 1909.

North Coast Limited

OBSERVATION CAR 950 is depicted (bottom) in rare Barney & Smith builder view taken in 1900. Floor plan and interior photos show observation room, barbershop with adjoining tub bath.

Barney & Smith, courtesy NP.   Barney & Smith, courtesy NP.

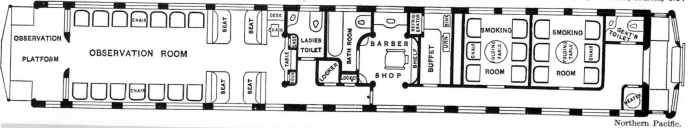

Northern Pacific.

Barney & Smith, courtesy NP

NORTH COAST LIMITED

The Northern Pacific route to California

WHEN the *North Coast Limited* was placed in service in 1900 it was intended as a summer-only service. However, the train's instantaneous popularity resulted in the decision in 1902 to operate it the year around.

For the first Seattle World's Fair, the Alaska-Yukon-Pacific Exposition of 1909, the *North Coast* was newly equipped by Pullman. Because of the heavy World's Fair traffic, the train carried only sleeping-car passengers. Through cars from Chicago to the Puget Sound which operated westbound in the new train No. 3, the *Northern Pacific Express* (via the Burlington Route), returned east in the *North Coast Limited*. The Portland sleeper, which in the past had been operated via Tacoma was now routed over the Spokane, Portland & Seattle from Spokane.

December 17, 1911, began an interesting chapter in the history of the *North Coast Limited*. Effective that date, the train departed from the magnificent new Chicago passenger terminal of the Chicago & North Western Railway and operated via the North Shore suburbs, Milwaukee, and the North Western's

new high-speed line via Wyeville, Wis., to the Twin Cities.

The year 1915 brought important developments. Completed in that year for the great Panama-Pacific International Exposition in San Francisco was the final link in the *North Coast Limited* route to California. The Great Northern Pacific Steamship Company (jointly owned with the Great Northern) placed in service the "Twin Palaces of the Pacific," *S.S. Northern Pa-*

COAL mounds high in tender of 1909 Baldwin Pacific 2162 behind crew who pose at head of seven-car *North Coast Limited*.

1707, on steel-sheathed train of '20's, was B&S car rebuilt by Pullman in 1922. NP photo.

TRADITIONAL pose by Charles Evans Hughes in 1916. NP photo.

cific and *S.S. Great Northern*. These twin beauties, America's fastest steamers, were 524 feet long and carried 800 passengers from Portland to San Francisco in 30 hours — 3 hours faster than the Southern Pacific's fastest express.

World War I changed many things. The *North Coast Limited* was no exception. The Great Northern Pacific's floating palaces became troop transports. The *S.S. Northern Pacific* caught fire at sea and was a total loss. (The *S.S. Great Northern* returned to the Pacific Coast in 1922 under new ownership.) Government control of the railroads ended the North Western routing into Chicago. Starting in 1918, the operation (which has continued until the present) from Chicago to the Twin Cities was via the Burlington's wonderfully scenic route along the banks of the Mississippi River, "where nature smiles 300 miles."

321

CLASS Q-5 Pacific 2233, 1920 product of Brooks Works, wheeled the North Coast Limited with 73-inch drivers in the 1920's.

STEEL R.P.O. 1401 was turned out by Pullman in 1915. It was 74 feet long and contained special racks for transporting fish.

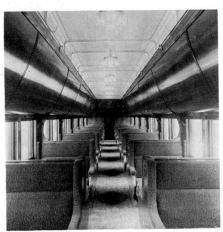

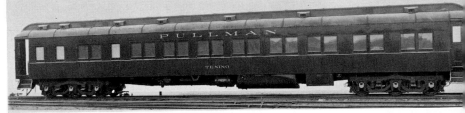

TENINO, 1915 Pullman sleeper of 12-1 arrangement, also had wide letterboard.

WILLAPA was one of first passenger cars built with wide letterboard and no upper sash, or so-called "Gothic." The sleeper (Pullman 1915) had 16 sections (left) and was one of last cars constructed under NP-Pullman joint ownership arrangement terminated in 1917. It was rebuilt by Pullman for Mexican service in 1934, was renamed Rio Mazatlan.

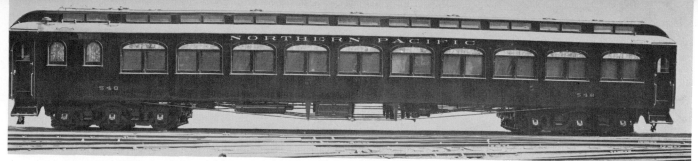

TOURIST CAR 548 came out of shops of Barney & Smith at Dayton, O., in 1906; contained 16 sections and a cooking range.

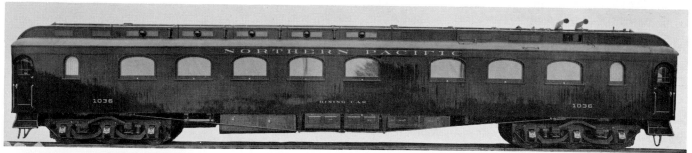

DINING CAR 1036'S unusual features included high windows, Old English interior (left) with beamed ceiling and lanterns. It was B&S-built in 1905.

North Coast Limited

DINING CAR 1674 had unique arch windows rarely seen in an all-steel car and seated 30 persons in mahogany interior (right) with recessed light fixtures.

BIG POWER: 2661 was one of eight 1938 Baldwin A-3 4-8-4's. NP photo.

NORTH COAST LIMITED

One of America's fine trains

> The crowning achievement of transportation service in the Northwest, today's *North Coast Limited* is termed by travelers everywhere, "One of America's Fine Trains." — *The North Coast Limited*, brochure, 1926.

NO ONE in the Northern Pacific offices at 5th and Jackson streets in St. Paul was surprised when Queen Marie of Romania selected one of the *North Coast*'s new observation cars as the royal "reception room" for her 1926 American tour. These 83-foot-long beauties ranked among the most splendid lounge cars ever built. They were the crowning touch to an admirable train.

On May 14, 1930, with much fanfare, new sets of sleeping, parlor, and dining cars were placed in service. Features of the new equipment included roller bearings, brass windows with sash cushioned in rubber, radios, separate bath and shower rooms for men and women, barber shop, soda fountain, and soft interiors of rose and green and walnut. New Pullman parlor cars with revolving chairs were operated between the Twin Cities and Mandan, N. Dak., and between Billings and Missoula, Mont.

PLUSH new roller-bearing-equipped North Coast is shown on exhibit at Chicago Union Station in this NP photograph of 1930.

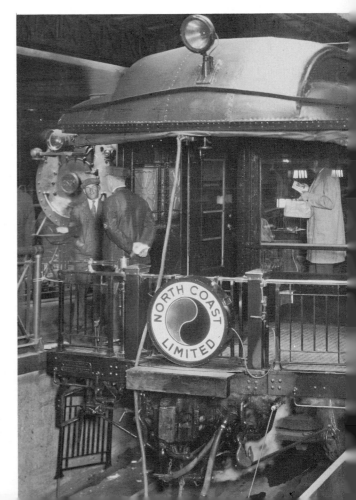

324

BABE RUTH, home run king of American baseball, was caught in classic observation-car pose. NP photo.

NP A-2 4-8-4 2657 came from Baldwin in 1934, was 104 feet long. Passengers could "inspect the iron horse" at certain long station stops. NP photo.

Pullman-Standard.

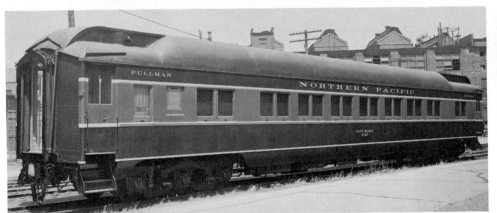

Pullman-Standard.

TOURIST SLEEPING CAR 3140 was remodeled in 1941 from 12-1 standard sleeper Phaeton. Tourist sleepers were especially popular during the depression years of 1930's and contained modestly furnished sections.

North Coast Limited

DINING CAR 1697 was home of "famously good" meals. Thirty-six-seat, 84-foot-long Pullman-Standard car constructed in 1930 provided simple elegance of upholstered chairs and parchment-shade lamps (left).

Northern Pacific.

Pullman-Standard.

326

CHIEF BAPTISTA was one of 35 Pullman sleepers named for Northwest Indian chiefs. In car: 10 sections, 1 compartment, 1 drawing room; walnut-grained sections (below).

OBSERVATION CAR 1710 had elegant lounge (above); was equipped with baths, barber, soda fountain, open platform with searchlight. It became a U. S. Army hospital car in '43.

NORTH COAST LIMITED

The Vista-Dome North Coast

ON November 28, 1946, the Northern Pacific board of directors authorized an expenditure of 9.8 million dollars for 6 Electro-Motive diesel locomotives and 78 lightweight streamlined passenger cars from Pullman-Standard, all for the *North Coast*. An additional 10 cars ordered by the Burlington and 2 cars ordered by the Spokane, Portland & Seattle completed the line. Delivery of this new equipment during 1947 and 1948 marked the start of a program which today continues to feature the most advanced techniques in passenger service.

The year 1952 marked the train's first two-nights-out schedule and the inauguration of the present striking two-tone green livery designed by Raymond Loewy.

Twenty dome coaches and sleeping cars, the first built to run in the Northwest, came from the Edward G. Budd Company and were placed in service in 1954. They permitted breathtaking views of the 1406 miles of rivers and 28 mountain ranges which are visible from the train between Chicago and the Puget Sound.

June 1955 marked the introduction of stewardess-nurses. Although similar service is available on other railroads, the *North Coast* alone in the Northwest carries registered nurses. These charming young ladies, all of whom have impressive hospital records, are a truly outstanding feature.

The famed *Lewis and Clark Traveller's Rest* buffet-lounge cars were also added in 1955. Named for the explorers' favorite campsite, and decorated in the pioneer spirit of the old Northwest, these beautifully unique cars serve popular-priced meals and beverages.

In 1958 six luxurious dining cars were purchased from the Budd Company at a cost of 2 million dollars. Most impressive feature of NP dining service is the friendly and courteous steward who personally assists in the ordering of each guest's meal.

In November 1959 the *North Coast* introduced the popular Slumbercoach to the Northwest. During a year marked by a general decline in passenger service, the Northern Pacific served notice that it was actively seeking long-haul passenger business.

These constant betterments have been happily reflected in NP passenger revenue which has climbed steadily since 1958. The *North Coast* in 1962 carried 297,982 passengers and earned $5,770,852 (excluding head-end and dining car revenue).*

Says NP President Robert S. Macfarlane:

It is my conviction that a substantial segment of the transportation market is made up of people who prefer to travel by train, if first-class service and equipment are provided. Through aggressive passenger advertising and personal calls, we actively solicit their business.

We have maintained our Vista-Dome *North Coast Limited* as one of the finest trains in the world, staffed by friendly, courteous personnel who provide the very best in service. As long as the traveling public continue to use our passenger service, we will maintain our high standards of comfort, safety, convenience, and service. **I**

*Car consist of the *North Coast Limited* between Chicago and Seattle-Portland on a selected day (July 10, 1962) during the Seattle World's Fair was: 403 — water baggage (Pullman-Standard) ; 425 — mail-dormitory (Pullman-Standard); *Loch Ness* — Slumbercoach (Budd) ; 551 — dome coach (Budd) ; 589 — day-nite coach (Pullman-Standard) ; 554 — dome coach (Budd) ; 571 — day coach (Pullman-Standard) ; 591 — day-nite coach (Pullman-Standard) ; 495 — *Lewis and Clark Traveller's Rest* (Pullman-Standard, rebuilt by Northern Pacific) ; 460 — dining car (Budd) ; 355 — Pullman 8-6-3-1 (Pullman-Standard) ; 311 — dome sleeper 4-4-4 (Budd) ; 369 — Pullman 8-6-3-1 (Pullman-Standard) ; 312 — dome sleeper 4-4-4 (Budd) ; 361 — Pullman (extra car) 8-6-3-1 (Pullman-Standard) ; 392 — observation-lounge 4-1 (Pullman-Standard).

CURVE is negotiated up Butte Mountain near Spire Rock, Mont. NP photo.

OMES provide a front-row seat for a Montana sunset a scene caught by an NP photographer during a North oast's journey from Chicago to the North Pacific Coast.

Northern Pacific.

NORTH COAST LIMITED

SIDETRACKED NP freight train cools its heels while dome cars of eastbound North Coast Limited pass near Bozeman, Mont.

Northern Pacific.

LOCH LEVEN, Budd Slumbercoach 326, contains 24 single rooms, 8 double rooms, each with full-length bed, toilet, washstand.

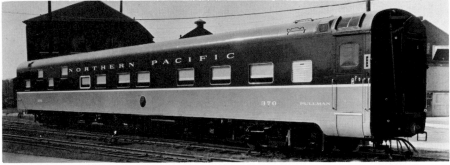

Pullman-Standard.

SLEEPING CAR 370 has 8 duplex roomettes, 6 roomettes, 4 double bedrooms; was delivered by **Pullman-Standard** in 1954. Butte (below), renumbered 358, has 8-6-3-1 plan.

Pullman-Standard.

OLD WEST decor in *Lewis and Clark Traveller's Rest.*

Budd Company.

DOME COACH 559 seats 46 on main level and 24 in dome; is wired for background music, p.a. system. Car is owned by **SP&S.**

330

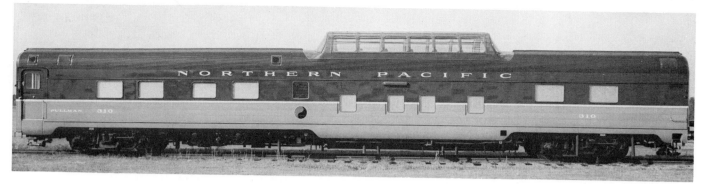

Budd Company.

SLEEPING CAR 310 is Budd-built dome car which provides 4 roomettes, 4 duplex single rooms (under dome), 4 double bedrooms.

Budd Company.

DINING CAR 463, one of six such Budd cars, seats 48 persons in luxuriously appointed room (below). Menu features Northwest specialties such as baked apples, fresh salmon, "Big Baked Potato," and Northern Pacific's famous individual lemon meringue pie.

Northern Pacific.

Northern Pacific.

Northern Pacific.

Pullman-Standard.

MONTANA CLUB came from Pullman in 1948, was renumbered 394. It has observation lounge, 4 double bedrooms, 1 compartment.

The International

Proving that "train travel can be fun"

GT 4-6-0 972 with *International Limited* at Beaconsfield, Que., in 1901 in photo from collection of Andrew Merrilees, distinguished Canadian rail enthusiast.

I   AS a result of the great increase in passenger traffic between Montreal, Toronto, and the United States at the turn of the century, the *International Limited* was inaugurated on May 25, 1900, by the Grand Trunk Railway. Since that date the *Limited* has been universally recognized as one of North America's foremost trains.

The history of the *International Limited*, presently operated by the Canadian National-Grand Trunk Western, is inseparably linked with the development of the provinces of Quebec and Ontario and their U. S. commerce.

The Grand Trunk Railway of Canada was incorporated by an Act of Parliament in 1852 to develop a railway system in Canada. The term "Grand Trunk" signified the line running from Quebec to western Ontario connecting the Atlantic ports of Montreal in the summer, and Portland, Me., in the winter, with the railroads in the central United States.

Immediately after its incorporation, the Grand Trunk proceeded with construction of a 5-foot 6-inch broad-gauge line between Montreal and Toronto, and this route was opened for traffic in 1856. In 1857 the first sleeping cars to operate in Canada were placed in service on this line.

Continuing westward, the road in 1859 reached the outskirts of Sarnia, Ont., where an international ferry service across the St. Clair River to Fort Gratiot (Port Huron) was established. The year 1859 also marked the opening of the famed 9155-foot-long Victoria Bridge across the St. Lawrence River at Montreal.

The broad-gauge system proved to be unsatisfactory, and with herculean effort was changed over to the standard 4-foot 8½-inch gauge almost overnight in 1874.

When the Michigan Central Railroad was acquired by the Vanderbilt interests in 1878, it became necessary for

Limited

GREAT WESTERN coach by Harlan & Hollingsworth.

the Grand Trunk to establish its own more reliable outlet into the United States. This was finally accomplished in 1880 after minor hostilities during which the Vanderbilts sought in vain to prevent the entrance into Chicago of the Canadian road's affiliate, the Chicago & Grand Trunk Railway (now the Grand Trunk Western).

The Grand Trunk's main rival in western Ontario was the Great Western Railway of Canada whose main line ran from Niagara Falls to Windsor, Ont., with a branch from Hamilton to Toronto. This rivalry was ended in August 1882 when the two roads were amalgamated. The Hamilton-Toronto "branch line" is now the most heavily traveled section of the Canadian National system, and over its rails each day the *International* operates as it travels the main highway of commerce between Canada and the United States.

From Montreal the train skirts the upper St. Lawrence, past Brockville, on to Kingston, Belleville, and Toronto. From Toronto the train continues to Hamilton, London, and Sarnia, then into the United States via Port Huron, across central Michigan and northern Indiana into Chicago.

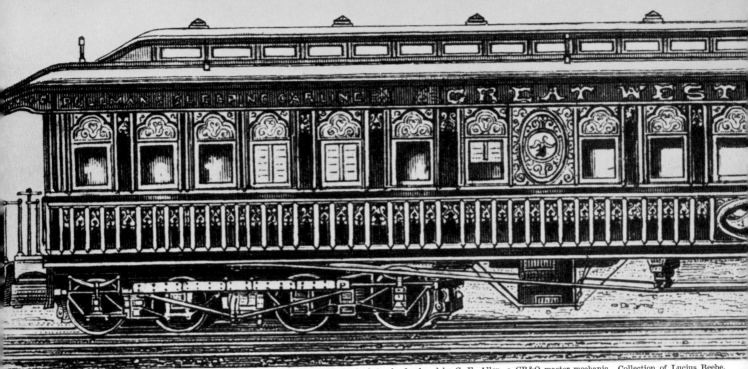

VICEROY, an early Canadian-built Pullman of 1867, was equipped with 8-wheel trucks developed by C. F. Allen, a CB&Q master mechanic. Collection of Lucius Beebe.

Canada's finest and fastest train

"THE 'limiteds' of the Grand Trunk Railway System, the great International Double Track Route, are the equal of any railway system in the world, and operate through a country filled with interest to the tourist, sportsman, and traveler," stated a brochure of the Grand Trunk Railway in 1913.

Effective May 25, 1900, GT train No. 1 leaving Montreal at 9 a.m. for Toronto was newly christened the *International Limited*. It carried a Pullman wide-vestibuled sleeping car, composite cafe-parlor car, and "Superior" new first-class coaches. Through tickets were sold from Portland, Me., and Boston to Chicago (via connecting train to Montreal). From Toronto the train was No. 15 bound for Chicago via Detroit, where an overnight Detroit-Chicago Pullman was added. The eastbound

The International Limited

Collection of Andrew Merrilees.

TYPICAL turn-of-the-century Grand Trunk consist is dusted by the smoke of black and burnished 4-6-0 No. 980.

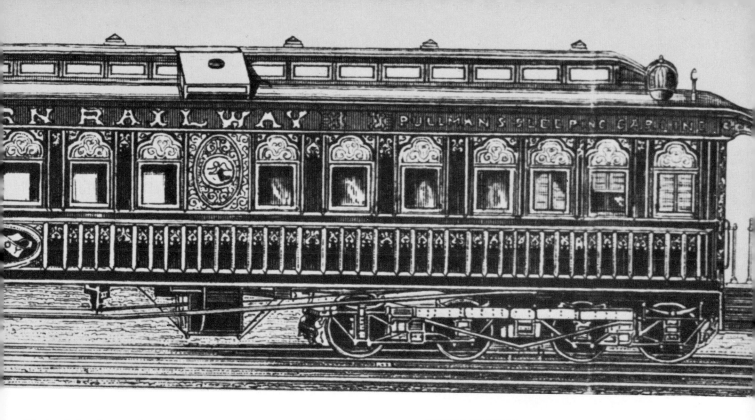

Montreal sleeping car for years returned on unnamed train No. 4 via Port Huron. During this era the *International* was a westbound-only operation. (Not until World War I was GT train No. 14 eastbound specifically termed *International Limited*.) During the 1904 Fair in St. Louis, the *International* carried through cars Montreal-St. Louis via IC at Harvey, Ill.

One of the features of the new train was the "improved Stone type" of electric lighting operated by belt-driven dynamo and storage batteries under the car. The new system was advertised as being the same as that installed on the royal train of King Edward VII. "In fact," the brochure continued, "the English Government has even gone so far as to use the power in the Government postal cars for melting the wax for sealing the mail bags en route, all without any appreciable effect on the motive power."

The Grand Trunk (and Great Western of Canada) ranked among George Pullman's earliest customers. Although the other great Canadian roads owned their own sleeping cars, the GT-GW lines operated Pullman equipment, some of which was built in Grand Trunk's Point St. Charles shops in Montreal.

The Sea-Side *and* White Mountains Special

OPERATED BY THE

GRAND TRUNK RAILWAY SYSTEM
and PULLMAN'S PALACE CAR CO.

A Pullman Vestibuled Train. ⚹ The Finest in the World.
Author's collection.

1896 announcement of International ancestor.

AT Battle Creek, 50-cent, 20-minute meal stop.

It is reported that George Pullman greatly admired the workmanship in the Canadian-built cars.

By 1870 Pullman sleeping cars were assigned to Grand Trunk lines between Montreal and Boston, Portland, Quebec, Detroit, and Springfield, Mass. The contracts with Pullman for operating several of these routes have remained in effect until the present time.

In 1896 the Pullman company and the Grand Trunk placed in service the *Sea-Side and White Mountains Special* between Chicago, Toronto, Montreal, and Portland, Me. This short-lived train de luxe featured a bathtub and an observation lounge car. Although it was not an outstanding success, the *Sea-Side and White Mountains Special* pointed the way for the *International Limited*.

TEN-WHEELER 1014 of the Grand Trunk, built by Schenectady in 1906, featured unusually long smokebox and generous cab proportions.

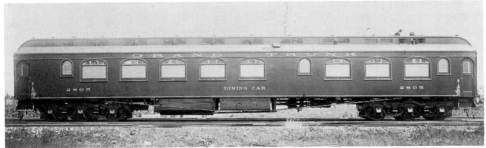

COACH No. 2203 was built by Pullman in 1908, possessed arch windows and an interior finished in quartered oak, featured "a large and comfortable smoking room . . . where lovers of the fragrant weed can enjoy their smoke with luxurious ease and comfort." Seldom was an invitation to light up delivered with more finesse to railroad travelers, aboard coaches or Pullmans.

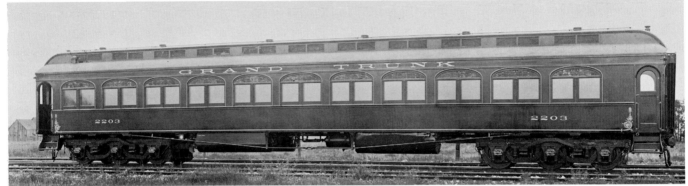

DINING CAR No. 2805 was 70 feet 7 inches long, seated 30, was delivered by Pullman in 1904, became Canadian National 1283, and was steel sheathed in 1928. The interior (right) was finished in African and Mexican mahogany with green-tinted ceiling. Tea was served here.

CAFE PARLOR No. 2609 was also built by Pullman in 1904, was 73 feet long, and was fitted with Krupp steel-tired wheels. Interior (right) was finished in African mahogany with inlaid and marquetry design, trimmings of statuary bronze; two-tone green carpeting and hassocks.

SABARA cost $16,714 and was one of five 12-section, 1-drawing-room sleepers built by Pullman in 1891 for Grand Trunk service. Each of the cars was lettered "Grand Trunk Route" and "Chicago and Boston." In these early years Pullman cars operating over the Grand Trunk were owned by the Pullman Company but maintained by the railroad under an agreement dating to 1867.

The International Limited

ORNATE interior of a Grand Trunk diner built by Pullman in 1899 contained niches for growing plants as well as handsome brass lamps. There were tables for two as well as for four.

VERY plush Grand Trunk parlor car of the early 1900's featured bay windows, window drapes, and linen antimacassars. Was this parlor the inspiration for today's bay-window cabooses?

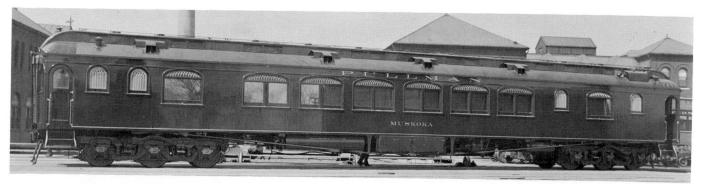

MUSKOKA, a 12-section, 1-drawing-room Pullman built in April 1907 for Grand Trunk service, was named for the Muskoka Lake districts of Ontario. The elegant 12-wheeler was not dismantled until 1935, outliving many a locomotive contemporary of its birth.

NORTHERN 6122 heading 9-car *International* of 1934 "raced" elderly biplane in publicity stunt. Author's collection.

Canada's Train of Superior Service

ADVERTISED as "Canada's Train of Superior Service," the *International* fulfilled her destiny of welding firmly the bonds uniting Canada and the United States. The *Limited*, "an extra fine train without any extra fare," served as the standard-bearer of the newly formed Canadian National Railways after the amalgamation of 1923.

In the first years of the CNR, the *International* (trains 14 and 15) perpetuated the former Grand Trunk traditions. Pullman sleeping and observation cars, former GT arch-windowed parlor cars, and diners operated over the new government-owned road.

The first major change in the train's consist appeared in

1924 with the arrival of Canadian National's famous 6000-class 4-8-2 locomotives. For a time these 326-ton mammoths were the largest locomotives in the British Empire. With the addition of heavy steel equipment, the *International* slowly acquired the new image of the National system.

The CNR was one of the first railways to equip its trains with radio. In 1924 it installed receiving equipment and headsets in the observation cars of most through trains. Experienced operators rode on each radio-equipped car to "handle the dial." In order to assure suitable entertainment, a radio department was organized by the Canadian National, and 11 railroad-owned broadcasting stations were built throughout Canada. The first two call letters of each station were appropriately CN.

The year 1929 was an important one for the *International*. Entire trains, completely new from the 6100-class Northern locomotives to the Pullman solarium cars, were placed in service on one of the world's fastest scheduled runs — Montreal-Toronto, 334 miles in 6 hours — resulting in the spirited speed war of the early 1930's with the Canadian Pacific.

The 6100-class 4-8-4's were designed for fast passenger and manifest freight service on the Canadian National System. These handsome giants were designed to haul the *International* with 12 cars at speeds of 80 mph on 511-mile run from Montreal to Sarnia, the longest continuous run without change of engines in Canada. For operation between Port Huron and Chicago, similar models numbered in the 6300 series were built for the Grand Trunk Western. The United States version, slightly heavier and more powerful, did not include the boosters provided on the Canadian model.

The car equipment of the 1929 train reflected the trend toward quiet luxury and refinement characteristic of the period. The coaches and dining and parlor car were railroad owned,

CN.

MOUNTAIN type 6030 bridges the Ottawa River in another pre-streamlining classic of a public relations photograph.

The International Limited

CANADA'S FIRST streamlined steam locomotives were five 4-8-4's of Canadian National's class U-4A delivered by the Montreal Locomotive Works in June 1936 and numbered 6400-6404. The 77-inch-drivered machines were a design compromise between the system's earlier high-speed Hudsons and slower but more powerful 73-inch-drivered 4-8-4's. Exhaustive wind tunnel tests were responsible for their streamlining, one aim of which was to lift smoke and cinders over the cab when the engine was drifting.

but the sleeping cars and solarium-observation car were furnished by Pullman. Three sets of equipment for the one-night, one-day operation included through cars from both Chicago and Detroit for Montreal.

Popular features of the train were a soda fountain, parlor cars (between Montreal and Toronto), valet service, and Vita-glassed sunroom "where in perfect ease and comfort you view river and lake and verdant valley as you wing your way along, the while you reap in full the health-giving benefits of the rays of the sun, the world's greatest doctor."

339

MOUNTAIN TYPE No. 6055 was built by the Montreal Locomotive Works in 1930 and typified International Limited motive power of her era. Unlike rival Canadian Pacific, CN exploited the 4-8-2 wheel arrangement and purchased it right up until dieseldom.

CN'S U. S. subsidiary, Grand Trunk Western, purchased 4-8-4's of the same general specifications as those of its parent — but from American builders. No. 6300 — GTW's original 4-8-4 — came from Alco in 1927.

POPULAR exhibit at B&O's Fair of the Iron Horse in 1927 was Canadian National's first 4-8-4, No. 6100. For a season the prototype Northern also bore the name Confederation.

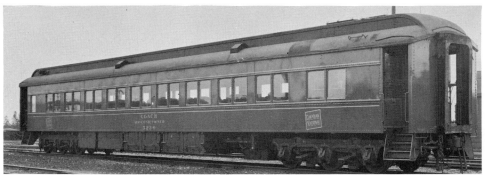

COACH No. 5230, an air-conditioned steel car, seated 50 in the body of the car and 16 in its smoking section. It contained a ladies' powder room. The coach is shown in CN livery of the 1930's: light green body, black roof, red and gold CN insigne.

DINING CAR No. 1244 was built by Pullman in 1918 and seated 30 patrons.

DINING CAR No. 1334 was built by Canadian Car & Foundry in 1938, seated 40 in wood-paneled interior.

PORT COLBURN, later changed to Port Colborne, was one of a series of CN Pullmans (14-section cars) named for Canadian ports.

Pullman-Standard.

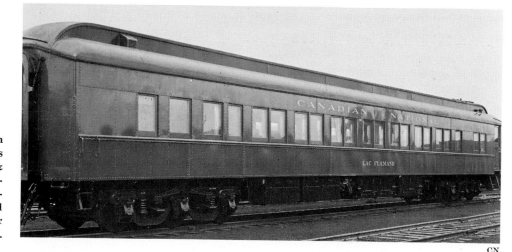

LAC FLAMAND, a parlor car with 26 seats and a compartment, was built in 1919 by Canadian Car & Foundry and operated between Montreal and Toronto. It served as a hospital car during World War II and was completely rebuilt as a parlor car by Canadian National in 1947.

CN.

RIVERDALE PARK, one of a series of 8-section, 1-drawing-room, 2-compartment cars named after Canadian parks, built by Pullman-Standard.

Pullman-Standard.

ALEXANDRIA BAY (twin cars: Georgian Bay and Murray Bay) contained a drawing room, 2 compartments, 3 single bedrooms, and a lounge equipped with soda fountain-buffet, radio, and solarium fitted with Vitaglass, wicker chairs.

Pullman-Standard.

The International Limited

SOLARIUM lounging put one in a real heads-back-and-feet-out mood to judge from drawing in this 1930 CN brochure.

Author's collection.

SOLARIUM-PARLOR cars Nos. 879-888, built in 1929, had plush, swivel chairs.

Collection of Andrew Merrilees.

341

THE *International Limited* in streamlined dress drawn by a pair of 1500 h.p. GM diesel units. CN photo.

As modern as this minute

THE severity of the depression, together with the length of World War II (which lasted for six years in Canada), precluded large orders for new passenger cars for the Canadian National during the 1930's and 1940's.

After the end of the war CN was desperately in need of new passenger equipment, but an industrial boom of unprecedented proportions demanded that available funds and materials be used for freight equipment and locomotives.

At last it became possible to obtain firm prices for the enormous quantity of car equipment which the railroad required, and in 1953 the Canadian National contracted for one of the largest passenger-car orders ever placed by a railroad on the North American continent. A total of 359 cars costing 59 million dollars included 218 coaches from the Dominion (Montreal) plant of Canadian Car & Foundry, and 141 sleeping, parlor, and dining cars from Pullman-Standard in Chicago. By the end of 1954 all CN mainline passenger trains were operating with the handsome new streamlined rolling stock.*

Every effort was made to ensure that the new cars would satisfy the public. A Canadian affiliate of the Gallup Poll

*Consist of the eastbound *International Limited*, No. 14, for December 4, 1962, was: GTW diesels 4910, 4931, 4136; 8858 (GTW) — baggage, Flint mail and express; 8254 (CN) — baggage, Toronto storage; 8811 (GTW) — baggage, Lansing mail and express; 8474 (GTW) — baggage, Toronto express; 9081 (GTW) — baggage, Port Huron express; 9683 (GTW) — R.P.O., Port Huron; 9004 (CN) — baggage, Toronto; 5494 (CN) — coach, Toronto; 5601 (CN) — coach, Toronto; *City of Findlay* (NYC&StL) — 10-6 (extra), Toronto; *Eleazer Lord* (E-L) — 10-6 (extra), Toronto; *American Sunset* (C&NW) — 6-6-4 (extra), Toronto; *Glacier* (SR) — 12-1 (extra), Toronto; *Cape Chignecto* (CN) — 2-2-L, Toronto; *Green Hill* (CN) — 6-4-4, Toronto; *Greening* (CN) — 6-4-6, Toronto; *Green Court* (CN) — 6-4-6, Port Huron; *Green Brook* (CN) — 6-4-6, Detroit; 4888 (CN) — coach, Detroit. (Four extra sleeping cars from the Pullman pool were added when Trans-Canada Air Lines was grounded.)

surveyed the travel market and worked closely with CN to develop the design of the new cars. One of the most important considerations of the government-owned road was that all of Canada should benefit by the modernized trains. Remote car routes together with the well-patronized transcontinental and international routes were re-equipped. Delivery of the new equipment was accompanied by considerable publicity with widespread use of advertising material in both English and French languages.

In 1957-1958 CN conducted another extensive survey of the Canadian travel market. Results indicated that the best avenues for making passenger-train travel more attractive would be fare reductions and a form of "packaging" to provide rail transportation, sleeping car accommodations, and meals — all for a lump sum.

These findings were put to the test in two major programs — one on the transcontinental line, and the other in the Atlantic provinces. Both are now a success.

An "All-Inclusive Travel Plan" offering rail fare, all meals, tips, and berth at reduced rates has yielded substantially improved earnings for the cross-country *Super-Continental*.

The celebrated "Red, White and Blue Plan" on lines east of Montreal is a revolutionary pricing system which boosts travel, levels peaks, and has increased passenger volume. The three colors identify three new fare structures — bargain, economy, standard — which offer savings according to the day traveled. Red (bargain) tickets, effective 163 days a year, offer the biggest savings of all (up to 44 per cent) and provide transportation, bed, and meals at less cost than by any other means of commercial travel — in most cases less than by private automobile. "Red, White and Blue" fares have attracted travelers in numbers which have astounded even the most optimistic. The crack Montreal-Halifax *Ocean Limited*, for

example, has enjoyed a passenger traffic increase of 77 per cent.

Canadian National Passenger Sales Manager Pierre Delagrave states: "Our view is this: we have good things to sell — and the people of Canada are going to buy these things in increasing numbers and be glad they did. We'll show that train travel can be fun — and we'll prove that trains can be as modern as this minute. Yet in doing this, we will sacrifice nothing of the emphasis on safety which always has been an outstanding feature of passenger trains. We're in the passenger business to stay!" I

CN.

FIRST train to appear in Canadian National's new-image color scheme of black and off-white with red-orange was the Ocean Limited on the Maritimes run. Nose of Montreal-built cab unit displays continuous-line CN introduced systemwide as insigne.

343

COACH No. 5515, shown in new-image color scheme, was built by Canadian Car & Foundry; seats 80 (52 in body of car, 28 in smoking section); has interior walls covered in easy-to-maintain plastic material.

CN.

LAKE CHAPLEAU, a 34-chair parlor car. Between Montreal and Toronto the International is a daytime pool train operated by CN and CP and carries both roads' rolling stock.

Unless otherwise indicated, all photos Pullman-Standard.

DINING CAR No. 1338, a 40-seat car, is shown in former CN standard dress of black and olive green, red and gold maple leaf herald at end.

GREENMOUNT, Pullman-operated streamlined sleeper with 6 sections, 6 roomettes, and 4 double bedrooms, is similar in layout to famous S-type Pine-series sleeping cars purchased in 1953 by Chicago & Eastern Illinois, Louisville & Nashville, and Nashville, Chattanooga & St. Louis for service between Chicago, Atlanta, and New Orleans in such trains as Georgian and Humming Bird.

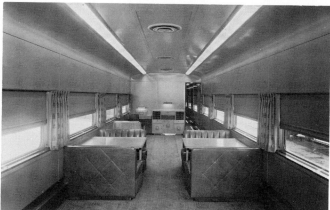

CAPE CHIGNECTO (twin of Cape Tormentine) has 2 double bedrooms, 2 compartments, and buffet-lounge. Scene inside unfurnished lounge (left) was taken at Pullman-Standard before shipment to Canada, where CN installed balance of lounge furniture.

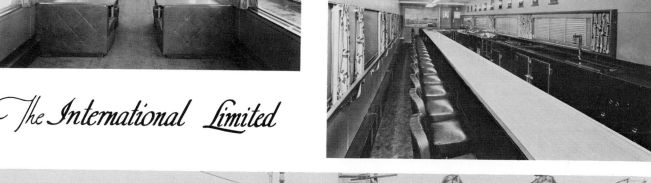

The International Limited

DINETTE No. 429, unique and popular "drug store counter on wheels," is operated between Montreal and Toronto, serves full-course hot meals as well as snacks, pleases the economy minded while trimming the railroad's dining-car deficit. The car contains kitchen, crew's dormitory, and a long counter seating 26. Again, exterior is shown in pre-new image dress of black and green.

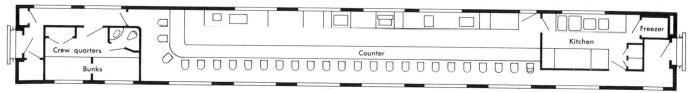

INTERURBAN

Original ink drawing by George Krambles.

NORTH SHORE LINE'S Prairie State Special: very de luxe indeed.

CLASSICS

For a season the interurbans possessed their own "classics"

1 ONE of the curious phenomena of American history was the spectacular rise, rapid decline, and almost complete disappearance of the electric interurban railways which once laced the land.

At the turn of the century the United States experienced a boom in the construction of small electrified traction lines built to attract short-haul passengers and light freight. In most cases these lines were the result of locally promoted get-rich-quick schemes which assured speculators of a "conservative investment."

In time the smaller roads were consolidated into large systems by farsighted men who contemplated high-speed electric railroads operating de luxe passenger and long freight trains with steam railroad precision. In many

Collection of George Krambles.
A GIBE at steam roads was "faster than express" blurb.

instances throughout the country the visions were transformed into realization. In the densely populated areas of the East, across the prairies and plains of the mid-continent, and through the canyons and valleys of the Pacific Coast classic interurbans raced against history.

A selected group of those interurban classics offered facilities for dining or sleeping, or for lounging in individual easy chairs. Private or party cars were also available for charter, but these are not covered in this volume.

Author's collection.
STOCK OFFERING of appeal to "conservative investor."

Almost as extraordinary as the story of the interurbans is the interest in their history generated by an ever-increasing legion of dedicated traction enthusiasts. As the number of operating companies dwindled, organizations such as the Electric Railroaders Association (New York) and the Central Electric Railfans' Association (Chicago) have been formed and there are now numerous electric railway museums as well. Indeed, for the photographic and documentary coverage in this chapter the author is indebted to George Krambles and William Janssen, two of the land's outstanding traction enthusiasts.

347

All photos, collection of George Krambles.

MARCELLA observation was originally built in 1902 as a motor car by the G. C. Kuhlman Car Company for exhibition at the Detroit Convention of the American Street Railway Association

and was purchased in 1903 for use by Clifford Beebe, president of the Auburn & Syracuse Electric Railroad. Car was later remodeled as trailer for parlor-car service and renamed the Syracuse.

Empire United Railways

THE Empire United Railways system was organized between 1913 and 1916 by Clifford Beebe of Syracuse, N.Y., who consolidated several electric lines operating from Rochester, Syracuse, Auburn, and Oswego in upper New York state. The principal road in the Beebe syndicate was the Rochester, Syracuse & Eastern Railroad, a high-speed double-track route which paralleled the New York Central between Rochester and Syracuse.

In the era preceding World War I, competition from the Vanderbilt's steam trains for the through traffic was severe. Although the EUR route was 6 miles longer, the electric line

introduced a fast parlor-car service to stimulate traffic and to attract a greater share of the business. An important contributing circumstance was the company's ownership of two attractive private cars which were easily convertible for parlor-car operation. Both cars were typical business cars designed for official use on the line. Each was beautifully finished and well equipped to afford the utmost in travel luxury. Their use as official cars, however, brought no return on a considerable investment. By refurnishing kitchens and staterooms with easy armchairs, both were remodeled for revenue service.

After their conversion, the two cars were placed in regular operation in 1915. They were operated in two-car trains with coaches and ran the 86 miles between Rochester and Syracuse in 2 hours 40 minutes. A flat charge of 25 cents was made for a seat in the parlor car, regardless of the distance traveled. An average of 100 passengers per day traveled aboard the luxurious equipment, contributing to a $7500-per-year increase in revenue with practically no additional investment.

The experiment was short lived. Business throughout the country slumped during 1916 and electric railway receipts decreased accordingly. The Empire United failed and Beebe withdrew from the company. After the advent of World War I, the parlor cars were discontinued and were converted to freight equipment. In 1927 the Rochester & Syracuse again attempted a limited train service with remodeled coaches, but the new cars were a far cry from the earlier luxurious equipment of the famed Beebe syndicate.

NO. 999, a 56-foot, 45-ton private car containing 6 rooms finished in African mahogany or mission oak, was turned out by

G. C. Kuhlman in 1910 for the Beebe-controlled roads, then rebuilt as the parlor car Rochester in 1915 for Empire United service.

348

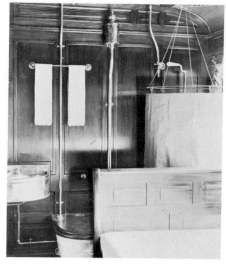

MOTORMAN of Marcella received high-level supervision (above left) from brass seated in wicker chairs in forward observation room. Stateroom quarters were adequate but close (center) with bed adjoining shower stall and toilet. The lounge, finished in mahogany, was equipped with a paneled built-in refrigerator and buffet (above right) for the comfort of trolley-bound guests.

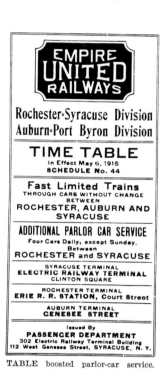

TABLE boosted parlor-car service.

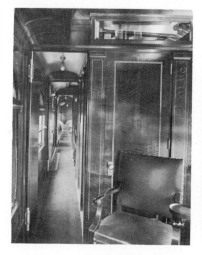

SELECTION of four interior views of the 999 reveals a lavatory of Gibraltar-like strength . . . a corridor view . . . the smoking room finished in mission oak . . . and a parlor compartment sprinkled with wicker chairs fitted with plush cushions.

349

PILOT, newsreel cameramen, C&LE "Red Electric" await beginning of famed rails vs. wings speed dash of 1930 in which interurban lighwteight outpaced Fleet biplane by hitting 97 mph. There was a fond farewell (below) as bus delivered Meteor passengers.

Cincinnati & Lake Erie Railroad

IN 1929 the Cincinnati & Lake Erie Railroad was created from several western Ohio interurbans by Dr. Thomas Conway, a finance-professor-turned-railroader, who set out to produce a thoroughly modern interurban road. New lightweight cars were ordered from the Cincinnati Car Company following a series of experiments designed to produce faster and more comfortable interurban equipment.

Twenty superb "liners of the rails" arrived in 1930. Ten of these were beautifully appointed with an observation and smoking lounges equipped with individual upholstered chairs to provide a comfortable trip across Ohio's rolling countryside from Cincinnati to Toledo. Three cars per day operated through to Detroit. Each of the new blue ribbon trains was given a name in a competition held among company employees. *Valley Queen, Meteor, Rocket, Golden Eagle,* and others were selected from more than 1200 entries.

Considerable publicity was generated by the new high-speed cars. In a spectacular race with an airplane filmed by Pathé News Weekly, the interurban traveled 97 mph to outdistance the plane. Shortly afterward in a speed contest with a racing

automobile, the interurban won by 15 lengths. Author Christopher Morley described his experiences aboard the "Red Electric" in a national magazine. The *Electric Railway Journal* commented, "What is perhaps the most interesting and significant experiment of recent years appears to be a pronounced success."

NO. 121 was 43 feet 9 inches long, weighed 47,800 pounds, had Westinghouse traction motors, and was painted red with gold and black striping. Observation lounge (above) was furnished with mohair-covered chairs, Wilton carpet, reading tables with lamps.

NO. 602, a Barney & Smith 56-footer, was rebuilt in 1925 (for Buckeye-Hoosier Special) as a chair car with wicker seats.

All photos, collection of George Krambles.

Dayton & Western Traction Company

THE Dayton & Western Traction Company completed its 38-mile line between Dayton, O., and Richmond, Ind., in 1903. The strategic route provided a direct connection between the Schoepf-McGowan systems in Ohio and Indiana. For that reason it was soon absorbed into the syndicate's Ohio Electric Railway network. In 1920, when Ohio Electric became insolvent, Dayton & Western reverted to its independent status.

During the 1920's the road developed considerable interline freight and passenger business in conjunction with the Terre Haute, Indianapolis & Eastern Traction Company, second largest of the Hoosier interurbans. Fast through freight trains containing as many as six box trailers rumbled westward from Dayton bound for Richmond, Indianapolis, and Terre Haute.

In 1922 D&W and THI&E co-operated in the development of a unique interurban passenger operation. Through limited trains known as the *Buckeye-Hoosier Specials* darted between Dayton and Indianapolis three times daily each way using Dayton & Western equipment. In 1924 D&W car No. 602 was remodeled as a chair car with individual wicker seats. A white-jacketed porter was in attendance. The new car operated in the 8 a.m. run out of Dayton and returned via the 1:30 p.m. trip from Indianapolis. Seat fare for the 108-mile journey was a modest 50 cents. Like many another traction service it was unable to withstand the pressure of highway competition and ceased operation after several years.

PARLOR CAR No. 500 of CD&M was 62 feet long, weighed 50 tons, seated 35 in parlor chairs, 8 in smoker, was crimson-cream.

INSIDE was found the luxury for claim of "finest interurban parlor cars in the world": deep, plush swivel chairs.

Columbus, Delaware &
Marion
Electric Company

AN interurban line from the Buckeye State capital north to Marion, an important industrial center, was completed in 1903 by the Columbus, Delaware & Marion Electric Company, an Ohio light and power utility. The new road "through the heart

of Ohio" formed a link in the chain of traction lines extending from Cleveland to Cincinnati.

In the mid-1920's CD&M planned a de luxe service for through travelers. Two steel parlor cars were ordered from American Car & Foundry's Jeffersonville (Ind.) works. The new cars, Nos. 500 and 501, were delivered in 1926. They were similar in design to the luxurious equipment completed by AC&F for Indianapolis-Louisville service on the Interstate Public Service.

Sparkling in their crimson and cream livery, the CD&M cars were advertised as "The Finest Interurban Parlor Cars in the World." They made five round trips daily except Sunday as the *Capitol* (southbound) and the *Northern* (northbound). The 49-mile trip took 1 hour 40 minutes.

Unhappily, the luxury service was short lived. Abandonment of connecting traction lines during the depression severely reduced CD&M revenues, and after operating with deficits for four years, the road was abandoned in 1933.

351

ACROSS the Wabash River near Logansport, Ind., goes the Peru, Union Traction car No. 298, operating as the Indianapolis-bound Kokomo Traveler. The 298, containing (below) smoker, buffet, solarium, was one of three parlor-buffets (others: 296-197) built by Cincinnati Car Company in 1906-1907 for Union Traction routes out of Indianapolis to Marion, Muncie, Logansport.

Union Traction Company

UNION TRACTION, the largest electric road in the Hoosier State, operated 454 miles of interurban and street railway. The line was established in 1897 by Charles Henry who reportedly popularized the term "interurban." In 1902 Union Traction became part of the Schoepf-McGowan syndicate. The line was expanded throughout the Gas Belt and rich farmland north and east of Indianapolis, paralleling every steam railroad in the area.

Two of the most important interurban routes connected Indianapolis and Fort Wayne, Indiana's two largest cities. In the absence of direct steam road service, Union Traction instituted joint operation with Fort Wayne & Wabash Valley Traction Company and its successor, the Indiana Service Corporation. In 1923 Union Traction inaugurated the *Hoosierland* limiteds over the 125-mile route via Anderson and Muncie. North of Bluffton the train operated over ISC lines into Fort Wayne. In 1925 one *Hoosierland* each way carried one of the arch-roofed cars originally built by Jewett Car Company for Stark Electric (O.) which were remodeled into solarium-observation-parlor-buffet-trailers and were named *Indiana* and *Purdue*.

HOOSIERLAND sports red livery and flags, striped awning, and a bevy of smiling, waving Hoosier lassies entranced by traction.

352

TRACTION LIGHT
INDIANA Service CORPORATION

COMPLETED in 1904 at a cost of over 1 million dollars, Indianapolis Traction Terminal was a 9-story Byzantine-style office and station building conceived by Hugh McGowan and designed in the style of Louis Sullivan. Even Erie honored it with a ticket office. Today the ponderous interurbans have vanished but the building still stands; contains bus terminal, offices.

Indiana Service Corporation

THE *Wabash Valley Flyers*, trains 12 and 25, were operated by the Indiana Service Corporation (Indiana Central Lines) between Indianapolis and Fort Wayne via the 136-mile route through Kokomo and Peru. They were advertised as "High Class Steel Trains . . . making County Seat stops only." The big cars were ordered when Samuel Insull acquired the ISC and re-equipped the line. Motor cars 375-379 and parlor-buffet cars 390 and 391 (*Little Turtle* and *Anthony Wayne*) were built in 1926 by the St. Louis Car Company and were painted sand yellow trimmed with green. The interior of *Little Turtle* contained 24 parlor chairs, men's lounge, and kitchen. Maneuvering about must have presented a challenge to the waiter.

WABASH VALLEY FLYER was trailed by Little Turtle parlor-buffet, which contained (below) 24 parlor chairs and kitchen.

COMING at you, the Flyer stands on State Boulevard in Fort Wayne, Ind., in June 1926 — the acme of big-time Hoosier traction.

DIE-CUT breakfast menu advertised "Indiana's Finest Parlor-Dining Car Service" with such Hoosier specialties as corn meal mush (25 cents) and griddle cakes with broiled ham (80 cents).

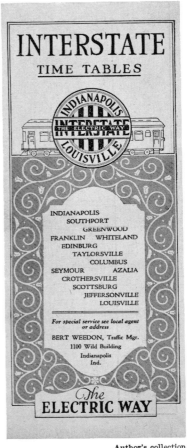

INTERSTATE
TIME TABLES

INDIANAPOLIS
INTERSTATE
LOUISVILLE

INDIANAPOLIS
SOUTHPORT
GREENWOOD
FRANKLIN   WHITELAND
EDINBURG
TAYLORSVILLE
COLUMBUS
SEYMOUR   AZALIA
CROTHERSVILLE
SCOTTSBURG
JEFFERSONVILLE
LOUISVILLE

For special service see local agent
or address

BERT WEEDON, Traffic Mgr.
1100 Wild Building
Indianapolis
Ind.

The
ELECTRIC WAY

Author's collection.
TIMETABLE: "The Electric Way."

354

Collection of George Krambles.

Interstate Public Service Company

"THE Interstate Public Service Company presents the perfect, modern transportation system via the Interstate Electric Railway — Indianapolis to Louisville. The Interstate Electric passenger service guarantees convenience, comfort, speed, safety. No finer or more complete passenger service in America, including the famous *Hoosier* and *Dixie Flyers* with dining and parlor car service, local cars and by night between Louisville and Indianapolis; the perfect, restful sleeping car service." — *Interstate advertisement*, 1926.

DIXIE FLYER, Interstate train No. 102 from Indianapolis to Louisville (117 miles in 3 hours 45 minutes), borrowed the famous steamroad name. Northbound counterpart on the Interstate was Hoosier Flyer.

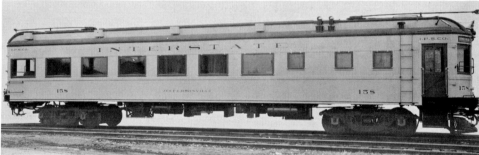

Both photos, collection of George Krambles.

JEFFERSONVILLE, 62-foot, 92,500-pound parlor-dining car No. 158 — first of Interstate's de luxe steel equipment — was named after on-line town that was also its birthplace. Built by American Car & Foundry's Jeffersonville (Ind.) plant in November 1923, No. 168 was prototype for five similar Interstate motorized cars painted orange with green trim and red mineral surfaced roof.

Both photos, author's collection.

SCOTTSBURG, sleeping car No. 167, was built by ACF in 1926; contained 10 sections (with windows in upper berths); was 62 feet long; weighed 62,200 pounds. It and sisters Indianapolis and Louisville ran on IPS 1926-1931, went to Pacific Great Eastern.

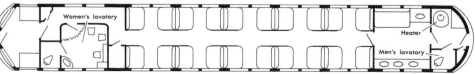

355

Chicago South Shore & South Bend Railroad

WHEN Samuel Insull purchased the bankrupt Chicago, Lake Shore & South Bend Railway at public auction in 1925, he was determined to rebuild the line into a first-class railroad. Within days the company had a new management, a new name (Chicago South Shore & South Bend Railroad), and a new image (the old Pullman green livery was changed to orange and maroon). The roadbed was rebuilt, the electrification system was changed, and new steel equipment was ordered.

Two dining cars and two parlor cars were completed by Pullman-Standard in January 1927 and were delivered to South Shore Line for operation. The de luxe services were an immediate success and contributed to a constant rise in passenger traffic which increased from 1.8 million passengers in 1924 to 3.2 million in 1929. A handsome yellow railroad-style timetable advertised the named limiteds: *Industrial, Notre Dame, St. Joe Valley, Fort Dearborn, Grant Park, Garden City, Duneland, Indiana,* and *Illinois.* In 1929 the South Shore was awarded the coveted Charles A. Coffin Award for its "outstanding contribution to the convenience of the public and benefit of the [electric transportation] industry."

Collapse of the stock market and depression brought about the downfall of Samuel Insull's empire and difficult times for the South Shore. Dining service ended in 1931 and parlor-car operations were discontinued the following year. Although the South Shore Line grew stronger and prospered as an important industrial carrier, the luxury trains that were Samuel Insull's pride became only a memory.

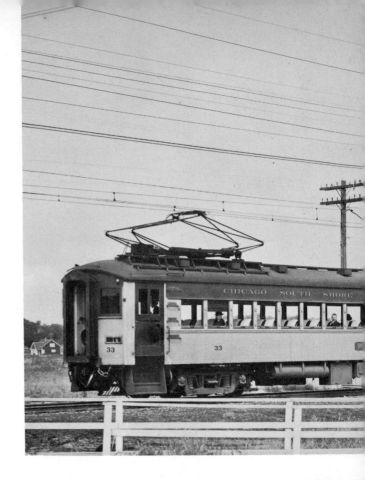

All car views, Pullman-Standard.

PARLOR CAR No. 352, completed by Pullman January 17, 1927, rode on Commonwealth 6-wheel trucks; weighed 111,400 pounds; faced its passengers (right) in easy chairs.

Women's toilet · Lounge · Men's toilet · Buffet · Heater · Smoking room

DINING CAR No. 302, completed by Pullman January 27, 1927, was — at 113,400 pounds — heaviest nonmotor interurban car; seated 24; had an over-all length of 64 feet 1½ inches.

Kitchen · Pantry · Dining room

Collection of George Krambles.

ILLINOIS LIMITED eastbound in 1929 on a schedule that put away the 90 miles between Chicago-South Bend in 2 hours 20 minutes — respectable going for Insull's cars.

Author's collection.

TIMETABLE dated April 26, 1931.

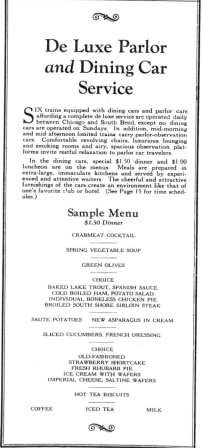
Author's collection.

SIRLOIN steak cost just $1.50.

Chicago Aurora & Elgin Railroad

CONSTRUCTION work on the Aurora, Elgin & Chicago Railroad — "The Great Third Rail Route" — was started in 1900 by the Pomeroy-Mandlebaum syndicate of Cleveland. By 1905 a contract was negotiated with the West Side Elevated Railway permitting AE&C trains to enter downtown Chicago. For the first time, passengers from the well-to-do western suburbs were able to ride to the Chicago Loop without a change of cars.

Parlor-buffet service on the AE&C was instituted on August 30, 1904, in an early attempt to offer such luxury on an electric line. *Carolyn*, newly completed by Niles Car & Manufacturing Company, contained wicker chairs seating 24 in smoking and parlor compartments separated by a kitchen.

In 1919 the "Great Third Rail Route" went into receivership, but it was reorganized during 1922 as the Chicago Aurora & Elgin Railroad under the direction of Dr. Thomas Conway of Philadelphia. Samuel Insull purchased the line in 1925 for his growing utility empire and planned to rebuild the road for high-speed operation.

High-speed limited trains composed of maroon all-steel cars raced between Chicago and the Fox River Valley. CA&E timetables listed the *Cannonball*, *Watch City Flyer*, *Fox Valley Flyer*, and *Chicago Loop Flyer*. But economic depression and the development of the automobile intervened. Service was cut back, and by 1929 the parlor-car equipment was permanently withdrawn.

Interruption of service because of postwar express highway construction crippled the road once known as the Sunset Lines. Passenger service came to an end July 3, 1957. On July 6, 1961, the road was officially abandoned; the first of Samuel Insull's three great Chicago interurbans passed on.

FUNERAL CAR No. 109 carried remains to West Side cemeteries; had special next-of-kin compartment; was painted a somber black.

All photos, collection of George Krambles.

WESTBOUND limited approaching Elmhurst, Ill., in the 1920's is led by steel-sheathed buffet-parlor car No. 600 which was rebuilt in 1923 with de luxe appointments (below) for diners.

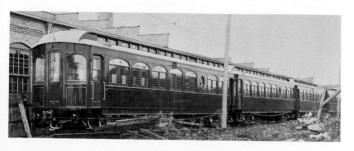

CAROLYN, end car in a lineup at Wheaton (Ill.) shops in 1905, was possessed of a luxurious interior finished in Flemish oak stained apple green and inlaid with both holly and maple.

Author's collection.
CA&E timetable: "very low fares."

359

ELECTROLINER sprints past the camera of George Krambles on Skokie Valley Route.

Chicago North Shore & Milwaukee Railroad

THE predecessor company of the Chicago North Shore & Milwaukee Railroad commenced operation in 1895 from Waukegan, Ill., south to neighboring North Chicago. This small line was soon expanded southward along the Shore Line Route to Evanston and then north toward Milwaukee. Interstate operation was established during 1908 by limited trains equipped with new cafe-parlor cars which connected at Evanston with rapid-transit service of the Chicago Elevated Railways.

In 1916 the then-bankrupt North Shore Line was reorganized by Samuel Insull. The new company embarked on a building and rehabilitation program which produced new steel equipment including parlor and dining cars and trackage rights over the elevated line directly into downtown Chicago. For these efforts the "Road of Service" was awarded the 1923 Charles A. Coffin Medal "for distinguished contribution to the development of electric transportation." During June 1926 the high-speed bypass route through the Skokie Valley was completed. The new line was put to the test June 24, 1926, on the occasion of the International Eucharistic Congress when North Shore moved more than 250,000 persons to Mundelein and back in a single day. Between 5:35 a.m. and 11:15 p.m. 810 trains composed of 2608 cars ran over the 40-mile route.

In the prosperous era after World War I the railroad developed extensive de luxe train services. Named limiteds — *Gold Coast, Eastern, Badger, Interstate, Cream City, Prairie State* — provided luxury equipment which was well patronized. North Shore dining cars served over 77,000 meals during 1926.

The impact of the depression ended the luxury trains on most interurban roads, but not on the North Shore. Although the open-observation cars were permanently withdrawn, modified meal service continued throughout the lean years and expanded as prosperity returned to the country.

"America's first all-electric luxury trains," the *Electroliners*, entered revenue service on February 9, 1941. These two red-and-green streamliners — constructed by St. Louis Car Company at a cost of $300,000 — were inaugurated with fanfare which included on-line exhibitions and press runs.

During World War II, North Shore trains were filled to capacity with military traffic from Fort Sheridan and Great Lakes Naval Training Station, two of the country's largest permanent service installations. But the return of peace and consequent demobilization were accompanied by a drastic reduction in traffic. The company's woes were further compounded by a

91-day strike by employees in 1948 and the construction of express highways paralleling the North Shore right of way.

The last decade was one of agony for the company and its passengers. Curtailing of service by management was accompanied by constant legal maneuvering. Unfortunately, all ef-

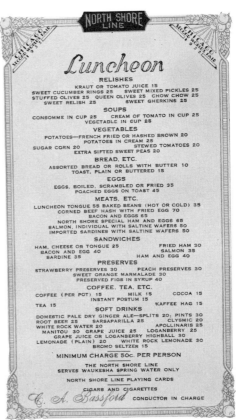

Author's collection.

1933 World's Fair menu was a la carte only.

360

LIBERTY LINER, ex-*Electroliner*, in 1964. Red Arrow Lines photo.

forts to save the line failed. Train operations ceased on Sunday, January 20, 1963, ending service on one of the country's greatest interurban roads.

One bright spot in the unhappy turn of events was the sale late in 1963 of the two *Electroliners* (Nos. 801-802 and 803-804) along with other abandoned North Shore equipment for $6400 to the Philadelphia Suburban Transportation Company (Red Arrow Lines) for service on the line to Norristown, Pa. After a complicated journey eastward via the Chicago & North Western and Pennsylvania lines, the liners underwent a $100,000 overhaul at Red Arrow's Upper Darby (Pa.) shops. Exteriors and interiors were completely refinished under the supervision of Horace A. Paul, a Philadelphia artist who created the strik-

ing new red, white, and gray livery. The tavern-lounge facilities were retained for morning coffee and evening bar services. The refurbished trains — renamed *Liberty Liners* and subtitled *Valley Forge* and *Independence Hall* — made their maiden voyages on the Red Arrow Lines on January 26, 1964.

Both photos, author's collection.

DINING CAR No. 416 was built by Cincinnati Car Company in 1926 as a trailer but equipped with trolley pole and third-rail

shoes. Interior is of a series 404-406 car built in 1917 for the Gold Coast. These were the road's first steel dining cars.

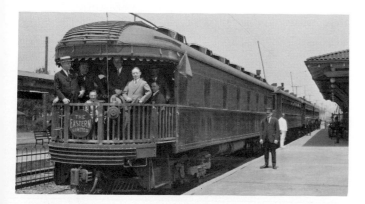

EASTERN LIMITED connected with Century, had a highly popular brass-railed observation-parlor, judging by this Kenosha scene.

Both photos, collection of George Krambles.

CARDINALS SPECIAL, draped by Marshall Field & Company, carried clergy to International Eucharistic Congress [see page 380].

LAKE SHORE LIMITED carried drumhead on chin of No. 99.

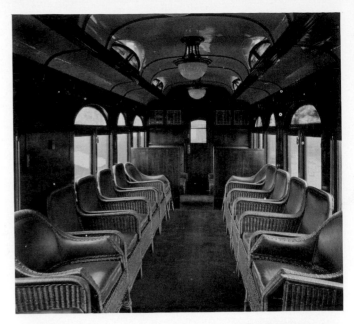

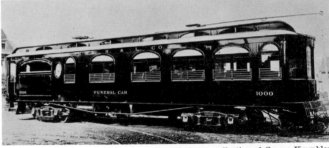

All photos, collection of George Krambles.

TMER&L and Milwaukee Northern

An electric railway and motor coach transportation system affording fast and frequent service, travel comfort, and convenience at low transportation cost. — *TMER&L timetable,* 1929.

THE Milwaukee Electric Railway & Light Company, affectionately known as the TMER&L, was an interesting system which operated nearly 200 miles of interurban line from Milwaukee throughout the rolling countryside and lake region of southeastern Wisconsin.

During the 1920's Milwaukee Electric embarked on a multi-million-dollar building and rehabilitation program. Private high-speed right of way was purchased; lines to Chicago, Lake Geneva, and Madison were projected; and the independent Milwaukee Northern Railway was finally acquired. Electrical facilities were standardized, older rolling stock was modernized, and parlor and dining car services were established.

But the glory of the handsome yellow and olive green cars of the TMER&L began to diminish after the crash of the stock market. Service was cut back drastically. Much of the uncompleted high-speed line was abandoned and all of the de luxe cars were soon discontinued. Service was curtailed on one route after another until the last line was abandoned in 1951.

ONE of the costliest interurbans ever built, TMER&L private car Milwaukee (below) was constructed by the St. Louis Car Company in 1904 for Wisconsin utilities promoter John Beggs. It was subsequently rebuilt by TMER&L as funeral car No. 1000 (above), then sold in 1923 to Milwaukee Northern, which rebuilt it as parlor car No. 99 with facing wicker chairs for de luxe runs.

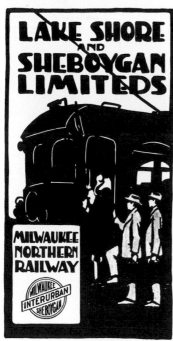

LAND O'LAKES parlor car in Milwaukee terminal at 3rd and Sycamore streets.

BELIEVED to be the first articulated interurban, dining car 1198-1199 was built in Milwaukee Electric's shops in 1928. Rear unit carried dining section, all-electric kitchen. Dining service, Milwaukee to Kenosha and Watertown, lasted only two years.

MENDOTA, one of four coaches rebuilt into parlors in 1924 (others: Menominee, Waubasee, Winnebago), ran on Watertown line with drumheads of the Land O'Lakes and Inter-City limiteds, offering a "luxurious, delightful, and comfortable mode of travel." But service was short lived.

Collection of William C. Janssen.

FRANCIS (twin of Theodore) was one of two unique convertible parlor-sleeping cars invented by and built for Harris F. Holland in 1903 by Harlan & Hollingsworth. Cars went to Illinois Traction in 1907 after Mr. Holland went bankrupt.

IT SLEEPERS had berths 6 inches longer than Pullmans and safety deposit boxes.

Collection of William C. Janssen.

Author's collection.

ROOMS en suite were a feature of traction sleepers.

Illinois Traction System

THE Illinois Traction System, later known as the Illinois Terminal Railroad System, was one of the largest electric railroads in the United States. It operated over 450 miles, connecting Peoria, Springfield, Champaign, and St. Louis. Its de luxe limiteds once raced across the Illinois prairie offering observation-parlor-dining cars and sleeping cars equipped with sections and private bedrooms.

FIVE-CAR Owl trundles down Madison Avenue in Granite City, Ill., early one morning with motor car, three sleepers (from Peoria and Springfield), and an observation-sleeper out of Champaign.

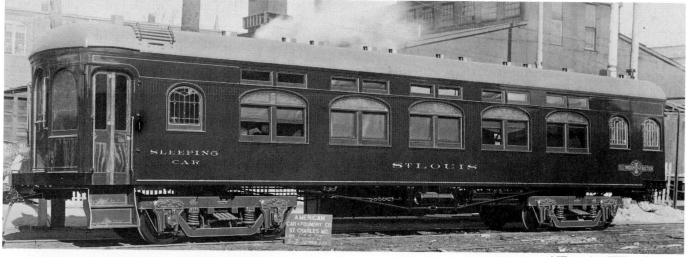

ACF, courtesy William C. Janssen.

ST. LOUIS, an IT sleeper with traditional upper-berth windows, was completed March 7, 1910, by St. Charles (Mo.) plant of ACF.

Interior photos, collection of William C. Janssen.

INSIDE an IT sleeper. Upper berths had windows, too.

365

Paul Stringham, courtesy George Krambles.

PENSIVE passengers at Lee Siding on the IT in August 1926.

LAST interurban cars built for U. S. service were eight blue-and-silver streamlined units delivered to IT in 1948 by St. Louis Car Company. They offered reclining coach seats, reserved observation seats, and a la carte dining service; operated as the City of Decatur, Fort Crevecoeur, and Mound City; survived in service until 1956 when Illinois Terminal abandoned its passenger service.

Collection of George Krambles.

a la carte

SOUPS
Clam Chowder, Split Pea, Bean, Beef Noodle, Cream of Tomato, Chicken Noodle,
Vegetable, Cream of Mushroom, Genuine Turtle
(includes crackers or bread) .25

CEREALS
Toasted Corn Flakes, Grape Nuts, All-Bran, Shredded Wheat, Puffed Wheat or
Rice (with cream) .25

RELISHES, APPETIZERS
Queen Olives .20   Tomato Juice .15   Orange Juice .15

MEATS
Choice Steak 1.35   Choice Loin Pork Chops (2) .95
Bacon or Ham and One Egg .75   Bacon or Ham and 2 Eggs .85
Egg, any style (1) .20   Eggs, any style (2) .35
Eggs, any style (3) .45

SANDWICHES
Fried Ham .45   Cold Meat .30
Cheese .30   Combination .45

BREAD
White, Whole Wheat, Rye (with butter) .10   Toast (buttered) .15

HOT DISHES
Chili Con Carne (includes crackers or bread) .30
Baked Beans, Hot or Cold .25   Spaghetti .25

FRIDAY SUGGESTIONS
Egg Salad Sandwich .30
Flaky Tuna Salad (Served with Potato Chips) .65

SALADS
Head Lettuce with Dressing .30   Sliced Tomatoes (in season) .30

VEGETABLES
French Fried Potatoes .20   Cottage Fried Potatoes .20

DESSERTS
Pie, liberal cut .20   Pie, liberal cut with cheese .30
Cake .20   Sliced Bananas with cream .25
Ice Cream .25

COFFEE, TEA, MILK
Coffee (cup) .10   Coffee (pot) .20   Tea (pot) .20
Milk (half-pint bottle) .15   Iced Tea .10

TO OUR PATRONS - - -
Thank you—The Illinois Terminal appreciates your patronage, and we trust it
will be our privilege to serve you often.
The above prices include Illinois Retailers' Occupation Tax.

CREVECOEUR • ILLINOIS TERMINAL COMPANY • MOUND CITY

Collection of George Krambles.

"A CHOICE STEAK" on the Illinois Terminal sold for $1.35.

RAILROAD ILLINOIS TERMINAL SYSTEM

FRESHLY painted in tangerine, IT's Capitol Limited — motor 273 and observation-parlor car Lincoln (No. 514) — poses for

All photos, collection of George Krambles.

company photographer at Decatur shops. Both cars typify pre-World War I arch-roof IT design. Both were later air-conditioned.

ILLINOIS was one of two cars remodeled into 9-bedroom sleepers by St. Louis Car Company in 1929. Each room contained a spring bed, upholstered chair, individual toilet facilities, reading lamp, and fan.

Collection of William C. Janssen.

PARLOR-CAR luxury (above); sleeping-car aisle (right).

BROADSIDE of observation-parlor 102 photographed in 1928 by Wilbourne B. Cox. Big steel interurban was painted blue and cream.

Waterloo, Cedar Falls & Northern Railway

PREDECESSOR company of the Waterloo, Cedar Falls & Northern Railway — the Cedar Valley Road — was chartered in 1895 to construct and operate an electric street railway and interurban between Waterloo and Cedar Falls, Ia. The line was thoughtfully conceived and carefully built to high standards. In time it developed into the second largest interurban in the Hawkeye State; in 1958, it was the last to abandon its passenger operations.

The three Cass brothers of Waterloo, developers of the road, realized the importance of interchange business with local steam railroads and actively sought freight and passenger business from the neighboring Chicago & North Western and Chicago Great Western roads at Cedar Rapids. It is reported that during the peak years the Cedar Valley Road operated a through Pullman sleeper Chicago to Waterloo via C&NW.

For the newly completed Waterloo-Cedar Rapids line, the road in 1915 purchased all-steel equipment "of the latest design" from McGuire-Cummings Manufacturing Company of Paris, Ill., for use on high-speed limited trains. Three of the new cars, Nos. 100–102, were observation-parlor cars fitted with buffet and wicker chairs for de luxe service in the rich farm country. Meal service lasted for only a few months. Receipts from parlor-car operation totaled only $8000 during 1917 and shortly afterward the service was discontinued.

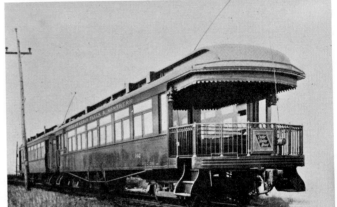

MARKERS of two-car limited were brought up by parlor car No. 102; inside (below) the ladies had wicker-chair compartment.

OBSERVATION-PARLOR CAR No. 100 posed for builder photo at Paris (Ill.) plant of McGuire-Cummings Manufacturing in 1915.

368

INTERURBAN BUILDING in downtown Dallas was busy during World War I, but lineup of automobiles forecast future implications.

Texas Electric Railway

PARLOR-CAR SERVICE on the Texas Electric Railway was inaugurated on May 1, 1917. It was advertised as "a distinct innovation on interurban lines in the Southwest." Three coaches — originally built by Niles for Stone & Webster-controlled Dallas Southern Traction Company — were rebuilt for de luxe service at the shop of the newly organized Texas Electric. The elegantly fitted cars were equipped with 22 large roomy chairs of the latest parlor type. A commodious smoking room was provided, along with an enclosed observation compartment "affording a splendid means of viewing the Black Land Belt" from Dallas north to Denison and south to Waco. Patrons aboard the cars were served by a "courteous porter whose sole duty [was] to cater to their every want."

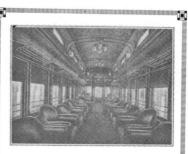

THE Parlor Car service inaugurated by Texas Electric Railway on May 1st affords a distinct innovation on interurban lines in the Southwest. These cars are operated on fast limited schedules between Dallas and Waco, and between Dallas and Denison.

The cars are elegantly fitted throughout for the comfort and convenience of patrons, each car being equipped with twenty-two large, roomy chairs of the latest parlor car type, furnishing the maximum of ease and comfort.

A commodious smoking room is provided, together with an observation compartment, thus affording a splendid means of viewing the magnificent "Black Land Belt" country traversed by these lines.

Patrons will find a courteous porter on the cars, whose sole duty is to cater to their every want. The cars are supplied with the current magazines to add to the pleasure of the trip.

This service supplements the hourly Local and Limited service operated between Dallas and Denison, Dallas and Waco, and Dallas and Corsicana.

LOOKING down aisle of parlor chairs to enclosed observation.

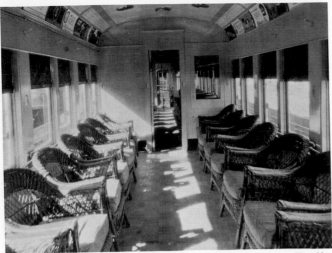

Collection of George Krambles.

LOOKING into the "Salounge Car" with its facing wicker chairs.

Northern Texas Traction Company

WHEN Northern Texas Traction Company completed the 35-mile Fort Worth-Dallas Division in 1902, the population of Dallas was 45,000 and of Fort Worth about 32,000. During the next 25 years the combined population of the two cities rapidly grew to a half million. Service on the interurban line kept pace with the towns' extraordinary growth. More than 50 million passengers rode the line which in 1924 received the Coffin Award for its contribution to the electric transit industry.

In 1927 the Northern Texas road introduced the *Crimson Limited*, proclaimed to be "the finest intercity transportation service in the country." The new two-car trains cost $47,000 and departed from Fort Worth and Dallas "hourly on the half," 7:30 a.m. to 6:30 p.m. The trail car was divided into two sections. The forward portion was furnished with revolving upholstered chairs. The rear section was termed the "Salounge Car" and was furnished with comfortable wicker seats. When hard hit by the depression seven years later, the road discontinued all service in 1934.

Collection of William C. Janssen.

CRIMSON LIMITED really ran downtown on timetable.

Collection of George Krambles.

TWO-CAR Crimson Limited's arch-roof and arch-window equipment of 1927 was "finest intercity transportation in the country."

COMFORT SPECIAL posed in January 1931 in front of PE's 2-million-dollar terminal at 6th and Main streets in Los Angeles with parlor 1254 on the point. This car was rebuilt from O&C 502 (below), leading West Side local through Portland, Ore., in rain.

Angelus Studio.

NIGHT scene on timetable of 1931.

Pacific Electric Railway

THE Pacific Electric Railway was the largest intercity electric road in the United States and was proclaimed the "Largest Electric Interurban System in the World." It operated 2600 trains per day on 615 miles of track during its peak years. Guiding genius of the company during its formative period was Henry Huntington, grandson of Southern Pacific's Collis P. Huntington. Southern Pacific controlled Pacific Electric during most of PE's history.

In 1929 PE inaugurated de luxe "Comfort Specials" on the boat trains operating between Los Angeles and Wilmington primarily for use in the service to and from steamers at Los Angeles harbor. Six reserved-seat parlor cars (extra fare, 25 cents) were rebuilt coaches purchased from Southern Pacific interurban lines in Oregon — the Red Electrics of Portland.

Thirty-nine deeply upholstered leather and mohair individual seats were placed in parlor-car fashion, facing the aisle. Wilton carpeting, silk shades, and dome lighting added touches of luxury. A separate room seating 11 accommodated smokers. Among the innovations was the service of a white-coated porter whose duty was "to look after the comfort of travelers." *Electric Traction* magazine commented that the new equipment "exceeded in refinement any similar type of car introduced by electric railways in the West."

BOWLER HATS predominate on observation of Kootenai, which brings up rear of five-car No. 9, the Shoshone Flyer, in Spokane.

Spokane & Inland Empire Railroad

"THE Spokane & Inland Empire Railroad is a standard-gauge railroad, electrically operated, and its lines comprise over 200 miles radiating south and east from Spokane. Unsurpassed anywhere in the United States in its freight and passenger equipment, it intersects the fertile fruit belt of southern Spokane county and serves the principal towns in the Palouse county." — *Spokane & Inland Empire advertisement, 1914.*

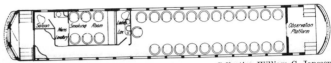

Collection William C. Janssen.

The 57-foot Kootenai was built by Brill in 1906 for Coeur d'Alene & Spokane, IE predecessor; later went to the North Coast Lines.

Harold Hill, courtesy of William C. Janssen.

WOODEN CAR 525 at Tacoma station with its observation platform closed in for winter service on Tacoma-Seattle Limited.

Asahel Curtis, courtesy Washington State Historical Society.

PARLOR CAR 523, built by St. Louis in 1907, brings up rear of three-car train at the Seattle station on Occidental at Yesler Way.

Puget Sound Electric Railway

BETWEEN Seattle and Tacoma in Washington the Puget Sound Electric Railway operated 36 miles of high-speed line. "The Scenic Route of Puget Sound" was built to high standards under the direction of Stone & Webster, engineering and management consultants of Boston. Track was laid through a countryside of scenic splendor located about 3 miles inland from Puget Sound west of the Cascade Range. The line, completed in 1902, was one of the earliest third-rail operations and employed trolley wire only while running on city streets.

Before the construction of paved highways, the company experienced a large volume of traffic. It inaugurated observation-parlor car service (extra fare, 25 cents) on limited trains in

Asahel Curtis, courtesy Washington State Historical Society.

INSIDE car 523 were tub chairs, velvet drapes, brass spittoons.

1907 using arched-window cars with unique open platforms that were closed in during wintertime. The Seattle-Tacoma limiteds proved a profitable operation until automobile and bus competition forced the road into receivership and abandonment in 1928.

Collection of George Krambles.

COMET pauses at Temescal Siding with unique big-windowed double-platform observation car Moraga bringing up its drumhead sign.

Sacramento Northern Railway

THE 94-mile trip from the Key System Ferry Pier in San Francisco through the Sacramento Valley via the "Sacramento Short Line" included two ferryboats and the luxury of Sacramento Northern's observation-parlor-buffet car *Moraga*. The heavy dark green car was built in 1913 by the Wason Car Company of Worcester, Mass., for SN predecessor Oakland, Antioch & Eastern which later became the San Francisco-Sacramento Railroad. *Moraga* was built with unique double-end platforms because of the inability to turn the car around at

Sacramento. It was rebuilt to a more conventional plan in 1927 when the new Union Station facilities were completed.

Sacramento Northern catered to state legislators and businessmen en route to the state capital and advertised service "to the door of the legislature." Dining and parlor-car service was offered on the *Comet*, *Meteor*, *Capitol*, and *Sacramento Valley*.

Lean years of depression forced the end of dining cars in 1934 and regularly scheduled parlor cars in 1938. Direct entry into San Francisco over the Bay Bridge in 1939 did not help stem the tide. Revenue continued to dwindle and regular passenger service on the Sacramento Northern ended in 1941.

TIMETABLE issued August 1923.

HAM-and-eggs club breakfast: 75 cents.

SN timetable dated January 1938.

373

Oregon Electric Railway

THE Oregon Electric Railway operated from Portland to Eugene, 122 miles through the heart of the Willamette Valley via Salem and Albany. The line to Salem was opened in 1908, and in 1910 the company was acquired by the Spokane, Portland & Seattle Railway (jointly owned by Great Northern and Northern Pacific). Heavy new equipment was ordered for operation over the new line to Eugene which was opened in October 1912.

Two buffet-observation-parlor cars, *Sacajawea* and *Champoeg*, arrived in September 1910 from Niles Car & Manufacturing Company. Two sleeping cars, *Santiam* and *Calapooia*, were delivered by Barney & Smith in October 1912. Because the sparsely populated territory could not support such luxury services, three of the de luxe cars were sold to the Pacific Great Eastern Railway, a steam road in British Columbia. The fourth car, *Sacajawea*, had been destroyed by fire at Fellers, Ore., in 1924. **⌶**

Ken Kidder.

SANTIAM, 10-section sleeping car No. 1010 built in 1912 by Barney & Smith, was sold to Pacific Great Eastern (above) in 1925.

PORTLAND-EUGENE limited with smoker, first-class coach, and observation-

Collection of George Krambles.

374

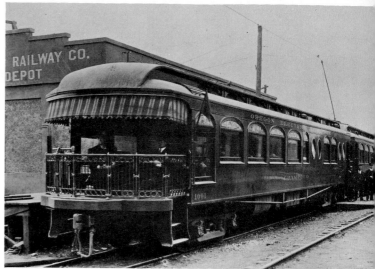

CHAMPOEG, parlor-observation car 1001, was built by Niles in 1910; measured 62 feet long; possessed an interior "of selected dark figured mahogany" as well as "Gothic and deck sashes glazed with leaded art glass." Something for steam roads to envy.

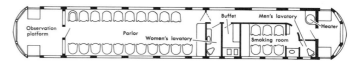

parlor built by Niles in 1912. Collection of William C. Janssen.

SACAJAWEA, sister of the Champoeg, appears to have a capacity load inside and outside as its OE train traverses cutover land.

A Trip Through CUBA with PULLMAN COMFORTS

When the Pullman Company threw open the gates to Cuba in 1925

The gates of Cuba have been opened by the Pullman Company to those discriminating travelers who wish to explore the Island Republic and enjoy its lovely climate with the minimum of effort and the maximum of comfort.

A specially prepared all-Pullman train has been assembled to make this dream come true. It is equipped with all those comfort-producing accessories that make Pullman travel the most luxurious in the world. — A Trip Through Cuba with Pullman Comforts, brochure, 1924.

1 DURING the winter of 1924-1925 newspapers throughout the United States featured stories about the *Cuban Special.* This gorgeous train was operated by the Pullman Company in conjunction with the United Railways of Havana and the Cuba Railroad. Between January and April 1925 it made leisurely weekly trips from Havana to Santiago and return on a schedule that enabled passengers to see the island under the most comfortable conditions.

Every Monday evening the *Special* was parked at the dock in Havana awaiting the arrival of the Peninsular & Occidental steamship *Cuba* from Key West. One hour later it slowly departed on the 535-mile run to Santiago which was reached on Wednesday morning after a stopover at Camaguey where auto trips and a formal dinner dance were provided.

After a day of sight-seeing at San Juan Hill and another formal dinner dance in Santiago, the train was run into the cool mountains for the evening.

On Thursday afternoon, the *Special* departed from Santiago bound for Matanzas and more sight-seeing. Following a short ride on Friday afternoon, the cars arrived in Havana where they were parked for occupancy until Monday, allowing several days in Havana.

The train used for this tour was a beauty. It was composed of six handsome wooden Pullmans (A, B, C, D, E, and F) — kitchen car, dining room car, and four observation-sleepers. All except the kitchen car were open-platform observations which had formerly served on various crack limited trains in the States before being redecorated for the novel and luxurious *Cuban Special.* Each car was served by a porter-valet who was thoroughly educated to the needs of the traveling public by years of experience in the United States. The Cuban railways provided an interpreter, and a representative of the Pullman Company supervised all arrangements.

Car A was the kitchen car with dormitory for the crew. It was formerly named *Honorius.*

Dining room car B was the former observation-parlor car *Port Chester,* a veteran of the New Haven's *Merchants Limited.* It was redecorated with staggered round tables and old Cordovan chairs upholstered in red leather.

Car No. 3, C, was the *Louisiana* of St. Louis World's Fair fame. It contained six luxurious compartments.

Cars 4 and 5, D and E, were the former *Kaaterskill* and *Knickerbocker,* 8-compartment observation cars of the celebrated New York-Chicago *Twentieth Century Limited.* They were placed in the *Special* with observation platforms meeting to form an "awning-covered, palm-decorated patio."

The last car, No. 6, F, was the 10-section observation-sleeper, formerly *Ben MacDhui* of the *Golden State.*

The standard Pullman mohair plush covering was replaced by "cool and seasonable French denim of pretty pattern," and throughout the train all decorations were in keeping with the land in which it operated.

One of the enthusiastic passengers was onetime Congressman Joseph R. Knowland, publisher of the Oakland *Tribune,* and father of former Senator William Knowland of California. The senior Knowland said this of the train: "I have traveled in many places that have been highly praised. This trip equals the best of my travels."

KAATERSKILL — car D of the *Special* — was an 8-compartment observation. Photo from Pullman-Standard.

A Trip Through CUBA

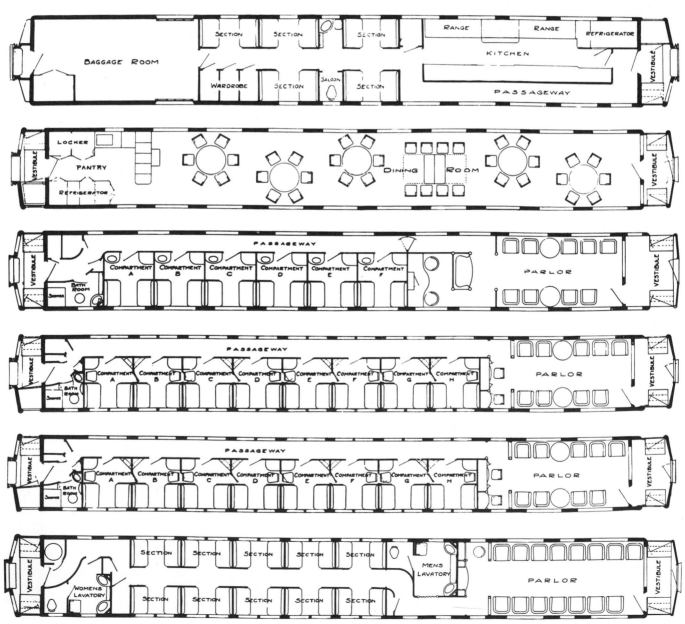

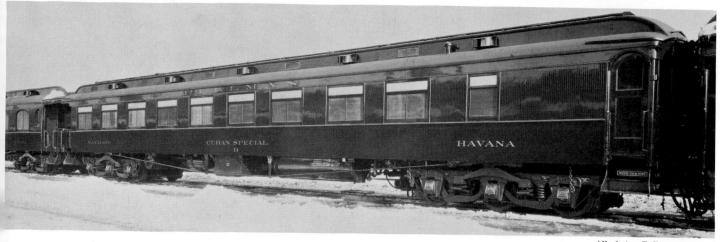

All photos, Pullman-Standard.

A VETERAN of the Merchants Limited, the former observation-parlor Port Chester served the Cuban Special as dining room car

B. Figured silk drapes, black and white tiling, and old leather chairs (left) enhanced the beauty of mobile dining in Cuba.

QUITE TROPICAL was a compartment in car C, formerly the Louisiana, with its electric fans and comfortable wicker chairs.

BEYOND the draped window in the observation-parlor of car C were palm trees and other examples of "sub tropical verdure."

CUBAN SPECIAL, tied to a steam line and parked alongside snowbanks, pauses for Pullman photographer before shipment to Cuba.

NEWLY repainted in cardinal red, the *Cardinals Train* stands at the Calumet (Ill.) shops of Pullman in June 1926.

The Cardinals

SCHEDULE OF
The Cardinals Train

		Eastern Standard Time
Leave New York. June 16, 1926. . 10:00 A.M.		
Arrive Albany...	"	.. 1:40 P.M.
Leave Albany....	"	.. 1:50 P.M.
Arrive Utica	"	.. 4:15 P.M.
Leave Utica	"	.. 4:25 P.M.
Arrive Syracuse.	"	.. 5:45 P.M.
Leave Syracuse ..	"	.. 5:55 P.M.
Arrive Rochester	"	.. 7:50 P.M.
Leave Rochester..	"	.. 8:00 P.M.
		Central Standard Time
Arrive Elkhart ...June 17, 1926..6:10 A.M.		
Leave Elkhart	"	..6:20 A.M.
Arrive South Bend	"	..6:55 A.M.
Leave South Bend.	"	..7:05 A.M.
Arrive Porter	"	..8:10 A.M.
Arrive Chicago..	"	..9:50 A.M.

TIMECARD over New York Central.

While they are with us may they enjoy the warmth of our hospitality, may they take with them and diffuse everywhere the kindliest memories of the hours they spent in our midst during the days when the Eucharistic Christ "pertransivit benefaciendo et sanando omnes." — George Cardinal Mundelein.

I   ON June 16, 1926, at 10 a.m. a most extraordinary train departed from Grand Central Terminal in New York City bound for Chicago. This amazing operation was known as the *Cardinals Train*. It consisted of seven stunning cars newly painted in cardinal red trimmed with gold. There were six Pullmans and a New York Central-operated dining car, each appropriately named for the occasion.

The XXVIII International Eucharistic Congress held in Chicago on June 20-24, 1926, was the first such event to occur in the United States. Delegates, both clergymen and laymen, came from all parts of the world to attend.

To accommodate the Cardinals and their party on their journey from New York to Chicago, the New York Central Railroad and the Pullman Company supplied the *Cardinals Train* as their contribution to the national welcome extended to the distinguished visitors.

New York bade an impressive farewell to the departing Cardinals and their suites. An hour before the train was scheduled to depart, a crowd of 10,000 gathered in the concourse of Grand Central Terminal and greeted the individual Cardinals with wave after wave of applause as they arrived. Cardinal Von Faulhaber, the Archbishop of Munich, Germany, was the first to board the train. Cardinal Bonzano, the Papal Legate, was given a prolonged ovation when he arrived. As the train departed, Cardinal Bonzano's last visible gesture from the observation platform of the rear car was one of blessing.

At town after town, the party was greeted by local dignitaries accompanied by bands and cheering crowds.

Train

Seven cars in red

Ten thousand gathered at the station in Albany. Thirty thousand persons cheered the Cardinals at Syracuse where Cardinal Bonzano bestowed the papal blessing while the people knelt on the stone pavement about the station.

The special arrived at Rochester at 7:50 p.m. where a throng of 50,000 had gathered at the station plaza and there Cardinal O'Donnell, the Primate of Ireland, spoke.

With nightfall, the occupants of the gorgeous Pullmans witnessed an unusual demonstration. At crossings and local stations, and even in plowed fields, crowds had gathered to cheer the Cardinals. The beams of automobile headlights were thrown on the "red special," and bonfires illuminated the landscape as the train passed. Elkhart and South Bend greeted the party on the morning of June 17 with crowds which cheered and then knelt reverently to receive the Cardinals' blessings.

The train was switched onto Michigan Central tracks at Porter, Ind., for the last 44 miles into Chicago's Park Row Station of the Illinois Central where it arrived at 9:45 a.m., 5 minutes ahead of scheduled time.

Cardinal Mundelein, Mayor Dever, and the Chicago City Council in morning dress were at the station to extend a civic greeting. Cheering thousands filled the station and the sidewalks of Michigan Boulevard. Cardinal Mundelein walked through the train, officially greeting each Cardinal as he proceeded, and finally received the Papal Legate. The Cardinals then left the historic train.

Students of car names may be interested to know the regular Pullman names of the cars in the *Cardinals Train*. These cars were painted red and were renamed in June 1926. During July they were repainted standard Pullman green and their original names were restored: *Charles Carroll of Carrollton* (ex-*Eagle Cliff*), *Cardinal Bonzano* (ex-*Sunderland*), *Cardinal Hayes* (ex-*Glen River*), *Bishop Quarter* (ex-*Glen Flora*), *Father Marquette* (ex-*Glen Ellyn*), and *Pope Pius XI* (ex-*Superb*).

All photos, Pullman Company.

CLUB CAR Charles Carroll of Carrollton was named for Catholic leader, B&O director, Declaration of Independence signer.

CARDINAL BONZANO, a 10-compartment car, was named for Papal Legate to the XXVIII Eucharistic Congress held in Mundelein, Ill.

CARDINAL HAYES, a 6-compartment, 3-drawing-room Pullman, was named for one of the passengers — the Archbishop of New York.

ST. MARY OF THE LAKE, the New York Central-operated dining car, was renamed for the seminary at Mundelein. Elaborate menus with red covers and silk ribbons were furnished for the journey and a hand-picked crew served the distinguished riders.

BISHOP QUARTER, a "6-3" car, named for first Chicago Bishop.

Cardinals Train

FATHER MARQUETTE, another 6-compartment, 3-drawing-room car, was named for famous missionary explorer of the Midwest.

POPE PIUS XI, the Cardinals Train's observation, served as private car for Cardinal Bonzano, who presided over the Congress.

MEET ME IN ST. LOVIS,

When Pullman displayed a traveler's paradise

1 IN 1803 Napoleon ceded the 1-million-square-mile Louisiana Territory to the United States. The centenary of this momentous event was celebrated by the St. Louis World's Fair of 1904, or as it was officially designated, the Louisiana Purchase Exposition. "Meet me in St. Louis" was the byword of the day.

One of the chief points of interest for the sight-seer at the Fair was the prize-winning exhibit of the Pullman Company. This display contained 10 elaborate specially built cars which were placed on two tracks in the center

GRAND prize awarded to Pullman train.

of the Transportation Building—one of the most expensive exhibit buildings at the Fair.

The richly fitted Pullmans were attended by uniformed employees of the company who were stationed in each of the cars to answer visitors' questions. Exterior color was Pullman standard dark olive green with plain striping, all highly varnished. Small cathedral windows of leaded art glass constituted a special feature of the train's appearance.

In naming and numbering the cars, selections were made appropriate to the Louisiana Purchase. All cars were built to Pullman standards in every respect and were solidly framed with continuous blocking, channel iron truss planks, iron-plated side and end sills and steel plat-

forms with wide vestibules and anti-telescoping devices. All cars were equipped for lighting by either gas or electricity, and for heating by circulating hot water. All cars except the 70-foot tourist car were 80 feet long.

Car interiors were simple but elegant, with an attempt made to depart from the conventional car design and to create the effect of a fine residence.

The exhibit trains were widely acclaimed and received Grand Prize honors at the Fair. Many of their innovations

MEET ME AT THE FAIR

STELLAR ATTRACTION: Pullman exhibit with uniformed attendants. Illustrations, these pages, Pullman Company.

became design prototypes for the carbuilding industry.

Because of the great variety of Pullman cars in the celebrated exhibit, no attempt was made by the company to keep the trains intact after the close of the exposition. Most of the cars were refitted and renamed for general service, although several of the more elegant cars were retained for special Pullman operations.

Composite car *Jefferson* and dining car *Monroe* operated in the 1906 *Havana Limited*, a once-a-week de luxe

tourist service from Chicago to Cuba via the Chicago & Alton and Mobile & Ohio railroads in connection with the Munson Steamship Line from Mobile to Havana. Observation-compartment car *Louisiana* was the last of the St. Louis cars to survive as a Pullman. It served in the fabled *Cuban Special* of 1925 (which is described in detail elsewhere in this volume) and was carried on the Pullman roster until November 1931 when dismantled, ending a glittering chapter in the saga of carbuilding.

MONROE, a dining car, possessed a strikingly designed interior (below) of Antwerp brown oak finished and carved in "Flemish Style." Other features of note: high leaded windows containing clear glass for viewing the outdoors, condiment-bottle niches under windows, leather chairs, and art-glass lamps.

LIVINGSTON contained 12 sections, a drawing room, and a stateroom; was finished in "L'art Nouveau Style" (above); had electric reading lamps. It became a tourist car in 1918, was destroyed in 1919.

All photos, Pullman Company.

JEFFERSON, composite baggage and smoking car, was renamed Viceroy in 1905 and dismantled in 1928. It contained a smoker with 12 overstuffed leather chairs, a buffet, and a barbershop with white-tiled bath. Olive carpet and dark brown koko wood (right) were done in "Modern Style" of North German Lloyd express steamships.

NAPOLEON, a parlor car, had dark vermilion wood walls (right) inlaid with marquetry in colonial style, rose upholstered chairs, and cut-glass ceiling lamps.

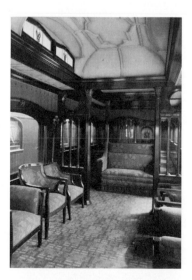

LOUISIANA, an observation-lounge, was highlighted by 6 compartments, each finished in a different exotic wood. Observation room (left) contained novel lights that represented flowers budding out of stems entwined with leaves. A special feature of the 12-wheeled car was an office "containing a writing table, bookcase, and typewriting outfit."

387

CHAIR CAR NO. 1903 carried 72 in reclining seats (below) amidst Cuban mahogany trim, was rebuilt to parlor Felicia in 1906.

CENTENNIAL, a cafe-smoking car, served as combination diner and club; had a smoking room (above) finished in Old English-style carved oak as well as leaded windows containing clear glass.

COACH NO. 1803 accommodated 72 passengers on Scarrit reversible green plush seats (right) as constructed, was rebuilt in 1906 to the parlor car Florelia.

MISSISSIPPI, tourist (or second-class) sleeper, was 70 feet long; had 16 sections finished in rattan; small galley.

MEET ME IN ST. LOVIS,

PRESIDENT at $30,000 was twice as expensive as typical Pullman of 1904; contained three private rooms, a white-tiled bathroom, a dining room, and an observation room — all finished in Louis XIV style. Renamed Plymouth Rock after the Fair, it operated in Pullman private-car service until 1914, became Canadian Pacific office car Montmorency.

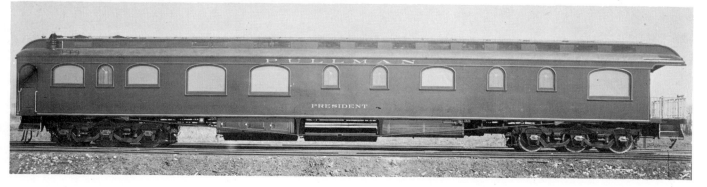

SOME CLA

How we got there prior t

1 THERE was a day in the recent past when *atomic* was a word of the scientist and *turbojet* meant nothing at all. It was a time when one could lie in bed and hear the wail of a steam whistle pierce the silence of the night. It was the day of the observation car with its glistening brass railing and illuminated drum sign. Enormous *Official Guides* listed page after page of de luxe named trains. And *Twentieth Century Limited* meant magic and wonder. It was the Railway Age, the era of the classic cars.

A classic is defined as a work of the highest order, of acknowledged excellence. The classic cars — the parlor cars and Pullmans, coaches and club cars; baggage cars and buffets — are note-

Q'S CHICAGO-DENVER LIMITED of 1926 carried Pullman-built solarium-parlor car Burlington Bridge. The beginning of the end was at hand for the open platform.

CHICAGO DENVER LIMITED

SSIC CARS

pavement and the Model A

worthy because of their design, construction, or interior furnishings. Big
wooden cars and heavy steel cars, they
are from a period in which an ordinary
chap with the price of a railroad ticket
could live in splendor that rivaled the
luxury of a king's castle across the sea.

These classics were operated in all
parts of the country, in all types of
trains. They have passed before our
eyes, taken for granted and all too often
unnoticed. Now, for the most part, they
have disappeared. Like the steam locomotive which pulled them, they have
been replaced by sleek new standardized models from a mass production
line.

Like the vanished steam locomotive,
they are missed.

IN 1906 the Rock Island's Chicago-Denver
Rocky Mountain Limited ended splendidly
with the picture window and brass railing of observation car 1664 (see page 397).

391

The P70: standard of standards

OLD WORKHORSE passenger car of the Pennsylvania was the P70. One of the early varieties of this famous design, No. 8055, is shown at American Car & Foundry in April 1914 before shipment for service on the old Vandalia Lines. A predecessor of the P70 built in 1906 for what was to be fireproof service

in the new tunnel under the Hudson River into the then new Pennsylvania Station in New York City was one of the first steel cars built in the U. S. Variations of the P70 have been constructed over the years, but the basic design — 4-wheel truck, window arrangement, Tuscan red — has changed little.

Where the drummers rode

THIS IS THE CAR the drummer rode with his sample cases, 5-cent "seegars," and the latest story about the Farmer's Daughter. Chair car No. 800 was one of a brace of mail, baggage, coach, and cafe-observation cars built by Pullman in 1905 to run behind the five new Brooks Atlantics in the Wisconsin Central's last bid for the Twin Cities–Chicago service. Four years later WC passed into the limbo of railroads leased (by the Soo) but not forgotten. The 800 was painted a deep wine, lined and lettered in gold leaf. Its high-back reclining seats were red plush.

The roof identifies it as "Harriman"

"HARRIMAN" COACH was the namesake of E. H. Harriman, ruler of the railway network built around Illinois Central, Southern Pacific, and Union Pacific. Harriman cars were distinguished by the arch or turtle-back roof, distinctive ventilators, and opaque Gothic window sash. There were straight coaches, parlor cars, club-lounge cars, and diners, all built in the period before World War I — mostly by ACF and Pullman. Illinois Central combination passenger-baggage

car 880 was built in 1913 at Jeffersonville (Ind.) works of ACF for Chicago-Florida service on the crack Seminole Limited. Interior trim was Mexican mahogany, and the 76-foot 1-inch length seated 40 in reclining seats in the passenger compartment, 8 in the smoker. Many of the Harriman coaches are still in active service. Some, like buffet-lounge 3857, have been extensively rebuilt. All were an important contribution to the art of carbuilding.

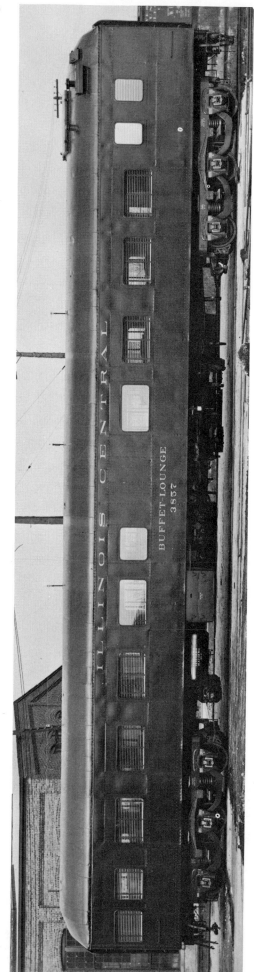

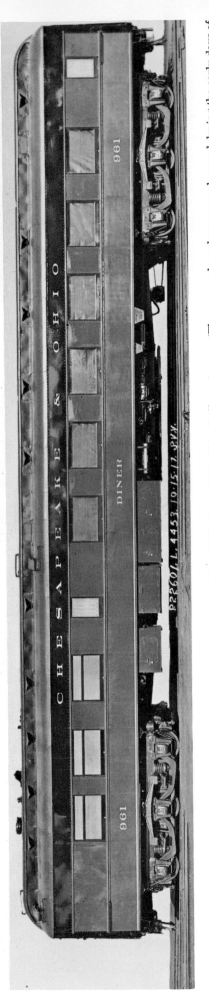

Dinner hour on the F.F.V.

CHESAPEAKE & OHIO diner 961, was one of a group of cars ordered to upgrade the famous *F.F.V. Limited* — the *Fast Flying Virginian*, named after the F.F.V. (First Families of Virginia). The car was painted in the long-gone orange-and-maroon scheme introduced in 1889 by M. E. Ingalls when he was president of C&O.

(The same color scheme was also used during the early days of the Big Four, of which Ingalls was also president.) Diner 961 was one of the first cars built with a wide letterboard replacing art-glass Gothic upper window sash. No. 961 looks modern, younger than her age. Probably for this reason she has survived the ravages of time, is still in active service on C&O.

CHESAPEAKE & OHIO diner 961, built by Pullman in November 1917,

Unobtrusively steel

GRANDFATHER smoked the "weed" here. Buffet car 449 was built by Pullman in 1910 for New York Central's *20th Century Limited* in the days of Chauncey Depew. Cars of this type served as the prototype for Lionel and Ives trains of the 1920's. Quote from the 1925 Ives catalog: "There's nothing like a well-managed Buffet car for making passengers boost the road they travel on." The lining of the steel plates (see the rivets) simulated wood. Passengers on the first steel cars, especially on electrified operations, were fearful of being electrocuted in severe thunderstorms.

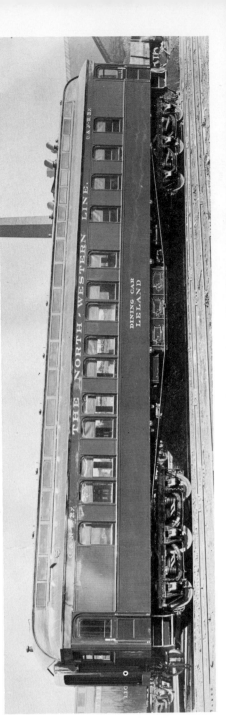

"Splendor of great Kublai Khan"

LEAVING Chicago daily at 6:30 p.m. bound for St. Paul and Duluth in the company of a Chicago & North Western 900-class 4-4-0, a buffet car, and three of Wagner's finest Palace sleepers, the 1896 *Leland* — one of the "new electric-lighted dining cars on the *North Western Limited*" — was a feast for hungry travelers, literally and figuratively. With her green and yellow livery sparkling, she was the Best of Everything in the Best of the West. Featured on the Dollar Dinner were blue points, green turtle soup, fried frog saddles, roast quail, grouse — Macedonia style, rabbit pie, beef or turkey, plum pudding, and charlotte russe. The wine list included five imported champagnes, six clarets, Bass Ale or Guinness Dublin Porter. Hunyadi water, imported cigars, and Turkish cigarettes were also stocked. Page 4 of the menu read as follows:

A flying palace that outshines
The splendor of great Kublai Khan,
Rich with the woods of Orient
And cunning handiwork of man,
Stored with the rarest of old wines
And foods for dainty nourishment —
King Luxuries winged caravan,
The North Western Limited.

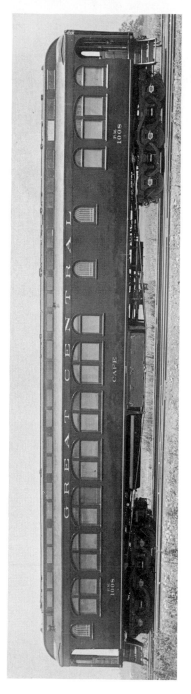

quette, together with Chicago, Cincinnati & Louisville (now C&O of Indiana), formed the Great Central Route reaching from Cincinnati on the south to Northern Michigan, and from Buffalo on the east to Springfield, Ill. This venture was short-lived, ending in receivership in 1907. In 1916, CH&D was purchased by B&O, concluding forever dreams of a Great Central. No. 1008, slated originally to run on the *East Coast Flyer* (Chicago-Grand Rapids), was built as a portion of Pere Marquette's contribution to the grandiose scheme.

For a grandiose scheme

A CLASS of car popular at the turn of the century is shown in this rare shot — one of the few in existence from this little-known railroad system, the Great Central Route. No. 1008, a cafe-chair car, was outshopped in June 1905 at Pullman in preparation for the newest railroad consolidation of the day. Cincinnati, Hamilton & Dayton and Pere Mar-

Leaded glass and brass cuspidors

EXTRAORDINARY yellow and red beauty, *Wauwatosa*, and her partner, *Winneconne*, each rolled up an astounding record of nearly 40 years of de luxe service in the consist of Milwaukee Road's *Pioneer Limited* between Chicago and the Twin Cities. They survived two World Wars; depression; and complete re-building in the 1920's, including steel plating and change of name (*Wauwatosa* became *Minneapolis, Winneconne* became *Chicago*). Built by Barney & Smith Car Co. of Dayton, O., in 1909,

they were retired only upon inauguration of post-World War II streamlined *Pioneer*. Interior fittings included a library, buf-fet, and lounge furnished with red carpet, leaded glass windows, brass cuspidors, tapestries, mahogany and guancasta paneling, Spanish leather club chairs, and eventually, air conditioning. Of interest are reporting marks CM&PS, indicating ownership by Chicago, Milwaukee & Puget Sound — the Milwaukee's West Coast extension, over which *Pioneer Limited* never operated.

The Saint and the Angel

SANTA FE parlor car No. 1204 was built by Pullman in December 1910 for the San Diego–Los Angeles section of trains 15 and 16 (the *Saint* and the *Angel*) which operated overnight on the Los Angeles–San Francisco line via Barstow, Bakersfield, and Fresno, a total of 719 miles in 21 hours. The exterior was painted white, and inside furnishings included wicker chairs. Among the refinements were the SANTA FE insigne stenciled near the car numbers, leaded glass bells set into each window Gothic, and the brass railing on the observation platform.

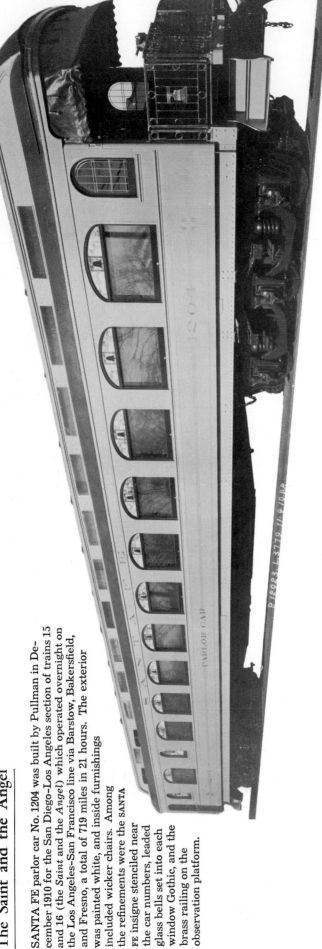

"A joy to look upon"

CONTEMPORARY advertising brochure described Union Pacific's Chicago–Omaha–Denver *Columbine*, inaugurated in 1930, in these glowing terms: "There are trains and trains. Some are just another means of going somewhere. Others are a joy to look upon, a delight to ride. In this last class comes the *Columbine*, the latest word in trains. In its name lies the whole secret. Colorado's state flower is the dainty blue-and-white columbine. A train named for it must be beautiful to be worthy of its namesake. . . . Its decorative motif comes from the flower — combined with the state crest of Colorado. From the nickel–trimmed locomotive to the blue, silver, and gold observation car, representing the state flag of Colorado bearing the state crest, it breathes the beauty of a great state." The exterior of the *Colorado Club* was painted in broad bars of silver and blue, striped with gold — colors of the state flag of Colorado. Within were three lounges: the sun parlor with sunroom furniture; and two parlor lounges with ebony furniture upholstered in gold mohair. Radio fans could listen to "Amos 'n' Andy" on the 8–tube radio; a soda fountain served "prohibition–type" cocktails and ice cream sodas. There was a complete barber and valet shop. Off the barber shop was a large dressing room, and a tub-shower ("piping hot, ice cold, or just the degree you prefer").

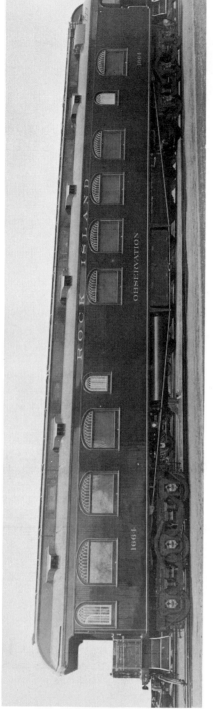

Anyone for an Antonio y Cleopatra?

PRIOR to World War I a razor-keen competition for the Chicago–Denver business existed. Each rival road had its *Colorado Special* or *Colorado Limited.* For the summer of 1909 Rock Island placed brand-new equipment in service on trains 7 and 8, the *Rocky Mountain Limited.* A westbound traveler was greeted in the then new La Salle Street Station in Chicago by the brass rail end of 1664 backed into the terminal. After depositing his luggage in his Pullman, he began to inspect what would be his home for 31 hours. He soon found his way into library-buffet-observation car 1664, then into its paneled smoking room.

For a railroad that is no more

phena. The caption which appears with it reads: "The only observation cars running thro' the Rocky Mountains of Colorado. These cars are attached to trains leaving Denver and Ogden and Salt Lake every morning, running through without change and passing through the Rocky Mountains by daylight."

TRYPHENA was one of the earliest observation cars built by Pullman. She and sister *Tryphosa* cost $17,034 each. Interior view of *Tryphena* shows the lavish ornamentation in the 8-section sleeper and observation car. Back cover of the March 1904 Colorado Midland public timetable shows a photograph of *Try-*

Green curtains, upper berths, "George"

THE 12-1 (12 sections, 1 drawing room) standard Pullman is perhaps the dean of all classics. Built by the thousands, it was run throughout North America wherever there was 4' 8½" track and a friendly white-jacketed porter, invar-

iably called "George." The green curtains, smoke-filled men's room, and undressing in an upper berth were as much a part of the Roaring '20's as were flapper girls and bathtub gin. These views show the development of the car from pre-World War I to the end. Pictured are *Puerto*, an early model dating from 1917; *Oostanaula*, built

in 1921 for Central of Georgia, one of a few roads which owned sleeping cars outright (rather than leasing them from Pullman); *Poplar Bluff*, a depression rebuild in an attempt to convert some of the open sections into bedrooms (note air-conditioning bubble); and *Deep South*, a GM&O redesign for the 1940 *Gulf Coast Rebel*.

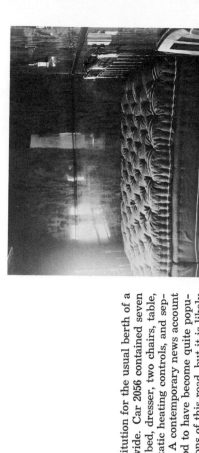

All-room car, circa 1888

DECEMBER 1888 issue of *Official Railway Guide* startled the railroad world (and most of all George M. Pullman) with this announcement: "Union Palace Car Co. . . . will commence operating SLEEPING AND PARLOR CARS on about 15,000 miles of railroad in January 1889." Formed by Job H. Jackson of Jackson & Sharp, Union Palace Car Co. was in effect a consolidation of Woodruff Sleeping & Parlor Coach Co. and Mann Boudoir Car Co. These two companies operated a total of 34 cars on about 5000 miles of railroads in the East, South, and Midwest. In January 1889 Union Palace was purchased by Pullman Palace for 2.5 million dollars. The *Maryland*, a 70-foot black and gold beauty with compartment-like boudoirs (built in 1888 by Jackson & Sharp — now ACF), was included in the sale, with all of Mann's and Woodruff's patents. Strangely, all-room cars and trains were 50 years away.

Bedsteads to Boston

DURING the winter of 1910 the New Haven established what was undoubtedly the most luxurious passenger service, exclusive of private cars, on any railroad in the U.S. Equipment, built by Pullman, consisted of a corridor-compartment car which was attached to each of the *Second Midnight Expresses* leaving New York and Boston simultaneously at 1 a.m. Distinguishing feature was the substitution for the usual berth of a full-length brass bed, 4 feet wide. Car 2056 contained seven compartments, each with brass bed, dresser, two chairs, table, electric fan, individual thermostatic heating controls, and separate enclosed toilet room. A contemporary news account stated: "The service is understood to have become quite popular with the discriminating patrons of this road, but it is likely to remain unique for some time, since it is doubtful there is another place in the country that would sustain such a service."

De luxe traction

BETWEEN the turn of the century and World War I many of the progressive electric traction lines throughout the country introduced parlor, dining, and even sleeping car services in an effort to compete with steam railroads. An interurban which offered these de luxe services was famed Illinois Traction System operating from central Illinois to St. Louis. Parlor-observation car 514, *Lincoln*, was one of six similar units (five of which were built in 1911 by Danville Car Co.) designed by J. M. Bosenbury, superintendent of motive power and equipment for ITS. These cars contained 19 parlor chairs upholstered in green Spanish leather, African mahogany paneling with inlaid trim, thick green Wilton carpet, and a porter who was paid $50 a month. In addition, there were sections for card playing and smoking. The exterior was dark green lined with gold. A particularly decorative feature was the bulkhead separating the parlor room from the card playing section. In the center of this bulkhead was a large oval-shaped stained art-glass design incorporating the initials of the road. In later years these cars were thoroughly rebuilt. Buffet service was added, the upper Gothic sashes were blocked off, and air conditioning was furnished. Eventually they were painted traction orange, and they ran in this livery after ITS became Illinois Terminal. For years the cars operated on the *Capitol Limited*, Nos. 96 and 97, between Peoria and St. Louis, until the advent of the short-lived post-World War II streamliners. Railroad enthusiasts and particularly traction buffs lament the passing of these fine cars and the railroad over which they operated.

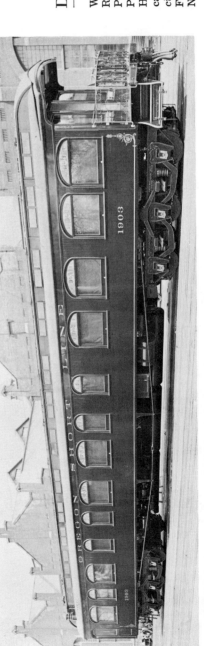

Dignity, grace, and beauty

WHEN Edward Henry Harriman ruled the Oregon Short Line Railroad at the turn of the century he surveyed the line to Portland from his own luxurious private car *Arden*, built by Pullman in 1899 and named after his palace in the Ramapo Hills north of New York City. The rest of the OSL brass rode in car 1903 on the rear of train No. 2, the *Chicago–Portland Special*. In one man's opinion, old "E. H." came out second best. Few cars ever built match the dignity, grace, and beauty of No. 1903, a Pullman Palace Car product of 1903.

SCARCE money and sparce settlement of North Dakota at the time of its admission to the Union in 1889 precluded the construction of many churches. Rev. William D. Walker solved the problem with a unique church on wheels. In 1890 Pullman built for the Episcopal Bishop's Church of the Advent the Cathedral Car of North Dakota—a 60-foot open-platform vehicle with pipe organ and Gothic stained-glass window which could accommodate 75 worshipers. Novel car was a familiar sight in small towns of the Great Plains from the Red River to the Montana border. In addition to officiating at church services, Bishop Walker conducted marriages and funerals. He attended to the stove, lamps, and housekeeping.

Pullman-Standard.

CATHEDRAL CAR OF NORTH DAKOTA: Church of the Advent

SOON after the United States entered World War II the wounded began to return home from the fronts of a global conflict. Accordingly, the U. S. Army Medical Department ordered six hospital ward cars from the Pullman Company. Parlor cars containing 28 chairs and a drawing room were stripped down and rebuilt for hospital train service. Typical was car No. 17, formerly the Pullman *Azalea*, shown at the Pullman car works in July 1942. A first-aid dressing room equipped with double doors replaced the drawing room. The main body of the car was fitted with 13 two-tier Glennon-type Army cots, a small kitchen, and office space.

Pullman Company.

U.S.A. 8917: United States Army Hospital Ward Car No. 17

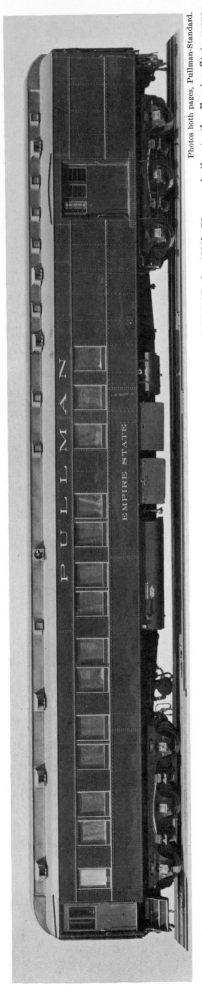

DURING the 1920's 76 cars similar to the *Empire State* were built under Pullman plan 3951. Most of them were named in series and assigned to crack trains: *Capitol* series for the *Capitol Limited*, *Liberty* series for the *Broadway* and *American*, and *Eagle* series for the *Florida Special*. In 1925 the *State* series (*Empire State, Bay State, Buckeye State, Hoosier State, Prairie State*) were completed for the *20th Century Limited*. Each contained leather club chairs, writing desk, card playing sections, buffet, barbershop, and men's bathroom with shower. The front section contained the baggage room complete with letter case and stretcher. Dispensing of alcoholic beverages in club cars during '20's was hampered by the Volstead Act.

EMPIRE STATE: Composite (Club) Car

THE classic "12 and 1" contained 12 sections — each having upper and lower berth — and 1 drawing room. The dean of heavyweight steel cars, 12-and-1 cars made up 4000 of the nearly 10,000 cars in the Pullman fleet in the peak year of 1931. Cars like *McBridesville* operated throughout North America offering Pullman ease and safety on almost all overnight runs.

MC BRIDESVILLE: 12 Sections, 1 Drawing Room

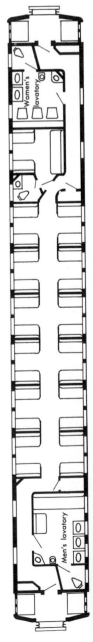

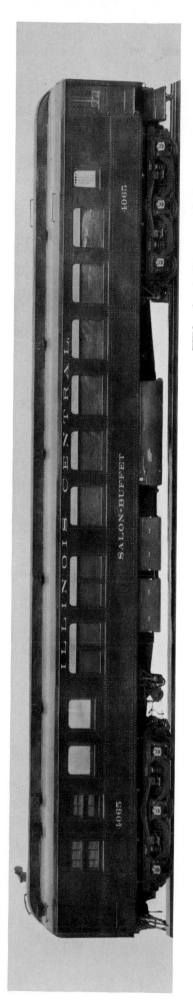

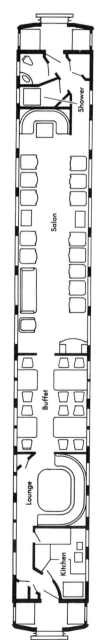

TWO salon-buffet cars with the atmosphere of a gentlemen's club were delivered to IC in March 1924. Passengers wishing to board the *Diamond Special* at St. Louis or Chicago several hours before its midnight departure found a number of conveniences awaiting them. These cars contained a white-tiled shower; club-salon with natural walnut paneling, easy chairs, and draped windows. Beverages, evening lunches, and breakfast were served in a dining section seating 20. The menu included broiled chops, bacon and eggs, sandwiches, fruits, cereals, and hot cakes. Upper window sashes fitted with white prism glass were among the last of this type used in carbuilding.

ILLINOIS CENTRAL NO. 4065: Salon-Buffet

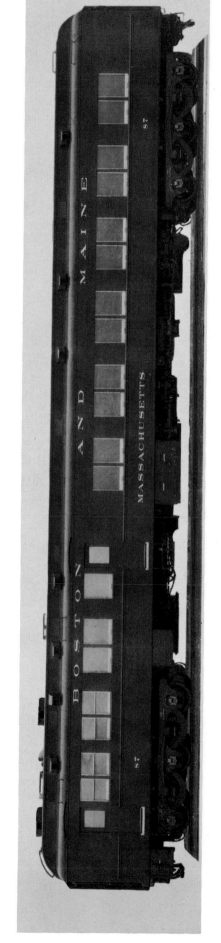

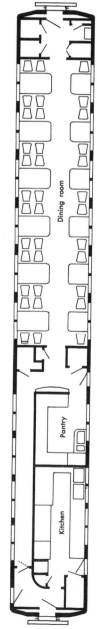

THE classic dining car included a kitchen with refrigerator, provision storage, broiler and range (operated by coal, charcoal, gas, or electricity), and steam table (fed from the train steam line). The pantry was equipped with dish warmer, sinks, bunkers for ice and ice cream, and buffet. The dining room seated 36 at six tables for two and six tables for four, and was decorated according to the specifications of the owning road. *Massachusetts* was built by Pullman-Standard in 1930 for the Boston & Maine *Minute Man*. Its colonial décor featured a Salem doorway, leaded glass sash, and bracket lamps. Railroads went to great lengths in the operation of dining cars to attract travelers who selected trains for the quality of meals.

MASSACHUSETTS: Standard Dining Car

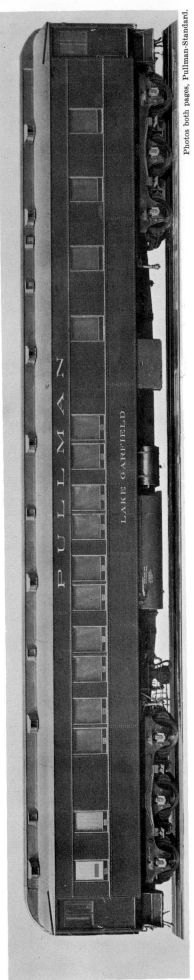

Photos both pages, Pullman-Standard.

LAKE GARFIELD: 10 Sections, Drawing Room, 2 Compartments

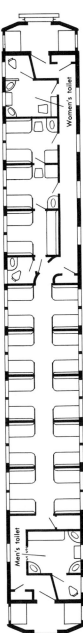

Men's toilet

Women's toilet

THIS Pullman plan was developed during the 1920's in order to provide more private rooms for long-distance runs. Over 500 cars of this type were built in the post-World War I years. Most were named for Army forts and camps, and lakes. Later-model *Chief* series eliminated one of the compartments and added more space to washrooms. Note Type 242 truck with pedestal and frame cast integrally, common in the early '20's.

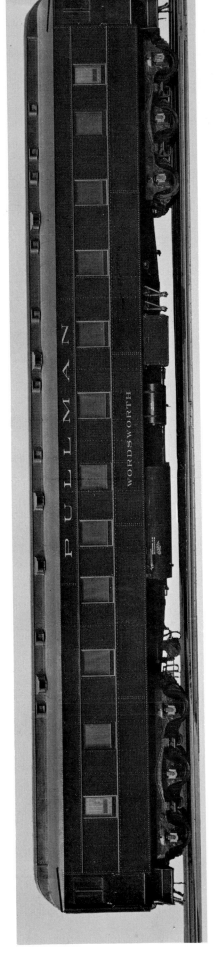

WORDSWORTH: 6 Compartments, 3 Drawing Rooms

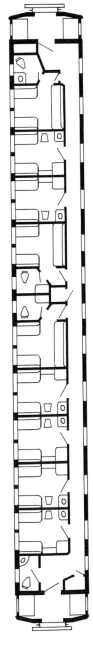

TWO hundred of these all-room cars were designed for luxury train service. All were named for famous men of the arts or in series with the prefix *Glen*. Variation of the 6-3 plan included cars with 7 compartments and 2 drawing rooms. Compartment-drawing room cars offered the most elegant accommodations in the finest trains. Many of these sleepers were assigned to the Pullman pool and were operated in vacation trains to the South in the winter and to Northern resorts in summer.

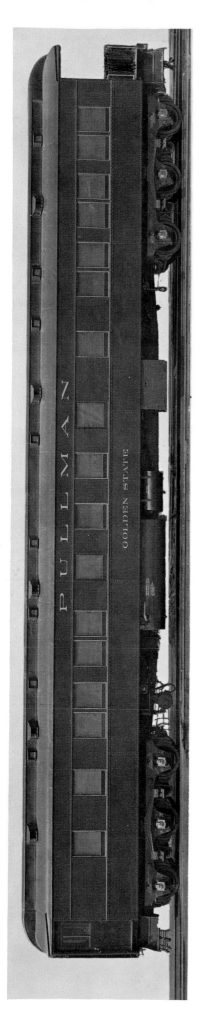

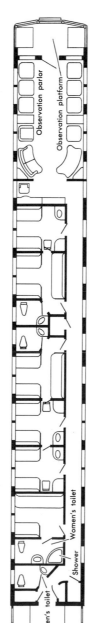

GOLDEN STATE: 3 Compartments, 2 Drawing Rooms, Lounge-Observation

BUILT in March 1924 under Pullman plan 3950, these cars contained 3 compartments, 2 drawing rooms, and ladies' lounge with shower bath and maid attendant. Known as the "3-2 obs," they were designed for service on de luxe trains. *Golden State* was assigned to Rock Island-Southern Pacific's *Golden State Limited*. Twin cars named in *Silver* series served in Santa Fe's *Chief*. *Sunset* series were assigned to *Sunset Limited*, *Central* series to NYC limiteds, *National* series to *National Limited*.

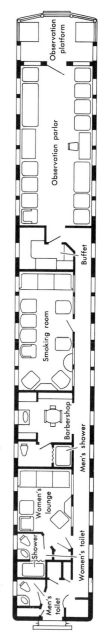

CITY OF EVERETT: Lounge-Observation Car

THIS full-length lounge-observation car was typical of equipment provided for crack Western transcontinental trains. *City of Everett* was one of 8 cars required to complete the Chicago-Seattle-Tacoma line for the Milwaukee Road *Olympian*. Plan (front to rear) provided men's toilet; women's shower bath and lounge with reed furniture and ladies' maid; men's club with shower, barbershop, and smoking room fitted with green morocco leather lounge chairs; soda fountain-buffet; observation parlor with high windows; and a roomy observation platform with movable searchlight for viewing scenery at night. When built in 1927 the new *Olympian* and *Pioneer Limited* cars were the first to have trucks equipped with roller bearings.

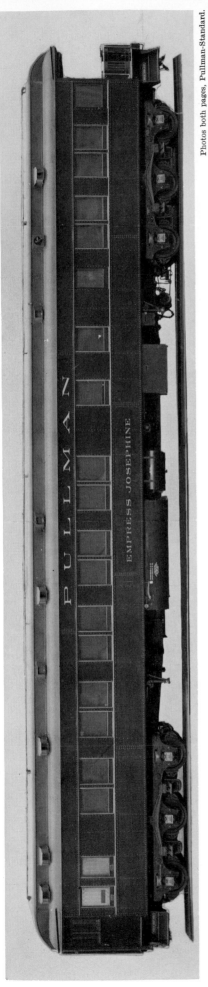

Photos both pages, Pullman-Standard.

EMPRESS JOSEPHINE: Observation-Parlor Car

THIS 20-chair lounge-observation-parlor car was built in March 1925 for service on the Louisville & Nashville *Pan-American* between Cincinnati and New Orleans. During the era of the '20's, before the advent of the highway and private automobile, the Pullman Company operated almost 1200 elegant parlor cars equipped for luxurious daytime travel. Most of them were named for ladies, flowers, or birds. *Empress Josephine*, a typical example, contained 20 revolving easy chairs, ladies' lounge and shower in the charge of a ladies' maid. Observation parlor had built-in radio with headphones.

ALEXANDER HAMILTON: Sunroom-Parlor Car

THIS 12-chair drawing room-buffet-lounge-sunroom car was built in 1930 for the re-equipping of the PRR New York-Washington crack daytime *Congressional Limited*. The heavyweight Pullman parlor car reached its zenith with *Alexander Hamilton* and twin car *Thomas Jefferson*. Both featured the new-design sunroom end known as the "Clipper" type first used on identical cars assigned to NH's *Yankee Clipper*. Remainder of cars served in PRR-NH *Senator*, B&O *Columbian*, C&NW *Viking* (later *400*), and SP&S *Empire Builder-North Coast* connection.

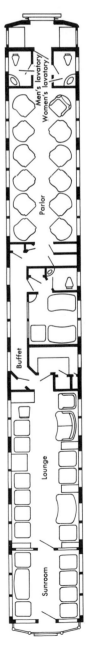

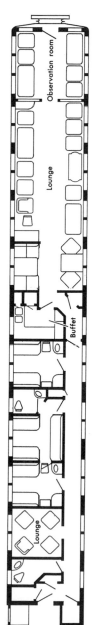

SUNBURST: Sunroom-Lounge-Sleeping Car

IN 1927 Pullman outshopped Lot 6076, one of the few orders of de luxe cars completed for assignment in the Southwest. Lot 6076 consisted of 8 cars for the *Sunshine Special* (MP-T&P) and 4 cars for the *Texas Special* (Frisco-Katy), built to Pullman plan 3975 (sunroom-lounge-buffet, 2 compartments, drawing room). Thirty-one similar cars served on some of the great trains of the land: UP *Pony Express*, B&O *Capitol Limited*, Dixie Route *Dixie Flyer*, IC *Seminole*, CNR-GT *International*, ACL *Everglades*, and L&N *Pan-American*. Then faster schedules and air-conditioning appeared. Most passengers preferred the safety and cleanliness of the sunroom to the open platform. The brass-railed observation passed from the American scene.

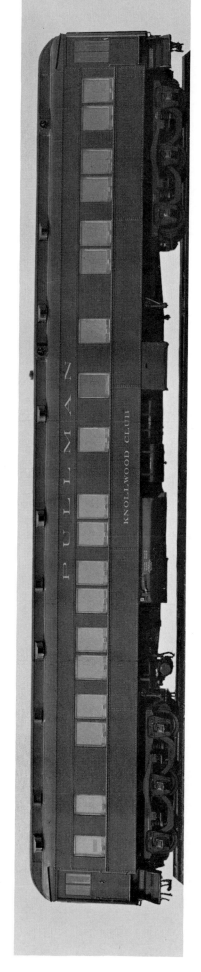

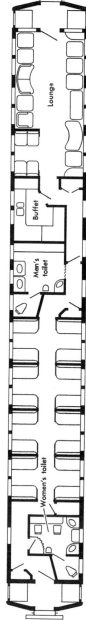

KNOLLWOOD CLUB: 8 Sections, Lounge-Buffet

AT the end of the 1920's railroads began to feel the effects of competition with the automobile. In the interest of economy the Pullman Company developed car plans which combined club and dining facilities with revenue-producing sleeping accommodations. Most of these cars were named for noted country or town clubs. *Knollwood Club* (named for the Lake Forest [Ill.] golf club) was built in 1929. It contained 8 sections, lounge, and buffet with soda fountain. Restaurant cars were equipped with a broiler-kitchen (in place of the buffet) and several tables. Prohibition repeal again permitted public sale of wine and liquor and increased the demand for *Club* series cars. By 1934 87 cars of this type were operating on 22 railroads.

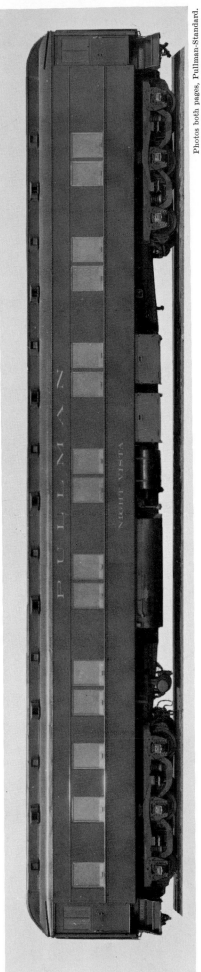

Photos both pages, Pullman-Standard.

BUILT in 1928, this early model individual room car provided 14 rooms for single passengers on an overnight journey. The single room contained a stationary bed crossways of the car (with box spring and mattress), complete toilet facilities, folding washstand with mirror, drop shelf for writing, luggage space, full-length mirror, Thermos water bottle, and individual heat control — all within 33.7 square feet. Forty-five heavy-weight all-single-room type cars were assigned to the following heavily trafficked overnight runs: New York-Chicago, New York-Detroit, New York-Washington, New York-Boston, Montreal-Toronto, Chicago-St. Louis, San Francisco-Los Angeles.

NIGHT VISTA: 14 Single Rooms

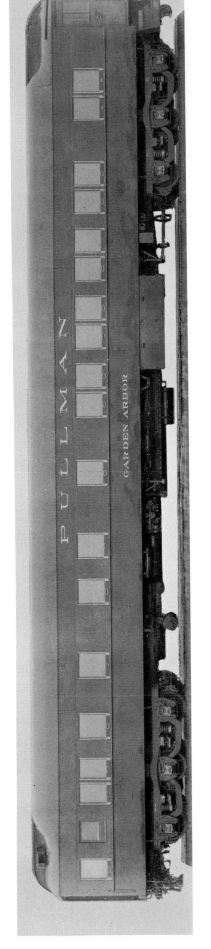

THE single room of 1927 was an instant success. For overnight runs which included daytime travel the stationary bed was replaced with a standard convertible Pullman sofa and the accommodation was called a bedroom. (A double bedroom also contained an upper berth.) To satisfy the demand for the new private rooms, hundreds of open-section cars were rebuilt with bedrooms during the depression years. Garden Arbor had 8 sections, 5 double bedrooms. It was formerly the 12 section-drawing room-compartment car Arnold built in 1910 for NYC.

GARDEN ARBOR: 8 Sections, 5 Double Bedrooms

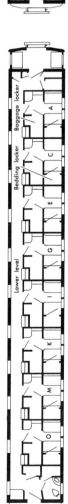

PULLMAN'S first full-length duplex cars, *Eventide* and *Nocturne*, were rebuilt from composite-club cars in 1932 and pioneered the development of bi-level Pullman equipment. They were initially assigned to the New York-Washington run on the Pennsylvania Railroad and remained on PRR until the 1950's. Plan of lower floor shows 8 single rooms with longitudinal berths, toilet facilities. Upper floor was similarly patterned.

EVENTIDE: 16 Duplex Single Rooms

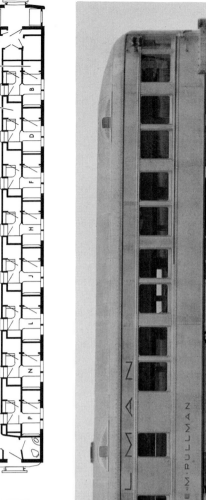

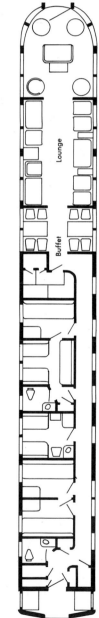

THIS classic observation-sleeping car marked the transition by Pullman from heavyweight to lightweight design in car-building. Built in 1933 for exhibition at the Century of Progress Exposition in Chicago, the new car contained features which were radical innovations at the time: lightweight aluminum construction (50 per cent lighter than a standard Pullman); four-wheel one-piece cast aluminum trucks (later replaced by conventional models); brushed aluminum exterior; interior décor featuring aluminum. *George M. Pullman* served on *Florida Arrow*, *Treasure Island Special*, and *Super Chief*. It paved the way for acceptance of the streamlined passenger car.

GEORGE M. PULLMAN: Lightweight Sleeping-Lounge-Observation Car

SLEEPING CAR *Forward*, outshopped by Pullman-Standard in November 1936, was the first car to be built on the steel alloy and truss frame construction principle used in the steel curtain-wall skyscraper. Pullman engineers, in an effort to produce a car of minimum weight and maximum strength, employed the welded truss type of side frame covered with light-gauged stainless-steel sheathing. *Forward* weighed less than 60 per cent of a standard heavyweight car. Stresses in the frame were carefully checked and tested until 220 per cent of the safe load was applied. Other features included early model tightlock couplers, upper-berth windows. *Forward* was sold to the Santa Fe in 1948, rebuilt to baggage-dorm No. 3437 in 1963.

FORWARD: 8 Sections, 2 Double Bedrooms, 2 Compartments

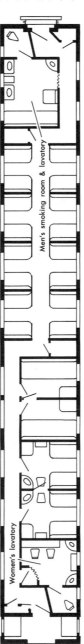

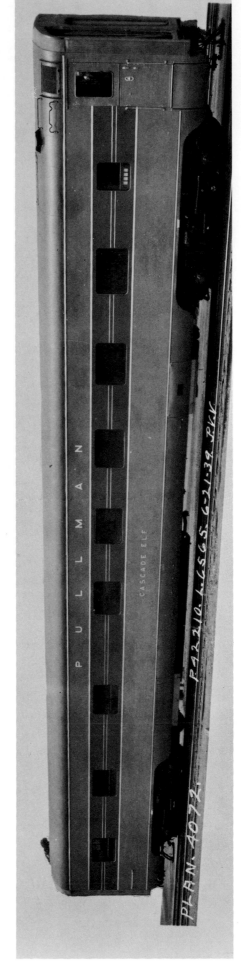

IN 1937 car architects at Pullman-Standard were presented with the problem of designing a sleeping car which would combine the two most modern sleeping accommodations — roomettes and bedrooms. The result was plan 4072, *Cascade* series, which produced a combination of 10 roomettes and 5 double bedrooms. The first models were rushed to completion in the spring of 1938, in time for inauguration of the new *Broadway* and *20th Century*. The *Cascade Elf* wore NYC's two-tone gray. Until 1941, 96 "10 and 5" cars were built for service on NYC, PRR, B&O, UP, and SP. Testimony to the soundness of their design is the fact that in 1964 almost all remain in active service. (NYC cars were sold to Canada and Mexico.)

CASCADE ELF: 10 Roomettes, 5 Double Bedrooms

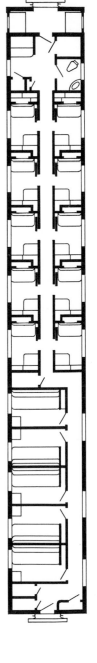

410

Both photos, Budd Company.

PULLMAN-STANDARD pioneered the all-roomette car. The experimental *Roomette I* was outshopped in August 1937. Successful on test runs throughout the country, the roomette offered a private room with complete toilet facilities for slightly more than the price of a lower berth. Before World War II 68 all-roomette cars were built. In 1948-1949 ACF, Budd, and P-S built 133 more of these cars for PRR and NYC. Their success was short lived. In the postwar boom, the demand was for higher-priced sleeping accommodations. NYC disposed of 68 cars including 44 which went to Canada. Ten *Harbor* cars were converted into sleeper-coaches. In 1963 50 of the *Ashtabula Inn* type were stripped down and rebuilt into coaches for PRR.

ASHTABULA INN: 21-Roomette Sleeping Car

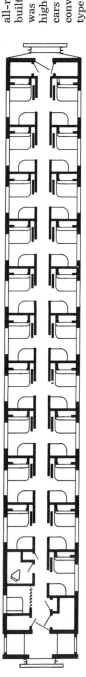

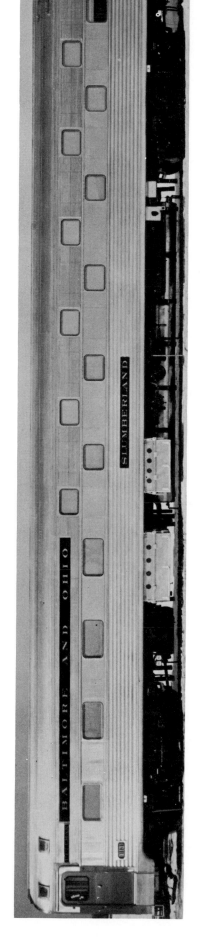

SINCE the earliest days of the sleeping car, railroads have provided low-priced service in colonist cars, second-class sleepers, and tourist cars. Present-day models offer budget-priced accommodations and are known as Slumbercoaches, Sleepercoaches, or tourist-roomette cars. The Budd Slumbercoach has 24 duplex single rooms and 8 double rooms offering economy-priced sleeping accommodations — each with private toilet facilities. B&O's *Slumberland* is one of five "24 and 6" cars operated by the B&O and Mopac on lines between Baltimore and Chicago, Baltimore and San Antonio. All five were built by Budd in 1958 and 1959. Similar models operated in 1964 on *Denver Zephyr, North Coast Limited,* NYC streamliners.

SLUMBERLAND: Slumbercoach (24 Duplex Single Rooms, 8 Double Rooms)

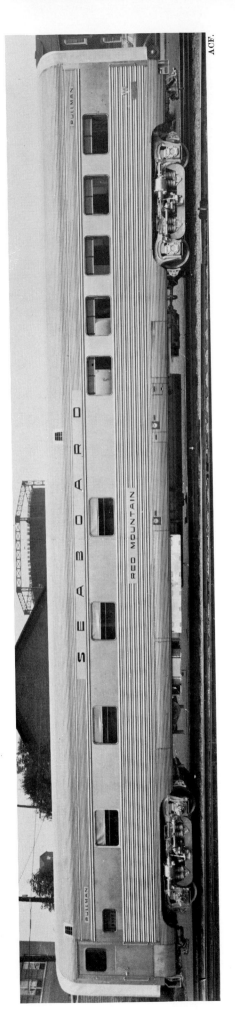

ACF.

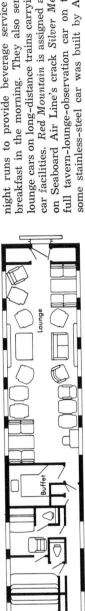

COMBINATION sleeping-lounge cars are operated on over-night runs to provide beverage service in the evening and breakfast in the morning. They also serve as supplementary lounge cars on long-distance trains carrying additional lounge-car facilities. *Red Mountain* is assigned as the forward lounge on Seaboard Air Line's crack *Silver Meteor* which carries a full tavern-lounge-observation car on the rear. The hand-some stainless-steel car was built by ACF for SAL in 1948.

RED MOUNTAIN: *6 Double Bedrooms, Buffet-Lounge* (Seats 23)

GN.

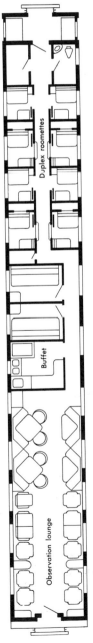

IN 1957 the Great Northern Railway shops at St. Paul re-modeled two *Glacier*-class sleeping cars for beverage and breakfast service on the *Winnipeg Limited* overnight from St. Paul to Winnipeg. One half of the car which formerly con-sisted of 16 duplex roomettes and 4 double bedrooms was re-placed with a broiler-type buffet and observation lounge. The new cars were renamed *Winnipeg Club* (ex-*Harrison Glacier*) and *Manitoba Club* (ex-*Oberlin Glacier*) and were newly painted in the green and orange livery termed the most beauti-ful in the land by rail enthusiast-historian Everett DeGolyer.

WINNIPEG CLUB: 8 Duplex Roomettes, 2 Double Bedrooms, Buffet-Lounge

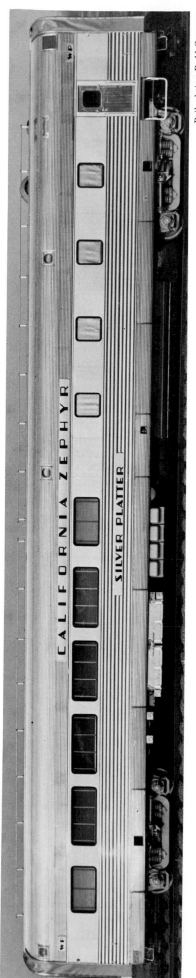

WESTERN PACIFIC'S 48-seat dining car was built in 1948 for *California Zephyr* service. Side and roof construction is of fluted stainless steel in the Budd manner. There are 32 seats in the main dining area flanked by four semi-private nooks termed banquettes, each seating four. Carpeted floor, leather upholstery, pastel walls and ceiling, sculptured plastics, and fluorescent lighting adorn the interior. Special features include telephone communication with lounge car for making dinner reservations and an "air curtain" at pantry entrance.

IN March 1950 SP invested 15 million dollars for five complete sets of stainless-steel cars to operate in the *Sunset Limited* between New Orleans and Los Angeles over America's second through transcontinental route. One of the outstanding cars in the new train was SP-owned full-length French Quarter lounge. Exterior is of stainless steel with red nameboard. Interior suggests New Orleans' famous Vieux Carré. White wrought-iron grillwork accentuates the French Quarter décor. Watermelon-red ceiling lends Mardi Gras atmosphere. When constructed, the car carried shower, valet, stewardess, and bar.

SILVER PLATTER: 48-Seat Dining Car

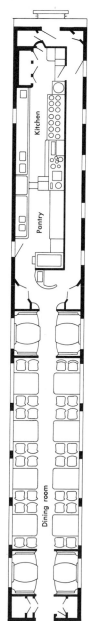

SOUTHERN PACIFIC NO. 2990: French Quarter Lounge

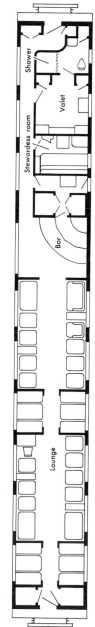

THIS ACF model "10 and 6" built in 1950 for PRR-MP-T&P Eagle service operated between the East Coast and Texas. Blue and gray livery was applied to all pool cars furnished by the three owning roads. Eagle Oak, one of 10 cars in the series, carried reporting marks of the Pennsylvania Railroad. Car has ACF riveted sides and smooth roof. Bedrooms are located at the door end of the car and offer choice of BC (bed crosswise) or BL (bed lengthwise). Ingenious planning permitted enclosed toilets, one more bedroom than the prewar Cascade car.

EAGLE OAK: 10 Roomettes, 6 Double Bedrooms

DURING the streamlined era the 10-roomette, 6-double-bedroom sleeping car served as the maid-of-all-work for the Pullman Company. Like the "12 and 1," its heavyweight predecessor, the "10 and 6" is the most universally operated style of lightweight Pullman. More than 600 "10 and 6" cars were built by Pullman-Standard, ACF, and Budd during postwar years. The major improvement over prewar Cascade-series cars was the enclosure of the bedroom toilet annex. Roomettes are placed at the door end of the car. Exterior is Budd shot-welded stainless-steel painted Tuscan red with the typical Budd fluted roof. Hollins College, one of 20 cars built by Budd in 1949 for N&W, serve on Pocahontas, Cavalier, Birmingham Special, and Pelican. All are named for N&W on-line colleges and counties.

HOLLINS COLLEGE: 10 Roomettes, 6 Double Bedrooms

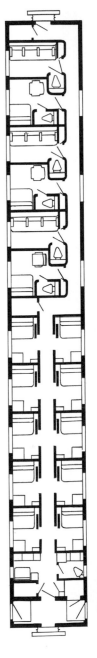

414

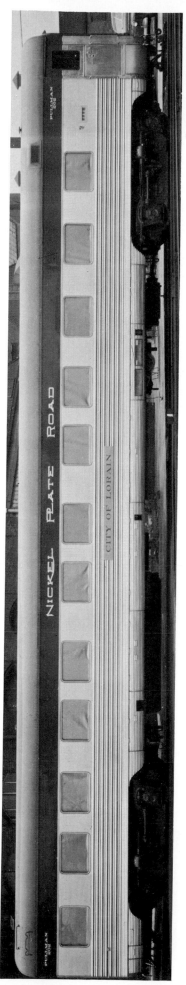

IN 1950 Pullman-Standard redesigned the "10 and 6" cars for the Nickel Plate and C&O. Exterior of the *City of Lorain* is stainless steel with extra-large window sash and blue letter-board. Car contains both name and number (209). Pullman-Standard construction includes combined fluted and smooth welded side plates and smooth roof. Higher priced bedrooms are located in smoother-riding center of car. Wash basins are fixed in place and separated from enclosed toilets in bedrooms.

CITY OF LORAIN: 10 Roomettes, 6 Double Bedrooms

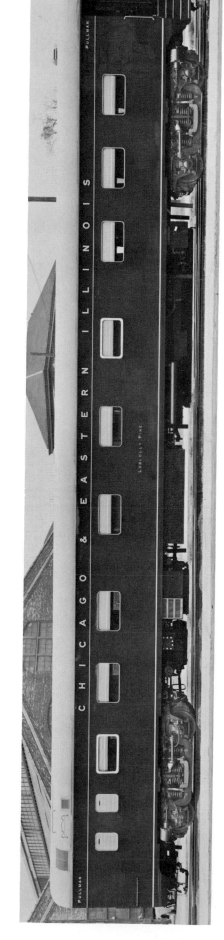

THE "S" (Standardized)-type sleeping car was developed by Pullman-Standard in 1953. The new plan featured a variety of accommodations and incorporated these features: cutaway bed in roomettes, fixed wash basin (eliminating danger of toilet articles going down the drain), and foot-operated faucets. Higher priced bedrooms were placed in the center. C&EI and L&N bought 29 S-type *Pine*-series cars and painted them blue and gold for service on the *Georgian*, *Gulf Wind*, *Humming Bird*, and *Pan-American*. CN purchased 20 more, named in the *Green* series. Seventeen similar cars built by Pullman-Standard's Worcester plant operated over NH, BAR, and B&M.

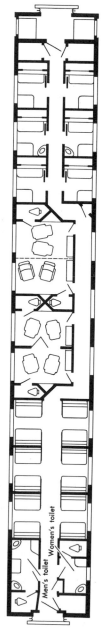

LOBLOLLY PINE: 6 Sections, 4 Double Bedrooms, 6 Roomettes

Men's toilet

Women's toilet

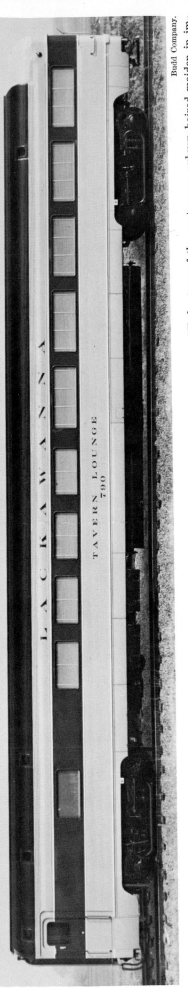

AT the turn of the century an auburn-haired maiden in immaculate white appeared on the American scene. Her name was Phoebe Snow and her white dress symbolized the cleanliness of travel on the Lackawanna Railroad, the "Road of Anthracite." Penrhyn Stanlaus and other celebrated portrait artists glorified Miss Snow on canvas. Vaudeville vocalists sang her praises. Poets and wags, too, contributed to her popularity with advertisements for the Lackawanna set to rhyme: "I won my fame and wide acclaim/For Lackawanna's splendid name/By keeping white and snowy bright/Upon the Road of Anthracite." In 1963 under the direction of Chairman William H. White, the Erie Lackawanna renamed trains 1 and 2, New York-Chicago, for Phoebe Snow. Bringing up rear is No. 790, red and gray Lackawanna tavern-lounge built by Budd in 1949. Original portrait of Phoebe hangs in tavern section.

LACKAWANNA NO. 790: Tavern-Lounge Car

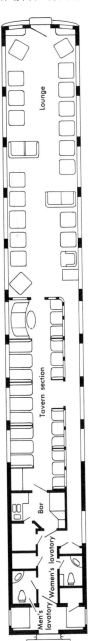

DE LUXE sleeping car Imperial Loch was built in 1948 at the Berwick (Pa.) plant of American Car & Foundry for Broadway Limited service. This model had enclosed toilet facilities in all rooms. These "4-4-2" cars were first developed in 1938 to provide de luxe accommodations for luxury streamliners: Broadway, 20th Century, City of Los Angeles, City of San Francisco, Golden State, Lark, Overland, Panama, and Super Chief.

IMPERIAL LOCH: 4 Double Bedrooms, 4 Compartments, 2 Drawing Rooms

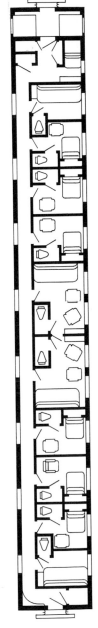

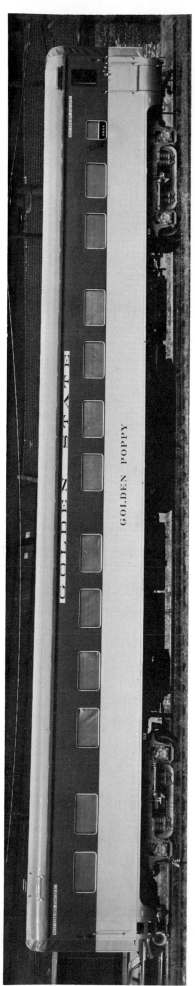

GOLDEN POPPY: 12 Bedrooms

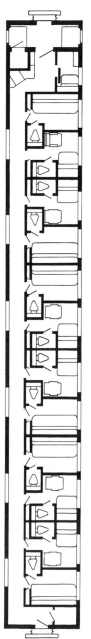

THE first lightweight all-bedroom cars were built in 1938-1939 for PRR's *Broadway*, NYC's *Century*, and SP's *Lark*. Postwar models were improved by the enclosure of toilet facilities in a separate annex room. With this addition the car became one of the most popular in the Pullman fleet. NYC's *Port* series and SP's *Golden Poppy* (silver and red) contain 12 rooms. Similar cars operated on C&O, IC, Seaboard, and UP contain 11 rooms. In 1963-1964 the Pullman Company rebuilt 12 duplex cars into all-bedroom configuration for service on Santa Fe.

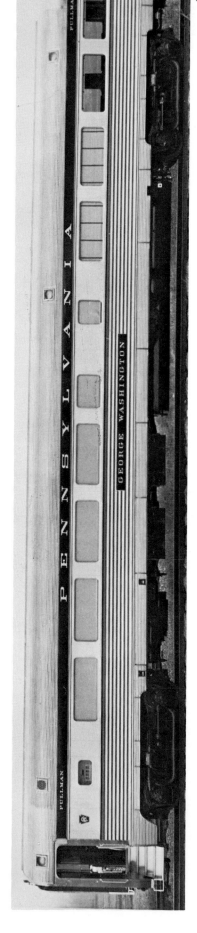

GEORGE WASHINGTON: 18 Chair-Bar-Lounge-Parlor-Observation Car

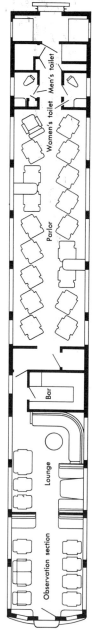

DESPITE competition with the private automobile and superhighway, there remain in 1964 a few railroads which operate parlor cars offering the daylight traveler a degree of comfort and relaxation unapproachable on today's crowded highways. Although the once vast Pullman fleet of nearly 1200 parlor cars is now a memory, one can still travel in spacious cars with soft-cushioned chairs and deep-pile carpeting. The *George Washington*, a modern parlor car built by Budd in 1952 for the all-new *Congressional*, operates between New York and Washington on the PRR. Panoramic windows, enclosed telephone room, drawing-room room car contribute to train's elegance.

IN 1954 the Canadian Pacific received the first of 173 stainless-steel cars built by Budd to re-equip its principal transcontinental trains. Included in the order were 18 dome-sleeper-observation-lounge cars, each containing 3 double bedrooms, 1 drawing room. They serve on the *Canadian* and the *Dominion* operating between Montreal-Toronto-Vancouver. The 18 cars were all named for Canada's national or provincial parks. Exterior is finished with unpainted stainless steel and trimmed in Tuscan red. Interior design includes special artistic treatments furnished by members of the Royal Canadian Academy of Arts. Original paintings, prints, murals depict facets of provincial botany, history, geography, and government.

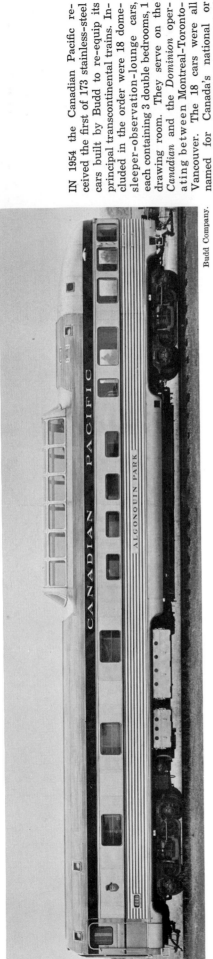

CANADIAN PACIFIC
ALGONQUIN PARK

Budd Company.

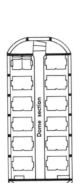

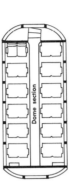

Dome section

Observation lounge

Beverage room

ALGONQUIN PARK: Dome-Sleeping-Observation-Lounge

THE first dome cars were introduced in 1945 by the Burlington. They were an instant success and more were ordered by railroads throughout the country. Restrictive clearances prohibited their use in most parts of the East. Known by various names — Vista-Dome (CB&Q, *et al.*), Astra Dome (UP), Strata Dome (B&O), Planetarium (MP, T&P), and Scenic Dome (CPR) — the dome car has attracted legions of travelers. The Pullman-Standard model shown was built in 1952 for MP-T&P *Eagle* trains. It seats 81 passengers: 24 in the dome, 42 on the main level, and 15 in lounge room below dome.

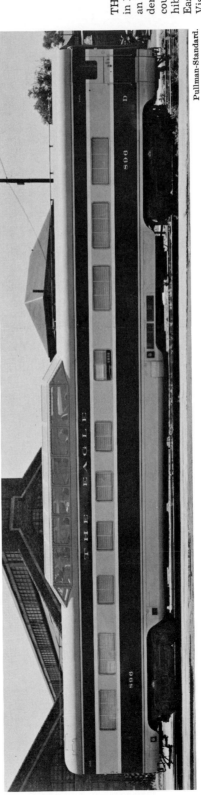

THE EAGLE
896

Pullman-Standard.

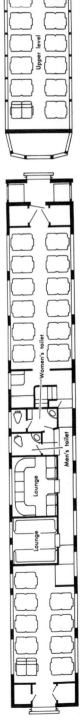

Upper level

Women's toilet

Men's toilet

Lounge

Lounge

PLANETARIUM COACH NO. 896: Dome Coach

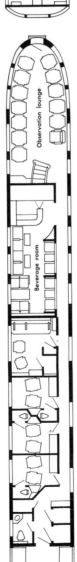

Pullman-Standard.

IN 1935 the Milwaukee Road established its first *Hiawatha* streamliner on the Chicago-Twin Cities run. In the following years additional *Hiawathas* were inaugurated throughout the Midwest. After World War II the Milwaukee was one of the first to re-equip its trains with a fleet of new cars. *Coffee Creek* was one of six Skytop Lounge Cars built in 1948 for the new *Olympian Hiawatha*. The orange and maroon tail-end car styled by Brooks Stevens sported a lounge room with green-tinted glass, a removable aluminum stretcher window, enclosed bedroom toilets, and special trucks with triple-coil bolster springs. All were sold to Canadian National in 1964.

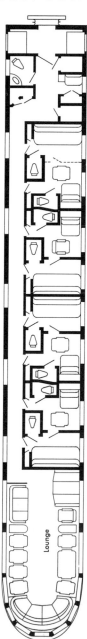

COFFEE CREEK: Skytop Lounge, 8 Double Bedrooms

Budd Company.

IN 1952 Pullman-Standard built the first full-length dome cars for the Milwaukee Road *Hiawatha* trains. Later models were built by Budd for Santa Fe and Great Northern. Southern Pacific operates similar cars built in its Sacramento shops. *Prairie View* is one of six built in 1955 for the Great Northern *Empire Builder* (CB&Q owns one). Each weighs 96½ tons and is carried on two six-wheeled trucks. Termed "Great Domes," these green and orange beauties seat 75 in dome, 34 in lower-deck cocktail lounge. Interiors are decorated in bright colors and Western American Indian décor.

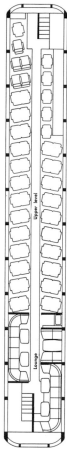

PRAIRIE VIEW (GN NO. 1394): Double-Deck Dome-Lounge Car

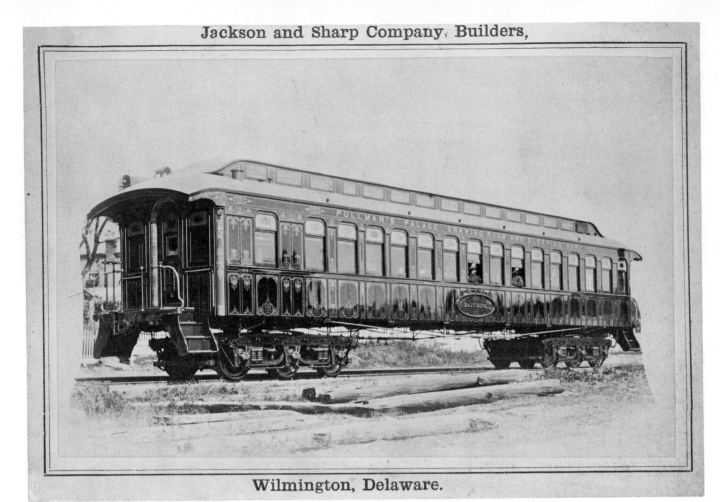

Wilmington, Delaware.

RARE builder card of the *Baltimore* by Jackson & Sharp. Author's collection.

HISTORY OF PALACE CAR

Mere numbers could never have so captured the imagination

I THE NAMES assigned to Pullman and railroad-operated passenger cars have long captured the public's imagination. Whether seen in the dim light of a whistle stop or the bright glare of a large Union Station, these names signify the best and most comfortable of railroad equipment.

Sunbury Inn, Cascade Pool, Quonset Point, Minnetonka, Imperial Chariot, Cimarron Valley, Dolly Madison, Pacific Union, Silver Arrow, Emerald Glade, Cadwallader C. Washburn, Kankakee River. . . . Thousands of words have appeared in print about such names. Stories about them have become part of the American folklore. Indeed, there has been speculation and endless rumor about their sources. Notwithstanding the romance and symbolism connected with these names, they are important to the accounting and car-service procedures developed over the years by the Pullman Company and the railroads.

Public interest in car names was shown in 1939 when a total of 780,000 were submitted to the Pullman Company in a 60-day period during a nationwide contest to select a name for the Pullman car exhibited at the New York World's Fair. (The winning name was *American Milemaster*.) After World War II, 240,000 persons in five states submitted names for cars on two New England trains. The Pullman Company receives a constant stream of requests to name cars after individuals, colleges, universities, cities, towns, counties, and a wide variety of institutions.

Car names are as old as railroading. However, the great palace car building and operating companies developed shortly after the Civil War. It was during the last half of the 19th century that George Pullman, Webster Wagner, William Mann, and T. T. Woodruff built their great fleets of luxury cars. By 1900 Pullman's Palace Car Company of Chicago had absorbed all of its competitors and — except for a small group of American and Canadian roads — was the sole operating company.

The earliest de luxe cars were numbered, but names were quickly adopted because of confusion with railroad-owned equipment. Pullman's first car, rebuilt in 1859 from a Chicago & Alton coach (built by Barney & Smith), was numbered 9. Later, in 1865, Pullman built his first original car and appropriately named it *Pioneer*. A Committee for Nomenclature was formed when this car became an apparent success and orders began to pour in. From that day on it has been the duty of this committee — in collaboration with railroad officials — to select car names, notwithstanding the fanciful and persistent rumor that Pullman's daughter Florence, later the wife of Illinois Gov. Frank Lowden, was given a gold piece for each car name she composed.

From the beginning, geography has been the wellspring for car names. This influence is clearly shown in names selected at random from Pullman rosters dating from the 1870's and 1880's: *Alamosa* (Denver & Rio Grande), *Calumet* (Hannibal & St. Joseph), *China* (Vandalia), *Kenosha* (Denver & South Park), *Maine* (Pennsylvania Railroad), *Tampa* (Atlantic Coast Line). A list of Wagner sleeping cars from 1882 indicates a similar geographical trend: *Albany* (New York Central), *Providence* (New Haven), *Council Bluffs* (Chicago & North Western). A Woodruff register from the same period lists *Chicago*, *Crestline*, *Crescent City*, and *Juniata*.

Early Mann cars were romantically named for operas or prominent actresses: *La Traviata*, *Rigoletto*, *Adelina Patti*, *Etelka Gerster*. When Woodruff and Mann were combined into the Union Palace Car Company and thence into the Pullman empire in 1889, all cars with duplicate names were renamed by the committee at Pullman.

Parlor cars and drawing-room cars were frequently named for women or flowers. Pullman operated *Andromeda*, *Irene*, *Tulip*, and *Godiva*. Wagner owned *Countess*, *Princess*, and *Early Rose*. Pullman-owned dining cars of the 19th century honored famous hotels: *Bellevue*, *Plaza*, *Victoria*, *Willard*. Southern Pacific once named a series of dining cars after grapes: *Catawba*, *Concord*, *Malaga*.

The number of Pullman-owned cars increased from 686 in 1885 to over 1700 in 1895 during the decade when the first sets of matched cars for the great named limited trains were built. In 1887 nine special sleeping cars were assigned to the *Pennsylvania Limited*, the first vestibuled train: *America*, *Austria*, *England*, *France*, *Germany*, *Ireland*, *Italy*, *Russia*, and *Spain*.

Author's collection.

North American Indian names have frequently appeared on cars. *Ojibwa*, *Muskoda*, *Pokegama*, and *Sahwa* were part of an early order for service on the Northern Pacific. In later years *Nagawicka*, *Nahma*, and *Minnetonka* operated on the Milwaukee Road. *Namaka* and *Nashwaakis* patrolled the Canadian Pacific.

In 1892 an order of 20 Pullman cars were named for important European cities: *Berne*, *Essen*, *Rheims*, *Belfast*,

NOMENCLATURE

BUILT BY BARNEY & SMITH MANUFACTURING COMPANY, DAYTON, OHIO.

ANOTHER rarity: the Pullman *Dayton* by Barney & Smith. Author's collection.

and so forth. Several months later a Lot of 21 cars were similarly named for great composers and writers — among them, *Chopin, Liszt, Goethe, Tennyson, Longfellow.*

Pullman and Wagner extended themselves building exhibition trains — each appropriately named — for Chicago's 1893 Columbian Exposition. The Pullman set included *America, Marchena, La Rabida, Ferdinand, Isabella.* Wagner's exhibit contained *Columbus, Ferdinand, Isabella, Pinzon,* and *San Salvador.*

Shortly after the start of the 20th century, the Pullman Company took over the Wagner operations. Pullman officials were dismayed to learn that over 300 of the newly acquired cars had names already on the Pullman roster. The problem was solved at the Chicago Public Library. *Lochinvar, Marmion, Hercules, Hyperides, Lysander, Prometheus,* and *Briareus* were chosen in haste.

Few early cars were named for persons except for figures of antiquity and famous men of the arts and letters. *Charlemagne, Rembrandt, Titian,* and *Van Dyke* appeared in 1901 along with *Chaucer* and *Shakespeare.* Among the first Americans honored were *Lowell* and *Whittier.* The 1903 *Colonial Express* contained *Edward Winslow, John Endicott,* and *Edward Hopkins.* These three cars were the first Pullmans with both Christian and surnames.

A significant development occurred in 1899. Ten observation cars were built for the Santa Fe *California Limited.* Each was named with the prefix *Ben: Ben Alder, Ben Avon, Ben Lomond.* Ten similar cars were built in 1902 for the Rock Island's *Golden State: Ben Ammi, Ben MacDhui.* Years later Pullman's Nomenclature Committee would remember these cars.

Shortly after World War I the Pullman fleet numbered nearly 8000 cars. All had performed strenuous service during the war and were in need of refurbishing. Many were old cars built of wood and were ready for replacement. Accordingly, several thousand cars were planned for construction as soon as possible.

By 1920, however, the naming of cars had become a painstaking job. Remembering earlier Santa Fe and Rock Island orders, a series of 50 new sleepers were named (with prefixes) for forts or military posts familiar to the returning - doughboy - turned - traveling - salesman. *Fort Adams, Fort Bliss, Fort Casey,* and so forth, began to roll from the shops at Pullman. These names were an immediate success. Twenty-five *Camps* were added, followed closely by 20 *Capes* and 20 *Mountains.* Continuing through the 1920's and 1930's, Pullmans by the hundreds were named after lakes, saints, clans, and points. Each prefix or suffix denoted a different type of car plan.

During the late 1920's and the 1930's, entire sets of custom-designed cars were built for the crack limited trains served by Pullman. Heavyweight and later streamlined lightweight trains brought forth many names suggested by the people and territories served by the new trains. Heavyweight observation cars for the *Twentieth Century Limited* were named for Eastern valleys: *Catskill Valley, Hudson Valley.* Later they were replaced by streamlined cars: *Bedloe's Island, Manhattan Island.* Heavyweight cars for the *Broadway* named for famous Revolutionary meeting places such as *Independence Hall* and *Faneuil Hall* were replaced by *Skyline View, Metropolitan View.*

The *City of San Francisco* received *Golden Gate Park, Chinatown, Nob Hill. Tsankawi, Saydatoh, Tapacipa,* and other Indian chiefs of the Southwest were honored on the *Super Chief.*

Until July 1, 1947, the Pullman organization both built and operated cars. On that date, however, the two functions were divided and were assumed by two separate companies as the result of a Government anti-trust action which consumed almost seven years in litigation. Henceforth, building Pullman cars became the function of Pullman-Standard Car & Manufacturing Company, American Car & Foundry, and the Budd Company. Operation of Pullman sleeping cars remained the business of the Pullman Company which was sold to a group of interested railroads.

Largely owing to the efforts of the late George A. Kelly, executive vice-president of the Pullman Company, the practice of using distinctive names for sleeping cars was continued under the new ownership by almost all of the participating railroads. Of more than 2000 streamlined Pullmans built since World War II, fewer than 200 (on NP, RI, and SP) are designated only by number.

PULLMAN NAMES

Listed below are representative names assigned to some of the principal Pullman car types, with the key words italicized.

HEAVYWEIGHT

Cape Flattery	10 sections, 1 drawing room, 2 compartments
Camp McCoy	10 sections, 1 drawing room, 2 compartments
Clover Meadow	8 sections, 5 double bedrooms
East Albany	12 sections, 1 drawing room
Emerald Glade	8 sections, 4 double bedrooms
Fort Mason	10 sections, 1 drawing room, 2 compartments
Glen Ellyn	6 compartments, 3 drawing rooms
Lake Pontchartrain	10 sections, 1 drawing room, 2 compartments
McGovern	12 sections, 1 drawing room
Mt. Rainier	10 sections, observation lounge
New Dominion	14 sections
Night Star	14 single bedrooms
Octagon House	13 double bedrooms
Point Lookout	10 sections, 2 drawing rooms
Poplar Dale	6 sections, 6 double bedrooms
Red Bird	12 sections, 1 drawing room
St. Ives	12 sections, 1 drawing room
Villa Palatial	10 sections, 3 double bedrooms
Wellesley College	10 sections, 2 double bedrooms, 1 compartment
Willow Dell	7 drawing rooms

LIGHTWEIGHT

American Patrol	6 sections, 6 roomettes, 4 double bedrooms
Cascade Pool	10 roomettes, 5 double bedrooms
Chartiers *Creek*	12 duplex single rooms, 4 double bedrooms
Chicopee *Falls*	6 double bedrooms, buffet, lounge
City of Ann Arbor	17 (or 18) roomettes
Kankakee *River*	10 roomettes, 6 double bedrooms
Green Brook	6 roomettes, 4 double bedrooms, 6 sections
Gunsight Pass	8 duplex roomettes, 4 double bedrooms, 4 sections
Huron *Rapids*	10 roomettes, 6 double bedrooms
Imperial Chariot	4 compartments, 4 double bedrooms, 2 drawing rooms
Indiana *Harbor*	22 roomettes
Long Leaf *Pine*	6 roomettes, 4 double bedrooms, 6 sections
National Colors	6 roomettes, 4 double bedrooms, 6 sections
Pacific Union	10 roomettes, 6 double bedrooms
Pine Lodge	10 roomettes, 6 double bedrooms
Quonset *Point*	14 roomettes, 4 double bedrooms
Regal Manor	4 double bedrooms, 4 compartments, 2 drawing rooms
Sunbury *Inn*	21 roomettes
Western Frontier	12 roomettes, 4 double bedrooms
Westchester *County*	13 double bedrooms

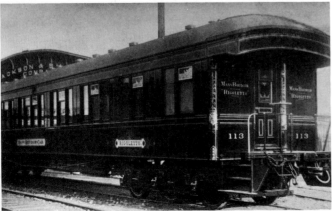

RIGOLETTO, handsome navy blue and gold Mann Boudoir car.

TOLTEC, narrow-gauge (3-foot) sleeping car for Denver & Rio Grande, rode transfer table at Pullman's Detroit shops in July of 1880.

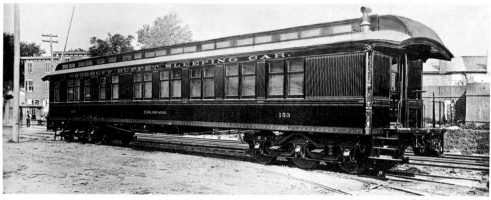

COLORADO, a Woodruff buffet-sleeping car assigned to the Wabash Cannon Ball, was constructed by Jackson & Sharp, numbered 153. Car was brown with ocher-yellow roof.

QUANTZINTECOMATZIN, a dining car built by Pullman in 1902 for the American Tourist Association's escorted tours of Mexico, bore longest single word ever applied to a railway car. Translated from Aztec Indian it meant, "the noble eater of the royal dish." Another long name is on NdeM sleeper: General Pedro Antonio De Leon. Short: PRR parlor Gap.

FERDINAND, a Wagner vestibuled dining car, was exhibited at the 1893 Columbian Exposition in Chicago.

ISABELLA, another exhibit at the Columbian Exposition, was a Pullman compartment-observation car.

BELLEAU WOOD was one of eight 7-drawing-room Pullmans built in 1920 for de luxe service on Santa Fe and named for World War I battles.

423

EXTERIOR PAINTING ARRANGEMENTS

The Pullman Company — November 1952

Since the earliest days of railroading, passenger rolling stock has been painted in colorful liveries. Variations are legion in number. The following selected list was prepared by Pullman Company in 1952 during transition from conventional heavyweight to lightweight equipment.

RAILROAD	CAR TYPE	COLOR SCHEME	SERVICE	RAILROAD	CAR TYPE	COLOR SCHEME	SERVICE
Atchison, Topeka & Santa Fe	Conventional	Two-tone gray, silver stripe			Lightweight	Yellow and green, black stripes	
	Lightweight	Two-tone gray, silver stripe		Delaware, Lackawanna & Western	Conventional	Green	
	Lightweight	Stainless steel			Lightweight	Gray and red, gold stripes	
Atlanta & West Point Western Railway of Alabama	Conventional	Blue		Denver & Rio Grande Western	Conventional	Orange and aluminum, black stripes	
	Lightweight	Stainless steel			Lightweight	Orange and stainless steel, black stripes	
Atlantic Coast Line	Conventional	Aluminum, purple letterboard			Lightweight	Stainless steel	California Zephyr
	Lightweight	Stainless steel, purple letterboard		Erie	Lightweight	Green	
Baltimore & Ohio	Conventional and streamlined conventional	Blue and gray, gold stripes			Conventional	Green, gray pier panel	
	Lightweight	Blue and gray, yellow stripes	Eagle	Florida East Coast	Lightweight	Stainless steel	
	Lightweight	Stainless steel, blue letterboard		Georgia	Conventional	Green	
Canadian National	Conventional	Green		Great Northern	Lightweight	Green and orange, gray and gold stripes	Western Star, Empire Builder
	Lightweight	Green		Gulf, Mobile & Ohio	Conventional and streamlined conventional	Maroon and red, gold leaf stripes	
Chesapeake & Ohio	Conventional	Gray and yellow, blue letterboard			Lightweight	Maroon and red, gold leaf stripes	
	Lightweight	Stainless steel and yellow, blue letterboard		Illinois Central	Conventional	Orange and brown, gold stripes	Used with lightweights
Chicago & North Western	Conventional	Yellow and green, black stripes	North Western Limited, Victory Train		Lightweight	Orange and brown, gold stripes	Panama Limited
	Lightweight	Yellow and green, black stripes		International-Great Northern	Lightweight	Blue and gray, yellow stripes	Eagle
	Lightweight	Two-tone gray, silver stripes	Overland	Kansas City Southern	Streamlined conventional	Green, red, and yellow	
	Lightweight	Yellow and gray, red stripes	City trains, joint UP		Lightweight	Green, red, and yellow	
Chicago, Burlington & Quincy	Conventional	Gray		Lehigh Valley	Conventional	Red	
	Conventional and streamlined conventional	Simulated flutes	Texas Zephyr	Louisville & Nashville	Conventional	Blue, simulated flutes	Humming Bird, Georgian
	Lightweight	Two-tone green	North Coast		Conventional	Blue	
	Lightweight	Green and orange, gray and gold stripes	Empire Builder, Western Star		Lightweight	Stainless steel	Joint SR
	Lightweight	Stainless steel			Lightweight	Tuscan red, gold stripes	Joint PRR
Chicago Great Western	Conventional	Maroon, imitation gold stripes		Missouri-Kansas-Texas	Conventional	Simulated flutes, red pier panels	
Chicago, Indianapolis & Louisville	Conventional	Gray and red, white stripes			Conventional	Simulated flutes, red pier panels	Texas Special
Chicago, Milwaukee, St. Paul & Pacific	Conventional	Orange and red			Lightweight	Stainless steel, red pier panels	
	Lightweight	Orange and red			Lightweight	Stainless steel, red pier panels, red roof, maroon skirting	Texas Special
Chicago, Rock Island & Pacific	Lightweight	Red and stainless steel	Golden State	Missouri Pacific	Conventional	Blue and gray, yellow stripes	
	Lightweight	Stainless steel			Lightweight	Blue and gray, yellow stripes	Eagle
Chicago, St. Paul, Minneapolis & Omaha	Conventional	Yellow and green, black stripes		Nashville, Chattanooga & St. Louis	Conventional	Blue, simulated flutes	Humming Bird, Georgian
	Conventional	Yellow and gray, red stripes	Joint UP		Conventional	Simulated flutes	

424

RAILROAD	CAR TYPE	COLOR SCHEME	SERVICE
National Railways of Mexico	Conventional	Light blue-green, red stripes, gray letterboard, gray roof	
	Lightweight	Dark red and cream, gray roof	Aztec Eagle
New York Central	Lightweight	Stainless steel	
	Lightweight	Two-tone gray, silver stripes	
New York, Chicago & St. Louis	Conventional	Pullman green	
	Lightweight	Blue and stainless steel	
New York, New Haven & Hartford	Conventional	Forest green	
	Conventional	Tuscan red	Joint PRR
	Lightweight	Stainless steel, orange pier panel	
Northern Pacific	Conventional	Two-tone green, gold stripe	
	Lightweight	Two-tone green, gold stripe	North Coast Limited
Norfolk & Western	Conventional	Red and brown, gold leaf stripes	
	Lightweight	Tuscan red, gold leaf stripes	Joint PRR
	Lightweight	Tuscan red and brown, gold leaf stripes	
Pennsylvania	Conventional	Tuscan red	
	Streamlined conventional	Two-tone Tuscan red, gold stripes	
	Streamlined conventional	Tuscan red	
	Lightweight	Blue and gray, yellow stripes	Eagle
	Lightweight	Tuscan red, gold stripes	
	Lightweight	Simulated stainless-steel flutes, red pier panel	American, Meteor, Texas Special
	Lightweight	Two-tone gray, silver stripe	Transcontinental, joint C&NW-UP
	Lightweight	Two-tone gray, silver stripe	Transcontinental, joint AT&SF
	Lightweight	Stainless steel, purple letterboard	Joint ACL
	Lightweight	Stainless steel	California Zephyr
	Lightweight	Stainless steel	Joint SAL
	Lightweight	Stainless steel	Joint SR
	Conventional and lightweight	Simulated flutes, stainless steel, Tuscan red letterboard	Congressional Limited, Senator
	Lightweight	Yellow and gray, red stripes	Joint UP
Pullman Pool	Conventional	Two-tone gray, silver stripes	Tourist cars
	Conventional	Standard green	
	Conventional	Two-tone gray, silver stripes	
	Conventional	Blue and gray, yellow stripes	Eagle
	Conventional	Dark gray	Remodeled conventional
	Conventional	Red and brown, gold stripes	Joint N&W
	Conventional	Standard green	Military troop sleeper
	Conventional	Maroon and gray	Orange Blossom Special (SAL)
	Lightweight	Two-tone gray, silver stripes	Pool
Richmond, Fredericksburg & Potomac	Lightweight	Stainless steel, purple letterboard	Joint ACL
	Lightweight	Stainless steel	Joint PRR
	Lightweight	Tuscan red, gold stripe	Joint PRR
St. Louis-San Francisco	Conventional	Simulated flutes, red pier panels	
	Conventional	Simulated flutes, red pier panels	Texas Special
	Lightweight	Stainless steel, red pier panels	
	Lightweight	Stainless steel, red pier panels, red roof, maroon skirting	Texas Special
Seaboard Air Line	Conventional	Pullman green	Seaboard on letterboard
	Conventional	Two-tone gray, silver stripe	Seaboard on letterboard
	Conventional	Gray and blue, gold stripe	Joint L&N
	Conventional	Two-tone gray, silver stripe	Pullman at center of letterboard
	Conventional	Maroon and gray	Orange Blossom Special
	Lightweight	Stainless steel	
Soo Line (Minneapolis, St. Paul & Sault Ste. Marie)	Conventional	Red	
Southern Pacific	Conventional	Pullman green	
	Conventional	Two-tone gray, silver stripes	Overland
	Conventional	Two-tone gray, silver stripes	Golden State
	Lightweight	Two-tone gray, silver stripes	Lark, Cascade
	Lightweight	Two-tone gray, silver stripes	Overland
	Lightweight	Yellow and gray, red stripes	City of San Francisco
	Lightweight	Red and stainless steel	Golden State
	Lightweight	Stainless steel, red letterboard	Sunset Limited
Southern	Conventional	Aluminum bronze	
	Conventional	Simulated flutes	
	Lightweight	Stainless steel	
Spokane, Portland & Seattle	Conventional	Dark green	
	Lightweight	Orange and green, gray and gold stripes	Western Star, Empire Builder
	Lightweight	Two-tone green, gold stripes	North Coast Limited
Texas & Pacific	Conventional	Blue and gray, yellow stripes	Eagle
	Lightweight	Blue and gray, yellow stripes	Eagle
	Lightweight	Blue and gray, yellow stripes	
Union Pacific	Conventional	Two-tone gray, silver stripes	
	Lightweight	Two-tone gray, silver stripes	
	Lightweight	Yellow and gray, red stripes	
Wabash	Conventional	Blue	Banner Blue Limited
	Conventional	Blue	
	Lightweight	Blue	
	Lightweight	Yellow and gray, red stripes	City trains, joint UP
Western Pacific	Lightweight	Stainless steel	California Zephyr

425

Index

CAR NAMES:

428

Acknowledgements

Without the generous help of the following persons — railroad enthusiasts and railroaders alike — this book would not have been possible. For their considerable assistance the author acknowledges his gratitude:

Wallace W. Abbey, Soo Line; R. L. Baker, Florida East Coast; John W. Barriger, Pittsburgh & Lake Erie; Lucius Beebe; Henry Benz, Pullman Company; Sidney W. Bone, New York Central; Clarence E. Boone, American Car & Foundry; Ralph Buckingham, Chester Budzinski, Pullman Company; Frances Burton; Joseph M. Canfield; Avis Cantagallo; Clarence S. Carbaugh, Southern Railway; Arthur C. Carlson, Illinois Central; Joyce Crawford; Gordon Crofoot; Owen Davies; Everett L. DeGolyer Jr.; Samuel Deloian, Pullman Company; William J. Dewan, Grand Trunk Western-Canadian National; Richard F. Dole, Maine Central; John P. Dowey, New York Central; Clarence C. Ehlert, Chicago & North Western; Rosemary Entringer; Peter E. Falles, Pullman Company; Lawrence Fischer, Canadian Pacific; Charles E. Fisher; Robert F. Gehrt, Atchison, Topeka & Santa Fe; George A. Gloff; Otha Grant, Southern Pacific; Marc Green, Chicago, Milwaukee, St. Paul & Pacific; Howard F. Greene; Walter Gustafson, Northern Pacific; Grahame Hardy; Louis Henderson, Pennsylvania Railroad; Melvin Horn, Pullman-Standard; Freeman Hubbard; G. Raymond Jackson, Pullman Company; Samuel James; William C. Janssen; Alfred W. Johnson; Albert C. Kalmbach; Marguerite M. Kindregan, Budd Company; George Krambles; William Kratville; Ann Kuss, New York Central; Lawrence Luser; Marian Manasse; Donald T. Martin, Atlantic Coast Line; Alan D. McGiffin, Canadian Pacific; William A. McKenzie, Northern Pacific; Robert S. McKernan, New York, New Haven & Hartford; Andrew Merrilees; William D. Middleton; W. Llewellyn Millar, Pennsylvania Railroad; Bertrand J. Misek; David P. Morgan; John Murray, Pullman Company; Ingrid Nickel; Ted O'Meara, Chesapeake & Ohio; Evanthia Perperas; Frank F. Perrin, Great Northern; William E. Pyne, Baltimore & Ohio; Charles Rank, Chicago, Milwaukee, St. Paul & Pacific; William E. Robertson; Theodore E. Rose; Albert M. Rung, Chicago, Burlington & Quincy; Edwin C. Schafer, Union Pacific; Raymond P. Schaffer, Chicago & North Western; Roy Schmidt, Pullman Company; James G. Shea, Southern Pacific; Harry Spurrier, New York Central; L. F. Sweeny, *Official Guide*; E. L. Thompson, Baltimore & Ohio; Joseph Verona, Chicago & North Western; Robert Wayner; Loring Wilcox; Nora Wilson, Pullman-Standard; Edward Wojtas, Chicago, Rock Island & Pacific; D. W. Yungmeyer.

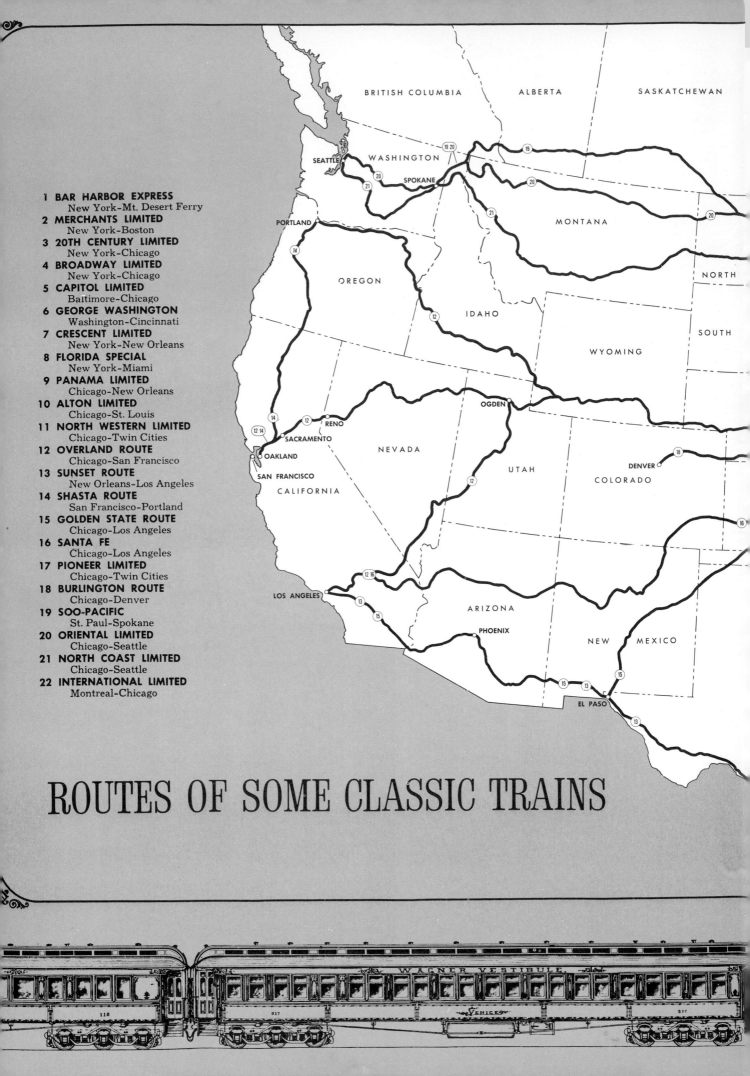

1 **BAR HARBOR EXPRESS**
   New York-Mt. Desert Ferry
2 **MERCHANTS LIMITED**
   New York-Boston
3 **20TH CENTURY LIMITED**
   New York-Chicago
4 **BROADWAY LIMITED**
   New York-Chicago
5 **CAPITOL LIMITED**
   Baltimore-Chicago
6 **GEORGE WASHINGTON**
   Washington-Cincinnati
7 **CRESCENT LIMITED**
   New York-New Orleans
8 **FLORIDA SPECIAL**
   New York-Miami
9 **PANAMA LIMITED**
   Chicago-New Orleans
10 **ALTON LIMITED**
   Chicago-St. Louis
11 **NORTH WESTERN LIMITED**
   Chicago-Twin Cities
12 **OVERLAND ROUTE**
   Chicago-San Francisco
13 **SUNSET ROUTE**
   New Orleans-Los Angeles
14 **SHASTA ROUTE**
   San Francisco-Portland
15 **GOLDEN STATE ROUTE**
   Chicago-Los Angeles
16 **SANTA FE**
   Chicago-Los Angeles
17 **PIONEER LIMITED**
   Chicago-Twin Cities
18 **BURLINGTON ROUTE**
   Chicago-Denver
19 **SOO-PACIFIC**
   St. Paul-Spokane
20 **ORIENTAL LIMITED**
   Chicago-Seattle
21 **NORTH COAST LIMITED**
   Chicago-Seattle
22 **INTERNATIONAL LIMITED**
   Montreal-Chicago

ROUTES OF SOME CLASSIC TRAINS

Of all inventions, the alphabet and the printing press alone excepted, those inventions which abridge distance have done most for the civilization of our species.
— Macaulay.

CONCERNING THE COLOR FOLDOUTS . . .

PULLMAN COMPANY advertising folder of the early 1920's, the original of which was printed by the now dissolved company-owned Pullman Press, featured the classic heavyweight steel sleeper Pleasant View. The exterior view reveals the traditional standard Pullman green paint (Pullman specification No. 70-10); gold-leaf lettering; No. 242 clasp brake trucks, with equalizer and pedestal cast integral with frame; the car's designation number in the corridor window; yellow step; and blue-uniformed conductor and porter. The interior view shows a 12-section, 1-drawing-room, 1-compartment configuration, briefly popular at the time. Subsequently the compartment was eliminated and the size of the washrooms increased. Gone today, though not forgotten, are the open sections, green berth curtains, safety ladder (for upper berths), walnut-grained metal trim, window cinder deflectors, nickeled lavatories, and the men's washroom ("the world's greatest story-telling forum"). This rare promotional piece is reproduced courtesy of Pullman Company.

ORIENTAL LIMITED of 1909 was promoted by a flamboyant example of railroad advertising produced for the Great Northern Railway by Poole Brothers, railway printers of Chicago. This outstanding example of the lithographer's art was prepared for distribution to sight-seers at the Seattle World's Fair of 1909 and is reproduced herein by courtesy of the Great Northern Railway.